Sages, Stories, Authors,
and Editors in
Rabbinic Babylonia

Program in Judaic Studies
Brown University
BROWN JUDAIC STUDIES
Edited by
Ernest S. Frerichs
Shaye J. D. Cohen, Calvin Goldscheider

Number 300
Sages, Stories, Authors, and Editors
in Rabbinic Babylonia

by
Richard Kalmin

Sages, Stories, Authors,
and Editors in
Rabbinic Babylonia

by

Richard Kalmin

Scholars Press
Atlanta, Georgia

Sages, Stories, Authors, and Editors in Rabbinic Babylonia

Library of Congress Cataloging-in-Publication Data
Kalmin, Richard Lee.
Sages, stories, authors, and editors in rabbinic Babylonia / by
Richard Kalmin.
p.   cm. — (Brown Judaic studies ; no. 300)
Includes bibliographical references and indexes.
ISBN 0-7885-0045-7
1. Talmud—Criticism, Redaction. 2. Amoraim. I. Title.
II. Series.
BM501.K36   1994
296.1'206—dc20   94-33649
                                                           CIP

Printed in the United States of America
on acid-free paper

For my family:

Freda, Rachel, and Michael

Table of Contents

APPENDICES

Preface

This book argues that the Talmud preserves identifiable sources which were not fully homogenized by later editors, and contains usable historical information regarding the centuries prior to its final editing. The problems involved in identifying and evaluating the historicity of diverse sources in a heavily redacted work are familiar to students of the ancient world, but the personalities, events, and literatures discussed in this book are unfamiliar to many. It will be helpful at the outset to define several terms used throughout and to delimit the chronological and geographical parameters of this study.

The study deals primarily with the Babylonian Talmud, also known as the Bavli, and to a lesser extent with the Palestinian Talmud, also known as the Yerushalmi. References to the Bavli are preceded by the abbreviation "b.," and references to the Yerushalmi by the abbreviation "Yer." When I refer simply to "the Talmud," or cite a source without an introductory abbreviation, I have in mind the Babylonian Talmud.

The Bavli and Yerushalmi are vast repositories of statements by and stories about the ancient rabbis, and these stories and statements are organized primarily in the form of commentaries on an earlier rabbinic book, the Mishna. Talmudic rabbis frequently author (1) halachic (legal) statements, (2) agadot (non-halachic statements), (3) interpretations of earlier sources, and (4) objections and questions about opinions expressed by other rabbis. Rabbinic statements and stories frequently purport to derive from a variety of different times and different places, but they have been woven together in the Talmud to form a series of coherent discourses.

Ancient rabbis are sages who advocated a life of devotion to and study of Torah, the traditional law and lore of the Jewish people, as interpreted by the rabbis themselves. Rabbis traditionally referred to as Babylonian Amoraim form the principal subjects of this book. Babylonian Amoraim are sages who lived under Persian rule, between the Tigris and Euphrates rivers in what is modern-day Iraq, from the early 3rd century C.E. until the early 6th century C.E.[1] Palestinian Amoraim (rabbis who lived in Israel under Roman rule between the 3rd and 5th centuries C.E.), and Tannaim (rabbis who flourished primarily in Israel prior to the 3rd century C.E.), also figure prominently in this research.

In addition to statements by Tannaim and Amoraim, both Talmuds also contain substantial amounts of unattributed materials. As several modern scholars have noted,[2] the anonymous sections of the Talmud are editorial in character.[3] They consist of an enormous commentary which

---

[1]These dates are based on *Seder Tannaim ve-Amoraim*, ed. Kalman Kahan (Frankfurt am Main: Hermon, 1935), pp. 4 and 6; and *Igeret Rav Sherira Gaon*, ed. Benjamin Lewin (Haifa, 1921), pp. 78, 95, and 97. Both works post-date the Talmud by hundreds of years, and the information they supply regarding Talmudic chronology has been challenged by modern scholars. See, for example, Jacob Neusner, *A History of the Jews in Babylonia* (Leiden: E.J. Brill, 1966), vol. 2, pp. 47-50. Yeshayahu Gafni ("Le-Heker ha-Khronologiah be-Igeret Rav Sherira Gaon," *Zion* 52 [1987], pp. 1-24; and *Yehudei Bavel bi-Tekufat ha-Talmud* [Jerusalem: Merkaz Zalman Shazar le-Toldot Yisrael, 1991], pp. 239-65), however, argues convincingly in favor of the reliability of some of this information. For my purposes, it matters little whether the geonic chronology is completely precise, and the traditional dates suffice to provide a chronological framework for the personalities and literatures discussed in this book. Even David Goodblatt, *Rabbinic Instruction in Sasanian Babylonia* (Leiden: E.J. Brill, 1975), pp. 39-40, who argues that the geonic chronicles are likely to describe the Talmudic period anachronistically, observes that comparison between the geonic dates and those provided by non-Jewish sources does not reveal significant differences.

[2]See, for example, Yizhak Halevy, *Dorot ha-Rishonim* (1897-1939; Reprint. Berlin: Benjamin Harz, 1923), vol. 2, p. 551; Meyer Feldblum, "The Impact of the 'Anonymous Sugya' on Halakic Concepts," *Proceedings of the American Academy for Jewish Research* 37 (1969), p. 20; Shamma Friedman, "Al Derekh Heker ha-Sugya," in *Perek ha-Isha Rabbah ba-Bavli* (Jerusalem: Jewish Theological Seminary, 1978), p. 20; David Goodblatt, "The Babylonian Talmud," in *Approaches to Ancient Judaism II: The Palestinian and Babylonian Talmuds*, ed. Jacob Neusner (New York: Ktav, 1981), pp. 154-56, and the literature cited there; David Halivni, *Mekorot u-Mesorot: Shabbat* (Jerusalem: Jewish Theological Seminary, 1982), pp. 5-18; Richard Kalmin, *The Redaction of the Babylonian Talmud* (Cincinnati: Hebrew Union College Press, 1989), pp. 1-5; and Baruch M. Bokser, "Talmudic Studies," in *The State of Jewish Studies*, ed. Shaye J.D. Cohen and Edward L. Greenstein (New York: Jewish Theological Seminary, 1990), pp. 91-93, and the literature cited there.

[3]This and other references throughout this book to the Talmud's anonymous commentary as "editorial" should not be understood as denial on my part that attributed rabbis played a role in the editing of the Talmud. Very likely they played an important role in this process, for example by (at least on some occasions) collecting and arranging earlier rabbinic sources in a particular order. (See also chapter 9, below.) The term "editorial," however, describes a (the?) central aspect of the anonymous commentators' enterprise, and is in all likelihood a less important part of the activity of attributed rabbis.

analyzes, explains, emends, and completes the attributed statements at the editors' disposal.

The Talmud does not assign dates to the rabbis, and students of the Talmud traditionally employ a system of relative chronology and divide the Amoraic period into seven generations.[4] This system will be utilized throughout this book, with the term "first-generation Amoraim" referring to rabbis who flourished during the first half of the 3rd century C.E., shortly after the final editing of the Mishna. The term "second-generation Amoraim" refers to rabbis who flourished immediately after the first-generation rabbis, and so on until the seventh Amoraic generation, which is comprised of rabbis who lived during the late 5th and early 6th centuries C.E.

There is little uniformity among scholars regarding the contribution of post-Amoraic generations to the Talmud. Post-Talmudic chronicles supply lists of names of rabbis who functioned during the post-Amoraic period, but these names appear only rarely in the Talmud itself. The duration of the period is likewise a matter of doubt.[5]

I would like to acknowledge the help of Professor Shaye J.D. Cohen, editor of Brown Judaic Studies, who suggested that I write this book and gave invaluable advice and encouragement every step of the way. His professionalism and high scholarly standards made the process of researching and writing a demanding but rewarding one. I would also like to thank Chancellor Ismar Schorsch and Vice Chancellor Ivan Marcus, of the Jewish Theological Seminary, who were unstinting in their support of this project. Several teachers, colleagues, and friends gave generously of their time and energy, most notably Professors Baruch M. Bokser, Michael Chernick, Shamma Friedman, Yeshayahu Gafni, David Goodblatt, David Halivni, Judith Hauptman, David Kraemer, Burton Visotzky, and Ben Zion Wacholder. I would also like to thank Rabbi Gail Labovitz for her fine work as my research assistant, and Ms. Adaya Henis for her proofreading and indexing. Finally, I wish to acknowledge the generous support of the Lucius N. Littauer Foundation, the Abell Publication Fund of the Jewish Theological Seminary, and the Stroock Faculty Fellowship.

Several parts of this book have already been published as separate articles, and have been revised and reorganized for inclusion in this

---

[4]Some divide the period into eight generations.

[5]For more on this obscure period, see, for example, Benjamin Lewin, *Rabbanan Saboraei ve-Talmudam* (Jerusalem: Ahiavar, 1937); Avraham Weiss, *Ha-Yezira Shel ha-Saboraim* (Jerusalem: Hebrew University, 1953), pp. 1-18; Yaakov Efrati, *Tekufat ha-Saboraim ve-Sifrutah* (Petah-Tikva, Israel: Agudat Benei Asher, 1973); and Kalmin, *The Redaction of the Babylonian Talmud*, pp. xv-xviii, 1-11, and 66-94.

book. I list here the relevant chapters together with the journals in which they originally appeared. Chapter 1: "Saints or Sinners, Scholars or Ignoramuses? Stories About the Rabbis as Evidence for the Composite Nature of the Babylonian Talmud," *Association for Jewish Studies Review* 15, No. 2 (1990), pp. 179-205. Chapter 2: "Changing Amoraic Attitudes Toward the Authority and Statements of Rav and Shmuel: A Study of the Talmud as a Historical Source," *Hebrew Union College Annual* 63 (1992), pp. 83-106. Chapter 7: "Quotation Forms in the Babylonian Talmud: Authentically Amoraic, or a Later Editorial Construct?" *Hebrew Union College Annual* 59 (1988), pp. 167-87. Chapter 8: "Talmudic Portrayals of Relationships Between Rabbis: Amoraic or Pseudepigraphic?" *Association for Jewish Studies Review* 17, No. 2 (1992), pp. 165-97; and "Rabbinic Attitudes Toward Rabbis as a Key to the Dating of Talmudic Sources," *Jewish Quarterly Review* 84, No. 1 (1993), pp. 1-27. Chapter 10: "Friends and Colleagues, or Barely Acquainted? Relations Between Fourth-Generation Masters in the Babylonian Talmud," *Hebrew Union College Annual* 61 (1990), pp. 125-58. Chapters 4 and 11 were originally published together as "Collegial Interaction in the Babylonian Talmud," *Jewish Quarterly Review* 82, Nos. 3-4 (1992), pp. 383-415.

Introduction

An important question facing modern scholars is the extent to which ancient documents contain diverse sources. To what extent is the New Testament comprised of sources which date from Jesus' lifetime, and to what extent is it the product of later authors and editors? Does the New Testament contain sources distinguishable along geographical lines, with different sections deriving from different Christian communities, and how do we best identify these sources?[1]

These questions confront scholars studying ancient rabbinic documents as well. The Babylonian Talmud, for example, is filled with statements attributed to and stories involving rabbis who lived prior to the Talmud's final redaction in the sixth or seventh century C.E.[2] It is also filled with statements which purport to derive from different localities, some Palestinian and others Babylonian, for example. Do these statements and stories derive from diverse periods and places, or were they invented by late, Babylonian pseudepigraphers?

Answers to these questions affect our understanding of the Talmud in a variety of important ways. If we cannot determine whether statements and stories are early or late, for example, our ability to understand the history of the Talmudic period is severely curtailed, if not rendered completely impossible. Does a particular story found in the Bavli depict an early Palestinian rabbinic court, or are late Babylonian judicial developments described? Do theological conceptions, eschatological beliefs, and legal concepts change during the course of the Talmudic period, or do differing views co-exist simultaneously?

---

[1]The literature on this question is enormous. See, most recently, John P. Meier, *A Marginal Jew: Rethinking the Historical Jesus* (New York: Doubleday, 1991).

[2]The term "final redaction" should not be understood to imply that the Talmud was completely closed and nothing new was added after the sixth or seventh century. On the contrary, words, phrases, and even lengthy discussions were added to the Talmud long after this date. The document presently before us, however, assumed recognizable shape at roughly this time, with all of its basic components fully intact and recognizable. The material added after this date was added to a pre-existent book and did not fundamentally alter its character, form, or content.

Modern Scholarly Approaches to the Dating and
Authorship of Talmudic Sources

Modern scholars have adopted a variety of different approaches to the question of diverse sources in the Talmud, and it will be helpful to describe several which are relevant to the present book. Many scholars maintain the likelihood of extensive editorial reshaping or fabrication of Talmudic stories and statements, and lament the scarcity of firm criteria by which to determine a source's date, authorship, or locality. According to this view, it is extremely difficult, often or usually impossible, to answer the questions raised above.[3]

One influential theory, that of Jacob Neusner, carries the above skepticism to an extreme. According to Neusner, the bulk of the Talmud was composed by late Babylonian editors. These editors had access to varied sources, but reworked them so extensively that at present they are generally impossible to distinguish in the Talmudic corpus.[4] The Bavli provides little access to the rabbis who flourished during the centuries preceding its final redaction.

A second approach claims that while the Talmud is a heavily edited work, it contains diverse sources which often can be identified and objectively described.[5] According to this approach, it is often possible to

---

[3]See the works cited in chapter 1, below. See also Louis Jacobs, "How Much of the Babylonian Talmud is Pseudepigraphic?" *Journal of Jewish Studies* 28, No. 1 (1977), pp. 46-59; and *Structure and Form in the Babylonian Talmud* (Cambridge, England: Cambridge University Press, 1991), pp. 6-17; and Baruch M. Bokser, *Post Mishnaic Judaism in Transition* (Chico, California: Scholars Press, 1980), p. 1. With regard to the Tannaitic period, see Gary Porton, *The Traditions of Rabbi Ishmael* (Leiden: E.J. Brill, 1982), vol. 4, pp. 212-25; Shaye J.D. Cohen, "Patriarchs and Scholarchs," *Proceedings of the American Academy for Jewish Research* 48 (1981), pp. 57-87 (see especially pp. 84-85, there); and *From the Maccabees to the Mishna* (Philadelphia: Westminster Press, 1987), p. 219; and Steven D. Fraade, "The Early Rabbinic Sage," in *The Sage in Israel and the Ancient Near East*, ed. John G. Gammie and Leo G. Perdue (Winona Lake, Indiana: Eisenbrauns, 1990), pp. 417-23, and the references cited in n. 2, there.

[4]See, for example, Jacob Neusner, *Making the Classics in Judaism* (Atlanta: Scholars Press, 1989), pp. 1-13 and 19-44; and *Sources and Traditions: Types of Compositions in the Talmud of Babylonia* (Atlanta: Scholars Press, 1992). Neusner repeats his arguments in numerous contexts, and I make no effort to cite them all here.

[5]See, for example, Goodblatt, *Rabbinic Instruction in Sasanian Babylonia*, pp. 4-5; and "Towards the Rehabilitation of Talmudic History," in *History of Judaism: The Next Ten Years*, ed. Baruch M. Bokser (Chico, California: Scholars Press, 1980), pp. 33-38; Lee Levine, *Ma'amad ha-Hakhamim be-Erez Yisrael* (Jerusalem: Yad Yizhak Ben-Zvi, 1985), pp. 4-5 (=*The Rabbinic Class of Roman Palestine in Late Antiquity* [Jerusalem: Yad Izhak Ben-Zvi, 1989], pp. 18-19); and David C. Kraemer, "On the Reliability of Attributions in the Babylonian Talmud," *Hebrew Union College Annual* 60 (1989), pp. 175-90; and *The Mind of the Talmud* (New York: Oxford

speak reliably about the distinct contribution of generations and localities, since each period, and certain localities, have their own unique features of thought, legal concepts, terminology, and formal expression. These unique features differ from one locality to another, or develop from one period to the next, a likely sign of organic growth rather than editorial manipulation.

According to a third approach, the issues of the dating and authorship of Talmudic sources present no problem. Some scholars see a one-to-one correspondence between ancient rabbinic texts and the historical events these texts purport to describe. Once miraculous elements and editorial accretions have been removed, these scholars believe, the "original source" which remains is an accurate reporting of historical events or a reliable recording of rabbinic dialogue.[6]

Why Would Later Generations Invent Information about Earlier Sages?

One could legitimately ask why later generations would invent stories about earlier rabbis, or why Babylonians would falsely attribute statements to Palestinian sages. A variety of different answers can be given, and I will suggest two which bear on the question of contemporary versus non-contemporary authorship. Perhaps schools founded by early rabbis persisted for several generations or even centuries, and late authors composed favorable stories about sages whom they considered to be their spiritual forbears. Perhaps late authors attacked rival schools by composing accounts which reflect poorly on the long-dead founders of these schools. By means of attacks

---

University Press, 1990), pp. 20-25. With regard to the Tannaitic period, see Robert Goldenberg, *The Sabbath-Law of Rabbi Meir* (Missoula, Montana: Scholars Press, 1978), especially pp. 245-47; and Jacob Neusner, *Judaism: The Evidence of the Mishna* (Chicago: University of Chicago, 1981), pp. 14-22.

[6]See the works cited in chapter 1, below. See also Saul Lieberman, "Martyrs of Caesarea," *Annuaire de L'Institut de Philologie et d'Histoire Orientalis et Slaves* 7 (1939-1944), pp. 395-446 (especially pp. 395-402); and *Hellenism in Jewish Palestine* (New York: Jewish Theological Seminary, 1950), pp. 83-99; David Halivni, *Mekorot u-Mesorot:* Eruvin-Pesahim (Jerusalem: Jewish Theological Seminary, 1982), pp. 91-95; Avraham Goldberg, "The Babylonian Talmud," in *The Literature of the Sages, Part One*, ed. Shmuel Safrai, Compendia Rerum Iudaicarum ad Novum Testamentum, sec. 2, vol. 3 (Philadelphia: Fortress Press, 1987), pp. 323-45; and Dov Zlotnick, *The Iron Pillar: Mishnah* (Jerusalem: Bialik Institute, 1988), pp. 8-9. I am not claiming that the above scholars consistently hold this position in all of their work.

on the character of Socrates, for example, the school of Socrates was attacked by rival schools after the sage's death.[7]

Analysis of a narrative which defends Mar bar Rav Ashi's right to rule in the city of Mata Mehasia will illustrate these points.[8] The narrative opens in Mahoza, where Mar bar Rav Ashi hears a madman declare that Tavyumi is head of the *metivta*[9] in Mata Mehasia. Mar bar Rav Ashi reasons that the position must be his, since he alone among the rabbis signs his name Tavyumi. He travels to Mata Mehasia, where the rabbis are about to appoint[10] Rav Aha Midifti as their head. Hearing of Mar bar Rav Ashi's arrival, rabbis are sent to seek his advice until ten are gathered in his presence. He delivers a formal address, thereby wresting control from Aha Midifti. Resigned to his fate, Aha applies to himself the proverb[11] that "whoever [the heavenly powers] harm, they do not quickly favor."[12]

---

[7]Patricia Cox, *Biography in Late Antiquity* (Berkeley, California: University of California Press, 1983), pp. 9-12.

[8]The story is found on Baba Batra 12b. For further discussion of the story's significance and its use as historical evidence, see Appendix 1, below. For earlier scholarly treatment of the story, see Solomon Rapaport, *Erekh Millin* (1852; Reprint. Warsaw, 1914), vol. 1, pp. 74-76; Heinrich Graetz, *Geschichte der Juden* (1853-1875; Reprint. Leipzig: O. Leiner, 1873-1900), vol. 4, pp. 371-72; Isaac H. Weiss, *Dor Dor ve-Dorshav* (1871-1891; Reprint. Jerusalem, 1964), vol. 3, pp. 188-89; Halevy, *Dorot ha-Rishonim*, vol. 3, p. 94; Neusner, *A History of the Jews in Babylonia*, vol 5, p. 254; and Avinoam Cohen, *Mar Bar Rav Ashi ve-Terumato ha-Sifrutit* (Ph.D. Dissertation, Yeshiva University, 1980), pp. 52-117.

[9]Little purpose would be served by entering here into the debate regarding the meaning of this term. It has been translated by different scholars as "academy" or as "study session." For an account of the theory that rabbinic instruction took place in the context of disciple circles, see Goodblatt, *Rabbinic Instruction in Sasanian Babylonia*, especially pp. 263-85; and "Hitpathuyot Hadashot be-Heker Yeshivot Bavel," *Zion* 43 (1978), pp. 14-38. For the theory that instruction took place in the context of academies, see Yeshayahu Gafni, *Yahadut Bavel u-Mosdoteha bi-Tekufat ha-Talmud* (Jerusalem: Merkaz Zalman Shazar, 1976), pp. 79-104; "'Yeshiva' u-'Metivta,'" *Zion* 43 (1978), pp. 12-37; "He'arot le-Ma'amaro Shel D. Goodblatt," *Zion* 46 (1981), pp. 52-56; "Ha-Yeshiva ha-Bavlit la-Or Sugyat B.K. 117a," *Tarbiz* 49 (1980), pp. 292-301; "Hiburim Nestorianim ke-Makor le-Toldot Yeshivot Bavel," *Tarbiz* 51 (1982), pp. 567-76; and *Yehudei Bavel bi-Tekufat ha-Talmud*, pp. 177-236. See also Saul J. Berman, "Adam Hashub: New Light on the History of Babylonian Amoraic Academies," *Dinei Yisrael* 13-14 (1986-1988), pp. 123-54; Kalmin, "Collegial Interaction in the Babylonian Talmud," pp. 383-415; and chapter 11, below.

[10]Or have already appointed.

[11]According to the Munich and Hamburg manuscripts, the text reads "Rav Aha Midifti said...."

[12]For a discussion of the variants of this story, see Cohen, *Mar Bar Rav Ashi*, pp. 52-93.

This story legitimates Mar bar Rav Ashi as head in Mata Mehasia at the expense of his contemporary and rival, Aha Midifti. The story views the madman's announcement at the beginning of the story as prophetic, in conformity with R. Yohanan's view that prophecy is in the hands of madmen and children since the destruction of the Temple. Mar, in wresting control from Aha, brings about the fulfillment of the madman's prophecy. He brings the actions of people in line with the will of heaven as expressed through the words of the madman. Aha Midifti's statement at the end of the story demonstrates his acceptance of the will of heaven in frustrating his ambitions to rule. "Whoever [the heavenly powers] harm, they do not quickly favor," says Aha, acknowledging defeat. He does not complain about the trick played on him by his unscrupulous rival, but rather accepts the bad fortune brought upon him by the will of heaven.

Was the story composed during Mar bar Rav Ashi's own time, however, or are later authors responsible? Is Mar bar Rav Ashi's own era depicted, or are events in a subsequent era the story's true subject? I will argue in subsequent chapters that in many instances these questions can be answered, but I see no way of answering them in the present case. The Talmud in this instance perhaps records polemics between rival schools in the form of a story involving the founders of these schools.

A unit of stories and statements on Baba Batra 22a further illustrates these points.[13] These stories and statements cast Rav Ada bar Ahava in an extremely negative light, but once again it is unclear whether they reflect contemporary hatred toward a particular individual, or competition between rival schools in a much later era.

The unit opens with a description of Rav Dimi Minehardea's arrival in the city of Mahoza.[14] Dimi carries figs for sale, and the exilarch directs Rava, one of the dominant rabbis in Mahoza, to determine whether Dimi is a sage worthy of special market privileges. Rava in turn directs Ada bar Ahava to "smell his bottle," i.e., to test Dimi's rabbinic learning. Ada obliges, greeting Dimi with a startling question: "If an elephant swallows a basket and expels the basket through its anus, what is the law?", i.e., does the basket become a vessel of dung which cannot become ritually impure, or is its status unchanged? Dimi is unable to answer, and asks whether Ada is Rava, whom he knows to be a leader in Mahoza. Ada

---

[13]For further discussion of this unit of stories, see Appendix 2, below.

[14]The story does not explicitly identify any geographical localities, but Rava's role in the story (see below) indicates that Mahoza is referred to. The Florence manuscript explicitly states that Dimi arrived in Mahoza, but this is most likely a later explanatory addition.

contemptuously strikes Dimi with his shoe,[15] declaring that "I am your master, and Rava is the master of your master." Dimi is not awarded market privileges, his figs spoil, and he complains to Rav Yosef. Yosef responds with a curse, promising that God will certainly requite this cruel treatment of Dimi.

As if in direct response to Yosef's curse, Ada dies. Yosef informs us that "I punished him, for I cursed him," while Dimi asserts that "I punished him, for he ruined my figs." Abaye announces that "I punished him, for he would say to the rabbis: 'Instead of gnawing bones in the house of Abaye, come and eat choice meat in the house of Rava.'" Rava claims that "I punished him" because Ada insulted Rava by demanding service ahead of Rava's attendant at the butcher's shop.[16]

Yosef's curse at the conclusion of the story reflects the narrator's unfavorable evaluation of Ada. Very likely, the unfavorable portrayal of Ada begins with the opening question to Dimi, continues when Ada gestures contemptuously and refers to himself as Dimi's master, and concludes when Dimi's produce is allowed to spoil.

Ada's opening question is most likely to be viewed as deliberately provocative and offensive. The Talmud's medieval commentators point out that the question is found verbatim elsewhere,[17] without any indication that it is shocking or inappropriate, so clearly it is a legitimate subject of rabbinic inquiry. Nevertheless, the question is very likely inappropriate as the initial greeting given to a visitor newly arrived in an unfamiliar locality. To use an imperfect modern analogy, discussion of the excretory functions of elephants might be perfectly appropriate in the context of a classroom or a professional conference. As the first words exchanged by two strangers, however, one of whom is a visitor from out of town, it is totally inappropriate.

Despite medieval protestations to the contrary,[18] furthermore, the rabbis who claim responsibility for Ada's death are most likely untroubled about their role in causing the death of a scholar. Rather, they are asserting the power of their curses in bringing about the punishment of a sage who shows insufficient respect for his fellow sages. Even though from a modern perspective Ada's offenses seem

---

[15]Or strikes Dimi's shoe. See Moed Katan 25a for Rashi's interpretation of the exchange between Rav Hisda and his son during Rav Abba's eulogy of Rav Huna. According to either interpretation, the gesture is one of contempt toward Dimi.

[16]See also Kiddushin 70a. Rav Nahman bar Yizhak also claims to have punished Ada, and his statement together with the accompanying story is examined in Appendix 2, below.

[17]Menahot 69a.

[18]See, for example, Tosafot and Ritba.

incommensurate with the punishment he suffers, from the Talmud's point of view his punishment is fully deserved. The text before us, in which Amoraim curse and kill as punishment for insults to the honor of rabbis, is by no means unique in the Talmudic corpus.[19]

This text tries to account theologically for the premature death of a scholar, and polemicizes against the practice of cross-examining scholars newly arrived in unfamiliar localities.[20] Separate from these issues, however, is the portrayal of Ada's death as deserved punishment for his humiliating treatment of Dimi Minehardea, and the orchestration of events to cast him in an unfavorable light. As with the story above involving Mar bar Rav Ashi, we are unable to determine the portrayal's date. Does it attest to contemporary hatred of Ada bar Ahava, or to later hostility between competing schools, one of which was closely identified with Ada and the second of which attacked the first by composing unflattering stories about its founder?

Later generations might compose accounts about much earlier rabbis for other reasons as well. They might choose as protagonists early rabbis who possessed or were said to possess some outstanding characteristic which particularly suited the author's message. The blindness of Rav Sheshet, a prominent Talmudic rabbi, might make him an especially fitting subject of a story which teaches that spiritual insight is far more powerful than physical sight.[21] Even long after his death, Sheshet might be made the protagonist of such a tale, for perhaps he had come to be the archetypical blind scholar, whose immense spiritual gifts more than compensated for his physical shortcomings.

A story featuring Sheshet and his contemporary, Rami bar Hama,[22] which casts Rami in an extremely unflattering light, will illustrate this point. Rami jealously lashes out at his former subordinate, Rav Yizhak bar Yehuda, who abandons Rami as his superior in favor of Sheshet. Yizhak bar Yehuda explains that Sheshet is preferable because he answers questions by quoting traditional sources. Armed with these sources, claims Yizhak bar Yehuda, Sheshet protects himself against

---

[19]See, for example, Berakhot 58b, Shabbat 108a, Yevamot 106a, Baba Kamma 80a, and Baba Mezia 84a. See also Neusner, *A History of the Jews in Babylonia*, vol. 3, pp. 61-81; and vol. 4, pp. 105-12 and 114-24, who discusses hostile traditions about the exilarch and rabbis portrayed as agents of the exilarch. See also chapter 1, below.

[20]See also Shabbat 108a, where the same practice leads to similarly tragic consequences in a story involving Rav and Shmuel.

[21]Berakhot 58a. See Yonah Fraenkel, "Bible Verses Quoted in Tales of the Sages," *Scripta Hierosolymitana* 22 (1971), pp. 94-98.

[22]Zevahim 96b.

refutation, for even if a contradictory tradition is cited the matter will end in a stalemate. Rami, however, responds with logical arguments, which are much weaker. He leaves himself vulnerable to attack, claims Yizhak, since a contradictory source will refute him. Rami challenges Yizhak to ask a question, expecting to demonstrate the power of his responses. Yizhak obliges, and Rami, true to form, counters with a logical argument. Yizhak quotes a contradictory source, and Rami, bowing to the superior authority of the source, acknowledges defeat.

The story is in part a didactic tale demonstrating the superiority of a style of learning which emphasizes knowledge of traditional sources in favor of logical reasoning. The story molds actual events or fabricates them entirely in an effort to influence the way rabbis learn and teach.

Does the story derive from the period of its protagonists, however? Or was it composed later by authors who chose stock characters equipped by tradition with attributes relevant to the lesson the authors wish to teach?

Once again, I see no way of answering these questions in the present case. Sheshet is elsewhere singled out for his remarkable erudition, his vast knowledge of traditional sources.[23] Rami, on the other hand, is said to possess keenness and sharp discernment, a positive quality which leads him into error, apparently causing him to rely too heavily on his intellectual gifts and neglect careful examination of several matters.[24] Perhaps Sheshet's legendary expertise, Rami's sharpness of intellect, and the criticism of Rami found in several sources[25] induced a late storyteller to choose them as protagonists and to cast Rami as the villain of the piece. Perhaps the author's exclusive concern was the story's message, and the personalities of Rami and Sheshet are relevant only insofar as they serve this larger concern.

Deciding between the Various Scholarly Approaches

Is it ever possible, however, to determine the date, authorship, and geographical provenance of Talmudic sources? Is it possible to decide between the contradictory scholarly approaches outlined above? With regard to the third approach, which accepts the historicity of Talmudic sources at face value, I will argue in chapter 1, below, that access to the original version of a passage (or, more accurately, access to the earliest version that modern scholarship is capable of reconstructing) does not guarantee access to the original words of the speaker or to the historical

---

[23]See, for example, Eruvin 67a, and Hanokh Albeck, *Mavo la-Talmudim* (Tel Aviv: Devir, 1969), pp. 312-13.
[24]See chapter 8, below.
[25]*Ibid.*

event, if any, which lies behind the passage. The historical core may not be recoverable, for opinions and events are frequently molded, colored, and distorted by the desires and beliefs of the original authors and their intended audience. Facile identification between text and history is an untenable scholarly approach.

Is it possible, however, to decide between the other approaches described above? Is it possible to determine whether contemporaries, near-contemporaries, or later editors originated the opinions or composed stories about the rabbis? Can we be reasonably certain that many sources which purport to derive from Palestine originate there and not elsewhere?

Perhaps the subtle character sketches and vivid portrayals of personalities and relationships found in Talmudic sources help us answer these questions. In discussing the famous story of Resh Lakish's conversion to the rabbinic way of life,[26] a student of mine once remarked that the story could not be the work of late, Babylonian editors because the characters were too real and the issues too immediate to be the invention of authors far removed, geographically and chronologically, from the events and personalities described.

This argument, unfortunately, fails to settle the issue. The character of R. Yohanan might be of pressing concern to a Babylonian author living centuries after the Palestinian sage's death, for example, if Yohanan had come to personify Palestinian learning and the late Babylonian author is passionately convinced of the superiority of Babylonian scholarship. By attacking Yohanan, this late author might simultaneously attack contemporary opponents who view themselves as Yohanan's disciples.[27] Similarly, competition between Sura and Pumbedita, Babylonian rabbinic centers of the Talmudic and post-Talmudic periods, might be expressed in the form of stories vividly depicting conflict between Rav Hisda and Rav Yehuda, important early representatives of these two cities. A story in which a student of Yehuda, Rami bar Tamari, demonstrates Hisda's inferiority to Yehuda,[28] might be an effective means by which late Pumbeditan storytellers propagandize in favor of their city and attack contemporary Suran foes, particularly since Hisda's connection to Sura

---

[26]Baba Mezia 84a. For further discussion of this story, see chapter 1, below.

[27]See Daniel Sperber, "On the Unfortunate Adventures of Rav Kahana: A Passage of Saboraic Polemic from Sasanian Persia," in *Irano-Judaica*, ed. Shaul Shaked (Jerusalem: Ben-Zvi Institute, 1982), pp. 83-100. See also Gafni, "Ha-Yeshiva ha-Bavlit la-Or Sugyat B.K. 117a," pp. 292-301.

[28]Hullin 110a.

and Yehuda's connection to Pumbedita are emphasized by the story itself.[29]

Part 1 of the present book, however, argues in favor of the second approach described above, namely that the Talmud is comprised of diverse sources which were not completely homogenized in the process of editing the Talmud.[30] More specifically, chapter 1 claims that several Talmudic stories reflect opposing polemical perspectives and most likely

---

[29]See also Yeshayahu Gafni, "Expressions and Types of 'Local Patriotism' Among the Jews of Sasanian Babylonia," in *Irano-Judaica II*, ed. Shaul Shaked and Amnon Netzer (Jerusalem: Ben-Zvi Institute, 1990), pp. 63-71; and *Yehudei Bavel bi-Tekufat ha-Talmud*, pp. 119-25.

[30]The literature on this subject is voluminous. See, for example, Yisrael Lewy, *Mavo u-Ferush le-Talmud Yerushalmi* (1895-1914; Reprint. Jerusalem, 1970), pp. 3-14 (introduction); Yaakov S. Zuri, *Toldot Darkhei ha-Limud be-Yeshivot Darom, Galil, Sura, ve-Nehardea* (Jerusalem, 1914), especially pp. 103-60; Haim Shaul Horowitz, "Die Komposition des Talmuds," *Monatschrift für Geschichte und Wissenschaft des Judentums* 63 (1919), pp. 122-30; Y.N. Epstein, *Mevo'ot le-Sifrut ha-Amoraim* (Tel Aviv: Devir, 1962), p. 12; and *Mavo la-Nusah ha-Mishna* (Jerusalem, 1964), pp. 353-493; Yaakov Zussman, *Sugyiot Bavliot le-Sedarim Zeraim ve-Tohorot* (Ph.D. Dissertation, Hebrew University, 1969), pp. 20-28, 30-30e, 110-11, 128-39, 161-62, 177-226, and 245-90; Goodblatt, *Rabbinic Instruction in Sasanian Babylonia*, pp. 63-196; and "The Babylonian Talmud," pp. 148-60, and the references cited there; Gideon Libson, "Al Mah Menadin," *Shanaton ha-Mishpat ha-Ivri* 2 (1975), pp. 298-342; and "Nidui u-Menudeh," *Shanaton ha-Mishpat ha-Ivri* 6-7 (1979-1980), pp. 177-202; David Rosental, "Pirka de-Abaye (Perek Sheni Shel Bavli Rosh Hashanah)," *Tarbiz* 46 (1977), p. 108, and the references cited there; "Arikhot Kedumot ha-Meshukaot ba-Talmud ha-Bavli," in *Mehkerei Talmud*, ed. Yaakov Zussman and David Rosental (Jerusalem: Magnes Press, 1990), pp. 155-204; and "'Benei ha-Talmud Hifsiku ve-Kafzu Lehakshot be-Tokh ha-Baraita': Bavli Ketubot 78a-b," *Tarbiz* 60 (1991), pp. 550-76; Bokser, *Post Mishnaic Judaism in Transition*, pp. 461-71; Michael Chernick, *Le-Heker ha-Midot "Kelal u-Ferat u-Kelal" ve-"Ribui u-Miut" ba-Midrashim u-va-Talmudim* (Lod: Makhon Haberman le-Mehkerei Sifrut, 1984), pp. 15-78; Eliezer Shimshon Rosental, *Massekhet Pesahim Talmud Bavli: Faksimilia mi-Ketav Yad (?) Provinza (?) 1442-1452* (London, 1984), pp. 5-16 and 39-53 (introduction); David Halivni, *Midrash, Mishnah, and Gemara: The Jewish Predilection for Justified Law* (Cambridge, Massachusetts: Harvard University Press, 1986), pp. 66-92; Kalmin, *The Redaction of the Babylonian Talmud*, pp. 5-7 and 38-65; Avraham Goldberg, "Derakhim Shel Zimzum Mahlokot Ezel Amoraei Bavel," in *Mehkerei Talmud*, pp. 135-53; Shaye J.D. Cohen, "The Modern Study of Ancient Judaism," and Bokser, "Talmudic Studies," in *The State of Jewish Studies*, pp. 63-64 and 89-94 respectively; Gafni, *Yehudei Bavel bi-Tekufat ha-Talmud*, pp. 11-16, 137-48, 187-90, 210-12, and 224-26; and Hermann L. Strack and Günter Stemberger, *Introduction to the Talmud and Midrash* (1991; Reprint. Minneapolis: Fortress Press, 1992), pp. 213-24.

For proof that Tannaitic sources contain pre-redactional elements, see, for example, Yaakov Zussman, "Heker Toldot ha-Halacha u-Megilot Midbar-Yehuda: Hirhurim Talmudi'im Rishonim la-Or Megilat 'Mikzat Ma'asei ha-Torah,'" *Tarbiz* 59 (1989), pp. 23-73.

derive from diverse sources. Chapters 2 through 7 argue that the Bavli attests to a variety of rhetorical, terminological, institutional, and attitudinal differences between early and later, Palestinian and Babylonian, and attributed and anonymous sources.

Chapter 3, for example, analyzes traditions in the Bavli dealing with dreams and attempts to show that Tannaitic sources approve, and Amoraic sources disapprove, of professional dream interpreters. Tannaitic sources depict rabbis interpreting the dreams of non-rabbis, even non-Jews, and Amoraic sources depict rabbis interpreting the dreams of other rabbis. Many traditions which the Bavli depicts as Tannaitic, therefore, are authentically Tannaitic (or at least relatively early), and many traditions which the Bavli presents as later are in fact later, and editors are not responsible for the change. Along these same lines, chapter 7 argues that quotation forms (technical terms which introduce a statement and do not form part of the statement) which introduce statements by early Amoraim differ from those which introduce statements by later Amoraim. Quotation forms which introduce statements by middle-generation Amoraim incorporate features of both early and later terminologies.

Comparison between the Bavli and Yerushalmi yields similar conclusions.[31] The Bavli, I attempt to show, contains Palestinian sources which were not completely Babylonianized in the process of transfer from one locality to the other. The two Talmuds, for example, sometimes portray Palestinian Amoraim in strikingly similar fashion, and agree that this portrayal distinguishes Palestinian from Babylonian Amoraim. In such cases, the most likely conclusion is that the Bavli preserves Palestinian sources, that the Bavli's unique portrayal of Palestinian

---

[31]For earlier comparisons between the Bavli and Yerushalmi which led to the conclusion that the Bavli preserves Palestinian sources, see, for example, Zussman, *Sugyiot Bavliot le-Sedarim Zeraim ve-Tohorot*, pp. 227-44; Zvi Moshe Dor, "Ha-Mekorot ha-Erez-Yisraeli'im be-Veit Midrasho Shel Rava," *Sinai* 52 (1962), pp. 128-43; *Sinai* 53 (1963), pp. 31-49; *Sinai* 55 (1964), pp. 306-16; "He'arah le-Ma'amaro Shel A. Goldberg," *Tarbiz* 34 (1964), p. 98; and *Torat Erez Yisrael be-Bavel* (Tel Aviv: Devir, 1971); Avraham Goldberg, "Hadirat ha-Halacha Shel Erez Yisrael le-Tokh Masoret Bavel ke-Fi she-Hi Mishtakefet mi-Tokh Perek Arvei Pesahim," *Tarbiz* 33 (1964), pp. 337-48; and "R. Zeira u-Minhag Bavel be-Erez Yisrael," *Tarbiz* 36 (1965), pp. 319-41; Goodblatt, "The Babylonian Talmud," pp. 148-51; Bokser, "Talmudic Studies," p. 89; Eliezer Segal, *Case Citation in the Babylonian Talmud: The Evidence of Tractate Neziqin* (Atlanta: Scholars Press, 1990), pp. 35-59; and Gafni, *Yehudei Bavel bi-Tekufat ha-Talmud*, p. 187. See also Strack and Stemberger, *Introduction to the Talmud and Midrash*, pp. 218-19, and the literature cited there.

discourse, institutions, and rabbinic relationships derives from Palestine.[32]

Another method used in this study to identify diverse sources takes as its starting point the Talmud's character as a literature of commentary.[33] Rabbis often comment on the statements, actions, and personalities of other rabbis, and do so in accordance with chronological data supplied by the Talmud itself. Rabbis depicted as later comment on statements by rabbis depicted as earlier, and contemporaries comment on statements by contemporaries. Rabbis depicted as early, however, do not comment on statements by rabbis depicted as later.[34]

These two factors, commentary and chronology, facilitate identification of several distinctions between rabbis portrayed by the Talmud as deriving from diverse time periods. Chapter 2, for example,

---

[32]For more on the relationship between the Palestinian and Babylonian Talmuds, see, for example, Zechariah Frankel, *Mavo ha-Yerushalmi* (1870; Reprint. Jerusalem, 1967), pp. 18b-53b; Louis Ginzberg, *Perushim ve-Hidushim ba-Yerushalmi* (1941; Reprint. New York: Ktav, 1971), vol. 1, pp. 86-87; Leopold Greenwald, *Ha-Ra'u Mesadrei ha-Bavli et ha-Yerushalmi?* (New York: Ha-Makhon le-Mehkar u-le-Mada ha-Yerushalmi, 1954), pp. 56-70; Epstein, *Mevo'ot le-Sifrut ha-Amoraim*, pp. 290-92; A. Steinzalts, "Ha-Kesharim Bein Bavel le-Erez Yisrael," *Talpiot* 9 (1965), pp. 294-306; Ronald Reuven Kimelman, *Rabbi Yohanan of Tiberias: Aspects of the Social and Religious History of Third Century Palestine* (Ph.D. Dissertation, Yale University, 1977), pp. 146-54; Baruch M. Bokser, "An Annotated Bibliographical Guide to the Study of the Palestinian Talmud," in *The Study of Ancient Judaism II: The Palestinian and Babylonian Talmuds*, ed. Jacob Neusner (New York: Ktav, 1981), pp. 187-91, and the literature cited there; Jacob Neusner, *The Bavli and Its Sources: The Question of Tradition in the Case of Tractate Sukkah* (Atlanta: Scholars Press, 1987), pp. 30-53; Pinhas Hayman, *Hitpathut ve-Shinuyim be-Torat R. Yohanan ben Napha be-Ha'avaratah mei-Erez Yisrael le-Bavel* (Ph.D. Dissertation, Yeshiva University, 1990; Ann Arbor: University Microfilms International, 1991), pp. 1-64, 71-82, and 89-95 (English section), and pp. 106-237, 275-401, and 429-56 (Hebrew section); Kraemer, *The Mind of the Talmud*, pp. 22-23 and 193-94; Catherine Hezser, *Form, Function, and Historical Significance of the Rabbinic Story in Yerushalmi Neziqin* (Ph.D. Dissertation: Jewish Theological Seminary, 1992), pp. 678-703; and Strack and Stemberger, *Introduction to the Talmud and Midrash*, pp. 218-19.

Martin Jaffee, "The Babylonian Appropriation of the Talmud Yerushalmi: Redactional Studies in the Horayot Tractates," in *New Perspectives on Ancient Judaism*, vol. 4, ed. Alan J. Avery-Peck (Lanham, Maryland: University Press of America, 1989), pp. 3-27, claims (pp. 23-24) that "the post-Amoraic editors of the [Bavli] had something much like the extant version of the [Yerushalmi] before them and reflected upon the logic of its construction as they composed their own commentary."

[33]See below for a detailed discussion of the term "commentary."

[34]There are some exceptions to this generalization, due to scribal error (see below) and editorial tampering. These exceptions do not contradict my claim that in general Talmudic discussions proceed along chronological lines.

attempts to show differences between early and later Amoraic attitudes toward the authority and statements of Rav and Shmuel, attitudes which are expressed in Amoraic commentary on Rav's and Shmuel's statements. Early Amoraim draw distinctions between the authority of Rav and Shmuel, and later Amoraim tend to view them as a unit. These differences, I argue, are evidence of distinct early and later Amoraic sources.

Distinctions between the anonymous and attributed sections of the Talmud, I claim, also show the diversity of the Talmud's source material.[35] Attributed rabbis, for example, express attitudes toward rabbis which differ from those reflected in unattributed statements. The anonymous editors tend to neutralize criticisms of rabbis contained in their sources, in contrast to attributed rabbis, who tend not to. These and other distinctions, I argue, support the claim of several scholars that by studying the anonymous and attributed materials independently we add significantly to our understanding of the Talmud's composition.

I have had little to say thus far about the historical or biographical value of the Bavli's sources. This omission has been deliberate, for a source's historicity is independent of its chronology or place of origin. Determining the latter is a necessary precondition for proper evaluation of a source's historicity, but Palestinian sources do not necessarily contain trustworthy evidence about Palestinian sages and institutions,

---

[35]See chapter 8, below, where I discuss this issue in greater detail. See also my explanation for why chapter 8's discussion of the anonymous parts of the Talmud, clearly relevant to Part 1 of this book, has been placed in Part 2. For further discussion of the Talmud's anonymous commentary, see Hyman Klein, "Gemara and Sebara," *Jewish Quarterly Review* 38 (1947), pp. 67-91; Feldblum, "The Impact of the 'Anonymous Sugya' on Halakic Concepts," pp. 19-28; Goodblatt, "The Babylonian Talmud," pp. 154-58; and "Towards the Rehabilitation of Talmudic History," pp. 37-38; Noah Aminoah, *Arikhat Massekhet Kiddushin* (Tel Aviv: E. Levin-Epstein, 1977); *Arikhat Massekhtot Bezah, Rosh Hashana, ve-Taanit ba-Talmud Bavli* (Tel Aviv: University of Tel Aviv, 1986); and *Arikhat Massekhtot Sukkah u-Moed Katan ba-Talmud Bavli* (Tel Aviv: University of Tel Aviv, 1988); Halivni, *Midrash, Mishnah, and Gemara*, pp. 66-92; Friedman, "Al Derekh Heker ha-Sugya," pp. 7-45; and *Talmud Arukh: Perek ha-Sokher et ha-Umanim ba-Bavli* (Jerusalem: Jewish Theological Seminary, 1991); Cohen, *Mar Bar Rav Ashi*, pp. 148-258 and 264-75; and "Bikoret Hilkhatit Le'umat Bikoret Sifrutit be-Sugiot ha-Talmud," *Asufot: Sefer Shanah le-Madaei ha-Yahadut* 3 (1989), pp. 331-46; Judith Hauptman, *Development of the Talmudic Sugya: Relationship Between Tannaitic and Amoraic Sources* (Lanham, Maryland: University Press of America, 1988); Kalmin, *The Redaction of the Babylonian Talmud*; Kraemer, *The Mind of the Talmud*; Bokser, "Talmudic Studies," pp. 93-95 and 98-101; Yaakov Elman, "Righteousness as its Own Reward: An Inquiry into the Theologies of the Stam," *Proceedings of the American Academy for Jewish Research* 57 (1991), pp. 35-67; and Strack and Stemberger, *Introduction to the Talmud and Midrash*, pp. 222-24.

nor do early sources necessarily depict the early period more accurately than do later sources.

What, if anything, can we say about the historical value of Talmudic sources? In tackling this question, it is necessary to take seriously the possibility that early and later sources attest to changes in how rabbis wish to portray themselves rather than to changes in their actual behavior. Or that sources reflect different Palestinian and Babylonian desires rather than different realities in the two centers.[36] Often the results of this study will be inconclusive, but on occasion historical and (very tentatively) biographical claims will be made.

As noted above, for example, we will conclude that the sources depict different early and later Amoraic attitudes toward the authority and statements of Rav and Shmuel. We will argue that the distinct sources in this instance most likely reflect historical reality and attest to an actual change in Amoraic attitudes.

It is possible, of course, that the attribution of these attitudes to particular sages is false, but this uncertainty has no significant impact on my conclusions in this instance. Even if the attributions are false, the attitudes themselves are most likely chronologically distinct. Pseudepigraphers rather than specific named Amoraim are perhaps responsible for the differing attitudes, but the sources nevertheless reliably depict a historical change, namely that different rabbinic attitudes are assignable to different historical periods.

Often, however, our historical conclusions will change if we take seriously the possibility that stories and statements have been fabricated. When we discover, for example, that stories involving early Amoraim presuppose distinct judicial and academic hierarchies, but stories involving later Amoraim do not (see chapter 4), we must ask whether the distinction between early and later sources is historically accurate. Do the judicial and academic hierarchies merge after the second generation, or do post-second-generation storytellers create a distorted picture, perhaps out of a desire to increase rabbinic power at the expense of the exilarch, whose importance in the judiciary is alluded to by several first- and second-generation stories?

---

[36]I wish to thank the participants in the History and Literature of Early Rabbinic Judaism section of the 1992 Society of Biblical Literature convention in San Francisco, California, for helping me formulate matters in this fashion. Special thanks are due Professors Daniel Boyarin, Shaye J.D. Cohen, and Robert Goldenberg. See also Christine Hayes, *Between the Babylonian and Palestinian Talmuds: Accounting for Halakhic Difference in Selected Sugyot from Tractate Avodah Zarah* (Ph.D. Dissertation, University of California at Berkeley, 1993); and Michael L. Satlow, *Talking About Sex: Rabbinic Rhetorics of Sexuality* (Ph.D. Dissertation, Jewish Theological Seminary, 1993).

Often we will see no way to answer such questions. We must not lose sight of the fact, however, that our choice is not, "Can we or can we not make use of Talmudic sources as historical evidence?" but rather what kind of historical use can we make of the sources. Even if the distinct early and later sources do not accurately reflect historical reality, they attest to a historical change, i.e., to a change in the way rabbinic storytellers depict the rabbinic movement.

The discussion thus far has focused on Part 1 of this book. While Part 1 contains numerous discussions of the historicity of the Bavli's sources, its main thrust is literary rather than historical. Its primary concern is identification and description of the Bavli's diverse sources, and only secondarily discussion of their possible historicity.

The major focus of Part 2, in contrast, is historical, containing, for example, chapter 9's historical explanation of a pattern revealed by the source analyses of Part 1. Chapter 9 argues that Part 1's consistent depiction of fourth-generation Babylonian Amoraim as transitional suggests that these middle-generation Amoraim may have been active editors of earlier Amoraic sources.

Chapters 10 and 11 continue the focus on history, examining the Talmud's portrayal of relationships between the rabbis who presumably produced and preserved the diverse sources analyzed in Part 1. Do Talmudic portrayals of relationships between Babylonian Amoraim, and of the organizational structures within which these rabbis interacted, correspond to the picture of diversity found in Part 1? Does the Talmud portray the Amoraim as a group likely to have authored and transmitted the diverse sources described in Part 1?

We will argue that it does, and that the correspondence between the two parts of this study argues in favor of the historicity of the Talmud's portrayals of a decentralized Amoraic movement. Part 2's conclusion that Babylonian Amoraim lacked unity and centralization strengthens Part 1's conclusion regarding diverse sources, and Part 1's conclusion regarding diverse sources reinforces and argues in favor of the historicity of Part 2's conclusions regarding the Talmud's portrayal of Amoraic diversity.

Definition of Terms

The terms "commentary," "dialogue," and "stories" play an important role in our analysis, and it will be helpful to define them at the outset of the discussion. The term "commentary" refers to remarks made by Rabbi X concerning either the statements or the character of Rabbi Y in situations where it is clear that the two rabbis are not speaking together and are not mentioned in the context of a single story. A discussion might begin, for example, with Rav ruling that it is forbidden to drink wine touched by an idolater. Rav Sheshet might follow with an objection against Rav's ruling, and according to all available evidence Sheshet had no direct contact with Rav. Sheshet's statement based on the statement by Rav falls under the category of "commentary" for the purposes of this study. Rav Yehuda, however, might respond to a statement by Shmuel, with all manuscripts and medieval commentators agreeing that Yehuda made his statement in Shmuel's presence, that "Rav Yehuda said to Shmuel," and with Yehuda's appearance in the presence of Shmuel a regular occurrence throughout the Talmud. In such circumstances, Yehuda's statement is considered "dialogue" rather than "commentary," for the term "dialogue" refers to the portrayal of actual communication, either when the Amoraim involved are depicted as speaking together in each other's presence, or when they communicate indirectly, via messenger.

Admittedly, dialogue and commentary are at times difficult to distinguish. A text which originally read "Shmuel said X. Said Rav Yehuda: But is it not the case that...?", i.e., which originally contained commentary by Yehuda based on Shmuel's statement, might be "corrected" by scribes to read "Shmuel said X. Said Rav Yehuda *to Shmuel*: But is it not the case that...?", i.e., might be transformed by scribes into dialogue. The opposite might also take place, with scribes transforming dialogue into commentary because of their assumption that the rabbis involved were not speaking in each other's presence.[37]

Several factors, however, reduce the significance of this uncertainty for my purposes. If two Amoraim appear frequently throughout the Talmud, and manuscripts and medieval testimonia agree that they never or only rarely appear in each other's presence, then we can conclude in individual cases with a fair degree of confidence that a particular passage depicts them as engaging in commentary and not dialogue when the

---

[37]See Eliezer Shimshon Rosental, "Rav Ben-Ahi R. Hiyya Gam ben-Ahoto?", in *Hanokh Yalon Jubilee Volume*, ed. Shaul Lieberman, E.Y. Kutscher, and Shaul Esh (Jerusalem: Kiryat Sefer, 1963), n. 1 on pp. 284-85; David Halivni, *Mekorot u-Mesorot*: Nashim (Tel Aviv: Devir, 1968), p. 17; and Friedman, *Perek ha-Isha Rabbah ba-Bavli*, p. 70, n. 3. See also chapters 8 and 10, below.

I refer throughout this book to the activity of "scribes." I do so for convenience, and not because I am certain that the phenomena under discussion are due to the activity of scribes rather than oral transmitters. For detailed discussion of this issue, see Eliezer Shimshon Rosental, "Toldot ha-Nusah u-Va'ayot-Arikha be-Heker ha-Talmud ha-Bavli," *Tarbiz* 57 (1988), pp. 1-36; and Yerahmiel Brody, "Sifrut ha-Geonim ve-ha-Text ha-Talmudi," in *Mehkerei Talmud*, pp. 237-303. See also Shamma Friedman's response to Brody and Rosental: "Le-Hithavut Shinuyei ha-Girsaot ba-Talmud ha-Bavli," *Sidra* 7 (1991), pp. 67-102.

passage contains no hint that they speak in each other's presence. Our confidence is increased if the sources supply chronological or geographical reasons why the two Amoraim most likely did not appear in each other's presence. Talmudic sources consistently maintain, for example, that R. Yirmiya spent much of his scholarly career in Palestine, and that Abaye and Rava lived their entire lives in Babylonia. When a text presents Abaye or Rava commenting on Yirmiya's statements rather than conversing with him, we can be reasonably certain that the text reflects the Talmud's dominant view regarding these sages and not scribal carelessness or misunderstanding.

The term "stories" refers to reports of events or actions, and also to actions or statements found within a narrative framework which begins with a description of the physical setting in which the action took place or the statement was made. The beginning of a story is clearly demarcated, with the description of setting or reported action marking the story off from its surrounding context. The conclusion of the story, however, is often difficult to discern. It is often unclear whether a statement placed at the conclusion of a story is part of the story or is commentary on the story. The chronological and geographical factors helpful above in distinguishing dialogue from commentary are not so helpful here, since the story might conclude with commentary by a rabbi from a different time or a different place, providing perspective on the events or opinions narrated in the body of the tale. Throughout this book, statements concluding stories will be considered doubtful commentary, but this uncertainty will not significantly alter my findings.

As noted in the Preface, this study deals primarily (though not exclusively) with Amoraic statements and activity recorded in the Bavli. Very likely, the statistics found throughout will have to be modified once parallels in other ancient rabbinic and non-rabbinic documents are more fully taken into account. Comparative study will serve to make the statistics more precise but will not, I am convinced, significantly alter my conclusions. Without a doubt, this conviction needs documentation, and substantial sections of the present study must therefore be viewed as preliminary statements which more detailed analysis will very likely confirm.

Part One

LITERARY STUDIES

1

Saints or Sinners, Scholars or Ignoramuses?

Stories about the Rabbis as Evidence for the Composite Nature of the Babylonian Talmud

In this chapter, I examine the Talmud's portrayal of the characters and personalities of several prominent Amoraim. I ask whether these Amoraim are presented as saints or as sinners, as scholars or ignoramuses, as friends and colleagues or as barely on speaking terms. My goal is to determine whether their portrayal aids us in identifying and describing some of the diverse sources that make up the Babylonian Talmud. I attempt to show that Talmudic accounts of the rabbis' personalities and the nature of rabbinic interactions contain contradictions that betray the existence of opposing sources. According to some sources, for example, Abaye is ignorant and incompetent while Rava is the greatest scholar of his generation. According to other sources, Rava is sinful and arrogant, cruel toward his contemporaries and disrespectful toward his teacher, in contrast to Abaye, who is a loyal and devoted disciple. According to my conclusions and the conclusions of other scholars, important aspects of the history of the Amoraic period need to be re-evaluated, since historians have tended to accept Talmudic stories as reliable evidence once miraculous elements and later editorial accretions have been removed.[1]

---

[1]The literature on the crucial subject of the use of Talmudic stories as evidence for history and biography is enormous, and a comprehensive bibliography will not be provided here. See, however, Wilhelm Bacher, *Die Agada der Babylonischen Amoräer* (Frankfurt am Main, 1913), pp. 34 and 114-15, who reconciles conflicting Talmudic accounts of the interaction between Rav and Shmuel and Abaye and Rava by claiming that their relationship was a peculiar combination of closeness and collegiality and intense competition. See also Moshe D. Herr, "The Historical Significance of the Dialogues Between Jewish Sages and Roman Dignitaries," and

Shmuel Safrai, "Tales of the Sages in the Palestinian Tradition and the Babylonian Talmud," *Scripta Hierosolymitana* 22 (1971), pp. 123-50 and 209-32 respectively. Safrai acknowledges differences in various versions of agadot, but they are "two accounts of the same event (p. 210)." Safrai assumes that "generally, too, the names of the Sages...are not confused in these narratives handed down by tradition, nor are the relations between them inconsistent with respect to the times *(ibid.)*. See also Graetz, *Geschichte der Juden*, vol. 4, pp. 258, 266-67, and 329-31; Ephraim Urbach, *Ha-Halacha: Mekoroteha ve-Hitpathutah* (Givatayim, Israel: Yad la-Talmud, 1984), pp. 192-216; Joshua Schwartz, "Tension Between Palestinian Scholars and Babylonian Olim in Amoraic Palestine," *Journal for the Study of Judaism* 11 (1980), pp. 78-94; and Yoel Florsheim, "Ha-Yahasim Bein Hakhmei ha-Dor ha-Sheni Shel Amoraei Bavel," *Zion* 51 (1986), pp. 285-93. Florsheim reconciles contradictory sources by assigning them to different periods of an Amora's life.

Jacob Neusner, by contrast, argues convincingly that at times the contradictions do not admit of reconciliation. See, for example, Neusner, *A History of the Jews in Babylonia*, vol. 3, pp. 50-94, and vol. 4, pp. 73-82 and 85-124, and *The Rabbinic Traditions About the Pharisees Before 70* (Leiden: E.J. Brill, 1979), especially pp. 184-341. See also Baruch M. Bokser, "Wonder-Working and the Rabbinic Tradition: The Case of Hanina Ben Dosa," *Journal for the Study of Judaism* 16, No. 1 (1985), pp. 42-92, and the references cited on p. 43, n. 2. See also Gafni, "Hiburim Nestorianim ke-Makor le-Toldot Yeshivot Bavel,"pp. 574-75, who analyzes stories about Babylonian rabbis and discovers motifs also present in Nestorian literature. Gafni argues that these parallels "do not necessarily attest to contact" between the two communities, but might be motifs absorbed independently into the two literatures. At least some of the biographical information preserved in the Talmud concerning Babylonian Amoraim, therefore, cannot be accepted at face value as historical fact. See also Sperber, "On the Unfortunate Adventures of Rav Kahana," pp. 83-100. Sperber argues persuasively that the story is a pro-Babylonian polemic and cannot be accepted as evidence for conditions in Palestine during the time of R. Yohanan. See also Gafni, "Ha-Yeshiva ha-Bavlit la-Or Sugyat B.K. 117a," pp. 292-301. See also Yonah Fraenkel, *Iyunim ba-Olamo ha-Ruhani Shel Sippur ha-Agadah* (Tel Aviv: Ha-Kibbuz ha-Meuhad, 1981). On p. 8, Fraenkel writes that he is not interested in the ancient rabbinic stories for the historical and biographical information they contain, but rather as sources for the rabbis' answers to eternal human questions. Whether or not such and such really happened to Hillel or R. Akiba is, for the purposes of Fraenkel's study, irrelevant. See also Fraenkel, "Bible Verses Quoted in Tales of the Sages," p. 89, n. 23, who writes that "It must be stated that in principle one should not rely on parallels in a literary analysis of Talmudic stories, but look for the intrinsic unity in every story. That is also why the general image of a sage can differ from one story to the next, which is natural if different narrators told the stories, and there is no need for any artificial harmonization." Most recently, see Yonah Fraenkel, *Darkhei ha-Agadah ve-ha-Midrash* (Givatayim, Israel: Yad la-Talmud, 1991), pp. 235-85. See also Anthony J. Saldarini, "The Adoption of a Dissident: Akabya ben Mahalaleel in Rabbinic Tradition," *Journal of Jewish Studies* 33 (1982), pp. 547-56. Saldarini observes that the story of Akabya's excommunication in Mishna Eduyot 5:6-7 fits the purposes of the editors of the Mishna. Whatever historical kernel that may be contained within the story, he concludes, is unrecoverable. See also William Scott Green, "What's in a Name - The Problematic of Rabbinic

This is not to say that every contradiction is proof of a distinct source. Yonah Fraenkel is very likely correct that the purpose of many Talmudic stories is not to advance a particular school's agenda or to promote the teachings of a particular master, but to teach a moral lesson, to make a statement about the nature of the world, or God, or the human predicament.[2] As such, the character of the Amoraic protagonist may be molded to fit the particular statement the author wishes to make. The same school or author, depending on the needs of the narrative, might portray the same rabbi in contradictory terms. Patricia Cox, examining Eusebius' biography of Origen, makes the same point. Eusebius' Origen, she writes, is "Janus-faced," meaning that a unified, coherent personality does not emerge from Eusebius' account of the life of Origen because the actual, historical Origen is refracted through the lens of Eusebius and the requirements of his narrative and the audience for whom he is writing.[3]

On several occasions, however, stories are told to promote or attack a particular rabbi or school, sometimes from contradictory polemical perspectives, and the most likely explanation is that the stories derive from opposing sources. In the final analysis, every narrative and every contradiction needs to be evaluated on its own terms.

'Biography,'" in *Approaches to Ancient Judaism: Theory and Practice,* ed. William Scott Green (Chico, California: Scholars Press, 1978), pp. 77-94; "Context and Meaning in Rabbinic 'Biography,'" in *Approaches to Ancient Judaism,* ed. William Scott Green (Chico, California: Scholars Press, 1980), vol. 2, pp. 97-111; and "Storytelling and Holy Man, The Case of Ancient Judaism," in *Take Judaism for Example,* ed. Jacob Neusner (Chicago: University of Chicago Press, 1983), pp. 29-43. See also Albert I. Baumgarten, "Rabbi Judah I and his Opponents," *Journal for the Study of Judaism* 12, No. 2 (1981), pp. 135-72. See also Zipporah Kagan, "Divergent Tendencies and Their Literary Moulding in the Aggadah," *Scripta Hierosolymitana* 22 (1971), pp. 151-70. Kagan finds that the versions of the story of the early years of R. Eliezer ben Hyrcanus' life divide into two groups. One group is "earlier and more authentic. The Aggadah in Group A was told close to the time when the events took place and for that reason it preserved a more realistic view of the figures, the plot, and numerous details. The Aggadah in Group B...was composed at a later time than the historical event (p. 168)." Finally, see Menahem Hirshman, "Li-Demuto Shel Shmuel ha-Katan," and Alon Goshen-Gottstein, "R. Elazar ben Arakh: Semel u-Meziut," in *Yehudim ve-Yahadut bi-Yemei Bayit Sheni, ha-Mishna ve-ha-Talmud,* ed. Aharon Oppenheimer, Yeshayahu Gafni, and Menahem Stern (Jerusalem: Yad Yizhak ben Zvi, 1993), pp. 165-72 and 173-97 respectively.

[2]See, for example, Yonah Fraenkel, "She'elot Hermeneutiot ba-Heker Sipur ha-Agadah," *Tarbiz* 47 (1978), pp. 139-72. See also the response by E.E. Halevi, "Od Al Genre Hadash ba-Sipurei ha-Agadah," *Tarbiz* 49 (1980), pp. 424-28, and Fraenkel's rejoinder ("Teshuva," p. 429, there).

[3]Cox, *Biography in Late Antiquity,* pp. 69-101.

It bears repeating that by the term "stories" I refer to reports of events or actions, and also to actions or statements found within a narrative framework which begins with a description of the physical setting in which the action took place or the statement was made. This description can be fairly elaborate, but more typically is extremely simple, consisting, for example, of the information that Rabbi X was sitting down when he made his statement.[4]

Before substantiating the above claims, it is necessary to say a few additional words about the criteria used in determining that stories derive from diverse sources. Since both favorable and unfavorable stories about an Amora often come to us as part of the same document, the Babylonian Talmud, it is frequently impossible to discern the existence of opposing sources. We must be wary about imposing western, twentieth-century values on the actions of ancient rabbis.

In one story, for example, Rava refuses to surrender the property of Isur the convert, who is lying on his death bed. Rava's plan is to take possession of the property when Isur dies. Rava wants to prevent his student, Rav Mari son of Isur, from taking possession of the property.[5] Rava discusses several ways in which ownership of property is normally transferred, and explains why each method has no efficacy in the present instance. Another student of Rava, Rav Ika b. d'Rav Ami, suggests a way in which Rav Mari can take possession even without Rava's cooperation. Word reaches the dying Isur, who follows the suggestion of Rav Ika b. d'Rav Ami and transfers ownership to his son. Word of what happened reaches Rava, and he angrily denounces his students for causing him economic loss.

Rava's conduct in this instance strikes us as reprehensible,[6] which might lead us to conclude that the story derives from circles hostile to Rava. More likely, the Talmud does not share our ethical standards in this matter. Rava is perfectly within his rights in holding on to Isur's property, since Rav Mari, born to Isur before he converted, has no claim to his father's inheritance according to Jewish law. Furthermore, it is not Rava's responsibility to tell Isur how he can transfer ownership to Rav

---

[4]See also Goodblatt, "The Babylonian Talmud," p. 165, and the literature cited in n. 51a, there; Hezser, *Form, Function, and Historical Significance of the Rabbinic Story in Yerushalmi Neziqin*, pp. 1-18 and 538-628; and Fraenkel, *Darkhei ha-Agadah ve-ha-Midrash*, pp. 15-17 and 481-99. See also the Introduction, above.

[5]Baba Batra 149a.

[6]See Graetz, *Geschichte der Juden*, vol. 4, pp. 332-33, who criticizes Rava's actions in this story. See the material collected by Mordechai Yudelowitz, *Mahoza: mei-Hayei ha-Yehudim bi-Zeman ha-Talmud* (Jerusalem, 1947), pp. 68-70. Yudelowitz concludes that relations between Rava and his students were strained.

Mari. Rava's students, in fact, can be faulted for using their halachic knowledge to influence the course of a monetary dispute they have no business getting involved in.[7] Our moral standards, therefore, are often quite different from those of the Talmudic rabbis. What strikes us as a hostile source often turns out not to be when viewed from the perspective of the Talmud itself.

Even the portrayal of behavior unattractive by the Talmud's standards, however, cannot always be taken as evidence of a hostile source. In ancient as in modern times, a complex personality evokes a variety of different responses, even among those most sympathetic to him. In ancient as in modern times, a single individual might be spoken of, by the same people, in terms alternatingly respectful and critical. This is not to say that we know enough about the psychology of Talmudic rabbis to draw exact parallels between the modern and ancient periods. We certainly do not. It is simply to say that caution is necessary when determining whether or not a source is hostile on the basis of its portrayal of an individual sage. The same individuals who praise a rabbi's scholarship might criticize his nasty temper, and might carefully preserve vivid descriptions of positive and negative aspects of his personality.

The situation is not totally hopeless, however. Occasionally we are on firm ground in determining that a story derives from a hostile source. One indication of this fact is the imputation to a rabbi of character traits which within the rabbinic value system mark the person off as *fundamentally* flawed or inadequate, provided that the character portrayal serves no larger moral or theological agenda. A rabbi might be portrayed as ignorant, a transmitter of unreliable traditions, or as violating fundamental rabbinic precepts, and the portrayal serves as a personal attack rather than as dramatization of some abstract truth.[8] Another important clue that a story derives from a hostile source is the presence in the story of rabbis who have clear motivation for portraying an Amora in unflattering terms (see below). Finally, if an Amora's portrayal in one story conflicts with his portrayal in another story, and the contradiction is not subservient to the message of the narrative, the existence of opposing sources may be the most likely explanation. Obviously, our argument is considerably stronger when more than one of these factors coincide.

---

[7]See Mishna Avot 1:8. See also Ketubot 52b, where R. Yohanan castigates himself for giving halachic advice to one of the parties in a monetary dispute, and thereby influencing the outcome of the case.

[8]See the discussion below.

It bears repeating that rabbis are often portrayed positively or negatively not because a story wishes to glorify or condemn a particular individual, but because the central purpose of the narrative is served by distorting or fabricating aspects of a sage's personality. In the discussion that follows, I focus only on cases in which no such larger purpose is discernible, or at least does not fully determine a sage's portrayal. I attempt to base the discussion only on cases in which a major point of the story is to enhance or undermine a rabbi's reputation independent of any other concern.

Talmudic stories about Geniva, a first- and/or second-generation Babylonian Amora, will serve as a case in point.[9] According to one story, Mar Ukba, identified in *Igeret Rav Sherira Gaon* as exilarch, complains to R. Elazar about certain individuals who are "vexing him greatly," and who he wishes to hand over to the Persian government.[10] Elazar counsels restraint; Mar Ukba should study Torah[11] and God will reward him with the destruction of his enemies. The story concludes with Geniva's imprisonment, confirming the wisdom of Elazar's counsel. God's hand is clearly at work, rewarding Ukba for his restraint in the face of Geniva's provocation. Ukba deserves praise for not taking matters into his own hands, for not involving the gentile government in an internal Jewish affair.

This story's negative attitude toward Geniva contrasts sharply with the sympathetic portrayal found in two other stories. According to one of the two stories, Rav Huna and Rav Hisda are seated together as Geniva passes by. One of the seated scholars[12] suggests that they stand before Geniva, a learned man, while the other wonders whether it is appropriate to stand before a man of division. Geniva approaches and greets them: "Peace be upon you, kings, peace be upon you, kings," which prompts Huna and Hisda to ask why he refers to them as kings and why he repeats his greeting. In response, Geniva quotes scripture and a statement by Rav, whereupon Huna and Hisda ask Geniva to join

---

[9]For earlier scholarly discussion of these stories, see Moshe Beer, "Rivo Shel Geniva be-Mar Ukba," *Tarbiz* 31 (1962), pp. 281-86; and *Rashut ha-Golah be-Bavel bi-Yemei ha-Mishna ve-ha-Talmud* (Tel Aviv: Devir, 1970), pp. 94-98; Neusner, *A History of the Jews in Babylonia,* vol. 3, pp. 75-81; Ephraim Urbach, "Al Iyun Histori ba-Sippur Al Moto Shel Rabbah bar Nahmani," *Tarbiz* 34 (1963-1964), pp. 160-61; Shamma Friedman, "La-Agadah ha-Historit ba-Talmud ha-Bavli," in *Sefer ha-Zikaron le-R. Shaul Lieberman* (Jerusalem: Saul Lieberman Institute of Talmudic Research, 1989), pp. 28-42; and Richard Kalmin, "The Talmudic Story: Aggada as History," *Proceedings of the Tenth World Congress of Jewish Studies* (1990) Division C, vol. 1, pp. 9-16.

[10]Gittin 7a.

[11]Or pray. See Tosafot, Meiri, and Maharam Shif.

[12]We are not told which one.

them in a meal. Again Geniva responds with a quotation of Rav, explaining why he cannot do so.[13]

Moshe Beer notes the close connection between this story and a similar story involving the same protagonists.[14] In this third story, Huna and Hisda are once again seated together as Geniva passes by. Again they debate whether to stand before Geniva, one arguing that he is a man of learning, the other that he is a man of division. Geniva approaches and asks what they are discussing. "Wind," they say, whereupon Geniva quotes a statement by Rav on the subject of wind.[15] Beer argues convincingly that a unified story featuring Huna, Hisda, and Geniva has been divided in two, each half placed in an appropriate context by a later editor.[16] Beer notes further that the story portrays Geniva as well-versed in the opinions of Rav, and claims that Geniva wishes to contrast his own expertise with Huna's ignorance, an ignorance made even more shocking by the fact that Huna was Rav's successor as head in Sura.

As indicated above, these stories reflect different perspectives on the merits of Geniva and very likely derive from diverse sources. The Mar Ukba tale (the first story described above) most likely derives from sources hostile to Geniva, as is indicated by its portrayal of Geniva's imprisonment as divine reward for Ukba's restraint. The Huna-Hisda stories, however, are sympathetic to Geniva and hostile to Huna and Hisda. The most striking proof of this claim is the portrayal of Geniva's superior knowledge of the opinions of Rav, contrasted by the ignorance of Huna and Hisda.[17] Other, subtler aspects of the narrative, however, also attest to its unfavorable opinion of Huna and Hisda. Huna and Hisda very likely betray the narrator's evaluation of their conduct when they inform Geniva that they were discussing "wind." Their debate about the wisdom of standing before Geniva was wind, worthless talk. Later on,[18] impressed by Geniva's responses, Huna and Hisda invite him to join them in a meal. By rejecting their invitation, Geniva turns the tables on them. Huna and Hisda, by their ignorance, are unfit to associate with him, not the other way around as they initially thought. Most likely, the Talmud preserves two (or three) stories about Geniva which derive from different sources.

Stories dealing with the character of R. Elazar ben Pedat and his relationship to R. Yohanan, Palestinian Amoraim of the second and third

---

[13]Gittin 62a.
[14]Beer, "Rivo Shel Geniva," pp. 281-86; and *Rashut ha-Golah,* pp. 94-98.
[15]Gittin 31b.
[16]See also Bacher, *Die Agada der Babylonischen Amoräer,* p. 72.
[17]Compare Beer, "Rivo Shel Geniva," pp. 282-83.
[18]Assuming that Beer is correct that the two accounts were originally one.

generations, further illustrate this point.[19] In two stories critical of R. Elazar, for example, Resh Lakish states an opinion and Elazar follows with an opposing view.[20] Later on, Resh Lakish repeats his opinion in the presence of R. Yohanan, and Yohanan states the view expressed earlier by Elazar. Resh Lakish, angry at being publicly contradicted by his teacher, denounces Elazar for stating an opinion and failing to attribute it to its author, Yohanan. According to these stories, Elazar's contemptible failure to attribute statements to their author leads to the public humiliation of a revered scholar, Resh Lakish.

One story which makes no mention of Resh Lakish repeats the familiar charge of plagiarism against Elazar, but from a strikingly different point of view. In this story Elazar once again states an opinion and fails to attribute it to its author, Yohanan.[21] Yohanan is angry with Elazar, but ultimately rejoices when R. Yaakov bar Idi brings about their reconciliation. Yaakov bar Idi cleverly compares the relationship between Yohanan and Elazar to that between the biblical heroes, Moses and Joshua. The relationship between master and disciple in both instances is so close that there is no need for the disciple to quote the master by name, argues Yaakov bar Idi. Just as the ancient Israelites knew that everything Joshua said he heard from Moses, so too everything Elazar says derives from his teacher, R. Yohanan. In the one context where the familiar charge of plagiarism is raised and Resh Lakish is not present, therefore, the criticism against Elazar is dismissed and he and his teacher are reconciled.

The various Talmudic narratives dealing with the character of Elazar, therefore, contain irreconcilable contradictions and most likely derive from diverse sources.

Most likely, it is no coincidence that when Elazar alone comes in contact with Yohanan, in all but two cases[22] their relationship is harmonious and Elazar is an exemplary student. By contrast, whenever Resh Lakish is also present, Elazar's actions are unbefitting a scholar, or bring him censure from his teacher.[23] In another story critical of Elazar,

---

[19]Compare Kimelman, *Rabbi Yohanan of Tiberias,* pp. 131-37.

[20]Ketubot 25b and Makkot 5b. For other stories depicting tension between them, see Yevamot 72b and Menahot 93b. Compare Zevahim 5a. See also Baba Kamma 100a and *Dikdukei Soferim,* n. bet (Henceforth, we will refer to this work as *DS.* Talmudic citations together with references to *DS* will be indicated as follows: Baba Kamma 100a [*DS* bet]), and Bekhorot 26b (The Munich, Florence, Vatican, and London manuscripts read R. Ilai instead of R. Elazar).

[21]Yevamot 96b. See also Yer. Berakhot 2:1 (and parallels).

[22]Hullin 19b and Keritut 27a.

[23]See Yevamot 35b-36a, where R. Elazar comments on a statement by Resh Lakish and displays no ill will toward him. See below for my discussion of the relationship between Rava and Rav Yosef. Rava's conduct was an issue for Rav

the well-known account of Resh Lakish's conversion to the rabbinic way of life, Elazar is portrayed as a student who continually supports the opinions of his teacher, Yohanan.[24] Elazar is contrasted unfavorably to Resh Lakish, who constantly challenges his teacher, spurring him on to greater and greater insight. In the eyes of Yohanan, say the transmitters of this story, Elazar is an unsatisfactory surrogate for Resh Lakish after the latter's tragic death.

In contrast, other narratives which make no mention of Resh Lakish portray an extremely close relationship between Yohanan and Elazar,[25] or show Yohanan, after his death, appearing to Elazar in a dream and supporting his interpretations.[26] On another occasion, Elazar states a halachic opinion, Yohanan follows with an objection, and Elazar successfully rejects his teacher's argument. When Elazar observes his teacher's unhappiness at having been defeated in argument by his student, Elazar skillfully soothes his injured pride.[27] In another context, Elazar is portrayed as a close disciple of Yohanan who knows how to interpret the moods of his teacher.[28]

Several other sages are portrayed unfavorably when found in the presence of a particular Amora, but come off much better when they appear in isolation or in the presence of a different Amora. Close examination of each individual story is necessary before final conclusions are drawn, but a likely explanation is that stories about these Amoraim derive from a variety of sources.[29] Rav Shila, for example, is portrayed

---

Yosef and/or his disciples (or later editors), but in statements attributed to Rava, we find no evidence of any tension between them.

[24]Baba Mezia 84a.

[25]Berakhot 5b, Yoma 53a, Hagiga 13a, and Baba Batra 7b.

[26]Bekhorot 5a and 56a.

[27]Ketubot 111b.

[28]Kiddushin 31b.

[29]We see this, for example, with the interaction between Rav and Rav Shila, R. Elazar and Shmuel, Rabbah and Mar Yehuda, Rava and Rav Papa bar Shmuel, Rava and Mar Zutra b. d'Rav Nahman, Rava and Rav Nahman bar Rav Hisda, and Rava and Rami bar Hama. With regard to Rav and Rav Shila, see Yoma 20b and Sanhedrin 44a, where Rav Shila appears in the presence of Rav and is portrayed unfavorably. See also Sanhedrin 109a. Compare Berakhot 49b, where Rav Shila quotes a statement by Rav. See also the references cited in Benjamin Kosowsky, *Ozar ha-Shemot* (Jerusalem: The Ministry of Education and Culture, Government of Israel, and The Jewish Theological Seminary, 1976-1983), p. 1546. With regard to R. Elazar and Shmuel, see Eruvin 74a and Hullin 111b, where Shmuel appears in the presence of R. Elazar and in both cases is portrayed unfavorably. On Ketubot 77a, they appear in each other's presence and Shmuel harshly rejects R. Elazar's tradition. With regard to Rabbah and Mar Yehuda, see Eruvin 61b and Kiddushin 58a. See the references cited in Kosowsky, *ibid.*, p. 1036. With regard to Rava and Rav Papa bar Shmuel, see Rosh Hashana 27a and

unfavorably when in the presence of Rav, but when Rav is not present or when Shmuel also figures in the story he is depicted more sympathetically. Rav Papa bar Shmuel invariably judges or acts incorrectly whenever Rava appears in his presence or is mentioned in the same story. Rav Papa bar Shmuel judges a case, for example, Rava objects in his presence, and Rav Papa bar Shmuel, in order to save face, asserts that he actually intended to say what Rava says. Rava follows with one or two additional objections, and again Rav Papa bar Shmuel adjusts his position, claiming each time that he intended to say what Rava says.[30] Elsewhere, however, when Rava is not present, Rav Papa bar Shmuel comes off quite well, as a community leader and judge, and as a student of Rav Yosef and Rav Hisda. In these cases as well, the contradictory portraits most likely do not admit of reconciliation and are evidence of opposing sources.

A story[31] which portrays conflict between Rav Yehuda and Rav Nahman, important Babylonian Amoraim of the second generation, further supports the contention that stories about the rabbis derive from diverse sources. This story disapproves of Rav Nahman and deliberately depicts him in an unflattering light. According to Jacob Neusner, the story's hostility to Nahman derives from his close association with the court and family of the exilarch.[32] Neusner divides the rabbinic movement into pro- and anti-exilarchic camps, and claims that this story's criticism of Nahman is criticism of the exilarch. It is difficult to agree with Neusner's interpretation, however, because Nahman's relationship to the exilarch is referred to only once in the story and the reference is not at all unfavorable. Nahman demands that Rav Yehuda appear before him in court, whereupon Yehuda goes to Rav Huna and asks if he should heed Nahman's summons. Huna answers that Nahman has overstepped his bounds, but Yehuda should go anyway so as not to offend the exilarch. There is nothing in this exchange which implies criticism or resentment towards Nahman on account of his connection to the exilarch. In general, Neusner's important early work on the history

---

34b, Baba Kamma 84a, Baba Mezia 60b and 109b, and Sanhedrin 26b. Compare Baba Batra 90b and Sanhedrin 17b. See the references cited in Kosowsky, *ibid*, p. 1226. With regard to Rava and Mar Zutra b. d'Rav Nahman, and Rava and Rav Nahman bar Rav Hisda, see the discussion below. In cases where Rava is not involved, reaction to the opinions of Mar Zutra b. d'Rav Nahman and Rav Nahman bar Rav Hisda follows no consistent pattern. Sometimes their opinions are rejected, other times they go unchallenged. See the references cited by Kosowsky, *ibid.*, pp. 1035-36 and 1104-05.

[30] Baba Kamma 84a. See *DS* shin.
[31] Kiddushin 70a-b.
[32] Neusner, *A History of the Jews in Babylonia*, vol. 2, pp. 61-75.

of the Jews in Babylonia overemphasizes the role of the exilarch in determining the tenor of relationships between rabbis. One important factor not considered by Neusner is competition between the rabbis themselves, independent of the exilarch. Most likely, internal rabbinic competition is the motivating factor behind this story's unflattering portrayal of Nahman. Throughout the story, Nahman repeatedly displays his ignorance of the opinions of Shmuel. Nahman's ignorance displays itself in a lengthy series of improper actions, and each time, Yehuda quotes Shmuel against him. Nahman quotes two statements by Rav, but Yehuda counters each time by demonstrating that Rav's opinion is not applicable in the situation at hand. Most likely, this story derives from sources sympathetic to Yehuda and hostile to Nahman, since one of the story's central concerns is to demonstrate the superiority of Yehuda, the Pumbeditan, whose mastery of the teachings of the great Nehardean sage, Shmuel, contrasts sharply with the ignorance of Shmuel's Nehardean successor, Nahman. The story also attempts to explain away Nahman's superiority in the judicial realm, even over Amoraim who were his academic superiors.[33] His pre-eminence in the judiciary, claims the story, is not due to any merit on Nahman's part. On the contrary, only out of respect for the house of the exilarch did Nahman's contemporaries subordinate themselves to him even though he was their inferior from the standpoint of rabbinic learning. Finally, the story is very likely trying to show the importance of adherence to the opinions of both Rav *and* Shmuel, to show that knowledge of the opinions of Rav alone will lead to the type of ignorant behavior exhibited by Nahman.[34] This conclusion is surprising, in view of the fact that elsewhere, Nahman is well-versed in the opinions of Shmuel, quoting him to a far greater extent, in fact, than he quotes the opinions of Rav.[35] This story, evidently, reflects a different view of Nahman and his relationship to Shmuel.

The Talmud's portrayal of the relationship between two important third-generation Amoraim, Rabbah and Rav Yosef, contains comparable incongruities. In one context, Rabbah and Yosef are described as candidates for the same position of communal responsibility.[36] At issue

---

[33]See below, chapter 4.

[34]For further discussion of this issue, see chapter 8, below.

[35]See Albeck, *Mavo la-Talmudim*, pp. 298-300. See also Florsheim, "Ha-Yahasim bein Hakhmei ha-Dor ha-Sheni," p. 282.

[36]Berakhot 64a. The traditional understanding of this story is that Rabbah and Rav Yosef were candidates for the office of head of the academy, but that understanding has been seriously called into question by recent scholarship. See the references cited in the Introduction, above. Compare Beer, *Rashut ha-Golah,* pp. 100-3.

here is who is the superior scholar, whose method of learning is preferable. The Babylonian rabbis send "there," to Palestine, for a decision, and word is sent back that Yosef is preferable. Yosef declines, however, out of humility[37] or due to an astrological prediction that he will rule for only two years and then die.[38] Rabbah rules in his stead, his tenure lasting twenty-two years, and Yosef rules after him. According to this story, Yosef was the superior scholar and it was his decision to delay assumption of a position that was rightfully his.[39]

This story is very likely an attempt on the part of sages who favor Yosef to explain why Rabbah was chosen to rule ahead of Yosef. This happened not because Rabbah was the superior scholar, these disciples or editors claim; on the contrary, Yosef was superior, and it was his decision to delay the appointment.[40] The Talmud thus preserves a polemical perspective regarding the relative scholarly merits of Rabbah and Yosef which most likely derives from sources sympathetic to Yosef.

Rava's claim in two contexts[41] that Rabbah and Yosef were unable to resolve a certain difficulty over a period of twenty-two years, and that only when Yosef became head was the matter resolved, is a clear echo of the story described above. Rava is alluding to the twenty-two years that Rabbah ruled and suggesting that only when the appropriate person came into power could the matter be satisfactorily resolved. Rava, or whoever placed these sentiments into Rava's mouth, shares the view that Yosef was greater than Rabbah. It is understandable that Rava would hold such an opinion (or that such an opinion would be attributed to Rava), since he was a student of Yosef but not of Rabbah.

The famous story of Rabbah's death[42] very likely derives from circles friendly to Rabbah.[43] Rabbah dies according to this story because God

---

[37]According to another interpretation, Yosef refuses out of a desire to avoid public office and to leave himself more time for study.

[38]See *DS* yud, on Berakhot 64a, and see Horayot 14a.

[39]Rav Yosef's denial of responsibility perhaps strikes us as less than heroic, unbefitting a man called upon to play a critical role in the leadership of his people. To the rabbis, however, Rav Yosef's actions were not in the slightest cause for criticism. Talmudic rabbis went to great lengths to delay entrance to the world to come, and frequently went to great lengths to avoid public office.

[40]Compare Mordechai Yudelowitz, *Yeshivat Pumbedita bi-Yemei ha-Amoraim* (Tel Aviv, 1935), pp. 21-22.

[41]Ketubot 42b and Baba Kamma 66b.

[42]Baba Mezia 86a. For proof that the Rabbah bar Nahmani mentioned in this story is to be identified with Rabbah, mentioned throughout the Talmud without the patronymic, see Shamma Friedman, "Ketiv ha-Shemot 'Rabbah' ve-'Rava' ba-Talmud ha-Bavli," *Sinai* 55 (1992), pp. 156-58.

[43]See Baruch M. Bokser, "Rabbah bar Nahmani," in *The Encyclopedia of Religion*, ed. Mircea Eliade (New York: Macmillan, 1987), vol. 12, p. 181.

and the scholars in heaven are deadlocked over an issue of ritual purity, and Rabbah's vote is necessary to decide the question. It was concluded above that several Talmudic passages reflect the view that Yosef was superior to Rabbah. If this is the case, then the story of Rabbah's death provides further support for the claim that the Talmud contains a variety of contradictory sources. It is difficult to imagine that people who transmitted stories whose major point is Yosef's superiority to Rabbah also transmitted a story which views Rabbah as a figure of cosmic importance.[44] Furthermore, Abaye and "all of the rabbis" attend to Rabbah after his death,[45] but Yosef is nowhere to be found. As Rabbah's colleague and successor in Pumbedita, his absence from the story is striking. According to some versions, in fact,[46] the story serves to legitimate Abaye, and not Yosef, as Rabbah's successor in Pumbedita. According to these versions, a message descends from heaven and falls upon the head of Abaye, designating him, and not Yosef, as Rabbah's successor. Very likely, whoever told the story of Rabbah's death does not consider Yosef to have been greater than Rabbah.[47] The Talmud preserves contradictory views regarding the scholarly status of Rabbah and Yosef which most likely derive from diverse sources.

Rava and his fourth-generation contemporary, Abaye (see above), are likewise the subjects of several polemical accounts which derive from diverse sources. Stories which emphasize Abaye's deficiencies as judge, teacher, and halachic decisor, and which contrast Abaye unfavorably with Rava, very likely derive from sources wishing to portray Abaye in an unfavorable light.[48] According to one story, for example, a student of Rava says "to the rabbis: 'Instead of grinding bones in the house of Abaye, come and eat choice meat in the house of Rava.'" In other words, study with Rava is rewarding, but study with Abaye is a waste of time. In two other stories, legal cases are brought before Abaye for judgment, whereupon Abaye procrastinates and fails to deliver a prompt verdict. The litigants are told by a student of Rava to go before Rava, whose

---

[44]Note, however, that on Moed Katan 28a Rava is portrayed as speaking highly of Rabbah. Perhaps on Moed Katan 28a only the opening statement derives from Rava, and the comparison of the differing fates of Rabbah and Rav Hisda which illustrates his claim was added by a later hand. This case is not unambiguous evidence, therefore, that Rava had (or was credited with having) a high opinion of Rabbah.

[45]Rava's presence there is very likely a scribal error, as Rabbinovicz, *DS* daled, already observed.

[46]See *DS* bet, and Gafni, "'Yeshiva' u-'Metivta,'" p. 25, n. 64.

[47]We must be wary, however, about placing too much weight on an argument from silence.

[48]Compare Yudelowitz, *Yeshivat Pumbedita*, p. 41.

"knife is sharp," and Rava delivers a prompt, and correct, decision.[49] Significantly, a single individual, Rav Ada bar Ahava, might be associated with all three of the sources hostile to Abaye.[50] Judging from the evidence of the Talmud, Ada bar Ahava was a zealous disciple of Rava who had an extremely low opinion of Abaye. The bulk of the Talmud's sources, however, display no such animus toward Abaye.[51]

---

[49]Yevamot 121b-122a (see *DS* yud on Hullin 77a), Baba Batra 22a, and Hullin 77a.
[50]In Baba Batra, the student referred to is Rav Ada bar Ahava, but in Yevamot and Hullin the manuscripts disagree as to whether Rav Ada bar Ahava or Rav Ada bar Matna is referred to. Friedman, "Ketiv ha-Shemot 'Rabbah' ve-'Rava' ba-Talmud ha-Bavli," p. 159, n. 5, decides in favor of the reading "Rav Ada bar Matna" because Rav Ada bar Matna appears much less frequently in the Bavli than does Rav Ada bar Ahava, and the scribes tend to replace unfamiliar names with familiar names. Against this argument, however, see immediately above for the criticism of Abaye and praise of Rava attributed to Ada bar Ahava on Baba Batra 22a. This source depicts Ada bar Ahava as convinced of Rava's superiority over Abaye, which would accord well with the attitude expressed in the Yevamot and Hullin stories. It is unlikely that the same conviction regarding the relative merits of Rava and Abaye, rarely expressed in the Talmud, would be attributed to two different Amoraim named Ada. In addition, Rav Ada bar Matna is elsewhere described as a student of both Abaye and Rava, while Rav Ada bar Ahava was only a student of Rava, and the latter would be more likely to express the view (or later editors would be more likely to attribute to him the view) that Rava is Abaye's superior (However, see Nazir 19b and Makkot 6a). See Yudelowitz, *Mahoza*, p. 85, and Bacher, *Die Agada der Babylonischen Amoräer*, p. 115, n. 8, and see the discussion below.

In the above-mentioned article, incidentally, Friedman casts some doubt on the conventional identification of Rava b. d'Rav Yosef bar Hama (referred to on Hullin 77a) as the well-known Amora, Rava.
[51]See Berakhot 56a, according to which Abaye's students went on to become disciples of Rava after the death of Abaye. Because of the miraculous elements contained in the story, and because of its obvious character as propaganda (serving to legitimate Rava as successor to Abaye), it is difficult to evaluate the historical value of this narrative (see also chapter 3, below). Nevertheless, the evidence of the Talmud supports Bar Hedya's claim that "Abaye will die and his *metivta* will go to you [Rava]. That is, most of Abaye's students went on to become students of Rava. Throughout tractates Berakhot, Pesahim, Bezah, Ketubot, Nedarim, Baba Mezia, Baba Batra, and Makkot, we find the following Amoraim active as Abaye's students: Abba bar Marta, Rav Ada bar Matna, Rav Aha bar Manyumi, Rav Idi bar Abin, Rav Huna b. d'Rav Yehoshua, Rav Huna b. d'Rav Moshe bar Azrei, Rav Zevid, Rav Hiyya b. d'Rav Huna, Rav Hinena b. d'Rav Ika, Rav Tavyumi, Rav Yemar bar Shelamya, Rav Yaakov bar Abba, Rav Kahana, Rav Menashya bar Geda, Rav Mari b. d'Bat Shmuel, Rav Nihumi bar Zecharya, Rav Papa, Rava bar Rav Hanan, Rava bar Sharshom, Rav Rehumi, Rav Sheravya, and possibly Rav Avya. Of these students, all were also students of Rava with the exception of Abba bar Marta, Rav Idi bar Abin (but see Moed Katan 16a), Rav Menashya bar Geda, Rav Nihumi bar Zecharya, Rava bar Sharshom, and possibly Rav Aha bar Manyumi (However, see Nedarim 47b).

One story which at first glance appears to praise Rava may in fact derive from a hostile source.[52] According to this story, Rava is in the habit of making an extravagant gesture of humility and submission to Rav Yosef whenever he leaves Yosef's presence. Yosef learns of Rava's practice and says to him: "May it be [God's] will that your head be elevated over the entire town." Yosef's blessing, when viewed in the context of Rava's entire career, is perhaps deliberately ironic. The transmitters of this story know full well that Rava never ruled in Pumbedita. Perhaps the story intends to contrast Rava's behavior while still a student, winning his master's favor and deserving of his blessing, with his behavior after he broke with Yosef and moved to Mahoza. Perhaps the implication is that Rava, had he wished, could have stayed in Pumbedita and ruled the entire city, thereby avoiding a painful break with his master.

That Rava's move to Mahoza was disapproved of by some is shown by a story which begins with Rava sending a halachic question to Yosef.[53] Yosef sends back a reply, and Rava issues a clarification, explaining that Yosef misunderstood his question. Yosef takes offense, complaining that Rava failed to show him proper respect. "If he doesn't need us," asks Yosef, "why does he send questions to us?" Rava learns that Yosef is offended and goes to him personally to make amends. Rava mixes Yosef's cup, like a student before his master, showing that he, Rava, still considers himself to be Yosef's student. Yosef then quotes a series of biblical verses and asks Rava to explain them, like a teacher examining his student. Rava willingly plays the role of a student in order to mollify his insulted teacher, interpreting the scripture quoted by Yosef as a warning against the evil of too much pride. By interpreting scripture in this manner, Rava in effect confesses his sin and accepts the blame for offending his teacher.[54]

Very likely, this story attests to rabbinic disapproval of Rava's decision to move to a new locality and assert independence from his master. Some rabbis unfavorably contrasted Rava with Abaye, Rava's older contemporary, who makes a brief appearance in the story. According to all available evidence, Abaye, unlike Rava, remained in

---

[52]Yoma 53b.

[53]Nedarim 55a. The long narrative on Nedarim 55a might be a combination of two stories, one of which is also found on Eruvin 54b. See also Friedman, "Ketiv ha-Shemot 'Rabbah' ve-'Rava' ba-Talmud ha-Bavli," pp. 159-62, for further discussion of this story.

[54]For more on the relationship between Rava and Rav Yosef, see Hullin 133a. See also the discussion of Ketubot 63a, below, and the discussion of Baba Batra 22a in the Introduction, above.

Pumbedita his entire life, a loyal disciple first of Rabbah and later of Yosef.[55]

Another story involving Yosef contains an unfavorable portrait of Rava as an independent sage. Very likely, Rava's appellation in this story aids us in detecting the presence of a hostile source. "The father of Rav Yosef b. d'Rava" sends his son to study with Rav Yosef, stipulating that the son stay away for six years.[56] The story is clearly critical of Rava for placing excessive demands on his son, demands which lead to family strife when the son comes home ahead of schedule, unable to meet his father's expectations.[57] It is peculiar that Rava, one of the towering figures in the Babylonian Talmud, should be referred to as "the father of Rav Yosef b. d'Rava." By referring to Rava in this manner, the narrator shifts attention away from the father and onto his son, as if the actions of Rav Yosef b. d'Rava, an obscure Amora who seldom appears in the Talmud,[58] are of greater interest than the actions of the father. By referring to Rava in this manner, the narrator creates the impression that the son is the story's protagonist and the father part of the supporting cast. Once again, Rava is independent of his teacher, Yosef, and his actions are worthy of condemnation, so much so that one scholar refers to this account as "truly one of the most appalling stories of a Rabbi's behavior in the Talmud."[59]

Perhaps we find evidence that not everyone in Babylonia considered Rava to be the dominant scholar of his generation in a passage which describes the students who study year-round in the houses of important rabbis.[60] According to this passage, the number of disciples studying with the dominant scholars in every generation steadily decreases as we move later in the Amoraic period. More disciples studied with Rav than with Rav Huna, and more studied with Rav Huna than with Rabbah and Rav Yosef. "When the rabbis left the house of Abaye," the text continues, "and some say the house of Rav Papa, and some say the house of Rav Ashi, two hundred rabbis remained, and they called themselves orphans

---

[55]For more on the relationship between Rabbah, Rav Yosef, and Abaye, see chapter 11, below, and Kalmin, "Collegial Interaction in the Babylonian Talmud," pp. 387-88 and 396-405.
[56]Ketubot 63a.
[57]See Fraenkel, *Iyunim ba-Olamo ha-Ruhani Shel Sippur ha-Agadah,* pp. 99-115.
[58]See Kosowsky, *Ozar ha-Shemot,* pp. 877-78.
[59]Daniel Boyarin, *Carnal Israel: Reading Sex in Talmudic Culture* (Berkeley, California: University of California Press, 1993).
[60]Ketubot 106a. Gafni, "Hiburim Nestorianim ke-Makor le-Toldot Yeshivot Bavel," pp. 574-75, notes that Christian sources preserve a strikingly similar account of the gradual decline of the Nestorian academy at Nicibis (Nezivin).

of orphans."[61] Most versions omit reference to Rava,[62] and it is quite possible that the omission is intentional. Perhaps whoever excluded Rava's name did not view him as worthy of inclusion alongside the other Amoraim mentioned on the list. Perhaps this passage provides further evidence that stories about Amoraim reflect a variety of perspectives and reached the Talmud from more than a single source.

Accounts of the interactions between Rav Papa, a prominent fifth-generation Amora, and Mar Shmuel,[63] who might have been an exilarch, further support this claim. According to the printed version of one story, Papa tells of a certain individual who criticized[64] Mar Shmuel after his death and had his skull crushed by a falling roof beam.[65] The implication is that Papa thinks highly of Mar Shmuel and views any insult to this great man as deserving of immediate retribution. Elsewhere, however, the interaction between Papa and Mar Shmuel consists of visits by Papa to the house of Mar Shmuel, where he discovers that the halacha is not correctly practiced there.[66] While Mar Shmuel himself is not directly criticized, he bears responsibility for the actions of his servants, and criticism of the servants is certainly criticism of the master.[67] Perhaps the Talmud preserves opposing perspectives regarding the relationship between Papa and Mar Shmuel, with one source viewing Papa as respectful, the other as critical, of Mar Shmuel. More likely, however, the manuscript versions of the first story are correct, according to which

---

[61]Goodblatt, *Rabbinic Instruction in Sasanian Babylonia,* pp. 56-57, basing himself on the chronology of Rav Sherira Gaon, dates the core of this passage, the section dealing with Rav, Rav Huna, and Rabbah and Rav Yosef, to the middle third of the fourth century C.E. Goodblatt views the concluding section as an attempt by students of Abaye, Rav Papa, and Rav Ashi to update the tradition so that mention would be made of their own teachers, whom they considered to be the greatest scholars of their generation.

[62]*Dikdukei Soferim ha-Shalem,* ed. Herschler, nn. on line 17, and n. 38 (Henceforth, we will refer to this work as *DS* Herschler). Note that a geniza fragment records Rava's name but not Abaye's. Note also that all versions omit reference to Shmuel, a prominent first-generation contemporary of Rav.

[63]Or Mar Shmuel Mar. The exact name of this Amora is not certain. See Albeck, *Mavo la-Talmudim,* p. 423.

[64]See Ritba for alternative interpretations of the phrase *mesaper ahar mitato.*

[65]Berakhot 19a.

[66]Bezah 14b (The printed text reads Rav Papi, but see *DS* tet. Variation between the names Papi and Papa is extremely common. Very likely, Mar Shmuel is consistently mentioned in connection with only one of the two Amoraim) and Menahot 34a (Rif and Piskei ha-Rosh read Rav Mari instead of Rav Papa. See also *DS* kuf).

[67]For discussion of the tendency of sources in the Bavli to criticize the exilarch indirectly, through criticism of his household or his servants, see Beer, *Rashut ha-Golah,* pp. 179-84.

Papa himself criticizes Mar Shmuel after his death and nearly (or actually!) has his skull crushed as punishment. The printed version most likely arose as a scribal attempt to remove the criticism of Papa found in the manuscript versions.[68]

No manuscript explicitly states that Papa both criticizes Mar Shmuel *and* is killed by the falling beam. Some texts relate that Papa criticizes Mar Shmuel and that he *almost* dies a violent death as a result. Other versions have Papa reporting the fate of another man, who criticizes Mar Shmuel and dies violently as a result. Perhaps a combination of variants yields the original version of the story, according to which Papa both criticizes Mar Shmuel *and* dies a violent death, despite the fact that no surviving text actually states this. Perhaps all extant versions alter the story in one way or another, differing over the extent to which they tamper with the original version and remove the harsh criticism of Papa. Very likely, therefore, the Talmud preserves diverse views regarding the relative merits of Papa and Mar Shmuel. According to one view, Papa observes and appropriately criticizes halachic violations in the house of Mar Shmuel. According to another view, Papa criticizes Mar Shmuel after his death and is punished or killed as a result.

As noted above, Mar Shmuel might have been an exilarch,[69] political head of the Jewish community in Babylonia[70] and representative of the Jews before the Persian government. The sources depicting strained relations between Papa and Mar Shmuel might therefore support Jacob Neusner's view regarding the existence of tension between the rabbis and the exilarch, and the presentation of this tension from diverse perspectives within the Talmud.[71] Neusner's claim that stories critical of the exilarch tend to involve an unnamed exilarch, however, would not be borne out by these sources.

---

[68]*DS* tet on Berakhot 19a. See also Perush ha-Rashbaz.

[69]See Albeck, *Mavo la-Talmudim*, p. 423; Neusner, *A History of the Jews in Babylonia*, vol. 5, pp. 55, 57, 258, and 260; and Beer, *Rashut ha-Golah*, pp. 206-9.

[70]In emphasizing the political role of the exilarch, I am not suggesting that the office of exilarch lacked religious significance. The religious and political realms were closely intertwined in the ancient world, and the exilarch's political and religious functions are not easily distinguishable. I use the term simply to indicate that the exilarch exercised several functions which in modern terms must be considered political.

[71]See, for example, Neusner, *A History of the Jews in Babylonia*, vol. 5, pp. 45-60, and see the discussion of Geniva above and in the appendix, below.

Generally, Talmudic Sources Exhibit No Clear-cut Polemical Perspective

The above arguments should not lead to an exaggeration of the extent to which Talmudic sources reflect polemical perspectives. A few scattered polemical stories have found their way into the literature, but for the most part sources display no clearly discernible polemical intent. All of the evidence for polemical distortion examined above is found in the context of stories, and virtually all of the stories are lengthy. Very likely, the authors and transmitters of lengthy stories often had free rein to engage in "creative historiography,"[72] to distort or invent facts to serve the purposes of their narrative and the moral, religious, and polemical message they wished to teach. The authors and transmitters of non-narrative materials and briefer stories, in contrast, worked under more rigid constraints.[73] They were evidently more limited with regard to the types of additions they could make to the facts and sources at their disposal.[74]

Even sources which are reported from a particular sage's point of view generally show no signs of polemical distortion in favor of the sage whose perspective they reflect. A glance at the interactions between several fourth-generation Babylonian Amoraim will illustrate this point.

I concluded in an earlier study that statements by the overwhelming majority of fourth-generation Amoraim are preserved in the Talmud primarily to the extent to which they have a bearing upon a handful of important Amoraim.[75] Statements by fourth-generation rabbis such as Rami bar Hama, Rav Huna bar Hinena, Mar Zutra b. d'Rav Nahman, and Rav Dimi Minehardea are preserved primarily to the extent to which they impinge upon Amoraim such as Abaye and Rava. In other words, fourth-generation Amoraim depend on Abaye and Rava for the preservation of their statements in the Talmud. And yet there is no

---

[72]See Yizhak Heinemann, *Darkhei ha-Agadah* (Jerusalem: Mezada, 1949/50), pp. 4-7 and 15-95.

[73]See Baumgarten, "Rabbi Judah I and His Opponents," pp. 141-42, and the literature cited in n. 28, there.

[74]The work of David Halivni, Shamma Friedman, and others in separating the additions of the anonymous editors from Amoraic legal dicta may contradict this suggestion. See the references cited in the Preface, above. However, we will not be in a position to fully appreciate the work of the anonymous editors in altering their Amoraic sources until the discrete analyses of individual discussions have been systematically analyzed and the full range of anonymous editorial activity catalogued and described. See Kalmin, *The Redaction of the Babylonian Talmud*, pp. 66-94, for a systematic analysis of the anonymous editorial commentary based on statements by the latest Amoraim mentioned in the Talmud.

[75]Kalmin, *The Redaction of the Babylonian Talmud*, pp. 54-65. See also Neusner, *A History of the Jews in Babylonia*, vol. 4, p. 74, n. 1; and pp. 287-89.

evidence of an attempt on the part of Abaye or Rava or their disciples, or on the part of later editors favoring Abaye or Rava, to systematically distort the nature of their interaction with most of their contemporaries. In one context, Rava judges a case and Rav Huna bar Hinena and Rav Huna b. d'Rav Nahman disagree with his decision.[76] Rava publicly announces his opinion and Huna bar Hinena and Huna b. d'Rav Nahman publicly announce their opposing opinion. Later on, Rav Nahman travels to Mahoza,[77] he and Rava discuss the matter, and Rava is surprised to learn that Rav Nahman agrees with Huna bar Hinena and Huna b. d'Rav Nahman, and that he, Rava, misunderstood his teacher. In another context, Huna bar Hinena judges a case, Rava objects in his presence, and the two sages publicly proclaim their contradictory opinions.[78] The text provides no indication that either point of view prevails. In fact, later Amoraic discussion takes notice only of the opinion of Huna bar Hinena in determining the law, and completely ignores the opposing opinion of Rava.[79] Elsewhere, Rava quotes Rav Nahman and fails to remember essential details of his teacher's opinion, details which Huna bar Hinena and Huna b. d'Rav Nahman remember. The sages through whom our sources are transmitted, therefore, or later editors on behalf of those sages, did not systematically distort the record of their interaction with most of their contemporaries. They did not, or

---

[76]Avodah Zarah 57b-58a.

[77]See *Tractate Abodah Zarah,* ed. Shraga Abramson (New York: Jewish Theological Seminary, 1957), p. 212, notes on line 18. See also Tosafot, s.v., *Ikla,* and Ritba, s.v., *u-le-Inyan.* My point is made even more decisively according to the reading of the printed edition.

[78]Avodah Zarah 40a.

[79]See also Shabbat 129a, Pesahim 58b, Bezah 6a, Ketubot 71b, Gittin 75a-b, Baba Kamma 6a and 42a, Baba Batra 21a (twice), Avodah Zarah 12a, 30a-b (the Munich manuscript reads Rav Papa instead of Rava), and 44b, Zevahim 96b, Menahot 35a (twice), Arakhin 22b, Niddah 24b, and possibly Yoma 72b. In these cases, Abaye's or Rava's statements are followed by opposing statements by Rav Dimi Minehardea, Rabbah bar Ulla, and the Nehardeans. Several of these opposing statements contain explicit objections against the opinions of Abaye or Rava, and yet statements by these Amoraim are included in the Talmud primarily to the extent to which they are transmitted in the proximity of opposing statements by Abaye or Rava. With regard to the Nehardeans, see David Goodblatt, "Local Traditions in the Babylonian Talmud," *Hebrew Union College Annual* 48 (1977), pp. 187-94. The disciples of Abaye and Rava who transmitted these disputes did not alter them to make it appear as if their masters had the final word, nor did they remove the explicit criticisms of their masters' opinions. See also the discussion below.

could not, systematically alter the sources to make them appear infallible.[80]

We see this even in their interaction with sages with whom they are portrayed as engaging in obvious conflict. For example, Talmudic sources portray conflict between Rava on the one hand, and Huna bar Hinena and Huna b. d'Rav Nahman on the other. In addition to the two confrontations described above, Huna bar Hinena performs a task on behalf of the exilarch,[81] and Rava follows after him and undoes his work. Elsewhere, Huna bar Hinena is about to publicly proclaim a law regarding vows,[82] and Rava sharply objects in his presence. Rava once rejects Huna bar Hinena's argument with the words, "Someone who does not know how to explain Tannaitic sources made this objection."[83] According to some versions in another context, Rava berates Huna bar Hinena for transmitting false opinions in Rav Nahman's name.[84] The Talmudic record is unambiguous in portraying opposition between Rava on the one hand, and Huna bar Hinena and Huna b. d'Rav Nahman on the other, and we noted above that statements by the latter two rabbis are included in the Talmud primarily to the extent to which they impinge upon Rava and a handful of other important Amoraim. This evidence for the existence of conflict between Rava and his contemporaries thus comes to us through the eyes of Rava, or his students, or later editors who favored Rava. Nevertheless, this evidence by no means presents an unambiguous picture of Rava as the dominant scholar of his generation. Instead, it presents a picture of Rava confronted by imposing adversaries who were on several occasions more than a match for him. When they clash, neither one consistently wins. The sages through whom our sources are transmitted, or later editors on behalf of those sages, did not systematically distort the record of their interaction with most of their contemporaries.

Quite plausibly, an important factor in Rava's clashes with Huna bar Hinena and Huna b. d'Rav Nahman was competition over who was

---

[80]For a discussion of the editorial techniques used by ancient authors around the time of the formation of the New Testament, see F. Gerald Downing, "Compositional Conventions and the Synoptic Problem," *Journal of Biblical Literature* 107, No. 1 (1988), pp. 69-85. Downing argues (p. 70) that in the ancient world, "even the most highly literate and sophisticated writers employ relatively simple approaches to their 'sources.'" J. Hornblower, *Hieronymus of Cardia* (London: Oxford University Press, 1981), p. 280, for example, writes that Diodorus Siculus "merely paraphrased or extracted, without addition or interpretation, except of the simplest kind...."
[81]Eruvin 25b.
[82]Nedarim 23b.
[83]Eruvin 67b.
[84]Hullin 50a-b. See also Baba Batra 155a and Avodah Zarah 24a (and parallel).

legitimate successor to Rav Nahman, a teacher common to all three. Other sources portray clashes between Rava and his contemporaries, and it is hard to view as mere coincidence the fact that several of these clashes pit Rava against sages whose fathers were dominant figures in the preceding generation. Such sages, by virtue of their lineage, would have had a natural claim to leadership within the rabbinic movement.

For example, the bulk of Rava's interaction with Mar Zutra b. d'Rav Nahman consists of quotations by the latter of his father's opinions reported by Rabbanan in the presence of Rava. Each time, Rava responds angrily, "Haven't I already told you not to attribute worthless opinions to Rav Nahman![85] This is what Rav Nahman said...."[86] Similarly, Rava several times comments on statements by Rav Nahman bar Rav Hisda, and on all but one uncertain occasion[87] the comment is a sharply worded rejection of Nahman bar Hisda's opinion which translates roughly as, "What a stupid thing to say."[88]

To reiterate, we have examined the Talmud's portrayal of several rabbis who flourished between the first and fifth Amoraic generations, most notably Geniva and Mar Ukba, R. Yohanan, Resh Lakish, and R. Elazar ben Pedat, Rabbah and Rav Yosef, Abaye and Rava, and Rav Papa and Mar Shmuel. We repeatedly found that Talmudic accounts of their characters and personalities and the nature of their interactions betray the existence of opposing sources.

---

[85]I have paraphrased Rava's statement. The literal meaning is, "Haven't I told you not to hang empty bottles on Rav Nahman!"

[86]Baba Batra 7a and 151b, and Avodah Zarah 37b. In addition, Rava rejects Mar Zutra b. d'Rav Nahman's argument on Gittin 50a. Interestingly, the two Amoraim are definitely depicted as interacting in each other's presence only on Hullin 94b, in which context we find no hint of competition between them. See also Bezah 34b and Bekhorot 54b.

[87]Horayot 10b (see *DS* hei). In that context, Rava simply objects against Rav Nahman bar Rav Hisda's view and folows with his own alternative.

[88]Ketubot 63b, Shevuot 12b, and Hullin 88b. With regard to the term *borkha*, see Jacob Levy, *Neuhebbräisches und Chaldäisches Wörterbuch über die Talmudim und Midraschim* (2nd ed., revised by Lazarus Goldschmidt. Berlin: Benjamin Harz, 1924), vol. 1, p. 203; Marcus Jastrow, *A Dictionary of the Targumim, Talmud Babli, Yerushalmi, and Midrashic Literature* (1886-1903; Reprint. New York: The Judaica Press, 1971), p. 150; and *Arukh ha-Shalem*, ed. Alexander Kohut (1878-1892; Reprint. Vienna, 1926), vol. 1, p. 193. In all three cases, Rava's comment is followed by a defense of Nahman bar Rav Hisda's opinion by Rav Nahman bar Yizhak. In both instances, no response is made to Nahman bar Yizhak's argument.

2

Changing Amoraic Attitudes Toward the Authority and Statements of Rav and Shmuel

The present chapter further supports the claim that the Bavli is comprised of diverse sources, by showing that early and later Amoraim exhibit different attitudes toward the authority and statements of Rav and Shmuel, prominent first-generation Babylonian Amoraim. The term "later" refers to post-third-generation Amoraim, and the term "early" refers to first-, second-, and third-generation Amoraim.

I examine whether these different attitudes are explicable as evidence of changes in the type of literature considered worthy of preservation for posterity. According to this explanation, Amoraic attitudes toward Rav and Shmuel appear to change because later Amoraim choose not to preserve certain kinds of statements authored in their own day, statements which earlier Amoraim consider worthy of preservation. In actuality, however (according to this explanation), attitudes toward Rav and Shmuel remain the same. In the discussion which follows, I will refer to this explanation as "literary explanation," since it claims that differences between early and later Amoraim are due to changes in the kind of literature preserved for posterity.

An alternative explanation, which accounts better for much of the evidence, views differences between early and later Amoraim as accurate reflections of historical reality. This explanation will be referred to as "historical explanation."

According to both literary and historical explanation, it is important to note, the differences between early and later Amoraim provide evidence of diverse sources. In addition, the terms "literary" and "historical" should not conceal the fact that according to both explanations the Talmud attests to a historical development. "Historical explanation" posits a development in attitudes toward rabbis; "literary explanation" posits a development in standards of literary preservation, and hence the term "literary."

The bulk of the evidence is poorly suited to literary explanation and is more easily accounted for on historical grounds. Nevertheless, I claim, historians have paid insufficient attention to literary factors in accounting for changes in Talmudic discourse. In some cases, I argue, changes in Amoraic literature which at first glance appear to reflect historical developments are just as easily explicable on literary grounds.

Systematic Preference for the Authority or Statements of Rav

As noted above, the Bavli depicts several differences between early and later Amoraim on the question of Rav's and Shmuel's authority, and these differences provide further evidence of diverse sources in the Talmud.[1] To be specific, the Bavli depicts differences between early and

---

[1]In addition to the phenomena described below, we also find differences between early and later Amoraim on the question of Rav's authority. To be specific, some early Amoraim acknowledge Rav's authority to disagree with Tannaitic opinions, and prefer Rav's halachic opinion to halachic opinions authored by Tannaim, whereas later Amoraim do not. On Hullin 122b, for example, Rav Shmuel bar Yizhak asserts that "Rav is a Tanna," which entitles him to disagree with a mishna found on 122a (with regard to Rav Shmuel bar Yizhak's chronology, see Albeck, *Mavo la-Talmudim*, pp. 264-65; and Halivni, *Mekorot u-Mesorot*: Shabbat, p. 114, n. 6, who writes that he was a student of Rav before moving to Israel). In addition, on Berakhot 49a Rav Zeira suggests that Rav Hisda could have defended himself against Rav Sheshet's objection by citing the halachic view of Rav. Rav Hisda expresses amazement at Rav Zeira's suggestion that he abandon "all of those Tannaim" and follow Rav. Rav's contradiction of the Tannaitic views, apparently, did not bother Zeira. On Baba Batra 170b-171a, Rav Huna quotes Rav's assertion that "the law follows neither R. Yehuda nor R. Yosi. Rather, the law is...." Rav bluntly rejects the views of two Tannaim, R. Yehuda and R. Yosi, and offers his own original view, prompting Rashi to explain that "Rav is a Tanna and disagrees." Rav Huna rejects Rav Nahman's effort to minimize the difference between Rav's and R. Yehuda's views, affirming Rav's prerogative to reject Tannaitic opinions (see also Urbach, *Ha-Halacha*, pp. 195-96, and n. 66 on p. 310).

See also Shabbat 40a and 53a (and Halivni, *Mekorot u-Mesorot*: Shabbat, pp. 114-15 and 156-57), Baba Batra 170b (and Urbach, *Ha-Halacha*, pp. 195-96), and Niddah 25a. See also Berakhot 23b-24a, where Rava or Rabbah (the printed text reads Rava, but see chapter 10, below) asserts that even though a Baraita contradicts the opinion of Shmuel, the law follows Shmuel. In these contexts, early Amoraim assert or presuppose Rav's authority in the face of contradictory Tannaitic opinions. Comparable attitudes regarding Rav's authority are never attributed to later Amoraim, which might further support my claim that the Talmud is comprised of diverse sources.

I phrase this tentatively because, as noted in chapter 8, below, late pseudepigraphers might have assigned praise of early rabbis to near-contemporaries of those rabbis. Similarly, and for the same reasons, late pseudepigraphers might have assigned their belief that Rav possessed Tannaitic

later Amoraim on the question of the relative authority possessed by Rav and Shmuel. Some early Amoraim regard Rav as more authoritative than Shmuel,[2] whereas later Amoraim do not systematically distinguish

---

authority to much earlier rabbis, according to which the above distinction between early and later Amoraim might not be indicative of diverse sources.

The Talmud's anonymous editors, like the early Amoraim, several times express the view that Rav possesses Tannaitic authority (Eruvin 50b, Ketubot 8a, Gittin 38b, and Sanhedrin 83b. See also Baba Batra 42a and Hullin 122b). Perhaps this commonality between the anonymous editors and the early Amoraim supports the view that some anonymous passages date from the early Amoraic period and are not exclusively post- or late Amoraic. At first glance it appears unlikely that an idea expressed by early Amoraim would disappear after the third Amoraic generation and resurface, anonymously, toward the end of the Talmudic period. More likely, it would seem, the anonymous and early Amoraic passages are contemporaneous, and the idea that Rav possesses Tannaitic authority disappears after the third generation, resurfacing only in the post-Talmudic period.

Upon closer examination, however, this argument fails, and a late date for the anonymous sources is easily maintained. The anonymous editors invoke the idea of Rav's Tannaitic authority exclusively in response to objections against Rav's statements, using it as an exegetical tool to extricate themselves from difficult interpretive situations. In contrast, with the exception of Hullin 122b, the Amoraic expressions of this idea are *not* motivated by the need to resolve objections. Quite likely, therefore, late anonymous editors revive an early Amoraic idea because it furthers their unique exegetical goals, namely, avoidance of the refutation of Amoraic statements. Late Amoraim are much less concerned with avoiding refutation of Amoraic sources than are the anonymous editors, which explains why the latter, and not the former, make use of the early Amoraic idea of Rav's Tannaitic authority.

It should be noted, furthermore, that the Amoraim and the anonymous editors use different terminology to express the view that Rav possesses Tannaitic authority. The editors say "Rav is a Tanna and disagrees," whereas Rav Shmuel bar Yizhak says "Rav is a Tanna and teaches [differently]."

[2]Once again, similarities between early Amoraic and anonymous statements permit no conclusions regarding the dating of anonymous material. On Bekhorot 49b, we find an anonymous halachic statement introduced by the term *ve-Hilkheta* which states that the view of Rav is authoritative in ritual matters while the view of Shmuel is authoritative in civil matters. Apparently, therefore, early Amoraim and anonymous editors distinguish between the halachic authority of Rav and Shmuel, whereas later Amoraim do not, which perhaps argues in favor of an early date for the composition of some anonymous passages.

However, Lewin, *Rabbanan Saborai ve-Talmudam,* pp. 46-53, notes that many, perhaps most of the anonymous legal decisions introduced by the term *ve-Hilkheta* are post-Talmudic additions to the text. Lewin cites numerous cases in which anonymous legal decisions are missing in several manuscripts, or originated in geonic sources and from there entered our texts of the Talmud. (See also Yaakov S. Spiegel, *Hosafot Meuharot [Savoriot] ba-Talmud ha-Bavli* [Ph.D. Dissertation, Tel Aviv University, 1976], pp. 152-219; and "Amar Rava Hilkheta--Piskei Halacha Meuharim," in *Iyunim be-Sifrut Hazal ba-Mikra u-va-Toldot Yisrael,*

between Rav's and Shmuel's authority. Even later Amoraim, of course, regard individual opinions by Rav as more authoritative than individual opinions by Shmuel, and vice versa, but they do not favor the authority of either Amora in systematic fashion.

A story on Shabbat 22a illustrates the claim that some early Amoraim view Rav as more authoritative than Shmuel.[3] Abaye informs us that "Mar," i.e., Rabbah, always followed the view of Rav, with the exception of three cases in which he followed the view of Shmuel.[4] Similarly, on Niddah 24b Rav Yirmiya bar Abba wishes to judge a case in accordance with the view of Shmuel. Rav Huna advises him to decide in accordance with Rav's opinion, for the law follows Rav in ritual matters.

Some later Amoraim, in contrast, consider R. Yohanan to be more authoritative than Rav or Shmuel, but never express the view that Rav is more authoritative than Shmuel, or vice versa. On Eruvin 47b, for example, Ravina, a fifth-generation subordinate of Rava, objects to a statement by Rava on the basis of a halachic principle which favors the halachic opinion of R. Yohanan over that of Shmuel. Apparently in response to Ravina's objection, Rava revises his position. Similarly, on Bezah 4a-b Rav Papa, also a fifth-generation subordinate of Rava, refers to a halachic principle which favors the halachic opinion of R. Yohanan

---

ed. Y.D. Gilat, C. Levine, and Z.M. Rabinowitz [Ramat Gan: Bar-Ilan University, 1982], pp. 206-14.) In addition, David Halivni and others have shown the anomalous nature of anonymous legal decisions, i.e., the contrast between these decisions and the overwhelmingly non-prescriptive character of the Talmud's anonymous commentary (see Kalmin, *The Redaction of the Babylonian Talmud*, pp. 1-11, 43-50, and 51-57). The anonymous editors, in contrast to the Amoraim, almost never author concise legal pronouncements, and the legal decision under discussion is very likely a post-Talmudic addition to the text. As such, it lies outside the purview of this study, and permits no conclusions regarding the dating of anonymous commentary.

 In addition, even if the anonymous legal principle under discussion is an integral part of the Talmud, no chronological conclusions are possible. The anonymous principle differs in one crucial respect from the Amoraic principles discussed above. The Amoraim, it will be recalled, prefer R. Yohanan's halachic authority to that of Rav, and prefer R. Yohanan's and Rav's authority to that of Shmuel. The anonymous editors, in contrast, assign to Rav and Shmuel their own separate spheres, ritual law to Rav and civil law to Shmuel, but express no consistent preference for the halachic authority of either Amora. The Amoraim play favorites, advocating the authority of one Amora over another, whereas the anonymous editors divide the halachic universe into two parts. The anonymous legal principle, while superficially similar to the Amoraic, is actually quite different, and fails to prove that anonymous passages date from the early Amoraic period.

[3]See also Shabbat 40a, Pesahim 101a, and Menahot 41b.

[4]See, however, Halivni, *Mekorot u-Mesorot: Shabbat*, pp. 69-70.

over that of Rav. On Bezah 4a, Rav Ada bar Ahava, likewise a fifth-generation subordinate of Rava, invokes the same principle.[5]

Rava and his school, therefore, are credited with the view that R. Yohanan is more authoritative than Rav and Shmuel,[6] but neither Rava nor any other later Amoraim consider Rav to be more authoritative than Shmuel, or vice versa. The difference between early and later Amoraim on the question of the relative halachic authority of Rav and Shmuel, therefore, is not attributable to literary factors, to the unwillingness of later generations to preserve later Amoraic expressions of preference for the halachic authority of particular Amoraim. We will return to this point in the conclusion below, and argue that the sources are most likely explicable on historical grounds, as evidence of actual changes in Amoraic attitudes toward the relative authority of Rav and Shmuel.

The Link between Geography and Authority

The sources also depict a difference between an early Amora and later Amoraim on the question of the link between the authority of Rav and Shmuel and their respective localities. Once again, this difference most likely attests to the existence of diverse sources.

Specifically, only Rav Nahman, an early Amora, distinguishes between the authority of Rav and Shmuel in their respective localities. On Baba Batra 153a, a case comes before Rav Nahman in Nehardea. Rav Nahman remands the case to Rav Yirmiya bar Abba in the city of Shum Tamya, refusing to rule in accordance with Rav in the locality of Shmuel. In other words, Rav Nahman accepts Rav's position but is unwilling to contradict Shmuel in his own locality.

In a related phenomenon, on Ketubot 54a Rav Nahman judges a case involving a Mahozan woman married to a Nehardean man. Rav Nahman discovers she is from Mahoza and declares that the case should

---

[5]I assume that the Rav Ada bar Ahava referred to is the fifth-generation subordinate of Rava by that name rather than the second-generation subordinate of Rav. It is unlikely that a subordinate of Rav who frequently quotes and comments on statements by Rav but rarely quotes or comments on statements by R. Yohanan (see below) would decide in favor of R. Yohanan in competition with Rav, or that later generations would credit him with such a view. In addition, Rava and his subordinates elsewhere prefer R. Yohanan's halachic authority to that of Rav and Shmuel, and the Rav Ada bar Ahava referred to in this passage is most likely a subordinate of Rava.

[6]For more on the special importance of R. Yohanan's traditions for Rava and Rav Papa, see Dor, *Torat Erez Yisrael be-Bavel*, pp. 11-78 and 79-115. See especially p. 13, n. 3, where Dor lists two cases in which Rava prefers Rav's view to the contradictory opinion of R. Yohanan. See also Urbach, *Ha-Halacha*, p. 214, and see chapter 5, below.

be judged according to the view of Rav. He reasons that Mahoza is in the vicinity of the city of Babylonia, and "[the city of] Babylonia and its environs follows [the view of] Rav." Rav Nahman next learns that the woman is married to a Nehardean man, and declares that the case should be judged in accordance with the view of Shmuel since "Nehardea and its environs follows [the view of] Shmuel." The link between the authority of Rav and his locality and the authority of Shmuel and his is unparalleled in sources attributed to later Amoraim.

A later Amora, in fact, refers to the locality of Rav and Shmuel as a single geographical entity. On Shabbat 37b, Mar Ukba Mimeshan suggests to Rav Ashi, a sixth-generation Amora, that "you who are close [i.e., in physical proximity] to Rav and Shmuel should act in accordance with Rav and Shmuel. We will act in accordance with R. Yohanan." In other words, the authority of Rav and Shmuel is preeminent in their locality; outside of this locality R. Yohanan's authority holds sway.

Once again, therefore, a difference between early and later Amoraim is not fully explicable on literary grounds. This difference is not attributable to the unwillingness of later generations to preserve for posterity later Amoraic opinions regarding the connection between authority and locality (see below).[7]

Fifth-generation Amoraim: An Unprecedented Tendency to Compromise

Further evidence of differences between early and later Amoraim indicative of diverse sources is provided by cases in which fifth-generation Amoraim display a tendency to compromise not discernible

---

[7]Once again, the Talmud's anonymous commentary warrants examination, and the data permit no conclusions regarding the date of this commentary. On Shabbat 19b, the anonymous editors discuss Rav Hamnuna's excommunication of an unnamed student who rendered a practical halachic decision in the city of Harta de-Argiz. The editors explain that Harta de-Argiz is "the locality of Rav," i.e., within his sphere of influence, and the student had no right to decide against Rav in his own locality. Also relevant are cases on Gittin 81a and 89b in which the anonymous editors assume that the practice in Nehardea reflects the view of Shmuel. When that practice contradicts Shmuel's own explicitly stated view, the editors make note of the contradiction and attempt to resolve it.

According to Shabbat 19b, therefore, the editors claim that at least during the third Amoraic generation (see Halivni, *Mekorot u-Mesorot:* Shabbat, p. 60) Rav's and Shmuel's authority applied with special force in their respective localities. The two anonymous sources in Gittin do not indicate clearly whether the link between authority and locality is operative in the present or past, in contrast to the Amoraim, who state clearly that an ongoing situation is referred to.

in sources attributed to earlier Amoraim.[8] Specifically, fifth-generation Amoraim occasionally express the view that disputes between early Amoraim admit of no final decision, and both positions are halachically valid. Action according to either position, they sometimes claim, fulfills one's obligation. On Gittin 60b, for example, Rav Huna bar Tahalifa asserts that "since the law has not been stated in accordance with Rav or Shmuel, whoever is stronger wins." On Shevuot 48b, Rav Hama declares that "a judge who acts in accordance with [a view held in common by] Rav and Shmuel has acted [validly], and a judge who acts in accordance with [the view of] R. Elazar has acted [validly]." This fifth-generation tendency to compromise was observed by earlier scholars, who note that it characterizes several statements by Rav Papa.[9]

Amoraic Quotation of and Commentary on Statements by Rav and Shmuel

Analysis of Amoraic quotation of and commentary on statements by Rav and Shmuel yields further evidence of differences between early and later Amoraim indicative of diverse sources.[10] Specifically, several early Amoraim quote and comment on[11] statements by Rav to the virtual exclusion of statements by Shmuel, and vice versa, whereas later Amoraim quote and comment on Rav's and Shmuel's statements to approximately the same degree. This difference as well is most likely explicable on historical grounds (see below), perhaps as evidence of the gradual dissemination of Rav's and Shmuel's teachings throughout Babylonia, perhaps as evidence of decreasing Amoraic preference for the statements of Rav to the exclusion of Shmuel, and vice versa.[12]

Several stories, all involving early Amoraim, support the picture arrived at through analysis of quotation and commentary patterns. For example, stories discussed above depict early Amoraim (1) exhibiting a

---

[8]See also Goldberg, "Derakhim Shel Zimzum Mahlokot Ezel Amoraei Bavel," pp. 135-53, especially pp. 135-37, 139-40, and 152-53.

[9]Weiss, *Dor Dor ve-Dorshav*, vol. 3, p. 181; and Albeck, *Mavo la-Talmudim*, p. 490. See also Halevy, *Dorot ha-Rishonim*, vol. 2, pp. 507-11.

[10]For documentation of this claim, see the Appendix, below.

[11]The expression "to comment on" refers to all cases in which statements by one Amora presuppose statements by another Amora in circumstances where it is clear that the former Amora is not engaging in dialogue with or does not appear in a story together with the latter Amora. Thus cases in which one Amora explains or interprets statements by another Amora are included under this rubric, as are cases in which an Amora states an opinion in opposition to the opinion of another Amora and explicitly refers to the rejected opinion. See also the Introduction, above.

[12]Compare Halevy, *Dorot ha-Rishonim*, vol. 2, pp. 480-94.

clear preference for the authority of Rav, and (2) expressing the view that a special connection exists between the authority of Rav and Shmuel and their respective localities. We find no comparable stories involving later Amoraim, supporting my contention that the quotation and commentary patterns outlined above are indicative either of the gradual dissemination of Rav's and Shmuel's statements throughout Babylonia, or of early Amoraic preference for the statements of Rav to the exclusion of Shmuel, and vice versa.

Amoraic Reactions to Challenges to the Authoritative Status of Rav's and Shmuel's Statements

Up until now, we have described differences between early and later Amoraic treatment of statements by Rav and Shmuel which are best explained historically. Some differences, however, are explicable on either literary or historical grounds. These differences attest either to changes in Amoraic attitudes toward Rav and Shmuel, or to changes in Amoraic literature not indicative of changing Amoraic attitudes toward Rav and Shmuel. I will return to these points in the conclusion of this chapter, and explain why a literary explanation may be applicable here but not above. Even according to literary explanation, it is important to reiterate, the phenomena provide evidence of diverse sources in the Bavli.

Specifically, only early Amoraim assert that contradiction of the views of Rav or Shmuel deserves punishment. On Shabbat 135a, for example, Rav Ada bar Ahava's son is accidentally castrated.[13] Rav Ada bar Ahava faults himself, exclaiming that "I deserve it [i.e., this accident is really punishment directed at me], for I transgressed [the view of] Rav." In addition, a story on Niddah 65a relates that Minyamin Saksanah wishes to judge a case in accordance with his interpretation of a view expressed by Rav, but dies before his decision can be carried out. Shmuel declares his death to be divinely ordained, applying to Rav the verse "No evil shall befall the righteous." That is, God sees to it that Rav plays no role, however remote, in the implementation of an incorrect decision. According to Shmuel, Minyamin is punished for attempting to rule in accordance with his incorrect interpretation of Rav's statement. Finally, on Baba Kamma 80a Rav might state that the mishnaic prohibition against raising small domesticated animals in Israel applies also in Babylonia.[14] Rav Ada bar Ahava asks Rav Huna why he raises

---

[13]The early Rav Ada bar Ahava is referred to, since Rav Nahman comments on his statement.

[14]According to an alternative version (see *DS* lamed), Rav Huna himself states that the prohibition against raising small animals also applies in Babylonia "from

such animals, and Rav Huna answers that his wife, Hova, guards the animals and sees that they do no damage. Rav Ada bar Ahava responds with a curse: "May Hova bury her children," and the story concludes with a report that "all the days of Rav Ada bar Ahava, Rav Huna had no viable children from Hova.[15] Rav Ada bar Ahava, therefore, might curse Rav Huna as punishment for his contradiction of the opinion of Rav,[16] a reaction without parallel in later Amoraic responses to contradiction of Rav's opinions.

Along these same lines, on several occasions early Amoraim react to perceived threats, challenges, or affronts to the authoritative status of Rav's and Shmuel's statements with shock, anger, or insults. Later Amoraim rarely react in comparable fashion. On Hullin 111b, for example, Rav Huna and Rav Hiyya bar Ashi perform actions which contradict the views of Rav. Both Amoraim object in harsh terms, referring to each other as "orphan," that is, bereft of a teacher. Similarly, on Kiddushin 81b-82a Rav Hisda angrily objects that his nephew, Rav Aha bar Abba, has "transgressed" the view of Rav by accepting betrothal for his minor daughter. Rav Aha bar Abba angrily responds that Rav Hisda is guilty of "transgressing" the view of Shmuel when he places the girl in his lap. On Avodah Zarah 39a, Hanan Hayta ridicules Rav Yosef, referring to him as "Yosef the poor" for his ignorance of an opinion expressed by Shmuel and his consequent inability to judge a case. On Hullin 107a-b, R. Zeira discovers R. Ami and R. Asi performing an action which contradicts the opinion of Rav and Shmuel. R. Zeira objects in amazement: "Two great masters like you err regarding [the view of] Rav and Shmuel?"

In sources attributed to later Amoraim, the harshness of these objections and insults is paralleled only on Yevamot 85a, where Rav Idi bar Abin derogatorily refers to Rav Papa and Rav Huna b. d'Rav Yehoshua as "children" because of their ignorance of an opinion expressed by Rav and Shmuel.

---

the time that Rav came to Babylonia." According to this reading, Rav Ada bar Ahava is bothered by the fact that Rav Huna's practice contradicts his own (i.e., Rav Huna's) expressly stated view. The printed edition, incidentally, has Rav Huna stating this opinion in the name of Rav. It is unlikely, however, that Rav would say "...from the time that Rav came to Babylonia," and the versions without Rav's name are therefore preferable. See *DS* nun. According to the version of the statement which lacks the phrase "...from the time that Rav came to Babylonia," however, the versions which have Rav Huna quoting Rav may be correct. See below.

[15]See also Nazir 57b and Halivni, *Mekorot u-Mesorot: Nashim*, p. 424, n. 3.
[16]See the discussion above.

The Importance of Knowledge of the Opinions of Rav and Shmuel

Further evidence of differences between early and later Amoraim with regard to statements by Rav and Shmuel is provided by several stories, all involving early Amoraim, in which special significance is attached to knowledge or understanding of the opinions of Rav and/or Shmuel. This difference as well is explicable on both historical and literary grounds, but according to both explanations the phenomenon provides evidence of diverse sources.

For example, stories involving early Amoraim on Gittin 31b and 62a emphasize the importance of expertise in the opinions of Rav.[17] Geniva repeatedly cites statements by Rav against the opinions and actions of Rav Huna and Rav Hisda, who each time are unable to respond. Geniva humiliates them by demonstrating their ignorance of the traditions of Rav, an ignorance made all the more shocking by the fact that Rav was their predecessor as head in Sura.

A story involving early Amoraim on Menahot 42a likewise attaches special significance to knowledge of the opinions of Rav.[18] This story relates that "after the death of Rav Huna, Rav Hisda entered and juxtaposed contradictory statements by Rav." Very likely, the story depicts Rav Hisda establishing his claim to rule in Sura after the death of Rav Huna by demonstrating mastery of the opinions of Rav. A story on Baba Kamma 21a is very likely explicable along the same lines. A question is sent to Rav Huna, who dies before he can respond. His son, Rabbah bar Rav Huna, responds in his stead with a quotation of Rav, perhaps also illustrating the importance attached to Rav's traditions at critical junctures in the transition from one generation to the next.

Summary and Conclusions

To reiterate, we have found that (1) some early Amoraim regard Rav as more authoritative than Shmuel, whereas later Amoraim do not systematically distinguish between Rav's and Shmuel's authority, (2) only an early Amora draws a special connection between the authority of Rav and Shmuel and their respective localities, (3) fifth-generation Amoraim tend to compromise between opposing opinions, a tendency not discernible in sources attributed to earlier Amoraim, (4) several early Amoraim quote and comment on statements by Rav to the virtual exclusion of statements by Shmuel, and vice versa, whereas later Amoraim quote and comment on their statements to virtually the same degree, (5) early Amoraim react to perceived threats, challenges, or

---

[17]For more detailed discussion of these stories, see chapter 1, above.
[18]See also the parallel on Eruvin 38b.

affronts to Rav's and Shmuel's authoritative status with shock, anger, insults, or punishments, whereas later Amoraim almost never react in comparable fashion, and (6) only in stories involving early Amoraim is special significance attached to knowledge or understanding of the opinions of Rav.[19]

As noted above, these differences further support my claim that the Talmud is comprised of diverse Amoraic sources. Can we say anything about their historical significance?

The evidence is explicable in one of three ways. Either (1) later editors composed, or radically altered, most of the Talmudic sources and created the above distinctions between early and later Amoraim, (2) Amoraic attitudes toward the authority and statements of Rav and Shmuel change during the course of the Amoraic period, and the sources accurately reflect these changes, or (3) Amoraic literature changes, but Amoraic attitudes toward the authority and statements of Rav and Shmuel remain the same. According to the latter explanation, the six distinctions noted above are a literary phenomenon. The kind of Amoraic material considered worthy of preservation changes during the course of the Amoraic period, leading to differences between early and later Amoraic statements not reflective of changing attitudes toward Rav and Shmuel.[20]

Which of these alternatives is correct? As most of the chapters in this study indicate, it is unlikely that a document as variegated as the Babylonian Talmud was subjected to the tightly controlled and consistent editorial manipulation posited by the first alternative. The first four distinctions noted above are also poorly suited to the third explanation, namely that these distinctions are a literary phenomenon. For example, it is unclear according to this explanation why only early Amoraic expressions of preference for the authority of Rav would be preserved (#1 above), given the fact that later Amoraim (according to this theory) would likewise hold such preference for Rav's opinions. In other words, it is unclear why later Amoraim would consider their own expressions of preference for Rav's authority unworthy of preservation. What changed

---

[19]We also found that some early Amoraim attribute Tannaitic authority to Rav, but later Amoraim do not. See above for explanation of why this difference is perhaps not indicative of diverse sources in the Bavli.

[20]I have distinguished throughout this book between the testimony of the sources and historical reality. The ability to identify diverse sources is no guarantee of the historical accuracy of those sources. It would seem, therefore, that a fourth alternative should be considered, namely that early and later sources are discernible, but these sources have no basis in historical reality. My reasons for rejecting this alternative were spelled out in the Introduction, above, and I will not repeat my arguments here.

after the third generation? Literary explanation, therefore, raises a question as serious as the one it attempts to resolve.

Literary explanation is particularly inappropriate here in view of the fact that later Amoraim do express preference for the authority of some Amoraim. Rava and his students, it will be recalled, regard R. Yohanan as more authoritative than Rav and Shmuel. The absence of later Amoraic expressions of preference for the authority of Rav over Shmuel, or vice versa, therefore, is difficult to attribute to literary factors, to an unwillingness on the part of later generations to preserve late Amoraic expressions of preference for the halachic authority of particular early Amoraim. Most likely, the difference between early and later Amoraim under discussion accurately reflects a change in Amoraic attitudes toward the authority of Rav and Shmuel.

It is also unclear, if we resort to literary explanation, why only early Amoraic expressions of the view that authority and locality are linked (#2 above) would be preserved. Here too, literary explanation raises a question as serious as the one it attempts to resolve.

Explanation on literary grounds is rendered even more problematic by the fact that later Amoraim are not silent on the question of the link between authority and locality. Mar Ukba Mimeshan, it will be recalled, asserts that the law follows R. Yohanan in his locality and Rav and Shmuel in theirs (viewed as a unit). The absence of similar later Amoraic distinctions between Rav and Shmuel (viewed separately), therefore, is difficult to attribute to literary factors, to the unwillingness of later generations to preserve such distinctions for posterity.

If we adopt historical explanations, however, then the sources are easily understandable. During the early Amoraic period, Rav's and Shmuel's authority applied with greater force in their own localities than in areas geographically removed. Later on, as their reputations and teachings spread, this connection between authority and locality weakened. To later Amoraim, much or all of Babylonia was the locus of Rav's and Shmuel's collective authority.[21]

---

[21]It is also difficult to explain on literary grounds why early Amoraim attribute Tannaitic authority to Rav, but later Amoraim do not (see above). Why were only early Amoraic expressions of this view preserved? What accounts for the suppression of or disregard for later Amoraic views on this subject?

If we adopt historical explanation, however, the evidence is easily accounted for. One might suggest, for example, that Rav's authority loomed large in the minds of early Amoraim, who possessed a living link to Rav or were themselves taught by rabbis who knew him firsthand. Later Amoraim, however, no longer possessed this living link. They were less in awe of Rav than their predecessors, and therefore did not attribute to him Tannaitic authority.

Similarly, if we adopt literary explanations it is unclear why later Amoraim display a unique tendency to compromise (#3 above), and why only early Amoraim quote and comment on statements by Rav to the virtual exclusion of statements by Shmuel, and vice versa (#4 above). If early and later Amoraim, historically speaking, are the same on these matters, why does the literature fail to record their similarities?

Historical explanation, in contrast, easily accounts for both phenomena. The tendency of later Amoraim to compromise corresponds to the fact that later Amoraim author relatively few prescriptive statements.[22] They are less likely than earlier Amoraim to say that such and such is the law, and their tendency to compromise is further manifestation of the relative infrequency with which they take halachic stands.

The fact that only early Amoraim quote and comment on statements by Rav to the virtual exclusion of statements by Shmuel, and vice versa (#4 above), admits of two possible historical explanations. It is evidence either of (1) decreasing Amoraic preference for the statements of Rav over those of Shmuel, and vice versa, or (2) the gradual dissemination of Rav's and Shmuel's teachings throughout Babylonia. Both developments are familiar to us from the discussion above, and my interpretations there are strengthened by the data presently under consideration.

In one sense, all four distinctions attest to the same development.[23] Early Amoraim tend to distinguish between Rav and Shmuel, crediting one or the other with greater or lesser authority, connecting Rav's and Shmuel's authority to their respective localities, and quoting or commenting on statements by one to the exclusion of the other. Later Amoraim, in contrast, tend to view the two Amoraim as a unit and to minimize distinctions between them. Later Amoraim do not distinguish between Rav and Shmuel on the basis of authority or locality. They quote and comment on their statements to approximately the same degree, and compromise between their opposing opinions. The Talmud thus supplies evidence of historical development in Amoraic attitudes toward Rav and Shmuel, supporting the conclusions of earlier scholars regarding the Talmud's value as a historical source.

The final two distinctions between early and later Amoraim, however, are explicable on either historical or literary grounds. We

---

[22]See David C. Kraemer, *Stylistic Characteristics of Amoraic Literature* (Ph.D. Dissertation, Jewish Theological Seminary, 1984. Ann Arbor: University Microfilms International, 1985), pp. 57, 64, 69-70, 80-81, and 109. See also Kalmin, *The Redaction of the Babylonian Talmud*, pp. 43-65.

[23]The unique tendency of early Amoraim to attribute Tannaitic authority to Rav easily conforms to the hypothesis suggested here.

found, it will be recalled, that early Amoraim react to perceived threats, challenges, or affronts to Rav's and Shmuel's authoritative status with shock, anger, insults, or punishments, whereas later Amoraim almost never react in comparable fashion (#5 above). In addition, only in stories involving early Amoraim is special significance attached to knowledge or understanding of the opinions of Rav (#6 above).

Clearly these distinctions are explicable on historical grounds. As noted above, perhaps Rav and Shmuel were overpowering presences in the minds of early Amoraim, who therefore react violently to challenges to their authority and tell stories emphasizing the importance of knowledge of their traditions. Later generations, however, know of Rav and Shmuel only indirectly, and are therefore less sensitive about threats to their authority and less impassioned about promoting knowledge of their traditions. Alternatively, perhaps Rav's and Shmuel's authority was challenged by some early rabbis and therefore had to be defended and promoted during the early Amoraic period. Later on, however, serious challenges to their authority ceased, and insults and punishments on their behalf were no longer necessary.

The evidence is also explicable on literary grounds, however. Perhaps the final two distinctions attest to changes in the type of literature considered worthy of preservation, but not to changes in Amoraic attitudes toward Rav and Shmuel. Perhaps if we could be transported back to the Amoraic period we would discover that later Amoraim react no less violently than do early Amoraim to challenges to the authority of Rav and Shmuel, and argue no less passionately than do early Amoraim that scholars must be well-versed in the opinions of Rav and Shmuel. Perhaps the Talmud preserves virtually no record of late Amoraic views on these subjects, however, because later Amoraim considered it less appropriate than did early Amoraim to preserve such material for posterity. They perhaps transmitted what they received from earlier generations, but not what was authored in their own day.

Some support for this conjecture is found in the fact that later Amoraim virtually never react to challenges to the authority of their predecessors, *whether near- or non-contemporary,* with insults, anger, or punishment.[24] Similarly, they virtually never tell stories emphasizing the

---

[24]Examination of Rav Yosef's statements, for example, reveals no cases in which later Amoraim react to challenges to Rav Yosef's authority with insults or punishment. Examination of Abaye's statements in tractates Berakhot, Shabbat, Eruvin, Pesahim, Rosh Hashana, Yoma, Sukkah, Bezah, Taanit, Megillah, Moed Katan, Hagigah, Yevamot, Ketubot, Nedarim, Nazir, Sotah, Gittin, Kiddushin, Baba Kamma, Baba Mezia, and Baba Batra reveals only one such case. On Moed Katan 12b, Rav Ashi ignores Abaye's opinion and immediately afterward narrowly avoids a serious accident. Rav Ashi's close brush with disaster is

importance of knowledge or understanding of statements by their predecessors, *whether near- or non-contemporary.*[25] Such stories and reactions are simply not a common part of the vocabulary of later Amoraim. The absence of comparable responses to the authority and statements of Rav and Shmuel, i.e., of insults and punishments on their behalf, therefore, might be part of a larger gap in the literature rather than evidence of changing attitudes toward Rav and Shmuel after the third generation. Perhaps this gap in the literature is part of a more general drop in the amount of non-halachic material attributed to and involving later Amoraim. That is, later Amoraim perhaps considered it less appropriate than did early Amoraim to transmit more than the halachic substance of Amoraic opinions uttered in their own day, but this issue is in need of further study.[26]

Perhaps it will be argued that since later generations transmitted what they received from earlier generations, it is unlikely that they would refrain from transmitting similar statements authored in their own day. Presumably later generations were aware of the implications of these early statements, and yet they willingly transmitted them. It is only a small step, one might argue, to suppose that on occasion later rabbis transmitted similar statements authored in their own day.

I disagree. Later Amoraim might very well transmit the early material but not the later. Early material bears the stamp of tradition and is difficult to systematically expunge, even when considered inappropriate from the standpoint of later generations. Later material, however, lacks the stamp of tradition, and will only survive if considered worthy of preservation by later standards.

---

viewed by the narrator of the story as a divine warning that his disregard of Abaye's opinion is inexcusable. Examination of Abaye's appearances reveals no stories involving Abaye in which adherence to the opinions of earlier Amoraim is underscored in comparable terms.

[25]Examination of statements by Rav Yosef, for example, reveals only one case in which later Amoraim emphasize the importance of knowledge or understanding of his statements. See Shabbat 46a-b, where Rava tries to humiliate Rav Avya by asking him to explain a statement by Rabbah and Rav Yosef. Rava hopes Rav Avya will fail, but Rav Avya successfully passes the test, prompting an expression of intense relief from Rav Nahman bar Yizhak.

Examination of Abaye's statements in the 22 tractates listed in the previous note reveals no comparable cases, either involving later Amoraim vis-a-vis Abaye, or Abaye vis-a-vis early Amoraim.

[26]Interestingly, Bacher, *Die Agada der Babylonischen Amoräer,* devotes pp. 1-107 to his survey of agadot involving and authored by first-, second-, and third-generation Amoraim, and pp. 107-47 to his survey of agadot involving post-third-generation Amoraim.

It could perhaps be argued that since *some* differences between early and later Amoraim examined above are best explicable on historical grounds (#1 through #4), it follows that *all* such differences demand historical explanation. Why employ historical explanations in some cases, and a literary explanation in others? Nothing compels us, however, to account for all of the phenomena in the same fashion. The historical fact that only early Amoraim regard Rav as more authoritative than Shmuel, for example (#1 above), does not imply the historicity of sources in which only early Amoraim react to challenges to the authoritative status of Rav and Shmuel with insults or punishment. The historical fact that only an early Amora maintains that the law follows Rav in his locality and Shmuel in his (#2 above) does not imply the historicity of sources in which only early Amoraim react to challenges to the authoritative status of Rav and Shmuel with insults or punishments. Quite possibly, historical explanations are appropriate for the former but not for the latter, and literary explanations are applicable in some cases but not in others.

The Transmission of R. Yohanan's Statements in Babylonia

We observed above that examination of commentary on and quotation of statements by and stories involving Rav and Shmuel reveals either (1) the gradual dissemination of their statements throughout Babylonia, or (2) decreasing Amoraic preference for Rav's statements over those of Shmuel, or vice versa. Comparison between commentary based on Shmuel's and R. Yohanan's statements reveals the same phenomenon, which admits of the same two possible explanations.[27]

Specifically, early Amoraim tend to comment only on statements by one or the other of the two rabbis, with early Babylonians commenting almost exclusively on statements by Shmuel. Later Amoraim, however, in particular the most prominent Babylonian Amoraim, tend to comment both on statements by Shmuel and on statements by Yohanan.

More specifically, no second-generation Amoraim comment both on statements by Shmuel and on statements by Yohanan, and no second-generation Babylonians comment on Yohanan's statements. Among third-generation Amoraim, only Rav Yosef, Rabbah, R. Ami, R. Huna, and Rabbah bar bar Hana comment on statements by both Amoraim, and only Yosef and Rabbah, both Babylonians, comment on statements by both Amoraim with any degree of frequency.

---

[27]For documentation, see the Appendix, below. For more on this issue, see Dor, *Torat Erez Yisrael be-Bavel*, pp. 11-84 and 94-113, and the references cited in the Introduction, above.

The integration of Yohanan's statements into the mainstream of Babylonian learning, therefore, or the decrease in Babylonian preference for the statements of Shmuel over those of Yohanan, begins in the third generation. In tractate Shabbat, Yosef and Rabbah comment on statements by Shmuel a total of 14 or 15 times, and on statements by Yohanan a total of 10 to 13 times. The process continues into the fourth generation, with Abaye and Rava accounting for most of the commentary on statements by Shmuel and Yohanan and commenting on their statements to almost exactly the same degree. Any generalizations we make regarding the fifth and seventh generations are of limited value due to the relative paucity of material, but in the sixth generation we again find two Amoraim (Rav Ashi and Ravina) accounting for most of the commentary on statements by Shmuel and Yohanan, and commenting on their statements to roughly the same extent.

3

Dreams and Dream Interpreters

The present chapter analyzes passages in the Bavli dealing with dreams, and attempts to show several differences between Tannaitic and Amoraic statements and stories indicative of diverse sources. The Bavli contains Tannaitic sources which have not been "brought up to date," i.e., changed in conformity with reality during later periods. I attempt to show that the Bavli depicts real changes in rabbinic attitudes toward dreams and dream interpreters, and attests to an increasing rabbinic desire to shield people, or rabbis themselves, from the harmful effects of dreams.

The Bavli also depicts differences between Palestinian and Babylonian rabbis on the subject of dreams, but for reasons which will be explained below, I am more convinced of the importance of chronological than of geographical factors.

It bears emphasizing that transitional rabbis (sages who lived during the one or two generations between the Tannaitic and Amoraic periods) conform to the patterns exhibited by Tannaim. For convenience's sake, the term "Tannaim" refers throughout this chapter to transitional as well as Tannaitic rabbis.

Differences between Amoraic and Tannaitic (and Palestinian and Babylonian) Rabbis According to the Bavli

(Babylonian) Amoraim and (Palestinian) Tannaim are distinguishable first in that one lengthy passage in the Bavli, which is most likely a combination of several independent traditions (see below), favorably depicts a (Palestinian) Tanna interpreting the dreams of a non-rabbi. (Babylonian) Amoraim, in contrast, are favorably depicted in several sources as interpreting only the dreams of other rabbis.

The Bavli depicts (Babylonian) Amoraim and (Palestinian) Tannaim as distinct in other ways as well. The lengthy, composite passage referred to above favorably depicts a (Palestinian) Tanna as an interpreter of symbolic dreams, dreams which consist of symbols and images rather than verbal utterances.[1] In contrast, several stories approvingly depict (Babylonian) Amoraim interpreting message dreams, which consist of verbal utterances.[2] In all but one case, these verbal utterances are verses from the Bible. One story *might* depict a (Babylonian) Amora interpreting a symbolic dream, but the story strongly condemns his activity.

The above distinctions between (Palestinian) Tannaim and (Babylonian) Amoraim, and the claim that the Bavli preserves (Palestinian) Tannaitic sources on this issue, are supported by parallels in the Yerushalmi and Palestinian midrashic literature. To be specific, in several Palestinian sources we find (Palestinian) Tannaim depicted as interpreters of the symbolic dreams of non-rabbis, in conformity with the Bavli's portrayal.

The Bavli distinguishes between Tannaim and Amoraim in other respects as well. Only Amoraim, both Palestinian and Babylonian, try to equip non-professionals to handle the dangerous and unsettling aspects of dreams on their own, thereby removing the need to consult professional interpreters. Finally, Amoraim, both Palestinian and Babylonian, tend to interpret dreams favorably. To a greater degree than Tannaim, Amoraim (according to the Bavli) tend to emend negative dream interpretations found in earlier sources, yielding positive interpretations.

---

[1]For additional distinctions between early and later rabbis on the topic of dreams, see Isaac Afik, *Tefisat he-Halom Ezel Hazal* (Ph.D. Dissertation, Bar-Ilan University, 1990), pp. 12, 17, and 23.

[2]See also E.R. Dodds, *The Greeks and the Irrational* (Berkeley: University of California Press, 1951), p. 107, who writes that Artemidorus and Macrobius and other writers of late antiquity refer to three types of dreams: (1) Symbolic dreams, which dress up in metaphors, like riddles, meanings which require interpretation, (2) *Horama*, or "vision," which are straightforward preenactments of a future event, and (3) *Chrematismos*, or "oracle," in which the dreamer's parent, or some other important personage, reveals without symbolism what will or will not happen, or what should or should not be done. See also pp. 108-9, there. See also A. Leo Oppenheim, "Mantic Dreams in the Ancient Near East," in *The Dream and Human Societies*, ed. G.E. Von Grunebaum and Roger Caillois (Berkeley, California: University of California Press, 1966), pp. 347-50. See also *The Interpretation of Dreams: Oneirocritica, by Artemidorus*, Robert J. White, translator (Park Ridge, New Jersey: Noyes Press, 1975), Book 4,1, pp. 185-86, who distinguishes between theorematic dreams (which "come true just as they are seen") and allegorical dreams (which "disclose their meaning through riddles"). See also Robert Karl Gnuse, *The Dream Theophany of Samuel* (Lanham, Maryland: University Press of America, 1984), pp. 16-23; and Maren Niehoff, "A Dream Which is not Interpreted is Like a Letter Which is not Read," *Journal of Jewish Studies* 43, No. 1 (1992), p. 60.

Rabbinic Attitudes toward Dreams: Chronological Changes (and Geographical Differences)

In the following pages, I attempt to document each one of these claims. I deal first with the claim that stories about (Palestinian) Tannaim differ from those involving (Babylonian) Amoraim. In a lengthy passage on b. Berakhot 56b, R. Yishmael b'R. Yosi,[3] a (Palestinian) Tanna, interprets several dreams reported to him by a "heretic" (*mina*).[4] The passage reads as follows:

A certain heretic said to R. Yishmael b'R. Yosi, "I saw myself pouring oil into olives." He said to him, "He had sex with his mother." He said to him, "I saw myself plucking a star." He said to him, "You stole from an Israelite." He said to him, "I saw myself swallowing a star." He said to him, "You sold an Israelite and consumed the profits." He said to him, "I saw my eyes kissing one another." He said to him, "He had sex with his sister." He said to him, "I saw myself kissing the moon." He said to him, "He had sex with an Israelite's wife." He said to him, "I saw myself walking in the shade of a myrtle tree."[5] He said to him, "He had sex with a betrothed girl." He said to him, "I saw shade above me and also below me."[6] He said to him, "You have intercourse upside-down." He said to him, "I saw crows returning to my bed." He said to him, "Your wife has whored with many men." He said to him, "I saw doves returning to my bed." He said to him, "You have defiled many women." He said to him, "I saw myself holding two doves and they flew away." He said to him, "You married two women and sent them away without a writ of divorce." He said to him, "I saw myself peeling eggs." He said to him, "You have stripped the dead [of their clothes]." He said to him, "I have done everything except for that, which I have not done." In the meantime, a woman came and said to him, "The cloak that you are wearing belongs to So-and-so, who died and you stripped him." He said to him, "I saw that they said to me, 'Your father left you possessions in Cappadocia.'" He said to him, "Do you have possessions in Cappadocia?" He said to him, "No." "Did your father ever go to Cappadocia?" He said to him, "No." "If so, *Kappa* is beam, *Deka* is ten. Go and check the tenth beam, which is full of money." He went and found that it was full of money.

As noted above, this passage is most likely a combination of several independent sources, according to which the Bavli's portrayal of the Tannaitic period, at first glance attested to by only a single story, is more likely based on several originally independent accounts. The composite nature of the Bavli's tradition is revealed first by the fact that a parallel in

---

[3]See *DS* vav.
[4]The printed edition reads "Sadducee," but see *DS* vav.
[5]See Rashi, s.v., *tuna de-asa*; Levy, *Wörterbuch*, vol. 2, p. 146; and Jastrow, *Dictionary*, p. 524. See also *DS* zayin.
[6]See the references cited in the previous note.

Yer. Maaser Sheni 4:6 consists of several discrete narratives involving a variety of different dreamers. Second, the conclusion of the Bavli's account (beginning with the discussion of possessions left in Cappadocia) is an independent narrative in the Yerushalmi and in Bereshit Rabbah.[7] In the latter two contexts, R. Yosi ben Halafta interprets the dream of "a man," in contrast to the Bavli where Yishmael b'R. Yosi appears to be continuing his conversation with the heretic. The composite character of the Bavli's account is shown further by the problematic nature of its conclusion. According to the Bavli, Yishmael b'R. Yosi sees to it that the wicked heretic, guilty of a wide variety of exotic sexual crimes and of robbing the dead, discovers a lost inheritance left to him by his father. This portrayal of a rabbi rewarding a wicked heretic is, to put it mildly, uncharacteristic of ancient rabbinic texts, further indication that the Bavli's account is a conflation of originally independent traditions.

In any event, the Bavli depicts a (Palestinian) Tanna as the interpreter of dreams by a non-rabbi. Stories in the Bavli involving (Babylonian) Amoraic dream interpreters paint a much different picture. To be specific, four stories[8] favorably depict (Babylonian) Amoraim interpreting dreams, and in each case the Amora interprets the dream of another rabbi. The four certain cases are as follows:

(1) On b. Taanit 24b, Rava[9] visits the city of Hegronia and declares a fast on account of drought. The fast fails and no rain falls, so Rava orders the fast to continue overnight. The following day, Rava asks whether anyone dreamed during the night of the fast, and Rav Elazar Mihegronia reports the following message, which was "read to him"[10] in a dream: "Greetings to the good rabbi from the good master, who from his goodness benefits his people." Rava announces that "it is a favorable time to ask mercy," and rain falls in response to their prayers.

(2) A story on b. Sotah 31a features two "disciples" who "sit before Rava" and report biblical verses read to them in a dream. "How abundant is the good that You have in store for those who fear You"

---

[7]See Yer. Maaser Sheni 4:6 and Bereshit Rabbah 68:12, ed. Theodor-Albeck, pp. 784-85.

[8]In addition to these four stories, see the similar story on b. Yevamot 93a-b involving R. Hiyya, a transitional rabbi whom I would expect to conform to the patterns exhibited by Tannaim. My point is not that only (Babylonian) Amoraim interpret their students' dreams, but rather that (Babylonian) Amoraim interpret *only* their students' dreams, unlike (Palestinian) Tannaim (and transitional rabbis) who *also* interpret the dreams of non-rabbis.

[9]See *DS* hei.

[10]The text literally states "read to us," but the speaker is probably using the editorial "we."

(Ps. 31:20),[11] reports one, and "But let all who take refuge in You rejoice" (Ps. 5:12), reports the other. Rava asserts that "you are both completely righteous rabbis, but one is motivated by love and the other by fear."

(3) According to a story on b. Hullin 133a, Rav Safra hears Proverbs 25:20 read to him in a dream ("Disrobing on a chilly day, like vinegar on natron, is one who teaches Torah to an evil heart"[12]). Safra fears that the verse indicates heavenly disapproval of his actions, and visits Rav Yosef, who assures him that he committed no offense. According to either Yosef or the anonymous editors, the dream expresses heavenly disapproval not of Safra, but of Rava.

(4) On b. Sanhedrin 81b-82a, Rav Kahana asks Rav a halachic question, but Rav is unable to recall the correct answer (he "forgets his tradition"). Kahana has a dream in which Malachi 2:11 is read, and he reports the dream to Rav. The verse jogs Rav's memory (he "remembers his tradition"), and his interpretation of the verse yields the answer to Kahana's question.

In all of these stories, (Babylonian) Amoraim interpret their students' dreams. In contrast to (Palestinian) Tannaim, (Babylonian) Amoraim are not favorably depicted as interpreters of the dreams of individuals clearly or even possibly outside of the rabbinic movement.[13]

I referred above to parallels in Palestinian literature to the lengthy composite narrative involving Yishmael b'R. Yosi on b. Berakhot 56b. I briefly summarize these and other relevant Palestinian stories, since they help us refine our understanding of the above-mentioned distinction between (Palestinian) Tannaim and (Babylonian) Amoraim. I will argue that this and other related distinctions indicate that the Bavli depicts (Palestinian) Tannaim as professional dream interpreters, and (Babylonian) Amoraim as hostile to professional interpreters.

In Yer. Maaser Sheni 4:6 we find the following thirteen stories involving (Palestinian) Tannaim:

---

[11]The translations of Biblical verses throughout this chapter are based on those of the Jewish Publication Society (Philadelphia, 1962, 1978, and 1982).

[12]I have translated the verse as Rav Safra appears to understand it. The Jewish Publication Society (p. 245) translates "...is one who sings songs to a sorrowful soul."

[13]See also Yer. Kilaim 32b (paralleled on Yer. Ketubot 35a), where a certain weaver reports his dream before R. Yohanan, a Palestinian Amora. Yohanan does not interpret the dream, however, and his interest in it stems from the fact that it demonstrates the greatness of one of his students.

(1-11) In eleven cases, rabbis interpret the dreams of a "person" (*bar nash*). In eight cases the interpreter is R. Yishmael b'R. Yosi, in two cases R. Yosi ben Halafta, and in one case R. Akiba.[14]

In one of these eleven cases, R. Yishmael b'R. Yosi asserts that the "person's" dream reveals his occupation: that of manufacturing ovens. In a second case, R. Yishmael b'R. Yosi curses the "person" whose dream reveals that he has murdered Jews. In a third case, R. Yishmael b'R. Yosi repeatedly refuses to interpret a "person's" dream unless he is paid a fee. The man refuses to pay and suffers monetary loss, which the story depicts as deserved punishment for his failure to pay.

In a twelfth case, (12) R. Yishmael b'R. Yosi interprets the dream of a Samaritan (*Kuti*),[15] and in a thirteenth case, (13) R. Eliezer (or R. Elazar)[16] interprets the dream of a woman.

Stories in the Bavli and Yerushalmi, therefore, depict (Palestinian) Tannaim (usually R. Yishmael b'R. Yosi) as interpreters of the dreams of non-rabbis, and even non-Jews. Several stories, in other words, depict (Palestinian) Tannaim as professional dream interpreters without a hint of criticism. Their services are available to all, and, if one story in the Yerushalmi involving Yishmael b'R. Yosi is any indication, they justifiably demand payment for their services.

Other distinctions between the Bavli's portrayal of (Palestinian) Tannaim and (Babylonian) Amoraim are connected to the distinction noted above. Confining the discussion to cases in which the texts claim that actual dreams are brought before rabbis for interpretation, we find sages, distinguishable along chronological and geographical lines, interpreting different kinds of dreams.

---

[14]The printed edition of Eikha Rabbah 1:1:16, where much of the Yerushalmi material is paralleled, reads R. Yohanan instead of R. Akiba, but see Solomon Buber's edition of Eikha Rabbah, p. 54, and n. 142, there.

[15]The text does not explicitly identify who interprets the Samaritan's dream, but Yishmael b'R. Yosi is most likely referred to, since he is the subject of a series of dream stories immediately above.

[16]Bereshit Rabbah, ed. Theodor-Albeck, pp. 1095-96, reads R. Eliezer. Other versions read R. Elazar, which can either refer to a Tanna or to the Amora, R. Elazar ben Pedat. The fact that no other stories depict later Palestinian sages as professional interpreters, however, and no other stories depict later professionals in positive terms increases the likelihood that an early rabbi is referred to here as well. According to Eikha Rabbah's version of this story, R. Yohanan's statement might be quoted at the conclusion of the story, according to which Elazar ben Pedat would appear to be referred to. In the Yerushalmi's version, however, Yohanan's statement is independent of the story, as are very similar statements recorded in the Bavli. There is thus no proof that the later Elazar is referred to.

To be specific, the four stories discussed above involving (Babylonian) Amoraim depict them interpreting explicit verbal utterances, in all but one case quotations of scripture.[17] The only story which perhaps portrays an Amora interpreting symbolic dreams (see below) condemns the activity in extremely harsh terms. In contrast, the composite account involving (Palestinian) Tannaim (see above) approvingly depicts a rabbi interpreting symbolic dreams (which consist, it will be recalled, of images which require translation in order to be intelligible).

How can we explain this difference between the Bavli's portrayal of (Palestinian) Tannaim and (Babylonian) Amoraim? While certainty is not possible, perhaps this distinction is further evidence of changing, or differing, rabbinic attitudes toward professional dream interpreters. (Babylonian) Amoraim tend not to be depicted as interpreters of symbolic dreams perhaps because such dreams were generally the domain of professionals. (Babylonian) Amoraim wish to clearly distinguish between their activities and those of professional interpreters. They interpret the message dreams of their students, which usually consist of scriptural verses, without fear of blurring the distinction between professionals and themselves. (Palestinian) Tannaim, in contrast, were not concerned with maintaining such a distinction. They did not share the (Babylonian) Amoraic disapproval of the activities of professional interpreters.

The Bar Hedya Story: A Polemic, but Against Whom?

I referred above to a story on b. Berakhot 56a-b which perhaps portrays a (Babylonian) Amora as a professional interpreter of symbolic dreams and strongly disapproves of his activity. According to this story, Abaye and Rava repeat their dreams before Bar Hedya, a dream interpreter who grants favorable interpretations to those who pay him, and unfavorable interpretations to those who do not.[18] Abaye pays a fee and is rewarded with favorable interpretations, while Rava does not pay and receives unfavorable interpretations. Bar Hedya's predictions come true, and Rava experiences a lengthy series of

---

[17]For discussion of the relationship between dream interpretation and scriptural exegesis, see Lieberman, *Hellenism in Jewish Palestine*, pp. 68-82; and Niehoff, "A Dream Which is not Interpreted," pp. 58-84.

[18]Compare Ken Frieden, *Freud's Dream of Interpretation* (Albany: State University of New York Press, 1990), pp. 79-82; and Afik, *Tefisat he-Halom Ezel Hazal*, pp. 178-424.

misfortunes, including the deaths of his wife and children.[19] He finally pays Bar Hedya's fee, and receives favorable interpretations in return.

One of Bar Hedya's interpretations, that Rava will experience a miracle, leads to his undoing. Travelling together with Rava on a ship, Bar Hedya worries that Rava's miracle might endanger him. Perhaps the ship will sink in a storm, and only Rava will be miraculously saved. Bar Hedya decides to flee, but as he leaves the ship a "book of dreams" (i.e., a dream manual) falls out of his pocket. Rava finds it, reads that "all dreams follow the mouth," and realizes that Bar Hedya has the power to determine whether dreams have good or bad consequences. Rava holds Bar Hedya responsible for the deaths of his wife and children,[20] and utters a curse: "May it be His [God's] will that this man [Bar Hedya] be handed over to the government, who will have no mercy on him." Bar Hedya cites the rabbinic teaching: "The curse of a sage, even when unprovoked, will come true," and reasons: "how much the more so" is this true in Rava's case, since Rava's curse is justified. Bar Hedya flees to Roman territory, where his greed eventually leads to his arrest and execution at the hands of the Roman government.

What is the story's message? According to one possible understanding, the story attempts to show that rabbis are more powerful than professional dream interpreters. The story is evidence of a power struggle between competing groups, rabbis on the one hand and professional interpreters on the other, both of whom sought control over the Jewish people in Babylonia. Like Bar Hedya's interpretation, Rava's curse is put into effect simply by being uttered, but in the end Rava's curse prevails and Bar Hedya dies a horrible death. The rabbis deserve the right to rule because they are more powerful.

According to a second possible understanding, Bar Hedya is a rabbi, and the story depicts a struggle between rabbinic proponents and opponents of professional dream interpretation, between rabbis who act as professional interpreters and rabbis who condemn the activity.

---

[19]In one hilariously funny scene, Bar Hedya predicts that Rava will receive two blows. Rava finds two blind men fighting and tries to intercede, and receives the two blows. The blind men are about to hit him again, but Rava protests, "I have enough. I saw two." This vignette seems to mock the entire notion of the efficacy and truth of dream interpretation, as if to say that Rava had to intercede in order to insure that the interpretation would come true. It seems to view Bar Hedya as nothing more than a charlatan. However, no other aspect of the story casts the slightest doubt on Bar Hedya's power and the truth of his interpretations. Furthermore, a geniza fragment lacks this detail. See *Ginzei Talmud Bavli*, ed. Abraham Katsch (Jerusalem: Rubin Mass, 1979), vol. 1, p. 16, for a photocopy of the fragment, and see p. 18 for Katsch's transcription.

[20]See *DS* resh.

I prefer the second understanding because we find a Bar Hedya engaging in standard rabbinic activity in three other contexts in the Talmud.[21] To judge from these sources, Bar Hedya is most likely a fourth-generation Amora, that is, a contemporary of Abaye and Rava who spent time in Palestine.[22] The sketchy biographical data about Bar Hedya found elsewhere, in other words, conforms to the story here, and Bar Hedya is most likely a rabbi.[23] It should also be noted that the story has Bar Hedya cite a rabbinic statement ("The curse of a sage, even when unprovoked, will come true"), which might reveal his character as a rabbi, but might also be a narrative device enabling the villain himself to admit guilt and acknowledge Rava's superior power.

One might object that the Talmud would be unlikely to portray a rabbi in such negative terms. This argument fails, however, because other portrayals of rabbis are similarly unflattering.[24]

We can be reasonably certain that the story's message is not: Go to a dream interpreter, but make sure you pay the fee. I reject this understanding because no one emerges from their encounter with Bar Hedya unscathed, including Abaye, who pays the fee at the outset. Once Rava finally pays the fee, Bar Hedya asserts that Abaye will die and his students will depart to learn with Rava. Everyone suffers from their encounter with the wicked dream interpreter, and playing by his rules and paying his fee ultimately affords little protection.

In any event, the story is important for my purposes because it involves (Babylonian) Amoraim and polemicizes against a professional dream interpreter. It is unclear, however, whether the story polemicizes against professional dream interpreters in general, or only against especially corrupt individuals who cynically use their power for personal gain.

Chronological versus Geographical Explanations

Before discussing other differences between rabbis on the subject of dreams, it will be helpful to explain my uncertainty regarding the role of geographical and chronological factors in explaining the above distinctions. It will be recalled that the lengthy, composite narrative

---

[21]Sukkah 43b, Moed Katan 18b, and Hullin 106b.
[22]See Hyman, *Toldot Tannaim ve-Amoraim*, p. 285.
[23]Hyman, *Toldot Tannaim ve-Amoraim*, p. 285, assumes, in my view correctly, that the Bar Hedya referred to on Berakhot 56a-b is the same Bar Hedya referred to elsewhere in the Talmud. Compare Neusner, *A History of the Jews in Babylonia*, vol. 4, pp. 343-46.
[24]See, for example, the stories involving R. Yohanan on Baba Kamma 117a-b and Baba Mezia 84a. It would be a simple matter to multiply examples.

which favorably depicts a professional dream interpreter involves a Palestinian Tanna. Sources involving Babylonian Amoraim favorably depict rabbis as interpreters, but not as professionals. The question arises as to whether chronology or geography is significant in accounting for this difference, or whether both factors play a role. Certainty on this issue is not possible, because the sources discussed above include no Tannaitic sources purporting to derive from Babylonia, and no Amoraic sources purporting to derive from Palestine.

However, other differences between rabbis on the subject of dream interpretation (to be discussed below) are most likely explicable along chronological rather than geographical lines. The fact that chronology is significant in some cases does not imply that geography plays no role in other cases, but it does make it difficult to exclude chronology from consideration in the ambiguous cases discussed above. I am convinced about the importance of chronological factors in the above cases, therefore, and less convinced about the importance of geographical factors, although the question is in need of further study.

Other Differences between Rabbis on the Subject of Dream Interpretation

As noted above, we find other differences between Tannaim and Amoraim closely related to the differences described above. Several statements, all by Amoraim (both Palestinian and Babylonian), equip non-professionals to handle dreams on their own and remove the need to resort to interpreters. It will be helpful to document this claim in detail.

On b. Berakhot 55b, a sixth-generation Amora (either Amemar, Mar Zutra, or Rav Ashi) asserts that one who "saw a dream but does not know what he saw" should repeat a formula which will insure a favorable outcome to the dream.[25]

Also on b. Berakhot 55b, Shmuel neutralizes bad dreams by reciting the biblical verse "Dreams speak vanity" (Zecharya 10:2), and encourages the fulfillment of good dreams by reciting the verse "Through a dream I will speak with him" (Numbers 12:6).[26] Similarly, on b. Berakhot 56b R. Yehoshua ben Levi lists verses one should recite to insure a positive outcome to a dream, lest different verses come to mind and cause a negative outcome. Along these same lines, on b. Shabbat 11a (and b. Taanit 12b), several later Babylonian rabbis refer to the practice of "dream-fasting," fasting in order to nullify a disturbing dream. Rav

---

[25]See also the sources cited by Alexander Kristianpoller, "Traum und Traumdeutung," in *Monumenta Talmudica,* ed. Karl Albrecht et al. (Vienna: Benjamin Harz, 1923), vol. 4, part 2, pp. 21-23.

[26]Compare Afik, *Tefisat he-Halom Ezel Hazal,* pp. 56-62.

Yehoshua b. d'Rav Idi refuses food from his host, Rav Ashi, because he is dream-fasting, and cites Rav's opinion that "A fast is as effective on dreams as fire is on kindling." Rav Yosef even goes so far as to to permit dream-fasting on the Sabbath.[27]

In the Yerushalmi (Berakhot 5:1), incidentally, R. Tanhum bei R. Hiyya, a Palestinian Amora, provides the text of a formula to be uttered by someone who sees "a difficult dream." Here as well, the individual is urged to handle the dream on his own, eliminating the need to consult an interpreter.

A statement by R. Yohanan on b. Berakhot 55b may serve the same purpose, although editorial additions to the statement make detailed examination necessary to appreciate its full significance. According to Yohanan, one who becomes depressed on account of a dream should "interpret" the dream (*yiftarenu*) in the presence of three people. Anonymous editors cite a statement by Rav Hisda against Yohanan's view, and explain that Yohanan really means to say that the dreamer should "make [the dream] good" (*yativenu*). The editors, or Yohanan, next provide the text of a formula which the dreamer is to recite before three people who love him,[28] thereby insuring that the dream will have favorable results.[29]

---

[27]See also b. Berakhot 14a and 60a-b, Pesahim 117a, and Nedarim 8a. See also Yer. Sanhedrin 28c (10:2), where the same idea is attributed to the wicked Menasheh. It is unclear whether the account there is Tannaitic or Amoraic, however.

[28]The printed edition lacks the phrase "who love him." See, however, *DS* lamed, and *Ginzei Talmud Bavli*, ed. Katsch, vol. 1, p. 14, for a photocopy of the fragment, and p. 14 for Katsch's transcription.

[29]See *DS* khaf, for a reading without the anonymous editorial objection on the basis of Hisda's view and the subsequent emendation or reinterpretation of Yohanan's statement. According to these versions, the text of the formula follows immediately after the opening part of Yohanan's statement, as follows: "If one has a dream which makes him sad, he should go and interpret it in the presence of three. Let him bring three who love him and say to them: I have seen a good dream, and they should say to him, Good it is and good may it be. May the Merciful One turn it to good...." In addition, Brigitte Stemberger, "Der Traum in der Rabbinischen Literatur," *Kairos* 18 (1976), p. 27, observes that the editorial insertion is problematic. The anonymous objection implies that a dream without interpretation is harmless, and yet the text continues on to supply a formula for neutralizing the ill effects of a dream, implying that a dream without interpretation is potentially very dangerous. The anonymous objection also distorts Hisda's view. The versions without the editorial insertion, therefore, would appear to be correct.

However, Afik, *Tefisat he-Halom Ezel Hazal*, p. 27, n. 3, argues persuasively that the reading without the editorial insertion is very likely attributable to homoiteloiton, and the editorial insertion is most likely an integral part of the text. In addition, Yohanan's statement until the words "and interpret it" is

If the formula is an original part of Yohanan's statement, then he asserts that the individual should take his dream to friends (people who "love him") who will be likely to interpret positively rather than to professionals who might interpret negatively. The role of the three friends is to repeat a fixed formula, leaving them with no initiative in the process whatsoever. If Yohanan is responsible for the formula, then he eliminates the need to consult a professional interpreter and empowers the individual to act on his own.

If later editors are responsible for the formula, then Yohanan (minus the editorial additions) specifies that the individual should take his dream before three people and "interpret it." Yohanan might be advising the dreamer to consult interpreters, who will decode his dream images into comprehensible speech, but just as plausibly he is advising the dreamer to go before individuals who will resolve, or dissolve, his dream. As Oppenheim observes in his classic study of dreams in the ancient Near East, the verb *ptr* (rendered above as "interpret") can refer to "the magic act of 'transferring' the evil power of a bad dream to a certain object." According to Oppenheim, the primary meaning of *pasaru* is "to remove," and a secondary meaning is "to solve." "The verb *pasaru* has...two aspects: one which refers to the 'translation' of the 'symbols' of the dream into an unequivocally worded message or announcement, and one which alludes to the fact that the evil implications of the mystery contained in such a 'symbolic' dream have been dissolved." The word *pasir* sometimes refers to "he who dispels (removes the consequences of evil) dreams."[30] Even if the text of the formula is not part of Yohanan's statement, therefore, there is no reason to assume that Yohanan advocates resorting to professional dream interpreters who will translate dream images into coherent speech.

---

entirely in Hebrew, while the formula itself as well as the introduction to the formula ("Let him bring three people and say to them") is in Aramaic. It is therefore unclear, no matter which reading we accept, whether or not the opening part of the statement and the text of the formula are the words of a single speaker.

[30] A. Leo Oppenheim, "The Interpretation of Dreams in the Ancient Near East with a Translation of an Assyrian Dream-Book," *Transactions of the American Philosophical Society*, New Series, 46, Part 3 (1956), p. 218. See also Stemberger, "Der Traum in der Rabbinischen Literatur," pp. 26-30; and Monford Harris, "Dreams in Sefer Hasidim," *Proceedings of the American Academy for Jewish Research* 31 (1963), pp. 68-71, who claims that Sefer Hasidim, a thirteenth-century German-Jewish work, also uses the terms *ptr* and *psr* in this sense.

Interpreting Dreams Positively

Finally, according to the Bavli, Amoraim (both Palestinian and Babylonian), are distinguishable from Tannaim in that Amoraim tend to minimize the force of negative dream interpretations found in earlier sources, and Amoraim tend more than Tannaim to interpret dreams positively.[31] These differences are very likely motivated by the forces which led to differing rabbinic attitudes toward professional interpreters, and which also motivated Amoraim to equip individuals to handle dreams on their own. Amoraim are much more concerned than are earlier rabbis with neutralizing the terrifying and potentially dangerous aspects of dreams. Amoraim view professional dream interpreters with suspicion or outright hostility because they fear the power of these individuals to interpret dreams negatively and thereby insure unfavorable consequences. The same impulse, namely fear of the inimical effects of dreams, also led Amoraim to interpret dreams positively.

In order to document this claim, I will survey the dream images and interpretations found on b. Berakhot 56b-57b, indicating, where relevant, whether a statement derives from an Amora or from a Tanna, or, at times, possibly from a dream manual.[32] The numbers and letters which begin each line are based upon the division of the material in Appendix 2, below, which contains a translation of the entire discussion.

Accompanying footnotes discuss the rationale for considering some of the statements on b. Berakhot 56b-57b as citations from dream manuals.[33] Briefly stated, my reasons are (1) the similarity between this

---

[31]Later rabbis also assign fixed positive interpretations to dream images on b. Baba Kamma 55a (R. Yehoshua ben Levi [see *DS* lamed]) and b. Sanhedrin 93a (Rav Papa).

[32]See also Ernst Ludwig Ehrlich, "Der Traum im Talmud," *Zeitschrift für die Neutestamentliche Wissenschaft* (1956), p. 143, and Stemberger, "Der Traum in der Rabbinischen Literatur," p. 13.

[33]My uncertainty is due to the fact that several statements referred to below very likely derive from dream manuals, but it is impossible to state this with certainty. We cannot be certain, therefore, that later rabbinic dream interpretations are uniformly positive. If the source designated below as 9A-R was authored by a later rabbi, for example, then some later dream interpretations are negative.

The reason for our uncertainty is that a source such as 16A-O is composed of numerous parts, some of which are obviously different from one another in form and content. These differences, furthermore, are *not* accompanied by the typical introductory terms and attributions usually indicative of a change of source in the Talmud. The shift in form or content might indicate a different source. That is, the shift in form or content might indicate that a source explicitly identified as Tannaitic (by means of terms such as *Tenno Rabbanan*) has concluded, and another, unidentified source (i.e., a dream manual) has resumed.

material and ancient non-Jewish dream manuals,[34] and (2) the anomalous nature of several of these statements. Both factors might indicate that some of these statements derive from sources not usually cited in the Talmud.

To be specific, the statements under consideration are declarative statements in Hebrew,[35] and therefore do not derive from the Talmud's anonymous editors. Statements by the anonymous editors are overwhelmingly argumentational, i.e., in question and answer form, and almost entirely in Aramaic. In addition, several of the statements appear to lack the introductory terms or attributions usually indicative of Tannaitic or Amoraic origin.[36] Several of these statements, in other words, are apparently neither Tannaitic, Amoraic, nor editorial, the usual sources cited in the Talmud. If they are none of the above, however, then what are they? Perhaps they are citations from dream manuals, the existence of which is attested to by the Talmud itself.[37]

Perhaps a statement on b. Berakhot 55b introduced by the technical formula "as it is said" strengthens this claim. The anonymous commentary based on this statement assumes that the formula introduces only biblical quotes, but the statement is not found in our texts of the Bible. Avraham Weiss conjectures, however, that the term "as it is said" introduces quotations from written texts, and perhaps the written text in this instance is a dream manual.[38] In fact, the statement in question, "All dreams follow the mouth," is referred to on b. Berakhot 56a as a citation from Bar Hedya's dream manual.

It is worthwhile noting that several unattributed cures found on b. Gittin 69b are very likely citations from medical manuals reported without introductory terminology. Supporting this claim is the fact that

---

[34]See *The Interpretation of Dreams, by Artemidorus*, I, 14ff., pp. 23ff. See also Philip S. Alexander, "Quid Athenis Et Hierosolymis? Rabbinic Midrash and Hermeneutics in the Graeco-Roman World," in *A Tribute to Geza Vermes: Essays on Jewish and Christian Literature and History*, ed. Philip R. Davies and Richard T. White (Sheffield, England: Journal for the Study of the Old Testament Press, 1990), pp. 117-19, and the literature cited on p. 123, n. 39, there.

[35]Statements by the anonymous editors, in contrast, are virtually always argumentational and in Aramaic.

[36]See below, and see the translation in Appendix 2, below. Compare Weiss, *Al ha-Yezira ha-Sifrutit Shel ha-Amoraim*, p. 268, who thinks that these sections are continuations of the statements by R. Yehoshua ben Levi, R. Hiyya bar Abba, and Rav Yosef.

[37]See the Bar Hedya story on b. Berakhot 56a, analyzed in detail above, and see the discussion below.

[38]Avraham Weiss, *Al ha-Yezira ha-Sifrutit Shel ha-Amoraim* (New York: Horeb, 1962), p. 266, n. 10. Compare Avraham Weiss, *Le-Heker ha-Talmud* (New York: Philipp Feldheim, 1954), pp. 51 and 55.

Rav Aha Midifti's and Rav Aha b. d'Rava's statements are based on these unattributed cures, whereas normally, named rabbis in the Talmud tend not to respond to unattributed statements.[39] In all likelihood, most unattributed Talmudic statements are not citations from other sources, but are editorial comments which originate in the Talmudic context itself.

The following is a subdivision of the material found on b. Berakhot 56b-57b:

(1)	Tannaitic (R. Hanina) – positive
(2)	Tannaitic (R. Natan)[40] – positive
(2a)	Amoraic Babylonian (Rava) – positive
(3)	Tannaitic or Amoraic (R. Hanan)[41] – positive
(3a)	Tannaitic (R. Hanina) – negative
(4A-K)	Amoraic Palestinian (R. Yehoshua ben Levi) – suggests verses to recite upon waking to ensure a positive outcome to a dream. A person is to say these verses before a negative verse occurs to him
(5)	Tannaitic – positive
(6)	Amoraic Palestinian or Babylonian (R. Zeira) – positive
(7)	Tannaitic – positive
(4L)	Amoraic Palestinian (R. Yehoshua ben Levi), or dream manual[42] – same as (4A-K), above
(8)	Tannaitic – positive and negative
(8a)	Tannaitic – positive and negative
(9A-R)	Dream manual[43] or Amoraic Palestinian (continuing R. Yehoshua ben Levi's statement [4A-K and 4L, above]) – positive and negative

---

[39]See, for example, Kalmin, *The Redaction of the Babylonian Talmud*, pp. 10 and 90-93, and the references cited in n. 33, pp. 157-58.

[40]Note that R. Natan's statement appears to be based on that of R. Hanina, which is chronologically impossible. This and other comparable difficulties will be discussed here only when relevant to my major contention.

[41]The fact that R. Hanina comments on this statement suggests that R. Hanan is not an Amora. See, however, *DS* nun.

[42]No source is specified, and this statement might derive from an anonymous dream manual. Part of the lengthy statement which I assigned above to R. Yehoshua ben Levi might likewise derive from such a manual. See, however, Weiss, *Al ha-Yezira ha-Sifrutit Shel ha-Amoraim*, p. 268, who claims that Yehoshua ben Levi continues to speak.

[43]Weiss, *Al ha-Yezira ha-Sifrutit Shel ha-Amoraim*, p. 286, claims that this statement is also the continuation of Yehoshua ben Levi's statement above (4A-K and 4L). Against this claim, however, it should be noted that 9A-R is entirely different from Yehoshua ben Levi's statement both in content and form. It is also difficult to view 9A-R as the continuation of the previous Tannaitic statements (8 and 8a).

(9H.a.)   Tannaitic – positive, with the exception of two images which
           are not positive
(10A-I)   Amoraic Palestinian (R. Hiyya bar Abba) – positive
(11A-P)   Amoraic Babylonian (Rav Yosef), or Tannaitic (*Teni* Rav
           Yosef)[44] – mostly positive, with three negative images (11G, L,
           and N)
(11B.a.)   Amoraic Palestinian (Ulla), or Tannaitic (*be-Matnita Tanna*)[45] –
           limits the circumstances under which an image is positive
(11L.a.)   Amoraic Babylonians (Abaye and Rava) – contradict the
           negative interpretation found in (11L), yielding a positive
           interpretation
(12)   A Tanna (a professional reciter of early traditions) recites a
           Tannaitic tradition before a Babylonian Amora (Rav Nahman
           bar Yizhak). The Tannaitic tradition contains a negative
           interpretation of a dream image
(12a-b)   The Babylonian Amora (Rav Nahman bar Yizhak) cites a
           Tannaitic tradition which interprets the same dream image
           positively, and proceeds to reconcile the contradiction,
           yielding a single positive interpretation
(13)   A Tanna recites a Tannaitic tradition before a Babylonian
           Amora (Rav Sheshet). The Tannaitic tradition contains one
           negative and two positive interpretations of three dream
           images
(13a)   The Babylonian Amora (Rav Sheshet) rejects the one negative
           interpretation and suggests a positive interpretation in its place
(14)   A Tanna recites a Tannaitic tradition before a Palestinian
           Amora (R. Yohanan). The Tannaitic tradition contains
           interpretations of dream images, one of which (wine) can be
           either positive or negative
(14a)   The Palestinian Amora (R. Yohanan) emends the Tannaitic
           tradition in (14), limiting the circumstances under which wine
           is a negative dream image
(15)   Amoraic Palestinian (R. Yohanan) – neither positive nor
           negative
(16A-G)   Tannaitic – positive and negative

The former (8) is a list of "five things said regarding an ox," and the latter (8a) is a
fragmentary Baraita ("If he rode him, he will die").
[44]*DS* dalet.
[45]With regard to the term *be-Matnita Tanna*, see Albeck, *Mavo la-Talmudim*, pp. 44-
45.

(16H-O) Tannaitic, or dream manual[46] – positive
(16H.a.) Amoraic Palestinian (R. Yehoshua ben Levi), or dream manual[47] – positive
(16K.a.) Amoraic Babylonian (Rav) – positive. His positive interpretation conflicts with the negative interpretation of an early source. The anonymous editors resolve the contradiction
(17) Tannaitic – positive and negative. The subject might not be dreams
(17a) Amoraic Babylonian (Rav Papa) – The subject might not be dreams, but if it is, Papa limits the circumstances under which a dream image is negative

According to the above survey, several Tannaitic statements contain negative dream interpretations, and most, and possibly all Amoraic statements contain only positive interpretations. In addition, on several occasions Amoraim emend negative interpretations by earlier rabbis and arrive at positive interpretations.[48] In another instance, Amoraim limit, or contradict, an earlier source's negative interpretation,[49] and in another case an Amora's positive interpretation contradicts an earlier source's negative interpretation.[50]

Dream Interpreters in the Greco-Roman World

Before concluding this chapter, it will be helpful to briefly survey attitudes toward dream interpreters in the Greco-Roman world, which will add perspective to the discussion above.

---

[46]I suspect that the statements in 16H-O are citations from a dream manual because they are formally distinct from the statements in 16A-G. The latter is a series of statements which begin, "There are three...." The former contains several statements (16H-M) linked together by the phrase "All kinds of X are good for dreams except for..." and concludes with two statements (16N-O) which are arranged according to numbers. In addition, the latter two statements are the only ones in the entire section which do not deal exclusively with dreams ("Five things are one-sixtieth: Fire, honey, Shabbat, sleep, and dreams...." "Six things are a good sign for a sick person: sneezing, sweat, a bowel movement, semen, sleep, and dreams....").

[47]The source cited here (16H.a.) is a requotation of the source cited above as part of (9).

[48]See 12a-b, 13a, and 14a above.

[49]See 11L.a., above. The earlier source reinterpreted by Abaye and Rava is either Tannaitic or Amoraic.

[50]See 16K.a. above. The earlier source is either Tannaitic or a citation from a dream manual.

While dream interpreters were popular, respected, and influential in many circles,[51] they were often criticized and disdained, particularly by the educated elite.[52] Ennius, for example, expresses a low opinion of dream interpreters already in the second century B.C.E.[53] Juvenal, a first- and second-century Roman satirical poet, writes that "Jewish beggar women...play on the credulity of Roman matrons by telling their fortunes.... For a very small fee these Jews will interpret your dreams for you to suit your taste."[54] Artemidorus, himself a professional interpreter, writes that dream interpreters were to be found in the marketplaces in great numbers, and many were considered vagrants and charlatans.[55] Artemidorus' dream manual is an attempt to answer critics of dream interpretation, and to establish its credentials as a respectable science.[56] Synesius, a second-century C.E. Platonist who converted to Christianity, asserts in his treatise on dreams that individuals must acquire discipline and skill at decoding dreams for themselves. The inability to do so means shameful dependence on interpreters, which belies a lack of understanding of divine revelation.[57] Divination through dreams was seen by officials of the Catholic Church as a mark of paganism, and was officially condemned by the Church in 314 C.E.[58]

Rabbinic disapproval of professional interpreters is thus paralleled by attitudes expressed in Greco-Roman sources, although the chronological picture is not identical. Some confirmation of my claim that rabbinic opposition increased over time is provided by the early fourth-century development in the Catholic Church, although the matter warrants further study.[59]

---

[51]Steven M. Oberhelman, *The Oneirocriticon of Achmet: A Medieval Greek and Arabic Treatise on the Interpretation of Dreams* (Lubbock, Texas: Texas Tech University Press, 1991), p. 38.

[52]Afik, *Tefisat he-Halom Ezel Hazal*, pp. 6, 72-73, and 346.

[53]See J.H.W. Liebeschuetz, *Continuity and Change in Roman Religion* (Oxford: Clarendon Press, 1979), p. 122, and the references cited there.

[54]Juvenal VI, pp. 542-47. Taken from Harry J. Leon, *The Jews of Ancient Rome* (Philadelphia: Jewish Publication Society, 1960), pp. 41f.

[55]*The Interpretation of Dreams, by Artemidorus*, I,1, p. 13.

[56]Oberhelman, *The Oneirocriticon of Achmet*, p. 39; and *The Interpretation of Dreams, by Artemidorus*, pp. 6-7 (introduction).

[57]See Benjamin Kilborne, "Dreams," in *The Encyclopedia of Religion*, ed. Mircea Eliade (New York: Macmillan, 1987), vol. 4, p. 487; and Oberhelman, *The Oneirocriticon of Achmet*, p. 32.

[58]Oberhelman, *The Oneirocriticon of Achmet*, p. 51.

[59]For further discussion of dreams and dream interpreters in the Greco-Roman world, see *Pauly's Real-Encyclopädie der Classischen Altertumswissenschaft*, ed. Georg Wissowa et al. (Stuttgart: J.B. Metzler, 1894ff.), vol. 18 (1st series), pp. 448-59, and vol. 6 (2nd series), pp. 2233-245.

Summary and Conclusions

To reiterate, the sources attest to differences between Tannaitic and Amoraic (and Palestinian and Babylonian) roles and attitudes. First, (Palestinian) Tannaim are favorably depicted as interpreters of the symbolic dreams of non-rabbis, but (Babylonian) Amoraim are favorably depicted only as interpreters of the message dreams of other rabbis. Second, a lengthy story involving (Babylonian) Amoraim polemicizes against professional dream interpreters in general, or against especially corrupt individuals who use their power for personal gain. Third, Amoraim equip individuals to handle difficult dreams on their own, removing the need to consult dream interpreters. Fourth, Amoraim, more so than Tannaim, tend to interpret dreams positively and blunt the force of negative interpretations found in their sources.

Most of these differences, we argued, attest to changing rabbinic attitudes toward professional dream interpreters, and to an increasing rabbinic desire to protect people, or rabbis themselves, from the inimical effects of dreams (or to differences between Palestine and Babylonia on these issues). Amoraim discouraged people from resorting to professional interpreters and took pains to show that they themselves were not professionals. Such men[60] were to be avoided, the rabbis believed, lest they interpret dreams negatively and insure an unfavorable outcome.

It is unclear whether the sources reveal a historical change in the rabbis' role vis-à-vis non-rabbis and even non-Jews, or attest instead to changes in the portrayal of the rabbinic role. (Alternatively, it is unclear whether the sources attest to differences between the rabbinic role in Palestine and Babylonia, or attest instead to differences in the portrayal of the rabbinic role in the two centers.) Perhaps (Babylonian) Amoraim frequently acted as professional interpreters, but the dominant attitude expressed in our sources regarding this period (or locality) strongly disapproves of professionals. This attitude, perhaps, led to the inclusion of stories which depict (Babylonian) Amoraim as interpreters of the message dreams of their students, and to the suppression of stories which show rabbis interpreting the symbolic dreams of non-rabbis.

In one sense, however, it matters little whether or not the stories are accurate portrayals of rabbinic activity. Even if fictional, the sources depict changing (or different) rabbinic attitudes. They attest to historical changes or differences, if not in the rabbinic role, then in the image of the rabbi which rabbinic storytellers wished to project.

---

[60]Unlike non-Jewish sources, ancient rabbinic sources provide no evidence that women ever engaged in dream interpretation.

One final implication of the present study remains to be discussed. This implication concerns Yeshayahu Gafni's claim that rabbis in Babylonia have powers which in Palestine were the domain of non-rabbis. In Babylonia, Gafni argues, officials in charge of education, the distribution of charity, and related matters are generally depicted as rabbis or agents of the exilarch. In Palestine, however, such positions are filled by local officials unaffiliated with the rabbinic movement or the patriarch.[61]

The findings of the present chapter are not in conflict with Gafni's conclusions, but they suggest that it would be a mistake to infer from the evidence he gathers that Babylonian rabbis had more power over non-rabbinic Jews than did Palestinian rabbis. In certain respects, the opposite may have been the case. As noted above, (Palestinian) Tannaim are depicted as interpreters of the dreams of non-rabbis, even non-Jews, whereas (Babylonian) Amoraim are depicted primarily as interpreters of the dreams of other rabbis. If these stories accurately reflect reality, they indicate that in some areas, rabbinic power over non-rabbis was more extensive in Palestine than in Babylonia. It should also be noted that the story on b. Berakhot 56a-b, analyzed in detail above, depicts Bar Hedya interpreting the dreams of a non-Jew (the wardrobe officer) only after he is exiled from Babylonia.

---

[61]Gafni, *Yehudei Bavel bi-Tekufat ha-Talmud,* pp. 101-9.

4

The Judicial and Academic Hierarchies

The present chapter argues that several traditions attributed to and describing the activities of first- and second-generation Babylonian Amoraim presuppose distinct judicial and academic hierarchies.[1] Traditions involving later Amoraim, however, preserve no record of this distinction, further supporting my claim that the Talmud is comprised of diverse sources. The sources reflect either a change in the organization of the rabbinic movement, or a change in the attitudes of rabbinic storytellers.

A narrative involving Mar Ukba and Shmuel, first-generation Babylonian Amoraim, provides the clearest portrayal of distinct judicial and academic hierarchies. This narrative describes Mar Ukba as Shmuel's subordinate when they engage in academic activity and as Shmuel's superior when judicial activity is involved ("When they sat and studied, Mar Ukba would sit before Shmuel.... When they sat in judgment, Shmuel would sit before Mar Ukba...").[2] The narrative conceives of Mar Ukba's court and Shmuel's school as separate realms, such that Mar Ukba's pre-eminence in the judiciary and his probable identity as the exilarch does not alter the fact that he is Shmuel's academic inferior.[3] Similarly, Shmuel's prominence as a teacher has no bearing on his status in Mar Ukba's court.

A story featuring Shmuel's[4] and Mar Ukba's interaction in another context is best explicable along these same lines, although at first glance the story seems to depict Mar Ukba as Shmuel's halachic superior.

---

[1]For earlier discussion of this phenomenon, see Graetz, *Geschichte der Juden,* vol. 4, p. 291; Neusner, *A History of the Jews in Babylonia,* vol. 2, pp. 100-2; Segal, *Case Citation in the Babylonian Talmud,* pp. 8-10; Yeshayahu Gafni, "Ma'asei Bet-Din ba-Talmud ha-Bavli," *Proceedings of the American Academy for Jewish Research* 49 (1982), pp. 23-40; and *Yehudei Bavel bi-Tekufat ha-Talmud,* pp. 100 and 226-32.
[2]Moed Katan 16b. See Beer, *Rashut ha-Golah,* pp. 69-70. See also Shabbat 55a.
[3]Compare Neusner, *A History of the Jews in Babylonia,* vol. 2, p. 100.
[4]Halachot Gedolot reads Abuha de-Shmuel, but based on their interactions elsewhere in the Talmud, Shmuel is the preferable reading.

According to this passage, Shmuel states a halachic opinion, against which Karna objects. In response to Karna's objection, "they said to [Karna]: 'Behold Mar Ukba and his court are in Kafri,'"[5] apparently implying that Mar Ukba's opinion is decisive as far as the final determination of the halacha is concerned.[6] Subsequently, however, the matter is sent before Rav and no further mention is made of Mar Ukba. Rav is evidently portrayed as an official in Mar Ukba's court,[7] and it is perhaps Rav's greatness (and not Mar Ukba's) which accounts for the decisive role this court plays in deciding a halachic question.

Judging from a similar case involving Rav Huna and Rav Nahman, however (see below), the intent of the question to Karna is more likely as follows: Since the halacha under discussion concerns judicial practice, Karna and Shmuel should find out how a superior court handles the issue. Karna and Shmuel, the halachic authorities, should hear from the judicial experts before rendering their halachic decision.

Several passages involving second-generation Amoraim presuppose the same dual hierarchy, which explains several peculiar features of the relationship between Rav Huna and Rav Nahman. On the one hand, Huna is clearly and consistently Nahman's superior in the academic realm.[8] Their interaction frequently consists of objections and questions by Nahman, in Huna's presence,[9] usually followed (presumably) by Huna's responses. Nahman frequently refers to Huna as "Huna, my colleague," but does so only when reporting their interaction after the fact and never to Huna's face. Even while referring to Huna as his colleague, furthermore, Nahman reports Huna's teachings like a subordinate quoting his superior.[10]

---

[5]Halachot Gedolot, however, reads "he said to him," according to which Shmuel himself is responding to Karna's objection.

[6]Compare Aminoah, *Arikhat Massekhet Kiddushin*, p. 149. See also Beer, *Rashut ha-Golah*, pp. 70-77.

[7]This point was made earlier by Beer, *Rashut ha-Golah*, pp. 70-77.

[8]See Halevy, *Dorot ha-Rishonim*, vol. 2, pp. 417-21. Compare Florsheim, "Ha-Yahasim Bein Hakhmei ha-Dor ha-Sheni Shel Amoraei Bavel," pp. 288-93. See also Baba Batra 51a. It is not clear who Nahman refers to as the author of the "superior words," and it is not clear what stage in their careers this narrative depicts.

[9]Berakhot 47b, Eruvin 69a, Rosh Hashana 29a, Bezah 22b, Ketubot 89b, Gittin 22b-23a, Baba Kamma 9a, Baba Mezia 43a and 101b, Baba Batra 136a and 141b, Avodah Zarah 72a, Zevahim 116b, Menahot 13b-14a, Hullin 40a-b, Arakhin 14a, and Niddah 6b.

[10]Ketubot 7a and 68b, Kiddushin 78b, Baba Mezia 70b and 71a, Baba Batra 47a and 138b (twice), and Niddah 28a. See Hyman, *Toldot Tannaim ve-Amoraim*, pp. 934-35.

In the judicial realm, however, Nahman is clearly Huna's superior.[11] In one context, Nahman judges Huna, strikingly, in accordance with a halachic opinion quoted by Huna himself in the name of Rav.[12] Nahman's verdict requires the creative application of Huna's halachic opinion to the situation at hand and requires a decision between a variety of halachic options. He uses halacha to form judicial precedent.[13]

Another dialogue likewise shows Nahman's character as a high-level judge, superior in this respect to Huna himself, while clearly portraying Huna as Nahman's halachic superior. The interaction begins with Huna's quotation of a statement by Rav juxtaposed to Nahman's contradictory quotation of Shmuel.[14] Nahman asks Huna whether the law follows "us" (Nahman and Shmuel) or "you" (Huna and Rav). "The law follows you," answers Huna, "for you are close to the gate of the exilarch." According to Huna, Nahman's halachic tradition, which concerns judicial practice, is preferable because of his judicial expertise.[15] Here Nahman's pre-eminence as judge spills over into the halachic realm, influencing the formation of halacha, but only by virtue of Huna's halachic authority. Very likely, we should understand the interaction between Shmuel and Mar Ukba, discussed above, in light of this fact.

In a third case which likewise portrays Nahman as Huna's judicial superior and halachic inferior, Huna quotes a halachic statement by Rav, and Nahman harshly objects. Huna asks: "And the master [Nahman], what is his view?", in response to which Nahman describes his conduct when relevant cases come before him in court.[16] Huna states his opinion first and Nahman follows with his own opinion only in response to Huna's explicit request. Significantly, Nahman does not respond to Huna's query with an abstract halachic opinion, but with a report of his conduct as a judge.

---

[11]Compare Florsheim, "Ha-Yahasim Bein Hakhmei ha-Dor ha-Sheni Shel Amoraei Bavel," pp. 292-93.

[12]Baba Batra 54b-55a.

[13]Shalom Albeck, "Ha-Dayyanim bi-Yemei ha-Talmud," in *Manhigut Ruhanit be-Yisrael*, ed. Ella Belfer (Tel Aviv: Devir, 1982), p. 54, claims that in general, decisions by judges are not used to decide the halacha, but that the results of the deliberations of the study houses are used by judges in rendering their decisions. Compare the discussion below.

[14]Baba Batra 64b-65a. See *DS* hei.

[15]See Rashbam, who explains, following R. Hananel, that Nahman acquired his expertise by observing the cases brought daily before the court of the exilarch, where many judges were to be found. Huna might also be claiming that Nahman's high position in the judiciary is a result of his service within the exilarch's beauracracy.

[16]Ketubot 19a.

The duality between the judicial and academic hierarchies may have ended after the time of Nahman, for we find no record of it in sources dealing with later Amoraim. On the other hand, perhaps the sources attest to a change in the rabbinic movement's portrayal by later Amoraic storytellers. The historical change attested to by the sources, therefore, may be in rabbinic self-presentation rather than in the structure of the rabbinic movement itself.

Perhaps the change in rabbinic self-presentation was motivated by a desire to minimize the exilarch's importance in the judiciary. The early Amoraic sources preserve echoes of the exilarch's importance in the judicial hierarchy,[17] although these echoes may have been deliberately muted. Mar Ukba, the subject of the first-generation stories, was very likely the exilarch,[18] although the Talmud portrays him as a member of the rabbinic establishment, albeit with special interests and powers. Rav Nahman, the subject of the second-generation stories, was closely associated with the exilarch, but no sources state explicitly that he derived his judicial authority from the exilarch (see above). Perhaps the post-second-generation rabbis carry this tendency further, deliberately minimizing the exilarch's importance in the judicial hierarchy by depicting a judicial system controlled by rabbis, whose qualifications to judge were based on their halachic expertise rather than on their connection to the exilarch.

Perhaps the impression we have of a single hierarchy during the later period is due to a widening gap between the two hierarchies. Perhaps distinct judicial and academic hierarchies continued even after the second generation, but individuals during the later period no longer linked the two hierarchies. Individuals such as Rav Nahman, an exilarchic judge and a prominent rabbi, are not to be found after the second generation, during which time there might have been an academic hierarchy presided over by rabbis who also acted as judges, and a judicial hierarchy composed of judges who were agents of the exilarch. The exilarchic judges, according to this theory, made no pretense about also being rabbis, and/or the rabbis did not accept their claims to be rabbis or authoritative judges. Exilarchic courts continued as before, and in the opinion of many were perhaps superior to rabbinic courts.[19] In the view of the rabbis themselves, however, the judges who presided over such courts had no standing within the rabbinic

---

[17]See also Beer, *Rashut ha-Golah,* pp. 57-58; and Gafni, "Ma'asei Bet-Din ba-Talmud ha-Bavli," pp. 31-34; and *Yehudei Bavel bi-Tekufat ha-Talmud,* p. 100.

[18]See *Igeret Rav Sherira Gaon,* ed. B. Lewin, p. 77; Neusner, *A History of the Jews in Babylonia,* vol. 2, pp. 96-107; and Beer, *Rashut ha-Golah,* pp. 65-77.

[19]See Beer, *Rashut ha-Golah,* pp. 58-65, 77-79, and 91-93.

community and their opinions were therefore not preserved. Talmudic sources, in other words, which reflect rabbinic perspectives, transmit a record only of the academic hierarchy during the later period, and read the judicial hierarchy out of existence.

One might argue that the absence of later stories depicting a dual hierarchy is due to the paucity of Talmudic material dealing with the exilarch. As noted above, the judicial hierarchy is closely associated with the exilarch, and the substantial gaps in the Talmud's portrayal of this hierarchy might simply be a function of our limited source material.

This argument, however, fails to explain why the gaps in the Talmud's portrayal are not more random. Why do we find a concentration of early stories depicting a dual hierarchy rather than a smattering of stories from various time periods? Most likely, therefore, the Talmud preserves evidence of a difference between early and later sources indicative of a historical change.

5

Palestinian Materials Preserved in the Bavli

The present chapter argues that the Bavli preserves recognizable Palestinian sources, and even at times preserves features of the Palestinian formulation of these sources.[1] Portrayals of the activity and discourse of Palestinian Amoraim in the Bavli differ significantly from those of Babylonian Amoraim. The two Talmuds depict important aspects of Palestinian activity, discourse, and technical terminology in strikingly similar ways, and agree that this activity sets them apart from Babylonian Amoraim. We find not only individual traditions shared by the two Talmuds, but more importantly distinct portrayals of Palestinian sages and institutions attested to in several traditions scattered throughout both Talmuds.

Palestinian Inferiors Observe Halachic Violations in Outlying Areas and Report Back to Superior Sages

The Bavli and Yerushalmi, for example, preserve several stories in which early Palestinian Amoraim witness improper halachic practices in outlying areas and either protest or remain silent. A superior sage hears what transpired (in all but one of the cases the inferior who witnessed the improper practice voluntarily goes before a superior), and passes judgment on the action of his inferiors. The superior sometimes expresses approval, sometimes disapproval, and occasionally orders his inferiors to return and make known the correct law. Very likely, the superior's concern in several stories is not merely to see that justice is done in the case at hand, but also to supervise the proper observance and teaching of halacha in areas outside of his immediate control.[2]

---

[1]See the references to earlier scholarly literature on this topic cited in the Introduction, above.
[2]See Levine, *Ma'amad ha-Hakhamim be-Erez Yisrael*, pp. 101-2 (=*The Rabbinic Class of Roman Palestine*, pp. 152-53) with regard to some of the stories discussed below.

Examination of both Talmuds reveals no comparable stories involving early (i.e., first- through third-generation) Babylonian Amoraim. We do find a similar story involving Rava, a fourth-generation Babylonian, the significance of which will be discussed below.[3]

In the following discussion, I first examine the relevant Babylonian Talmudic sources, and then examine the evidence of the Yerushalmi. In the following discussion, the stories are paraphrased. Full translations can be found in Appendix 2, below.

On b. Yevamot 46a (and parallel), R. Hiyya bar Abba visits Gabla[4] and silently observes three halachic violations committed there. Hiyya bar Abba "goes before R. Yohanan," who tells him to "go and announce that their children are illegitimate [*mamzerim*], their wine is prohibited as idolatrous wine, and their lupines are forbidden as food cooked by idolaters, since they are not people of Torah."

Similarly, on b. Sanhedrin 26a Resh Lakish accompanies R. Hiyya bar Zarnoki and R. Shimon ben Yehozedek on their mission to intercalate the year in Assia.[5] Resh Lakish points out two public violations of the Sabbatical year, but Hiyya and Shimon decline to interfere. Resh Lakish "goes before" Yohanan and complains, "People who are suspect regarding the Sabbatical year are fit to intercalate the year?" Yohanan is distressed, either at Resh Lakish for criticizing Hiyya and Shimon, or at Hiyya and Shimon for their failure to interfere.[6] Hiyya and Shimon "go before" Yohanan and complain about Yohanan's failure to respond to Resh Lakish's insulting reference to them as "cattle herders," but Yohanan dismisses their complaint.

Similarly, on b. Avodah Zarah 58b Resh Lakish visits Bozrah[7] and observes that (1) untithed fruit is eaten, and (2) water is consumed even though it had been worshipped by idolaters. Resh Lakish rules that the fruit and water are forbidden, but when he "goes before" Yohanan, Yohanan orders him to return to Bozrah and reverse his decisions.

Along these same lines, on b. Rosh Hashana 21a R. Aibo bar Nagri and R. Hiyya bar Abba visit "a certain locality" and are silent when they discover violations of a particular halacha. Yohanan "hears and is

---

[3]See also chapter 2, above.
[4]Regarding this locality, see *Arukh ha-Shalem*, ed. Kohut, vol. 1, p. 226; Jastrow, *Dictionary*, p. 207; and Shmuel Klein, *Sefer ha-Yishuv* (Jerusalem: Mosad Bialik, 1939), vol. 1, p. 26.
[5]Regarding this locality, see *Arukh ha-Shalem*, vol. 1, p. 179 and vol. 4, p. 229; Jastrow, *Dictionary*, p. 93; and Klein, *Sefer ha-Yishuv*, pp. 122-23.
[6]See R. Hananel and Yad Rama. Compare Jastrow, *Dictionary*, p. 1104.
[7]Regarding Bozrah (=Bostra), see *Arukh ha-Shalem*, vol. 1, pp. 156-57; and Klein, *Sefer ha-Yishuv*, pp. 23-24.

angry" and says to them that they should have made known the correct law.

The Yerushalmi's description of Yohanan's interactions with inferiors agrees with the Bavli's portrayal in several important respects. According to Yer. Sheviit 38b-c (8:11), for example, Resh Lakish visits Bozrah and sees people committing what he thinks is a halachic violation.[8] "Is this not forbidden?", he asks them, and he "goes and asks R. Yohanan," who informs him that their actions are permitted.

This story is similar to the narrative on b. Avodah Zarah 58b discussed above. While the versions in the two Talmuds differ on several details, they agree that Yohanan's inferiors confront a halachic violation in outlying areas and then appear before Yohanan, who passes judgment on their action.

The same is true of a story on Yer. Kiddushin 64d (3:12), which parallels b. Yevamot 46a (see above). According to the Yerushalmi's version, R. Hiyya bar Ba visits Tyre.[9] Returning from his visit, he goes before Yohanan, who asks him "What case came to you?" Hiyya answers, "A convert who was circumcised but not ritually immersed." Yohanan asks Hiyya why he failed to confront the convert with his violation of the law, whereupon R. Yehoshua ben Levi says, "Leave him alone! He did well not to attack him."[10] Once again, the versions differ on several details, but agree on the points of concern to us here.

A story on Yer. Avodah Zarah 42a (2:8) follows the same basic pattern. R. Hiyya bar Ba goes to Tyre and finds that R. Mana bar Tanhum permitted lupines there. Hiyya bar Ba "goes to R. Yohanan," who asks what case came his way. Hiyya bar Ba tells him of Mana bar Tanhum's ruling, and Yohanan asks why Hiyya bar Ba failed to confront Mana bar Tanhum with his incorrect ruling. Hiyya explains that Mana "is a great man who knows how to sweeten the Mediterranean Sea." Yohanan asserts that Mana is no miracle worker and Hiyya should have corrected his mistake.[11]

---

[8]For interpretations of this passage, see Zeev W. Rabinovitz, *Sha'arei Torat Erez-Yisrael* (Jerusalem: Weiss Press, 1940), p. 75; *Talmud Yerushalmi Massekhet Shevi'it Im Perush Kav ve-Naki* (Jerusalem: Feldheim, 1979), p. 183; and Yehuda Feliks, *Talmud Yerushalmi Massekhet Sheviit* (Jerusalem: Rubin Mass, 1986), vol. 2, p. 211.

[9]Regarding Tyre, see *Arukh ha-Shalem*, vol. 4, pp. 44-45; and Klein, *Sefer ha-Yishuv*, pp. 126-29.

[10]I translate the conclusion according to the interpretation of Penei Moshe. The story also supports my thesis according to the interpretation of Korban Eda, who emends the text and understands the conclusion as follows: "He said to him, 'R. Yehoshua ben Levi let the matter alone.' [R. Yohanan said to him, 'You] did well not to attack him.'"

[11]See also Yer. Sheviit 36d, according to which Resh Lakish travels to Bozrah and then reports to Yohanan, describing his interaction with the people there. Here as

A story on b. Hullin 6a involving Palestinian Amoraim other than Yohanan records a similar interaction. The story relates that R. Abahu sends R. Yizhak bar Yosef on an errand to a Samaritan community,[12] where he encounters a certain elder (or old man) who informs him that "there are no guardians of Torah here." Yizhak informs Abahu, who in turn informs R. Ami and R. Asi, and "they did not depart from there until they made them full-fledged idolaters."

As in the stories involving Yohanan, this story depicts an inferior rabbi journeying to another town where he confronts improper halachic observance. He reports back to a superior sage who responds to the halachic violations.

In two very similar stories on b. Bezah 9b and b. Niddah 24a, also involving early Palestinian rabbis, R. Hiyya's sons "go out to the towns." Upon their return, Hiyya asks them whether a case came before them. They relate the case and their verdict, and Hiyya orders them to "go out and reverse their decision."

Examination of statements by several prominent Babylonian Amoraim in the Bavli[13] reveals only one clear parallel.[14] The story, on b. Baba Kamma 117a, involves Rava, a fourth-generation Babylonian Amora who comments on statements by Yohanan more frequently than on statements by any other Amora. According to Zvi Dor, the Talmud depicts Rava as particularly receptive to Palestinian learning,[15] a theory supported by the present study's finding that the early Palestinian interactions described above are unparalleled in Babylonia until the time of Rava. Rava, apparently, or students or editors depicting Rava's activity, modelled his interactions after the stories involving Palestinian

---

well, Yohanan comments on the interaction and thus has the final word. In the Shevi'it story, the inferior rabbi's handling of halachic violations is not the issue, but we observe the same pattern of an inferior rabbi serving as his superior's link to the actions of Jews in outlying areas, and the superior supervising the activities of his inferior.

[12]*Bei Kutai.* See *Arukh ha-Shalem,* ed. Kohut, vol. 1, p. 50. Compare Ben-Zion Eshel, *Yishuvei ha-Yehudim be-Bavel bi-Tekufat ha-Talmud: Onomastikon Talmudi* (Jerusalem: Magnes Press, 1979), p. 62, who incorrectly understands *bei Kutai* here as a place name.

[13]Rav, Shmuel, Rav Huna, Rav Nahman, Rav Yosef, Rava, and Rav Ashi.

[14]Several stories describe Rav's travels, halachic decisions, and observations of people's practices, some of which are contrary to halacha, but we never hear of the travels of other Amoraim who subsequently report back to Rav, or of Rav reporting back to other scholars. See Shabbat 146b, Eruvin 100b, Yoma 18b (and parallel), Taanit 24a and 28b, Megillah 22a (and 22b), and Hullin 110a. See also Ketubot 50b and Baba Kamma 12a for interactions involving Rav Nahman.

[15]See the references cited in the Introduction, above. For another commonality between Rava and the situation in Palestine, see Gafni, *Yehudei Bavel bi-Tekufat ha-Talmud,* pp. 107-8.

sages, although we should be wary of placing too much weight on evidence supplied by a single source.

The story relates that Rav Huna bar Yehuda visits the town of Bei Avyonei.[16] Returning from his visit, he goes before Rava who asks what case came his way. Huna bar Yehuda describes the case of a Jew forced to show idolaters the property of another Jew. When idolaters seize or tax the property of the second Jew, he (Huna bar Yehuda) declared the first Jew liable. Rava orders Huna bar Yehuda to reverse his decision, however, since the first Jew acted under compulsion.

As in the cases involving early Palestinians, this story describes an inferior sage visiting an outlying area and being called upon to express his legal opinion. He goes before a superior sage, who passes judgment on his decision. The story involving Rava attests either to a change in the role of Babylonian teachers, or to a change in the portrayal of that role. In either case, Palestinian models inspired the change.

It is certainly believable historically that Yohanan and others supervised the activities of Jews in outlying areas by means of student emissaries. Nevertheless, the possibility that these stories were fabricated to bolster the reputations of the sages involved cannot be dismissed. They perhaps attest to a Palestinian desire to portray certain rabbis as impressive leaders who issued wise directives to their subordinates, who heeded their instructions. The fact that the same unique Palestinian characteristic is attested to in both Talmuds is no guarantee of its historicity, since the Babylonian stories most likely derive from Palestine. The Palestinian stories, in other words, are the source for, rather than independent confirmation of, the Babylonian accounts.

Palestinian Forms in the Bavli

We also find that several features of Palestinian discourse are accurately preserved in the Bavli. The Bavli, for example, preserves Palestinian usage of the Hebrew term *sha'al* ("he asked") to introduce questions by Palestinian Amoraim.

The following facts support this claim: (1) In the Bavli, questions by Babylonian Amoraim are introduced by the Aramaic term *ba'i*[17] ("he asked"), but not by the Hebrew term *sha'al*.[18] (2) Questions by Palestinian Amoraim in the Bavli are introduced either by *sha'al* or *ba'i*.

---

[16]Regarding this locality, see Eshel, *Yishuvei ha-Yehudim be-Bavel bi-Tekufat ha-Talmud*, p. 52; and Aharon Oppenheimer, *Babylonia Judaica in the Talmudic Period* (Wiesbaden: L. Reichert, 1983), p. 469.

[17]Or *ba'a*.

[18]See above for a list of the Amoraim examined.

(3) In the Yerushalmi, questions by Palestinian *and* Babylonian Amoraim are introduced either by *sha'al* or *ba'i*. (4) The term *sha'al* introduces Amoraic questions much more frequently in the Yerushalmi than in the Bavli. To give just one illustration of this fact, in the Yerushalmi the term *sha'al* introduces questions addressed to Yohanan a total of 34 or 35 times,[19] while in the Bavli the term introduces such questions only 7 times.[20]

The term *sha'al*, therefore, occasionally introduces questions by Palestinian Amoraim in the Bavli. The Bavli thus preserves an authentic feature of Palestinian Amoraic discourse which later scribes and editors did not consistently "correct" in conformity with standard Babylonian usage.

A closely related phrase found regularly in the Yerushalmi but only infrequently in the Bavli conforms to a similar pattern. Very likely, in this case as well the Bavli accurately preserves a feature of Palestinian terminology.

I refer to the following technical formula: *Amar Rav X: Ba'i*[21] *Rav Y* ("Said Rav X: Asked Rav Y"), which indicates that Rav X cites a question authored by Rav Y. The question introduced by the term *ba'i* ("he asked") serves as the first link in a quotation chain.[22]

The term "quotation chain," incidentally, refers to phrases which introduce a statement but do not form part of the statement. The primary function of such phrases is to identify the author of a statement and its tradent.[23]

Examination of the entire Bavli reveals a total of 11 or 12 cases in which a question introduced by *ba'i* is the first link in a quotation chain *(Amar Rav X: Ba'i Rav Y)*.[24] The tradent (Rav X) is Palestinian in 9 or 10

---

[19]Yer. Berakhot 4b, 6a, and 6b, Demai 22d and 25b, Kilayim 27d, Sheviit 36c and 38b-c, Terumot 40c, 44b, and 46b, Hallah 58c and 60a, Orlah 61b and 61d, Bikkurim 65a (twice), Shabbat 9c and 13c, Eruvin 25b, Pesahim 30d, Bezah 60d, Yevamot 3d and 14b, Ketubot 25c, Nazir 55c, 56a, and 56b, Baba Mezia 9d, Baba Batra 14a and 16a, Avodah Zarah 40b, 41a-b, and 41b, and possibly Berakhot 9a.

[20]b. Berakhot 33a and 38b, Shabbat 142b, Ketubot 7a, Baba Batra 154b, and Hullin 97a and 106a.

[21]Or *Ba'a*.

[22]One distinction between the Yerushalmi's and Bavli's versions of the form should be mentioned, the exact significance of which eludes me. In the Bavli, the verbs precede the names of the rabbis, as follows: Said R. X: Asked R. Y. In the Yerushalmi, the verbs generally follow the names of the rabbis, as follows: R. X said: R. Y asked.

[23]See also chapter 7, below.

[24]Shabbat 99b (R. Mayshe quoting R. Yohanan. Henceforth, I will list the rabbis involved in a quotation chain as follows: R. Mayshe-R. Yohanan, mentioning the tradent first, and the author second); Yoma 47b (R. Yohanan-R. Yehoshua ben

cases, and is Babylonian in only two cases. Rava is involved in one case, and a student of Rava is involved in the other, and the Bavli's portrayals of Rava's special links to Palestine were noted above.[25] In 1 of the 2 cases involving Babylonians, furthermore, the author of the question (Rav Y) is Palestinian. According to the Bavli, therefore, this quotation chain is primarily a Palestinian phenomenon,[26] a conclusion supported by the Yerushalmi,[27] where this quotation form is relatively common.[28]

Oza'ah [London 5508 reads R. Yehoshua Aza'ah]) and 52a (R. Yohanan-Yosef Ish Huzal); Yevamot 11b (R. Hiyya bar Abba-R. Yohanan); Baba Mezia 57a (Rava-Hasa-R. Ami [see *DS* bet and gimel]); Zevahim 20a (R. Yohanan-Ilfa) and 85b (R. Hiyya bar Abba-R. Yohanan); Menahot 52a (R. Hiyya bar Abba-R. Yohanan); Hullin 12b-13a (R. Hiyya bar Abba-R. Yohanan) and 53b (Rav Papi-Rav Bibi bar Abaye); Bekhorot 24a-b (R. Yohanan-Ahai be-Ribi); and possibly Menahot 60a (Rav Yizhak bar Yosef-R. Yohanan).

[25]All 9 or 10 cases which exclusively involve Palestinians, incidentally, are either quotations of Yohanan by third-generation rabbis, or quotations by Yohanan of earlier rabbis.

[26]Interestingly, in *no* cases do we find the same quotation chain preserved in both Talmuds. That is, while the form itself is preserved in both the Bavli and the Yerushalmi, none of the 11 or 12 cases preserved in the Bavli has an exact parallel in the Yerushalmi.

[27]Specifically, I surveyed statements by Rav Huna, R. Huna, R. Yohanan, R. Yonah, R. Mana, Resh Lakish, Shmuel, and R. Shmuel. See the following note.

[28]According to Frankel, *Mavo ha-Yerushalmi*, pp. 9b-10a, the terms *ba'i* and *ba'a* in the Yerushalmi mean "to object," "to conclude," and "to ask," but in the Bavli the terms always mean "to ask." For the meaning "to ask" in the Yerushalmi, see Yer. Berakhot 6:1 (R. Zerikan-R. Zeira); Kilayim 4:2 (R. Yona-R. Yoshaya); Sheviit 2:3 (R. Yosa-R. Avuna), 2:3 (R. Yona-R. Avuna), and 9:5 (R. Yosa b'R. Bun-R. Ba bar Memel); Shabbat 5:1 (R. Yona-R. Hoshaya); Pesahim 8:1 (R. Yaakov bar Aha-R. Zeira); Shekalim 6:4 (R. Yosi bei R. Bun-R. Ba bar Memel) and 7:3 (R. Yosa-R. Yohanan); Megillah 1:7 (R. Avuna-R. Yirmiya); Yevamot 2:2 (R. Yaakov bar Aha-R. Shimon ben Lakish); Ketubot 2:4 (R. Haggai-R. Zeira) and 3:4 (R. Zeira-Rav Hisda); Nedarim 7:3 (R. Yirmiya-R. Zeira); Gittin 2:1 (R. Elazar-R. Abin), 2:4 (R. Elazar-R. Abin), and 7:1 (R. Elazar-R. Abin); Kiddushin 1:2 (R. Bun bar Hiyya-R. Hoshaya); and Baba Mezia 3:8 (R. Huna-R. Yirmiya). The above references are to the Vilna edition of the Yerushalmi.

See also Peah 17d (R. Imi-Resh Lakish) and 18a (R. Yonah-R. Hoshaya); Kilayim 27d (R. Nahman-R Mana [The Nahman referred to here is not the well-known Babylonian Amora, Rav Nahman bar Yaakov, but a Palestinian Amora who frequently quotes R. Mana. See Hyman, *Toldot Tannaim ve-Amoraim*, p. 939; and Albeck, *Mavo la-Talmudim*, p. 398]) and 29b (R. Yonah-R. Yoshaya); Demai 21d (R. Huna-R. Yirmiya); Sheviit 33d (R. Yonah-R. Avuna); Terumot 45b (R. Yonah-R. Hoshaya); Orlah 62c (R. Abahu-R. Yohanan); Shabbat 7b (R. Yonah-R. Hoshaya), 10d (R. Ila-R. Yohanan), 13b (R. Abahu-R. Yohanan), and 23c (Shimon bar Ba-R. Yohanan); Eruvin 19c (R. Yonah-R. Hoshaya [See also Sukkah 52a]) and 22a (R. Huna-Rav Nahman bar Yaakov); Pesahim 34b (R. Shmuel-R. Zeira); Shekalim 50d (R. Yosa-R. Yohanan); Yevamot 2c (Yizhak bar Istaya-Resh Lakish), 3c (R. Yaakov bar Aha-Resh Lakish), and 9c (R. Abahu-Resh Lakish); Ketubot 26d (R. Aha-R. Shmuel); Gittin 43d (R. Hiyya bar Ba and Havraya-R. Yohanan) and

Very likely, the generational and geographical distribution of this form indicates that the Bavli preserves an authentic feature of Palestinian Amoraic discourse. In addition, it further supports Zvi Dor's thesis that middle-generation Babylonians, especially Rava and his disciples, are depicted as especially susceptible to Palestinian influence.[29]

The two cases involving Babylonians are as follows: On Baba Mezia 57a, Rava, a fourth-generation Babylonian, quotes Hasa, a third-generation Babylonian,[30] who in turn quotes R. Ami, a second-generation Palestinian. On Hullin 53b, Rav Papi, a fifth-generation Babylonian, quotes Rav Bibi bar Abaye, also a fifth-generation Babylonian.[31]

Other factors likewise indicate that the Bavli preserves authentic Palestinian forms which survived the process of editorial and scribal standardization. Once again, the Bavli and Yerushalmi employ different terminologies, but the Bavli preserves Palestinian usage in a small number of cases.

Specifically, a standard Palestinian quotation form found frequently in the Yerushalmi, *Rav X be-shem Rav Y* ("Rav X in the name of Rav Y"), is found twice in the Bavli. Both times the quotation form introduces statements attributed to Palestinian sages. On Baba Batra 19b[32] we find "Said R. Haga in the name of R. Yosi," and on Tamid 31b we find "Said R. Hanina in the name of R. Asi and R. Asi in the name of Rav Shmuel bar Yizhak."

This phenomenon admits of two explanations, both of which presuppose that the Bavli preserves authentic Palestinian terminology. According to one explanation, Palestinian statements generally reached Babylonia equipped with Palestinian quotation forms. These forms were changed or "corrected" by editors or scribes in accordance with standard Babylonian usage, but in two cases the original Palestinian form survived.

According to a second explanation, most Palestinian statements reached Babylonia without quotation forms, which were added toward the conclusion of the Talmudic period in Palestine as part of the

---

49c (R. Yonah-R. Hoshaya); and Baba Mezia 9b (R. Huna-R. Yirmiya). The references in this paragraph are to the Venice edition of the Yerushalmi.

[29]Perhaps the distinct Palestinian and Babylonian quotation forms indicate differences between Palestinian and Babylonian transmission of statements, or institutional differences between the two rabbinic centers. Given the limited state of our understanding of Talmudic quotation forms, however, I have no clue what these institutional or transmissional differences might be. See also chapter 7, below.

[30]See Albeck, *Mavo la-Talmudim*, p. 288.

[31]Hullin 53b.

[32]See also b. Baba Batra 25b.

Yerushalmi's editing. Most Palestinian statements reached Babylonia introduced only by the names of rabbis, as follows: R. Asi, Rav Shmuel bar Yizhak: X. Once in Babylonia, the statements were edited and equipped with Babylonian quotation forms, as follows: Said R. Asi said Rav Shmuel bar Yizhak: X. Some Palestinian statements, however, reached Babylonia at a relatively late date, at a time when Palestinian quotation forms had already been added, as follows: Said R. Asi in the name of Rav Shmuel bar Yizhak, and in two cases the Palestinian form survived.

As pointed out above, according to both explanations the Bavli preserves authentic Palestinian terminology. The only question is whether the terminology derives from the Amoraic period (first explanation) or from the period of the Yerushalmi's later editing (second explanation), but this question has no effect on the major point of concern to me here.

A third explanation is possible, although unlikely. Perhaps in two cases, Babylonian scribes or editors substituted a Palestinian quotation form for what had been a standard Babylonian form. That is, later scribes or editors changed the Babylonian form: *Amar Rav X Amar Rav Y*, to the Palestinian form: *Amar Rav X be-Shem Rav Y*, yielding the two exceptional cases referred to above. According to this explanation, these cases supply no evidence for the survival of Palestinian forms in the Bavli.

Absolute certainty on this question is not possible, but the first two explanations are preferable since scribes or editors would be unlikely to change a familiar Babylonian form to a less familiar Palestinian form.[33] In all probability, scribes or editors neglected at times to Babylonianize Palestinian terminology, but it is not at all likely that they Palestinianized Babylonian forms.

Interestingly, one of the two statements under discussion[34] is attributed to R. Yosi, a Palestinian Amora whose name is rendered elsewhere in the Bavli as R. Yosi bar Zevida.[35] The name as well as the quotation form most likely survived the journey from Palestine intact.

Palestinian Versions of Names in the Bavli

Further support for the contention that the Bavli sometimes preserves the Palestinian versions of names is provided by a case in

---

[33]Compare Richard Kalmin, "Quotation Forms in the Babylonian Talmud, Authentically Amoraic, or a Later Editorial Construct?" *Hebrew Union College Annual* 59 (1988), p. 182.
[34]Baba Batra 19b (and parallel).
[35]See Albeck, *Mavo la-Talmudim*, pp. 334-35.

which a statement by a Babylonian Amora[36] apparently reached Babylonia via Palestine.[37]

Specifically, on b. Bezah 8b we find the following introductory formula: "They said in the west [Palestine] that R. Yosi bar Hama and R. Zeira, and some say Rava b. d'Rav Yosef bar Hama and R. Zeira, said the following...."[38] According to the phrase, "They said in the west," the text claims to have reached Babylonia via Palestine, and the reference to Rava as Rava b. d'Rav Yosef bar Hama supports this claim.

In Babylonia, Rava is referred to simply as Rava, with no further specification. In Palestine, however, the name Rava refers to one of several Palestinian rabbis named R. Abba rather than to the Babylonian rabbi by this name. In Palestine, the Babylonian Rava is not called Rava, since it is not at all obvious which Rava is referred to. In the case cited above, in which the statement derives from Palestine, the name is rendered as Rava the son of Rav Yosef bar Hama to insure proper identification of the statement's Babylonian author.

This conclusion is strengthened by the fact that with the exception of the statement under discussion, Rava is referred to in the Bavli as the son of Rav Yosef bar Hama only when some narrative purpose is filled by doing so. Elsewhere in the Bavli, Rava is referred to in this fashion only when other rabbis wish to humble or belittle him, or in the context of stories which depict him as a youth.[39] Only in the present context does he bear the name for no apparent reason, most likely because the statement derives from Palestine and preserves the Palestinian version of his name. Significantly, editors and scribes did not change the name in accordance with standard Babylonian usage.

Rava's statement is also found in the Yerushalmi.[40] His name is rendered there as R. Abba bar Yosef,[41] supporting the claim that in

---

[36]See, however, Friedman, "Ketiv ha-Shemot 'Rabbah' ve-'Rava' ba-Talmud ha-Bavli," pp. 158-64, who expresses reservations about the conventional identification of Rava b. d'Rav Yosef bar Hama as Rava.

[37]See also Frankel, *Mavo la-Yerushalmi*, pp. 40b-41b.

[38]Other Talmudic rabbis are referred to in more than one way, which some scholars have taken as evidence of diverse sources. See, for example, Hanokh Albeck, *Mavo la-Mishna* (1959; Reprint. Tel Aviv: Devir, 1967), pp. 67-68, 70, and 72; William Scott Green, "Palestinian Holy Men: Charismatic Leadership and Rabbinic Tradition," *Aufstieg und Niedergang der Römische Welt* 2:19/2 (1979), pp. 642-44; Bokser, "Wonder Working and the Rabbinic Tradition," pp. 46-47, 51, and 59; Halivni, *Mekorot u-Mesorot: Shabbat*, p. 94, n. 2, for a discussion of the names R. Shimon and R. Shimon ben Yohai, and Rabbi and R. Yehuda ha-Nasi.

[39]Eruvin 54a, Yevamot 122a, Nedarim 55a, and Hullin 43b and 77a.

[40]Yer. Bezah 1:3. This is apparently the only appearance by Rava the Babylonian in the Yerushalmi. See Steinzalts, "Ha-Kesharim Bein Bavel le-Erez Yisrael," p. 301; Yisrael Francus, *Talmud Yerushalmi Massekhet Bezah im Perush Ehad ha-*

Palestine it is not enough to refer to him simply as Rava, and further identification is necessary.

Unique Characteristics of Palestinian Amoraim Attested to in the Bavli but Not Clearly Confirmed by the Yerushalmi

We also find respects in which early Palestinian discourse and/or interactions are portrayed as unique in the Bavli, but due to our incomplete understanding of Amoraic discourse in the Yerushalmi we are unable to determine at present whether or not the Bavli preserves Palestinian sources. In other words, the Bavli's portrayal of Palestinian Amoraim is neither corroborated nor contradicted by the Yerushalmi's portrayal, and any conclusions we draw based on the Bavli alone must be considered tentative.[42]

Unique Features of Palestinian Amoraim According to the Bavli

A. Dispute Dialogue[43]

According to the Bavli, for example, Yohanan's tendency to engage in dispute dialogue with Palestinian contemporaries, especially Resh Lakish, distinguishes him from other Amoraim.[44] The uniqueness of the Bavli's portrayal of Yohanan perhaps further indicates that the Talmud preserves Palestinian sources. For reasons which will be explained below, however, this feature of Yohanan's discourse *might* be an invention by late Babylonian editors.

Kadmonim Rabenu Elazar Azkari Ba'al Sefer Haredim (New York: Jewish Theological Seminary, 1967), p. 40, n. 100; Urbach, *Ha-Halacha*, p. 214; and Friedman, "Ketiv ha-Shemot 'Rabbah' ve-'Rava' ba-Talmud ha-Bavli," p. 163, and the references cited in n. 19, there.

[41]I find it very unlikely that the Bavli referred to Rava here by the Palestinian version of his name in order to conform his name to the tradition of the Palestinian provenance of the statement. When speculating about what an editor might have done, of course, anything is possible, but a Babylonian editor would be much more likely to change an unfamiliar Palestinian version of a name as common as Rava's than to tamper with a familiar Babylonian version.

[42]See also Frankel, *Mavo ha-Yerushalmi*, pp. 40a-45a; and Epstein, *Mevo'ot le-Sifrut ha-Amoraim*, p. 292, who argue that the Yerushalmi preserves Amoraic statements in a more original, i.e., less edited form than in the Bavli. If these scholars are correct, then certainly conclusions about Palestinian Amoraim cannot be based solely on sources found in the Bavli.

[43]The term "dispute dialogue" was used by Eliezer Diamond in a paper entitled "The Editing of Dialogue in Rabbi's Mishnah," delivered at the 1986 Association for Jewish Studies Conference in Boston, Massachusetts.

[44]See also chapters 10 and 11, below.

The term "dispute" refers to juxtaposed, contradictory Amoraic opinions. For example, when opinions by two rabbis are juxtaposed in the following dispute form: [1] "Said Rav X: A; [2] Rav Y said: B," the opinions (A and B) of two rabbis (X and Y) are contradictory. The term "dispute dialogue" refers to dialogue between Amoraim whose contradictory opinions are juxtaposed in dispute form, as follows: [1] "Said Rav X: A; [2] Rav Y said: B; [3] Said Rav X to Rav Y; [4] Said Rav Y to Rav X." In such cases, the two rabbis (X and Y) discuss their contradictory opinions (A and B) in each other's presence.

According to the Bavli, therefore, Yohanan and his most prominent contemporaries (i.e., Resh Lakish and R. Elazar), are unlike other Amoraim in that their juxtaposed, contradictory opinions are frequently followed by dialogues between them. To be specific, examination of the Bavli reveals a total of 35 to 40 cases in which Yohanan engages in dispute dialogue with Resh Lakish or Elazar.[45] In contrast, examination of well over half of the Bavli reveals only 15 or 16 dispute dialogues involving other Amoraim.[46]

---

[45]Eruvin 11b, Pesahim 34a, 84a (and parallel), and 84b-85a, Yoma 3b-4a and 74a, Sukkah 46b, Hagigah 7a, Yevamot 10b, 35b, 62a, and 81a, Ketubot 13b, Nazir 16b-17a, Kiddushin 57a and 59a-b, Baba Kamma 68b and 71b, Baba Mezia 84a and 90b-91a, Baba Batra 136b and 154a-b, Sanhedrin 111b, Avodah Zarah 6b and 41b-42a, Menahot 9a, 9a-b, and 23a, Hullin 74b, 75a, 119b-120a, and 123b-124a, Bekhorot 4b-5a, Niddah 41b and 62b, and possibly Ketubot 34b-35a, Gittin 47b, Zevahim 113a-b, Hullin 119b-120a, and Niddah 24a.

[46]I examined tractates Shabbat, Eruvin, Megillah, Moed Katan, Ketubot, Gittin, Kiddushin, Baba Kamma, Baba Mezia, Sanhedrin, Avodah Zarah, and Bekhorot, and all of the statements by Rav, Shmuel, Rav Nahman, Rav Yosef, and Rav Ashi, and found dispute dialogue between Babylonian Amoraim only on Shabbat 7b (Abaye and Rava) and 136a-b (Ravina and Rav Sheravya [or Rav Mesharshya. See Yevamot 36b-37a]); Moed Katan 2b (Rabbah and Rav Yosef); Ketubot 7a (Rav Papi and Rav Papa); Baba Kamma 56b-57a (Rabbah and Rav Yosef), 66a-b (Rabbah and Rav Yosef), and 75a (Rav and Shmuel); Baba Mezia 36b (Abaye and Rava) and 43a (Rav Nahman and Rav Huna); Sanhedrin 12b (Rav Nahman and Rabbah. The printed edition reads Rava, but Rabbah, a third-generation Pumbeditan sage, is more likely referred to. See DS resh, and see chapter 10, below); Avodah Zarah 35b-36a (Rav and Shmuel); Hullin 74b (Mar Zutra and Rav Ashi) Bekhorot 12a (Mar Zutra and Rav Ashi); and possibly Kiddushin 44b. On Shabbat 145b (see DS yud, and the parallel on Bekhorot 36a), some versions attribute the dispute dialogue to Palestinian sages and others to Babylonian sages. See also Baba Kamma 53a and DS khaf.

In addition, on Moed Katan 20b, we find dispute dialogue between two Palestinian Amoraim, R. Mana and R. Hanina. See Hyman, *Toldot Tannaim ve-Amoraim*, p. 886.

See also Ketubot 48b and Kiddushin 46a (Rav and Rav Asi), which are not cases of dispute dialogue since the two Amoraim involved in the dispute do not converse with one another. See also Ketubot 69a (Amemar and Rav Ashi), where the dialogue comes immediately after Amemar's statement and is followed by

Avraham Weiss sees Yohanan's dispute dialogue as authentically Amoraic.[47] His arguments, unfortunately, fail to convince. Weiss views Yohanan and Resh Lakish as the originators of the typical lengthy Talmudic discussion, noting that they alone among early Amoraim left behind a significant number of argumentational sequences which extend beyond a single tier of dialogue. Typically, Yohanan and Resh Lakish state contradictory views, and Resh Lakish follows with an objection against Yohanan (or vice versa). Yohanan (or Resh Lakish) responds, and the two Amoraim continue in this fashion until the discussion concludes after several rounds of give-and-take. In the face of evidence that at least some of their dispute dialogues are later editorial additions,[48] Weiss maintains the reliability of their attribution to Yohanan and Resh Lakish. He argues that if a later editor invented these extended dialogues and attributed them to Yohanan and Resh Lakish, why did he fail to do the same for earlier Amoraim? Why did later editors attribute lengthy arguments to Yohanan and Resh Lakish, argues Weiss, but not do the same for Rav and Shmuel?[49]

Weiss cites the story of Resh Lakish's conversion to the rabbinic way of life[50] as proof for his claim that Resh Lakish and Yohanan engaged in lengthy argumentation, and that a record of this argumentation is preserved in the Talmud. Perhaps, argues Weiss, we should take literally Yohanan's claim that "when I would state an opinion, Resh Lakish would follow with twenty-four objections and I would respond with twenty-four responses, and in this manner learning was increased."[51] Closer examination of this story, however, weakens it as evidence supporting Weiss' claims. On the contrary, this story contradicts the portrait found elsewhere of Yohanan's interaction with Resh Lakish. Elsewhere in the Talmud, particularly in contexts where they engage in dispute dialogue, Yohanan and Resh Lakish frequently relate toward one another as colleagues. According to the story of Resh Lakish's conversion to the rabbinic way of life, by contrast, Resh Lakish is

---

Rav Ashi's opposing view. See also Kraemer, *Stylistic Characteristics of Amoraic Literature*, p. 182.

[47]Weiss, *Al ha-Yezira ha-Sifrutit Shel ha-Amoraim*, pp. 10-23. For examination of a closely related issue, see Moshe Weiss, "Ha-Otentiut Shel ha-Shakla ve-Tarya ba-Mahlokot Bet Shammai u-Vet Hilel," *Sidra* 4 (1988), pp. 53-66.

[48]See the references to Tosafot cited by Weiss, *Al ha-Yezira ha-Sifrutit Shel ha-Amoraim*, pp. 14-15. See also Frankel, *Mavo ha-Yerushalmi*, pp. 35a-b.

[49]Weiss, *op. cit.*

[50]Baba Mezia 84a. See also chapter 1, above.

[51]Weiss, *op. cit.*, p. 21.

Yohanan's student from beginning to end.[52] The lengthy dialogues referred to by Yohanan at the conclusion of the story are dialogues between a teacher and his student, and not dialogues between near-equals. Yohanan states his view, Resh Lakish objects as a student, and Yohanan resolves his objections. Throughout the story, Resh Lakish departs from this rigid pattern only once, opposing Yohanan in a halachic dispute and confronting his teacher as a near-equal. As a result, however, a bitter argument breaks out between them, their relationship cannot stand the strain, and both end up dying tragic deaths. This story conflicts with the picture of their relationship reflected elsewhere in the Talmud, where Resh Lakish frequently confronts Yohanan as a near-equal, and does not support Weiss' claim regarding the authenticity of Yohanan's and Resh Lakish's lengthy dispute dialogues.

It will be recalled that Weiss bases his claim on the fact that Yohanan and Resh Lakish are unique among early Amoraim in that argumentation between them is lengthy. Why would later editors add substantially to argumentation by Yohanan and Resh Lakish, argues Weiss, but not to that by earlier Amoraim? However, Weiss' argument can be answered by pointing out the unique nature of dialogues between Yohanan and Resh Lakish. The unique nature of their dialogues might explain why later editors would add substantially to their dialogues but not to those involving earlier Amoraim. As noted above, most of the lengthy dialogues between Yohanan and Resh Lakish are dispute dialogues, based on their juxtaposed opinions in dispute form. There is reason to believe, furthermore, that subsequent commentary forms more frequently around such juxtaposed opinions than it does around other types of Amoraic activity,[53] for example, individual Amoraic statements

---

[52]See Fraenkel, *Iyyunim ba-Olamo ha-Ruhani Shel Sippur ha-Agadah*, pp. 74-77. Compare Eliezer Segal, "Law as Allegory? An Unnoticed Literary Device in Talmudic Narratives," *Prooftexts* 8 (1988), pp. 249-50.

[53]We find a total of 317 to 413 statements by Abaye and Rava recorded in tractate Baba Batra. On Baba Batra 17b and 137a, we find 2 disputes between them (totalling 4 statements) introduced by the term *Itmar* ("It was said"). Of the remaining 313 to 409 statements, 16 to 18 have extensive commentary based on them (Baba Batra 5a-b, 6a, 44a, 76b, 137a, 172b, 173a, 174b [twice], and possibly 80a), or 4 to 5 percent of the total. Both of their disputes introduced by the term *Itmar*, in contrast, have extensive commentary based on them.

If Baba Batra is typical of the Talmud as a whole, the implication is that lengthy commentary forms with relative frequency around juxtaposed, contradictory opinions in dispute form. The small number of disputes on which these conclusions are based, however, indicates that further examination is necessary before final conclusions are drawn.

Incidentally, commentary consisting of three distinct statements of normal length, or four extremely brief statements, has been considered brief. Commentary consisting of more than three distinct statements of normal length,

or dialogues between students and teachers. Perhaps only the basic core of the dialogues derives from Yohanan and Resh Lakish. Perhaps the dialogues were originally quite brief but were greatly augmented by later editors. Given the unique nature of dialogues between Yohanan and Resh Lakish and the greater tendency of later commentary to form around juxtaposed opinions, it is not surprising that later editors would add substantially to their dialogues but not to those of earlier Amoraim.

In my view, the greater length of the argumentation between Yohanan and Resh Lakish is not as significant as the fact that they (and, to a lesser extent, R. Elazar) regularly engage in dispute dialogue. In offering an argument for the authenticity of the basic core of their dispute dialogues, I would formulate Weiss' question as follows: Why would later editors regularly invent dispute dialogue between Yohanan and Resh Lakish, but not do the same for other famous pairs of Amoraim? Why would they attribute only a handful of such dialogues, for example, to Abaye and Rava, whose disputes fill the Talmud?

However, even this argument can be answered. David Goodblatt argues that rabbinic instruction in Babylonia during the Amoraic period did not take place in the context of academies.[54] Scholars agree, however, that some rabbinic instruction in Amoraic Palestine may have taken place in the context of academies.[55] If Goodblatt is correct about the situation in Babylonia, then Palestinian Amoraim, unlike their Babylonian counterparts, may have possessed the institutional framework for regular confrontation between the most important leaders of the rabbinic community. According to Goodblatt's theory, we can understand why later editors would add dialogue to Palestinian disputes but not to disputes involving Babylonians. If the later editors knew of the unique institutional framework which existed in Palestine, then it is

---

or more than four extremely brief statements has been considered extensive. This cut-off point is admittedly somewhat arbitrary. I therefore attempted to set the boundary at a point at which all would agree that everything identified as brief was in fact brief. In doing so, it is quite likely that the boundary has been set too low, and that a portion of what we have characterized as extensive commentary should in actuality be described as brief.

[54]See the references cited in the Introduction, above.

[55]Goodblatt, *Rabbinic Instruction in Sasanian Babylonia*, pp. 63-107; Bokser, *Post Mishnaic Judaism in Transition*, p. 466; Martin Goodman, *State and Society in Roman Galilee, A.D. 132-212* (Totowa, New Jersey: Rowman and Allenheld, 1983), pp. 75-81; and Levine, *Ma'amad ha-Hakhamim be-Erez Yisrael*, pp. 10-13 (=*The Rabbinic Class of Roman Palestine*, pp. 25-29). Goodman cites evidences that rabbinic education in late Tannaitic times took place in the context of disciple circles, and that the institution of the academy developed during the Amoraic period. See also Aharon Oppenheimer, "Batei Midrash be-Erez Yisrael be-Reshit Tekufat ha-Amoraim," *Katedra* 8 (1978), pp. 80-89.

understandable why they would attribute dispute dialogue to Yohanan and Resh Lakish but not to Babylonian Amoraim. For only in Palestine might rabbinic instruction have taken place in the context of academies which facilitated regular face-to-face contact between the leaders of the rabbinic movement.[56]

I am not claiming, it should be emphasized, that the unparalleled frequency with which Yohanan and Resh Lakish engage in dispute dialogue is explicable only if we deny the early Amoraic provenance of these dialogues and attribute them to later editors. I am simply claiming that the actions of such later editors make sense. We can understand why they would invent dialogues involving Palestinian, but not Babylonian, Amoraim. In the face of powerful arguments for and against the early Amoraic provenance of dispute dialogues between Yohanan and Resh Lakish, we must view the question of their authorship as unresolved.[57]

I mentioned above that examination of the Yerushalmi likewise fails to decide the question. To be specific, Yohanan and his most prominent contemporaries engage in 18 dispute dialogues,[58] whereas other post-Tannaitic[59] rabbis engage in 19 such dialogues.[60] Yohanan's prominence

---

[56]See also Hayman, *Hitpathut ve-Shinuyim be-Torat R. Yohanan ben Napha*, pp. 32-64, 87-95 (English section), and 119-456 (Hebrew section).

[57]Compare Kraemer, *Stylistic Characteristics of Amoraic Literature*, pp. 188-92; and Halivni, *Midrash, Mishnah, and Gemara*, p. 70, and p. 139, nn. 12 and 13.

[58]Yer. Terumot 44a, Maaserot 49d and 52a, Hallah 57d and 59b-c, Pesahim 29a and 35a, Taanit 68d, Yevamot 4a, Nedarim 36c, Nazir 52c-d, Baba Kamma 3c, Sanhedrin 23a and 29d, Shevuot 37a and 37b, Avodah Zarah 42d (See Moshe Kosowsky, *Ozar Lashon Talmud Yerushalmi* [Jerusalem: The Israel Academy of Sciences and Humanities and the Jewish Theological Seminary, 1985], p. 382), and Niddah 50d. See also Yer. Peah 18a-b, Yevamot 6b (R. Yohanan and R. Hanina), and Gittin 59c.

[59]The term post-Tannaitic (as opposed to Amoraic) includes transitional rabbis, sages who lived during the one or two generations between the end of the Tannaitic period (early third century C.E.) and the beginning of the Amoraic period. Such rabbis occasionally behave like Amoraim, for example when their opposing opinions, juxtaposed in dispute form, are accompanied by dispute dialogue (see, for example, Shabbat 5a [R. Hiyya and Bar Kappara]), and no term denoting a Tannaitic teaching introduces their statements. Such rabbis are included in the above statistics as post-Tannaitic rabbis. Cases in which terminology indicative of Tannaitic sources introduces their statements, however, are not included.

[60]Yer. Berakhot 10d (Yizhak bar Abba bar Mehasia and Rav Hananel), Sheviit 39d (R. Yuda and R. Yosi), Shabbat 3d (Shmuel and Rav) and 5a (R. Hiyya and Bar Kappara), Bezah 60b (R. Zeira and R. Abba bar Yosef), Megillah 70b (Rav Huna and Rav Yehuda) and 72b (R. Elazar and R. Yosi ben Hanina), Yevamot 6a (Rav and Shmuel) and 8a (Rav and Shmuel), Ketubot 28b (R. Yona and R. Yosi), Sotah

in the statistics is significant, but given the frequency with which he and his contemporaries are mentioned in the Yerushalmi, his prominence may be due largely to frequency of appearance.[61]

B. Yohanan Comments on Statements by Rabbis Well below Him in Status

The Bavli portrays Yohanan's interaction with his contemporaries as unique in another respect as well. Once again, examination of the Yerushalmi will neither confirm nor contradict the Bavli's portrayal, making it difficult to determine whether or not the Bavli preserves a Palestinian source.

To be specific, on several occasions, rabbis who in some contexts are depicted as well below Yohanan in status open by stating opinions in declarative, non-dialogic form ("Said Resh Lakish: X"), and Yohanan follows with a response. That is, after the inferior (at least as he is portrayed in other contexts) has spoken, Yohanan comments on the statement. To be specific, we find 17 to 19 such statements by Resh Lakish or R. Elazar followed by comments by Yohanan ("Said R.

16c (R. Yosi and R. Haggai), Gittin 44a (R. Ami and R. Zeira) and 46b (R. Ila and R. Abba bar Memel), Kiddushin 60a (R. Yirmiya and R. Zeira) and 66a (R. Hananya and R. Mana), Sanhedrin 21d (R. Haggai and R. Yosi [accepting the emendation by Masoret ha-Shas. Most likely, the name Yosi was mistakenly omitted by scribes]) and 30c (R. Yizhak and R. Hoshaya), Horayot 47c (Rav Hisda and Rav Hamnuna), and Niddah 49b (R. Hiyya and Rabbi). See also Eruvin 26c (two unnamed Amoraim) and Sukkah 52b (two unnamed Amoraim).

[61]See, for example, Levine, *Ma'amad ha-Hakhamim be-Erez Yisrael,* pp. 6-7 (=*The Rabbinic Class of Roman Palestine,* pp. 20-21). By way of preliminary observation, however, it should be noted that in the Yerushalmi tractate Yoma, Yohanan, Resh Lakish, and Elazar appear a total of 147 times, as opposed to 550 appearances by all other post-Tannaitic rabbis combined. In other words, other post-Tannaitic rabbis appear between 3.5 and 4 times more frequently than do Yohanan, Resh Lakish, and Elazar, but engage in roughly the same number of dispute dialogues. Yohanan's prominence in the statistics regarding dispute dialogue gathered from the Babylonian Talmud, however, is much more pronounced.

The following is a breakdown, by chapters, of the appearances by Yohanan, Resh Lakish, and Elazar in tractate Yoma: Chapter 1: 31 appearances; Chapter 2: 31; Chapter 3: 12; Chapter 4: 15; Chapter 5: 19; Chapter 6: 17; Chapter 7: 10; Chapter 8: 12. For other post-Tannaitic rabbis, the breakdown is as follows: Chapter 1: 88; Chapter 2: 70; Chapter 3: 66; Chapter 4: 58; Chapter 5: 95; Chapter 6: 54; Chapter 7: 28; Chapter 8: 91. (Statements quoted several times, or quoted once and then alluded to several times by later interpreters, are counted each time they appear or are alluded to. A statement quoted five times, for example, is counted as five appearance. Counting appearances in this fashion rather than as only one appearance has no significant impact on my conclusions.)

Yohanan: Y," or "R. Yohanan said to him: Y"). Typically, Yohanan objects against or interprets statements by Resh Lakish or Elazar.[62]

Comparison between Abaye's relationship with Rav Yosef and Yohanan's relationship with Resh Lakish will clarify these points. Abaye is routinely depicted as Yosef's inferior, and their interaction typically consists of an opening statement by Yosef followed by a comment by Abaye. Abaye will also frequently open with a question or objection, and Yosef will follow with a response. Only once in the entire Bavli do we find Yosef commenting on a declarative, non-dialogic statement by Abaye.[63] This one case is suspect as a scribal error since it runs counter to the hundreds of other dialogues between them scattered throughout the Talmud. In contrast, the pattern with respect to Yohanan and Resh Lakish is persistent enough to preclude its dismissal as the product of scribal error. Basing ourselves for a moment on the evidence of the Bavli alone, it is a unique feature of early Palestinian Amoraic discourse, without parallel among Babylonian Amoraim.

In the following discussion, I review in detail the 17 to 19 cases in which statements by Resh Lakish and Elazar are followed by comments by Yohanan. I begin with a survey of Babylonian sources and then examine the Yerushalmi.

(1) On Ketubot 111b, Elazar states that "*amei ha-arez* (Jews ignorant of rabbinic traditions and practices) will not live [eternally]," and he cites a biblical text in support of his view. Yohanan says, "It is not pleasing to their master [God] that you say this about them," and he follows with an alternative explanation of the verse. Elazar then cites another verse to support his original claim, and Yohanan is vexed over his inability to respond to Elazar's argument. Elazar salves Yohanan's wounded feelings by saying, "Rabbi, I have found a remedy for them [the *amei ha-arez*] from the Torah...."

Elazar speaks first and Yohanan reacts to his statement, despite the fact that Yohanan is depicted as the superior sage.

(2) On Makkot 5b, Resh Lakish states his opinion first and Yohanan responds, although Yohanan is again depicted as the superior sage. Resh Lakish and R. Elazar "sit before" Yohanan, their seating arrangement described in terms routinely used to describe inferiors in the presence of

---

[62]For more on the relationship between Yohanan and his contemporaries, see Frankel, *Mavo ha-Yerushalmi*, pp. 111a-112a; Halevy, *Dorot ha-Rishonim*, vol. 2, pp. 317-21 and 327-32; Hyman, *Toldot Tannaim ve-Amoraim*, pp. 660-62, 670-71, 1194-96, and 1199; Wolf Jawetz, *Sefer Toldot Yisrael* (1933-1936; Reprint. Tel Aviv, 1963), vol. 7, pp. 78-80, 84-88, and 94-95; Albeck, *Mavo la-Talmudim*, pp. 225-27; and Kimelman, *Rabbi Yohanan of Tiberias*, pp. 20-23 and 127-37.

[63]Zevahim 81a.

their superiors.[64] A case comes "before him," namely Yohanan, and Resh Lakish states his opinion. Yohanan objects, whereupon Resh Lakish angrily glares at Elazar, denouncing him for making the same argument earlier and failing to report it in Yohanan's name.[65]

(3) In 9 or 10 contexts, Yohanan objects against declarative, non-dialogic statements by Resh Lakish or Elazar. On Yevamot 106a and 121b, Ketubot 74a, and Zevahim 113a Resh Lakish interprets Tannaitic statements; on Sukkah 44a, Baba Kamma 68a-b, and Niddah 27b-28a and 41b Resh Lakish or Elazar state halachic opinions; and on Hullin 115a-b Resh Lakish derives a law from scripture, and each time Yohanan objects.

(4) On Berakhot 5a, Resh Lakish states that "whoever engages in Torah [study], afflictions stay away from him," and he supports himself with a biblical proof-text. Yohanan asserts that "even schoolchildren know that" and interprets the verse differently. Similarly, on Gittin 29a and Hullin 81b Resh Lakish interprets a mishna, Yohanan rejects the interpretation ("even schoolchildren know that"), and follows with an alternative view.

Along these same lines, in three contexts[66] Resh Lakish states his opinion and Yohanan asserts that "God disapproves of what you say...."

(5) On Baba Batra 135b, Elazar might open by stating a halachic opinion and Yohanan might follow by telling unnamed listeners to "be careful" of Elazar's opinion.[67]

These 5 categories yield a total of 17 to 19 cases.[68]

---

[64]Goodblatt, *Rabbinic Instruction in Sasanian Babylonia*, pp. 199-238; Gafni, *Yehudei Bavel bi-Tekufat ha-Talmud*, pp. 274-79; and Kalmin, "Collegial Interaction in the Babylonian Talmud," pp. 390-96 and 400-6.

[65]See also Ketubot 25b.

[66]Sanhedrin 111a (three times. See *DS* vav).

[67]Rav Shizbi interprets Yohanan's comment to mean "take this comment very seriously," that is, as an expression of support for Elazar's opinion. Yohanan might, however, be indicating his reservations about the opinion and perhaps means to say "be careful about accepting this opinion." Shizbi's decision to accept the version which has Yohanan commenting on Elazar's statement, therefore, may be incorrect.

[68]It should be noted that I am not referring to cases where Yohanan's opinions are juxtaposed to contradictory opinions by inferiors in dispute form, such that Yohanan's "reference" to the opinion of the inferior is no more than the word *af* or *afilu*, or other similar expressions. For example, on Baba Mezia 27b Resh Lakish says, "The mishna is the view of R. Meir," and R. Yohanan follows by stating that the mishna makes sense "*even* (*af*) if you say [it represents the view] of the sages." The phrasing of Yohanan's opinion in this fashion creates the impression that Yohanan knows Resh Lakish's view and disagrees with it. Simply by omitting the phrase "even if you say," however, we arrive at an independent statement with no necessary connection with Resh Lakish's

As noted above, examination of the Bavli[69] reveals that Babylonian Amoraim do not engage in the same interactions.[70] The closest parallels are cases in which Rav Ashi's subordinates author dialogic interpretations in Ashi's presence (see chapter 6, below), and cases in which one Amora "sits before" another and states an opinion, to which the second Amora reacts. On Shabbat 54b, for example, Rav Papa bar Shmuel "sits before Rav Nahman" and offers an interpretation, which Nahman rejects. The seating arrangement indicates that Papa is the inferior and Nahman is the superior,[71] and yet Papa states his opinion first and Nahman responds. Similarly, on Hullin 54a Rav Yizhak bar Shmuel bar Marta "sits before Rav Nahman" and states an opinion which Nahman rejects.

Even in these cases, however, the unique nature of Yohanan's interactions is clear. Nahman's and Ashi's presence is indicated at the outset, while in all but 1 of the 17 to 19 cases involving Yohanan the text initially supplies no indication of Yohanan's presence. True, this is

---

statement. I have not included such statements in this survey, since they are suspect as the result of editorial tampering with Yohanan's statement.

Some of the cases included in this survey might be the work of an editor who performed radical surgery on his sources. That is, perhaps he took independent statements and altered them by more than the simple addition of a linking phrase, creating the impression that Yohanan responds to statements by Elazar and Resh Lakish. It is difficult, however, to maintain that the phenomenon under discussion is entirely editorial. To maintain such a view, we would have to explain why later editors tampered with Yohanan's statements in this fashion but did not do likewise concerning other Amoraim. We would have to explain why they singled out Yohanan for special treatment.

[69]This claim is based on examination of statements in the Bavli attributed to R. Ami, R. Asi, Rav Ashi, R. Zeira, R. Hiyya, R. Yosi bar Hanina, Rav Yosef, R. Yannai, R. Yirmiya, Rav Nahman, Rav, and Shmuel, and on examination of the Babylonian tractates Shabbat, Ketubot, and Baba Batra. See the discussion below, and see Shabbat 54b (twice--Rav Aha bar Ulla and Rav Hisda, and Rav Papa bar Shmuel and Rav Nahman [DS pei]) and 82a (Rafram bar Papa and Rav Hisda), Eruvin 29b (Rav Aha b. d'Rav Yosef and Rav Yosef) and 63a (Ravina and Rav Ashi), Ketubot 75a (Rav Aha b. d'Rava and Rav Ashi), Kiddushin 53b (Rabin Saba and Rav), Baba Batra 133a (Rav Ada bar Ahava and Rava), 133b (Rav Ilish and Rava), and 141a (Rav Ashi and Rav Kahana), and Avodah Zarah 33a (Rav Aha b. d'Rava and Rav Ashi).

[70]In addition to the two cases discussed below, see also Bezah 26b, where Nahman objects against a statement by Rabbah bar Rav Huna. The term darash, however, which introduces Rabbah bar Rav Huna's statement, distinguishes this case from the cases involving Yohanan. As I noted in The Redaction of the Babylonian Talmud, pp. 129-30, the term darash introduces quotations of earlier material, even when no earlier author is mentioned by name, more frequently than is the case with the term amar.

[71]See DS pei.

"merely" a formal distinction, but it is crucial for evaluating the provenance of these exchanges, which is my main concern here.[72] This "merely" formal distinction, furthermore, very likely betrays an institutional and/or relational difference between Palestinian and Babylonian Amoraim, although I have no clear idea what this difference might be.

Central to my claim that Yohanan is unique is the assertion that some sources portray him as decisively superior to Elazar and Resh Lakish. In the discussion which follows I document this claim by analyzing sources which describe Yohanan's relationship with Resh Lakish.[73] Yohanan's superiority to Elazar is even more pronounced, and will not be surveyed in detail here.[74]

(1) According to stories on Ketubot 25b and Makkot 5b, Resh Lakish and Elazar "sit before R. Yohanan." As noted above, this seating arrangement describes interaction between a superior and an inferior. When a case comes before Yohanan, Resh Lakish states his opinion only to find that Yohanan disagrees. Resh Lakish glares angrily at Elazar, furious that Elazar stated the same opinion previously and failed to attribute it to Yohanan. The intensity of Resh Lakish's anger is due in part to his having been publicly contradicted by his superior, Yohanan.

---

[72]See also Eruvin 10a (and *DS* tet), Kiddushin 60a (Hyman, *Toldot Tannaim ve-Amoraim*, p. 912, thinks the names are reversed and that R. Asi explained the reasoning of R. Yohanan to R. Mesharshya b. d'R. Ami), and Baba Batra 57a. On Yoma 71b, Ravina provides the scriptural derivation of a law stated in a mishna, and Ashi follows with an objection, presumably in his presence (as indicated by the word *lei*). It should be noted, however, that many versions in this and in the parallel contexts have the names reversed, and I see no way to determine the correct reading. See Halivni, *Mekorot u-Mesorot: Yoma-Hagigah*, p. 122, n. 4. In addition, there may have been a fifth-generation Ravina distinct from the Ravina who regularly acts as Ashi's subordinate, and Ashi might converse with this earlier Ravina here. See Shalom Albeck, "Sof ha-Hora'ah ve-Aharonei ha-Amoraim," *Sinai*, Jubilee Volume (Jerusalem: Mosad ha-Rav Kook, 1958), pp. 57-60.

[73]See also Halevy, *Dorot ha-Rishonim*, vol. 2, pp. 317-21; Hyman, *Toldot Tannaim ve-Amoraim*, pp. 660 and 1194-96; and Kimelman, *Rabbi Yohanan of Tiberias*, pp. 20-23 and 127-28.

[74]The following Babylonian Talmudic sources depict Elazar as well below Yohanan in status: Yoma 53a, Yevamot 96b, Ketubot 25b, Baba Mezia 7b and 94a, Baba Batra 154b, Makkot 5b and 16a, Hullin 19b, and Keritut 25b and 27a. See also Frankel, *Mavo ha-Yerushalmi*, pp. 111a-112a; Halevy, *Dorot ha-Rishonim*, vol. 2, pp. 327-32; Hyman, *Toldot Tannaim ve-Amoraim*, pp. 194-95 and 661-62; and Albeck, *Mavo la-Talmudim*, pp. 225-26.

(2) On Yoma 9b, Baba Batra 7b, and Avodah Zarah 58b Resh Lakish "goes before R. Yohanan." Here as well Resh Lakish is described as an inferior in the presence of his superior.

Similarly, a story on Taanit 8a relates that Resh Lakish used to arrange his learning 40 times and then "enter before R. Yohanan." The story explicitly compares the 40 times Resh Lakish arranged his learning to the 40 days that Moshe waited on Mount Sinai to receive the Torah from God. *Mutatis mutandis*, Resh Lakish's relationship with Yohanan, his teacher, corresponds with Moshe's relationship with God.

(3) According to Baba Mezia 84a, Yohanan "taught [Resh Lakish] Bible and Tannaitic traditions and made him a great man." Clearly this story is not to be taken as objective history. It contains several unbelievable elements which serve the story's message rather than accurately transmit biographical facts. The story creates the impression, for example, that Yohanan was Resh Lakish's only teacher, and yet numerous other sources make it clear that he had other teachers as well.[75] The programmatic nature of the story, however, does not imply that all of its details are false. The story's portrayal of Yohanan as an important teacher of Resh Lakish is congruent with several other Talmudic sources which depict the same relationship between them.

Interestingly, the story depicts Yohanan's and Resh Lakish's relationship as unable to survive the strain of Resh Lakish's attempt to achieve near-equality with Yohanan.[76] Yohanan finds it intolerable that Resh Lakish contradicts him to his face, and the resulting clash between them leads to their tragic deaths.

Perhaps the story is in part a Babylonian reaction to the unprecedented nature of Resh Lakish's relationship with Yohanan. Some sources depict substantial hierarchical differences between them, and other sources depict them disputing with one another as near-equals. The Babylonians, unfamiliar with such a relationship, depict it as the cause of their downfall.

(4) On Meilah 7b, Yohanan objects against Resh Lakish's quotation of R. Oshaya. Yohanan boasts of having "cut off the legs of the child," i.e., of having levelled an irrefutable argument against the youngster (or the inferior), Resh Lakish.

(5) A story on Berakhot 31a relates that Resh Lakish refrained from laughter after hearing from "his master," Yohanan, that it was forbidden

---

[75]See Halevy, *Dorot ha-Rishonim*, vol. 2, pp. 317-20; Hyman, *Toldot Tannaim ve-Amoraim*, pp. 1194-96; and Kimelman, *R. Yohanan of Tiberias*, pp. 8-9, 20-23, and 128-29.

[76]See chapter 1, above.

to do so. On Hullin 139a, the anonymous editors also refer to Yohanan as Resh Lakish's master.[77]

To recapitulate the somewhat lengthy arguments advanced above, we attempted to show another respect in which Yohanan's interactions are unique. We found that rabbis who in some contexts are depicted as well below him in status open by stating opinions in declarative, non-dialogic form, and Yohanan follows with a response. Such interactions are formally distinct from interactions between Babylonian Amoraim.

It might be objected that perhaps we have not uncovered a unique feature of Yohanan's discourse, but rather found evidence that Yohanan's relationships with Resh Lakish and Elazar changed dramatically over the course of their careers. Perhaps Resh Lakish and Elazar were originally well below Yohanan in status, but eventually achieved near-equality with him.

This explanation is possible, but it does not affect my claim regarding the Bavli's unique portrayals of early Palestinian Amoraic interactions. Even according to this explanation, Yohanan's relationships with Resh Lakish and Elazar are unlike relationships between Babylonian Amoraim, undergoing dramatic changes not discernible in other relationships, for example, that between Abaye and Yosef (see above).

As noted above, the Yerushalmi also supplies evidence of this unique feature of Yohanan's discourse, although to a lesser extent than the Bavli.[78] Further study is necessary to determine whether the Yerushalmi confirms or contradicts the Bavli's portrayal. Any conclusions we draw based on the Bavli alone must be considered tentative.

Palestinian Rabbis and Institutions Versus Those in Babylonia

In addition to supporting my claims regarding diverse sources in the Bavli, the findings above perhaps contribute toward an emerging portrayal of Palestinian rabbinic institutions as more complex and sophisticated than comparable Babylonian institutions. As noted above, according to the Bavli Palestinian Amoraim engage in dispute dialogue far more frequently than do Babylonian rabbis, perhaps indicating that Palestinians interact in the context of an academy and thus possess the

---

[77]Resh Lakish himself refers to Yohanan as his master in several contexts, although he may do so simply out of respect for an esteemed colleague. See Frankel, *Mavo la-Yerushalmi*, p. 54a; Hyman, *Toldot Tannaim ve-Amoraim*, p. 221; and Albeck, *Mavo la-Talmudim*, p. 225, n. 146, and the references cited there.

[78]See Appendix 1, below.

institutional framework for direct contact between the most important rabbinic leaders. In addition, we found portrayals of early Palestinian Amoraim supervising the activities of Jews in outlying communities by means of student emissaries. This evidence of institutional complexity was attested to earlier and more frequently in Palestinian than in Babylonian sources.

Earlier scholars reached similar conclusions regarding the greater complexity of Palestinian institutions. As noted above, scholars who deny the existence of academies in Babylonia allow for their existence in Palestine. In addition, Yeshayahu Gafni argues that Palestinian traditions often mention or describe officials and institutions without parallel in Babylonian sources. He argues that several of the Bavli's discussions of Palestinian officials and institutions are entirely theoretical, or consist exclusively of Palestinian materials,[79] suggesting that governmental bureaucracy was more complicated in Palestine than in Babylonia. Further research is necessary to determine the extent to which differences between the two centers follow a consistent pattern, and whether or not Babylonia in certain respects surpasses Palestine in institutional complexity.

The findings of the present chapter also bear on the question, touched upon briefly in chapter 3, of the extent to which Amoraim had power over non-rabbis in the two rabbinic centers. Stories of student emissaries in outlying areas depict early Palestinian rabbis asserting their right to decide the legality of actions by non-rabbis.[80] These stories depict early Palestinian rabbis announcing their decisions publicly, imposing or attempting to impose their will over groups or individuals who did not voluntarily appear before them, or urging other rabbis to do so. If these stories are true, they further indicate that at least in some respects, Palestinian rabbis had more power, or at least asserted the right to have more power, over non-rabbis than did their Babylonian counterparts. Earlier studies, however, indicate that this is not a consistent difference between Palestinian and Babylonian rabbis.[81]

---

[79]Gafni, *Yehudei Bavel bi-Tekufat ha-Talmud*, pp. 104-5.
[80]Yer. Sheviit 38b-c, Yer. Kiddushin 64d, b. Yevamot 46a (b. Avodah Zarah 59a), b. Sanhedrin 26a, b. Avodah Zarah 58b-59a, and b. Hullin 6a.
[81]For example, Gafni's study, alluded to above, argues that many leadership roles which the Yerushalmi depicts as being held by non-rabbis are depicted by the Bavli as the domain of rabbis.

6

Unique Formal Characteristics of Later Amoraic Discourse

Other formal aspects of Amoraic discourse provide evidence of generational contrast indicative of the diversity of Talmudic source material. The present chapter argues that statements by later Amoraim are formally distinguishable from statements by earlier Amoraim in the following ways: (1) only later Amoraim (i.e., Rav Ashi and, to a lesser extent, his contemporary, Ravina) frequently listen silently while subordinates discuss a particular topic; (2) statements usually phrased as monologues are frequently rendered in dialogue form when attributed to subordinate contemporaries of Rav Ashi; and (3) dialogue chains involving Rava and Rav Ashi and a succession of different subordinates are relatively common, but are rare involving earlier Amoraim.[1]

---

[1]Throughout this chapter, I refer to "superior" Amoraim and to "inferior" or "subordinate" sages. If the interaction between two rabbis throughout the Talmud regularly consists of questions or objections by the one and responses by the other, if one Amora seeks and the other provides instruction, the former is most likely the inferior and the latter the superior. See also Kalmin, *The Redaction of the Babylonian Talmud*, pp. 5-6 and 38-65; and chapter 11, below.

In addition, when most interactions between two sages indicate the character of one as the inferior, it is likely (though not certain) that they possess the same relative status even in contexts where their precise hierarchical relationship is not obvious. Rav Aha b. d'Rava, for example, addresses objections and questions to Rav Ashi well over fifty times, and Rav Ashi usually responds (Kalmin, *Redaction of the Babylonian Talmud*, pp. 106 and 111), according to which Rav Ashi is most likely the superior and Rav Aha b. d'Rava his inferior. In a handful of cases, their interaction does not clearly reveal their relative status (see below), but Rav Aha b. d'Rava is probably the inferior in the latter contexts as well.

In rare instances, one or two interactions contradict the usual Talmudic portrayal of a rabbinic relationship, and a sage who is depicted as another's inferior throughout the Talmud is depicted as his superior. In such instances, the exceptional cases are attributable either to (1) textual corruption, (2) differences of opinion regarding the nature of the relationship, or (3) storytellers willing to bend the truth in order to make a particular point (see chapter 1, above). It should also be noted that in some sketchily documented cases, a clear pattern does not emerge regarding the relative status of two sages.

It is important to note that this chapter focuses primarily on comparison between Rav Ashi's statements and statements by other Amoraim. Generally, therefore, the term "earlier" refers to first- through fifth-generation Amoraim, and the term "later" to sixth- and seventh-generation Amoraim. In one respect, however, dialogues between Rava, a fourth-generation Amora, and his fifth-generation subordinates conform to the pattern followed by dialogues between Rav Ashi and his subordinates. The term "later," therefore, sometimes refers to fourth- and fifth-generation Amoraim as well. This usage reflects the fact that the fourth, fifth, and sixth generations are all "later" compared to the first, second, and third. My intent is to show that the earlier and later Amoraic periods are distinguishable, and it is unnecessary to draw the dividing line between these two periods at precisely the same point each time.

A. Rav Ashi and Ravina Sit Silently While Their Subordinates Speak

The traditional theory of the Talmud's redaction, which assigns to Rav Ashi the dominant role in the editing of the Talmud, held sway for almost a millennium.[2] Only in the twentieth century did scholars seriously challenge and ultimately reject this theory, pointing out that none of the salient features of Rav Ashi's discourse uniquely or necessarily identify him as an editor.[3] The correctness of this conclusion, however, should not cause us to minimize several unique features of Rav Ashi's discourse, one of which was pointed out by Yizhak Halevy, a proponent of the traditional theory of the Talmud's redaction.[4] The significance of this unique feature, unfortunately, was obscured by Halevy's attempt to interpret it in light of his theories about Rav Ashi's editorial role. Perhaps if we reexamine Rav Ashi's statements without a preconceived theoretical framework we will be better able to understand their significance.

What are these unique features? We find, first, that Rav Ashi frequently listens silently to discussions by rabbis who elsewhere

---

[2]See Goodblatt, "The Babylonian Talmud," p. 311.
[3]Julius Kaplan, *The Redaction of the Babylonian Talmud* (New York: Bloch, 1933), pp. 69-70, 79-80, 94, 104-5, and 127; and Avraham Weiss, *Hithavut ha-Talmud bi-Shlemuto* (New York: The Alexander Kohut Foundation, 1943), pp. 245ff.
[4]Halevy, *Dorot ha-Rishonim*, vol. 2, pp. 562-66, observes that Rav Ashi frequently listens silently without contributing anything to a discussion. According to Halevy, this proves that Rav Ashi presided over the editing of the Talmud. Halevy's understanding is possible, but by no means necessarily implied by the evidence, and is not supported by other features of Rav Ashi's activity and discourse. See also the discussion below.

regularly act as his subordinates.[5] As a rule, in contrast, earlier Amoraim are mentioned only when they actively participate in a discussion. To be specific, having examined statements by Rav Ashi, I found a total of 58 to 61 cases in which he listens to statements by subordinates and contributes nothing to the discussion.[6] In contrast, examination of statements by several prominent earlier Amoraim: Rav Huna, Rav Nahman, Rabbah, Rav Yosef, and Rava reveals only 10 or 11 such cases.[7]

---

[5]Compare Urbach, *Ha-Halacha*, pp. 220-21.
[6]In this note, I list the name of the Amora with whom Rav Ashi appears, followed by the relevant Talmudic citations in parentheses: Rav Abba (Yoma 48a, Ketubot 111a [*DS* Herschler, notes on line 14, and nn. 30-31; and Kalmin, *The Redaction of the Babylonian Talmud*, pp. 27, 103, 106, 120, and 172, n. 12], Baba Kamma 27b, and Baba Batra 147a and 148a); Rav Aha Saba (Kiddushin 21a and Zevahim 91a); Rav Aha b. d'Rav Avya (Nedarim 10b [*DS* Herschler, notes on line 14, and n. 36], Baba Mezia 96a, and Hullin 80a [An alternate version reads Rav Aha b. d'Rava. According to both versions, Rav Ashi listens while a subordinate speaks]); Rav Aha b. d'Rava (Yoma 25b and 32b, Kiddushin 21a, Baba Mezia 80a, Makkot 5b [and parallel], Menahot 5b, Hullin 137a, and possibly Gittin 32b); Rav Ati (Hullin 141b [*DS* het]); Rav Geviha Mibei Katil (Baba Batra 83a [twice], Hullin 64b, and Meilah 10a); Rav Hillel (Shabbat 109a, Bezah 40a, and Hullin 98a); Rav Hanan (Hullin 80a [*DS* het]); Rav Hanin Mahozna'ah (Gittin 85b [and parallel]); Rav Yemar (Gittin 78b and 89b, Baba Kamma 90a, Baba Mezia 80a, Baba Batra 148b, and Shevuot 37b); Mar bar Amemar (Sukkah 32b and 41b, Baba Batra 174a, and possibly Pesahim 74b); Mar Kashisha b. d'Rav Hisda (Gittin 87a, Baba Mezia 108a, and Baba Batra 7b); Rav Mordechai (Shevuot 37b and Menahot 21b-22a); Rav Sama (Baba Mezia 110a [*DS* zadi]); Rava Mibarnish (Shabbat 28a and Nazir 40a); Rava Miparzakia (Nazir 38b); Rabbah Zuti (Menahot 31b and 52a); Ravina (Bezah 40a, Nedarim 10b and 51b, Gittin 85b [and parallel] [twice], Baba Mezia 96a, Shevuot 37b, Menahot 21b-22a, Hullin 80a [see Richard Kalmin, *The Post-Rav Ashi Amoraim: Transition or Continuity? A Study of the Role of the Final Generations of Amoraim in the Redaction of the Talmud* (Ph.D. Dissertation, Jewish Theological Seminary, 1985. Ann Arbor: University Microfilms International, 1985), pp. 475-77], 137a, and 141b, and possibly Baba Kamma 114b [*DS* pei]).
[7]Shabbat 140a (Rav Ada Nersha'ah with Rav Yosef) and 150b (Rav Natan bar Ami with Rava); Megillah 8b (Rav Shmuel bar Yizhak with Rav Huna); Yevamot 12b (and parallels) (A *Tanna* with Rav Nahman); Gittin 83b (Rava with Rav Nahman); Baba Batra 113b-114a (Rabbah bar Hanina with Rav Nahman); Horayot 11a (Rava with Rav Nahman); Hullin 35a (Rav Yizhak bar Shmuel bar Marta with Rav Nahman); Keritut 7a (Rav Hananya with Rava) and 23a (Rava with Rav Nahman), and possibly Ketubot 53a (Rav Yemar Saba with Rav Nahman) (*DS* Herschler, notes on line 11, and n. 18). See also Shabbat 60a, where Rav Yosef interprets an earlier source, Abaye objects versus Rav Yosef in his presence, and Rav Ada Nersha'ah follows with an alternative interpretation in Rav Yosef's presence. Rav Yosef does not respond in any way to Rav Ada Nersha'ah's interpretation, but he does contribute to the discussion through his initial interpretation. See the similar format on Pesahim 13a involving Rav Yosef, Abaye, and Rav Ada bar Matna. See also Gittin 63b, where Rava's question to Rav Nahman builds on an earlier statement by Rav Nahman, and Rav Nahman offers no response to Rava's question. We find numerous cases, involving

Rav Ashi appears far less frequently than these earlier Amoraim, and yet listens without comment more than five times more frequently.

Rav Ashi's role as passive observer is illustrated by a discussion on Gittin 85b[8] which begins with the following question: If a husband writes "Behold you belong to yourself" on a divorce bill intended for his wife, what is the law? Is he severing all ties between them and thus fully divorcing her, or is he merely releasing her from the obligation to work for him, in which case they are still married? In response to this question, "Ravina says to Rav Ashi: 'Come and hear...'", and quotes a Tannaitic statement which rules that the phrase "Behold you belong to yourself" on a writ of manumission serves to release a slave from his master. Ravina reasons that if the formula works for a slave, who is the master's chattel, then it certainly works for a woman, who is not the husband's chattel. Rav Ashi offers no response, and the discussion ends. A related discussion follows, however, beginning with the following question by Ravina to Rav Ashi: "If [the master] said to [his slave], 'I have no business with you,' what is the law?" Is this or is this not a valid formula of manumission? Here as well Rav Ashi offers no response, and Rav Hanin (or Rav Hanin Mahozna'ah), presumably in Rav Ashi's presence, responds by quoting traditions to the effect that the formula in question is sufficient to free the slave. The two closely related discussions consist entirely of statements by subordinates of Rav Ashi, with Rav Ashi a silent listener from beginning to end.

Along these same lines, a Tannaitic statement on Hullin 137a cites R. Yosi's opinion that *leket* (a portion of the crop which drops from the tree during harvest, which the farmer must leave for the poor) is gathered by the poor only when the farmer cuts the produce from the stalk, but not if he plucks it off with his hands. Rav Aha b. d'Rava, in Rav Ashi's presence, asserts that when produce is normally harvested other than by cutting, R. Yosi believes that cutting is not a necessary condition for *leket*. Onions and garlic, for example, are usually picked rather than cut, and the poor collect *leket* from these vegetables when the farmer harvests them in their usual manner. Ravina, also in Rav Ashi's presence, asserts that "we teach likewise" in Mishna Peah 3:4. According to this mishna, R. Yosi states that *peah* (the corners of the field which the farmer must leave for the poor) is collected from onions. *Peah* and *leket*, both levied on the farmer to aid the poor, follow similar rules, reasons Ravina, and

---

Amoraim in every time period, in which a superior Amora expresses an opinion or offers an interpretation, following which an inferior Amora objects or asks a question, apparently in the superior's presence, and no response follows. I confine the discussion to cases in which the Amora contributes nothing at all to the discussion and simply listens to statements by others.
[8]See also the parallel on Kiddushin 6b.

R. Yosi therefore holds that the poor can gather *leket* fom onions even though they are picked rather than cut. Accordingly, the mishna supports Rav Aha b. d'Rava's understanding of R. Yosi's view.

Here as well, Rav Ashi merely listens as Rav Aha b. d'Rava and Ravina discuss R. Yosi's opinions. Rav Ashi's role, or rather lack of role, in this and other contexts is virtually without parallel in discussions involving earlier Amoraim. As a rule, the Talmud mentions earlier Amoraim only when they actively participate in a discussion.[9]

One might object that in all likelihood, earlier Amoraim sometimes appear to contribute to a discussion but in actuality they do not. Suppose that Rav Hisda objects in Rav Huna's presence. Rav Huna appears to respond, but it is likely that in some instances the discussion originally ended with Rav Hisda's objection and later generations added the "missing" response.[10] In all probability, therefore, there are more than 10 or 11 cases in which earlier Amoraim listen silently while their subordinates speak.

This objection can be easily answered, however, since the same likelihood of later addition exists with regard to exchanges between Rav Ashi and his subordinates. Granted that in all likelihood there are more than 10 or 11 cases involving earlier Amoraim, there are also more than 58 to 61 cases involving Rav Ashi. It is unlikely that the evidence presently inaccessible to us (i.e., that based on hypothesized "later additions") differs substantially from the explicit evidence of the sources. Even if we could identify all editorial additions, our conclusions would very likely remain substantially the same.

It bears mentioning that Ravina, Rav Ashi's sixth-generation contemporary, listens to statements by subordinates and contributes nothing to the discussion a total of 7 times.[11] Even this many cases is

---

[9]Gafni, "He'arot le-Ma'amaro Shel D. Goodblatt," pp. 53-54.

[10]As noted in the Introduction, above, the mere presence of the word *lei*, "to him," indicating direct discourse, is less than certain evidence of face-to-face contact. See also chapter 10, below.

[11]Baba Kamma 26a and Baba Mezia 66b (Rav Aha Midifti [In *The Redaction of the Babylonian Talmud*, p. 15, I concluded, along with earlier scholars, that Rav Aha Midifti interacts with a seventh-generation Amora named Ravina. I now believe that Rav Aha Midifti interacts with the sixth-generation Ravina. I hope to document this point in a separate study, and to demonstrate that in general, the contribution of the seventh-generation Ravina to the Talmud has been overestimated. The basic conclusions in my earlier work are unaffected by this reevaluation of the chronology of the late Amoraic period, however. As far as the present study is concerned as well, it makes little difference whether the sixth- or seventh-generation Ravina is referred to, since in either case the phenomenon is not uniquely characteristic of Rav Ashi's discourse]); Yevamot 8a-b (Rav Aha bar Bibi Mar); Hullin 33a (Rav Aha bar Rav [see *DS* bet]); Yevamot 45b (Rav Aha b.

significant, since the sixth-generation Ravina appears much less frequently than the earlier Amoraim mentioned above and yet listens silently almost as frequently. We are apparently not dealing with a unique characteristic of Rav Ashi's discourse, but with a distinguishing feature of later Amoraic discourse and/or interactions in general. Rav Ashi dominates the statistics during the later Amoraic period, however, because of the relative frequency with which he appears.

It will be helpful to explain why I consider Rav Ashi's and Ravina's tendency to sit silently and contribute nothing to the discussion as a characteristic of later Amoraic discourse rather than as a transmissional phenomenon. By the term "transmissional phenomenon," I refer to the possibility that Ashi originally said something but his statement did not survive.[12] The dialogue originally had closure, but it was imperfectly transmitted and eventually Ashi's contribution was forgotten. Viewed in this manner, Ashi's "tendency" is due to the peculiar fate his statements suffered at the hands of later generations rather than evidence of the distinctive discourse of later Amoraim.

I consider this explanation unlikely because it leads to the improbable conclusion that responses by later Amoraim regularly did not survive, whereas responses by earlier Amoraim generally did survive. We would expect the opposite, however. We would expect material originating close to the time of the final redactors to be better preserved than material of more ancient vintage.[13] Explanation of the phenomenon as a unique feature of later Amoraic discourse, however, obviates this difficulty, since Ashi's tendency to listen silently is characteristic of later Amoraic discourse and says nothing about lost or imperfectly transmitted dialogue.

---

d'Rava. The Ravina who reports what Rav Gaza said to him is not the same Ravina who listens to Rav Aha b. d'Rava tell a story about Amemar, since Rav Sheshet also reports what Rav Gaza said to him. We cannot rule out entirely that one or more of the names are corrupt. See, however, Eruvin 11b, where Rav Gaza is described as Rav Sheshet's attendant); Baba Mezia 81a (Huna Mar bar Maremar); and Zevahim 24a (Rav Sama b. d'Rav Ashi).

[12]See Halivni, *Mekorot u-Mesorot: Yoma-Hagigah*, p. 9 (introduction), and pp. 355 and 400-3; *Mekorot u-Mesorot: Shabbat*, p. 208; and *Mekorot u-Mesorot: Eruvin-Pesahim*, pp. 68, 268-70, and 348, n. 2. See also Kalmin, *The Redaction of the Babylonian Talmud*, pp. 84-85 and 190-92. The statistics regarding the chronological distance between the final editors of the Talmud and later Amoraim will have to be reevaluated, but my basic conclusions are not affected by the present findings. See also Fraenkel, *Darkhei ha-Agadah ve-ha-Midrash*, p. 576, n. 171. For an attempt to explain one case on other than transmissional grounds, see Weiss, *Le-Heker ha-Talmud*, p. 181.

[13]See Kalmin, *The Redaction of the Babylonian Talmud*, pp. 6-9 and 70-87.

According to Yizhak Halevy, Ashi's tendency is evidence of his role in the editing of the Talmud. Granted that this explanation is possible, nothing about the phenomenon necessarily indicates editorial activity, and Halevy's arguments are convincing only if one assumes Rav Ashi's editorial role and searches the Talmud for supporting evidence. If we approach the material with an unbiased eye, what, if anything, can we learn about later Amoraim? We will return to this question below, following examination of other factors distinguishing earlier from later Amoraim.

B. Statements by Inferiors Addressed to Superiors

Later Amoraim are also unique in that statements which are usually phrased as monologues (see below) are often rendered as dialogues when attributed to sixth-generation Amoraim. By the term "dialogues," I refer to statements addressed by one rabbi to another (for example, "Said Rav X to Rav Y"), whether or not the rabbi addressed offers a response. By the term "monologues," I refer to statements made by a single rabbi or a group of rabbis (for example, "Said Rav X," or "Said Rav X, Y, and Z"), provided that the text supplies no indication that the statement was addressed by one rabbi to another.

In the following discussion, the term "dialogic statements" refers to statements in dialogue form, and the term "dialogic interpretations" refers to interpretations in dialogue form. By "interpretations," I refer to statements which interpret, explain, or provide the reason for or derivation of earlier sources. Such statements relate directly to the sources upon which they comment and do not respond to these sources through the medium of some pre-existing statement.

Examination of statements by sixth-generation Amoraim reveals that subordinates of Rav Ashi regularly speak in dialogue form in situations where earlier Amoraim regularly speak in monologue form. Subordinates of Ashi regularly (1) address dialogic interpretations to their superiors which differ formally from dialogic interpretations by earlier subordinates to their superiors, and (2) make dialogic responses to statements not authored by the rabbi addressed. Dialogic responses by earlier Amoraim, in contrast, almost always come in response to statements and actions by the rabbi addressed.

It will be helpful to describe some specific examples. On Baba Batra 6a we find a dialogic response by a subordinate of Rav Ashi to a question not authored by Rav Ashi.[14] I first translate and then briefly explain the discussion.

---

[14]The discussion begins on Baba Batra 5b and continues on 6a.

(A) They asked: If the creditor claims payment sometime after the debt falls due, and the debtor pleads, "I paid it before it fell due," what is the law? Do we say that even where there is a presumption against him [namely, that people do not pay before the time], we plead [on his behalf], "Why would he lie [i.e., if he wanted to lie he could have made a different plea, and certainly would have been believed]," or is the rule that where there is such a presumption we do not advance this plea?...

(B) Said Rav Aha b. d'Rava to Rav Ashi: Come and hear: [If a man says to another], "You owe me a *maneh*," and the other says, "That is so," and if on the next day when the lender says, "Give it to me," the borrower pleads, "I have given it to you," he is exempt, but if he says, "You have nothing in my hand [i.e., the loan never took place]," he is liable to pay. Is it not the case that when he said, "I have given it to you," he said, "I paid when it fell due," and when he said, "You have nothing in my hand," he said, "I paid you before it fell due"; and we are told that in the latter case he is liable, which implies that where there is a presumption [against him, i.e., that a debtor does not pay before his time], we do not plead [on his behalf], "Why would he lie?"[15]

In this discussion, Rav Aha b. d'Rava quotes and interprets a Tannaitic statement in answer to the following halachic question: Suppose a document specifies that X owes Y money, and that the debt falls due on a particular date. If Y claims payment from X after the date specified, and X claims to have paid before the date specified, is X (the debtor) believed? Does the court believe the debtor's claim to have paid prior to the due date when he makes this claim after the due date? Working against the debtor is the presumption that people usually do not pay prior to the due date. Working in his favor is the fact that had he wanted to lie, he could have claimed to have paid on the due date and would have been believed. The question is, when he claims to have paid prior to the due date do we believe him in spite of the presumption against his claim?

Rav Aha b. d'Rava, in dialogue with Rav Ashi, responds by quoting the following Tannaitic statement: Suppose that A (a creditor) claims that B (a debtor) owes him money, and B agrees. Subsequently, A demands payment. If B claims, "I gave it to you," he is exempt from payment. If he claims, "You have nothing in my hand," he must pay. According to Rav Aha b. d'Rava, the debtor's claim, "You have nothing in my hand," is equivalent to the claim, "I paid you before it fell due." Rav Aha b. d'Rava uses the Tannaitic statement to answer the halachic question,

---

[15]This translation has been adapted from that of Maurice Simon, *Baba Batra* (London: The Soncino Press, 1935), pp. 20-21.

understanding the source to imply that the court does not believe the debtor's claim to have paid prior to the due date.[16]

Rav Aha b. d'Rava, therefore, is credited with authoring a dialogic response to a question not posed by his interlocutor, Rav Ashi. Such dialogic responses are almost totally without precedent in the names of earlier Amoraim. Dialogic responses by earlier subordinate Amoraim virtually always come in response to statements or actions by the superior rabbi addressed.

As noted above, sixth-generation subordinates of Rav Ashi also author dialogic interpretations far more frequently than do earlier Amoraim. A passage on Hullin 137a, discussed preliminarily above, will illustrate this point. A translation of the passage follows:

A) ...For it has been taught: [Scripture says,] "The gleaning of your harvest," but not the gleaning of plucking. R. Yosi says, Gleaning is only that which falls on account of reaping.

(B) ...Said Rav Aha b. d'Rava to Rav Ashi, R. Yosi agrees in the case of [harvesting] in the normal manner. For it has been taught: R. Yosi says, [Scripture says], "Harvest," from which I only know reaping. Whence do I know uprooting? The text therefore states, "To reap." And whence do I know plucking? The text therefore states, "When you reap."[17]

In this discussion, Rav Aha b. d'Rava addresses a dialogic interpretation to Rav Ashi, asserting that when produce is normally harvested other than by cutting, R. Yosi believes that cutting is not a necessary condition for *leket*. As noted above, dialogic interpretations addressed by earlier subordinate Amoraim to their superiors differ formally from those addressed to Rav Ashi by his subordinates.[18]

To be specific, 33 or 34 dialogic interpretations and responses are attributed to subordinates of Rav Ashi,[19] in sharp contrast to the 1 or 2

---

[16]It is possible that the interpretation derives from later, anonymous editors rather than from the Amora who quotes the baraita. It is highly unlikely, however, that all or even most of the 33 or 34 cases (see below) are explicable as additions by later editors.

[17]This translation has been adapted from that of Eli Cashdan, *Hullin* (London: The Soncino Press, 1935), p. 786.

[18]See the discussion below for further details.

[19]Rav Abba (Yoma 48a and Baba Kamma 27b); Rav Aha b. d'Rav Yosef (Niddah 69b); Rav Aha b. d'Rav Avya (Baba Mezia 96a and possibly Baba Batra 150a); Rav Aha b. d'Rava (Baba Batra 5b-6a and Hullin 20a-b and 137a); Rav Ati (Sukkah 8a); Rav Geviha Mibei Katil (Baba Batra 83a [twice] and Meilah 10a); Rav Hillel (Shabbat 109a and Avodah Zarah 69a); Rav Hanin Mahozna'ah (Gittin 85b [and parallel]); Rav Yemar (Baba Batra 148b); Mar Kashisha b. d'Rav Hisda (Sukkah 8a, Nedarim 24a, Gittin 50b and 87a, Baba Mezia 108a, and Baba Batra 7b); Rav Mordechai (Yevamot 94a [See Friedman, *Perek ha-Isha Rabbah ba-Bavli*, p. 399, n. 8, for variants. All versions agree, however, that the statement was made in Rav

such statements authored by subordinates of Rav Huna, Rav Yehuda, and Rava.[20]

What are the characteristic features of early dialogic interpretations, and how do they differ formally from those described above?

Examination of statements by Rav Huna, Rav Yehuda, and Rava[21] reveals that most dialogic interpretations attributed to earlier Amoraim[22] take the following form: Rav X quotes an interpretation by Rav Y and asserts that the statement was made in his presence.[23] On Shabbat 107b,

---

Ashi's presence], Gittin 89b, Baba Kamma 90a, Baba Mezia 80a, Baba Batra 174b, Makkot 13b, and Menahot 21b); Rava Mibarnish (Rosh Hashana 26b); Rabbah Zuti (Menahot 52a); and Ravina (Baba Batra 64a, Shevuot 37b, and Hullin 137a).

[20]Shabbat 150b (Rav Natan bar Ami to Rava) and possibly Yevamot 87b (Rav Yehuda Midiskarta to Rava). With regard to the latter case, I am uncertain which parts of this lengthy statement were made by Rav Yehuda Midiskarta, and which (if any) were made by Rava. If the entire statement derives from Rav Yehuda Midiskarta, such that Rava sits silently and contributes nothing to the discussion, then the statement prefigures in a striking way the kinds of statements which are routinely attributed to sixth-generation Amoraim.

[21]I used the lists of statements attributed to these Amoraim found in Kosowsky, *Ozar ha-Shemot*, pp. 376-89, 532-56, and 1372-411. I analyzed the statements by Rav Huna and Rav Yehuda found in the orders of Nezikin and Kodashim, and the statements by Rava found in the orders of Moed and Nashim and in tractate Berakhot.

Certainly some of the statements attributed to Rava were not made by him, and some statements presently attributed to Rabbah were actually made by Rava. See chapter 10, below. My purpose in the present chapter, however, is to compare a sizable collection of statements by early (in this instance, pre-sixth-generation) Amoraim to statements by sixth-generation Amoraim. For my purposes, therefore, it makes no difference whether the statements were actually made by or in the presence of Rava or Rabbah.

[22]See Berakhot 42b, Shabbat 48b, 74a, and 146b, Eruvin 3b, 61b, 71a, and 104a, Pesahim 20b, Rosh Hashana 27a and 34b, Yoma 41b, 53a-b, 77b, and 80b (twice), Bezah 28a, Taanit 4a, Megillah 10a, Moed Katan 10b, 18a, and 28a (twice), Yevamot 39a and 69b-70a, Ketubot 27b (and parallels) and 81a, Nedarim 11b-12a, 27a, 54b, and 91a, Gittin 28b, and possibly Ketubot 28a.

[23]We also find many cases in which one Amora makes an interpretation, a second Amora follows with an objection, presumably in the first Amora's presence, and concludes with his own alternative interpretation. I have not included a detailed discussion of such cases first because only the word *lei*, "to him," indicates that the second Amora speaks in the first Amora's presence, and this word might be scribal error (see the Introduction, above, and chapter 10, below). Second, even if the objection was made in the first Amora's presence, we have no reason to assume that the interpretation which follows was also made in his presence. Often the second Amora's alternative interpretation is introduced as follows: *Ela Amar Rav X* ("Rather, said Rav X"), without any indication that it was stated in the first Amora's presence. In addition, often the alternative interpretation is introduced simply by the term *Ela* (Rather), such that it might be an addition by a later editor rather than the continuation of the second Amora's statement. Third,

for example, Shmuel states that "one who puts his hand inside a beast and loosens the embryo in its womb [on Shabbat] is liable (i.e., is punished for a violation of Shabbat)." Based on Shmuel's statement, Rava reports that "Bar Hamduri explained to me: 'Did not Rav Sheshet say: "One who detaches cuscuta from shrubs and thorns is liable on account of [the prohibition of] uprooting something from the place of its growth," here as well he is liable on account of [the prohibition of] uprooting something from the place of its growth.'" That is, Rava quotes Bar Hamduri's explanation of Shmuel's statement and claims he heard it directly from its author.[24] Such statements are clearly distinguishable from dialogic interpretations by sixth-generation subordinates of Rav Ashi, first because the latter are authored by inferiors and the former are not, and second because the former are third-person reports of an event which took place sometime in the past and the latter are not.

Dialogic interpretations introduced by the formula *Savar Rav X Lemeimar Kamei de-Rav Y* (Rav X thought to say in the presence of Rav Y) are also different from dialogic interpretations by subordinates of Rav Ashi.[25] Both the presence of the introductory formula and the regularity with which such statements are refuted distinguish them from dialogic interpretations by subordinates of Rav Ashi, which lack the *Savar Lemeimar* formula and which are often not refuted. In addition, this formula implies that the Amora who "thought to say" is unsure of his opinion and/or awaits the reaction of his interlocutor. The later material, in contrast, does not have this tentative or anticipatory quality.

One final variety of dialogic interpretation found in the names of earlier Amoraim is also distinct from the sixth-generation material under discussion. I refer to dialogic interpretations addressed by superior Amoraim to their inferiors. Shmuel, for example, addresses dialogic interpretations to his subordinate, Rav Yehuda, as does Abaye to Rava and Rav Yehuda to Rav Ada Mashoha'ah, Rabin bar Rav Nahman, Ada Dayala, and Rabbah bar Rav Yizhak.[26] The statements by earlier Amoraim, furthermore, often take the form of commands or instructions

---

and most important, such cases are found in every Amoraic generation and do not uniquely characterize a particular period.

[24]See also Shabbat 125a, Eruvin 56b, Hagigah 11b, Yevamot 83b, Ketubot 48b, Nedarim 5b, Sotah 39b, Kiddushin 9b (and parallel) and 40a, Baba Mezia 8b and 70b-71a, Baba Batra 47b and 138b, Avodah Zarah 28b, Menahot 29a and 42b, and Niddah 28a.

[25]For examples of dialogues between Rav Ashi and a subordinate contemporary introduced by this formula, see Avodah Zarah 33a and Hullin 98a. Sometimes the phrase *Kamei de-Rav Y* ("in the presence of Rav Y") is not found.

[26]Yevamot 21b, Baba Kamma 15b and 36b, Baba Mezia 107a (three times) and 107b (twice), Sanhedrin 80b, Avodah Zarah 40b and 43b, Menahot 26b, and Niddah 25b.

regarding the proper interpretation of a source. On several occasions,[27] for example, Shmuel commands Rav Yehuda as follows: "Abandon the mishna and follow me. The first clause is [the view of] the sages and the final clause is [the view of] R. X."[28] The sixth-generation interpretations, in contrast, are addressed by inferiors to their superiors, and never take the form of commands or instructions.

C. Dialogue Chains

We also find that later Amoraim are unique in that interactions between Rava and Rav Ashi and their respective subordinates frequently take the following form: "Said Rav A to Rav Ashi: X (Rav Ashi may or may not respond). Said Rav B to Rav Ashi: Y (Again, Rav Ashi may or may not respond)." In these cases, Rav A speaks to Rav Ashi, following which Rav B speaks to Rav Ashi on the same or a closely related topic.

For example, on Avodah Zarah 71a Rav Ashi expresses the view that pulling an object toward oneself does not effect ownership in transactions between Jews and idol-worshippers. On 71b, Mar Kashisha b. d'Rav Hisda, in dialogue with Rav Ashi, cites a Tannaitic source in contradiction to Rav Ashi's view. A discussion ensues, the conclusion of which is that the contradiction can be resolved. Ravina, also in dialogue with Rav Ashi, quotes another source in contradiction to Rav Ashi's view, and the conclusion of the discussion is that Ravina is correct.

Examination of statements by Rav Ashi reveals 27 to 29 such dialogue chains involving Rav Ashi and a series of different subordinates,[29] and 13 cases involving Rava (a fourth-generation Amora)

---

[27]See, for example, Baba Kamma 15b. It would be a simple matter to multiply examples of this phenomenon.

[28]Some Amoraim make interpretive statements in the presence of other rabbis, but not in dialogue form. In several cases, the statement is introduced by a description of the seating arrangement of two or more Amoraim: "Rav X sat in front of Rav Y, and he sat and said..." or "Rav X sat behind Rav Y, who sat in front of Rav Z, and he sat and said...." One or more of the Amoraim present proceed to make a prescriptive or interpretive statement. See, for example, Baba Kamma 102a, Avodah Zarah 6b, and Hullin 111b (*DS* shin). Such statements are clearly distinguishable from the interpretive or prescriptive dialogues involving Rav Ashi and his subordinates because they are not rendered in dialogue form.

[29]In this note, I list the 27 to 29 cases. Each citation is followed (in parentheses) by the names of the rabbis with whom Rav Ashi appears: Eruvin 57a (Ravina and Rav Havivi Mahozna'ah), Sukkah 8a (Mar Kashisha b. d'Rav Hisda and Rav Ati); Bezah 40a (Rav Hillel and Ravina), Yevamot 10a (Ravina and Rav Kahana [There was evidently a sixth-generation Amora named Rav Kahana, inferior to Rav Ashi, in addition to the fifth-generation superior who more frequently comes in contact with Rav Ashi. See Kalmin, *The Redaction of the Babylonian Talmud*, pp. 103, 108,

and his subordinates.[30] In contrast, only 5 such cases involve Rav Huna, Rav Nahman, Rabbah, or Rav Yosef [31] and their respective subordinates.

Implications of the Formal Differences Between Earlier and Later Amoraim

To reiterate, we found that (1) Rav Ashi (and, to a lesser extent, Ravina) frequently listen silently while subordinates discuss a particular topic; (2) statements usually phrased as monologues are frequently rendered in dialogue form when attributed to subordinate contemporaries of Rav Ashi; and (3) dialogue chains involving Rava and

---

and 112. For discussion of manuscript variants, see *DS* Liss, notes on lines 14-15, and n. 36, and Halivni, *Mekorot u-Mesorot: Nashim*, p. 12, n. 2]), 22a (Ravina and Rav Kahana), and 115b-116a (Mar Kashisha b. d'Rav Hisda and Ravina); Nedarim 8a-b (Ravina and Rav Aha b. d'Rava [*DS* Herschler, notes on line 14, and n. 65]) and 10b (Ravina and Rav Aha b. d'Rav Avya [*DS* Herschler, notes on line 14 and n. 36]); Gittin 85b (and parallel) (Ravina and Rav Hanin Mahozna'ah) and 87a (Mar Kashisha b. d'Rav Hisda and Ravina); Kiddushin 21a (Rav Aha b. d'Rava and Rav Aha Saba); Baba Kamma 36a (Rava Miparzakia and Rav Aha Saba), 62a (Rav Yemar, Rav Aha b. d'Rav Avya [*DS* lamed], and possibly Rav Aha b. d'Rava), 106a-b (Rav Gamda and Rav Aha Saba), and 117a (Rabbanan and Rav Abba [*DS* yud]); Baba Mezia 77b (Rav Mordechai and Rav Aha b. d'Rav Yosef), 80a (Rav Aha b. d'Rava and Rav Mordechai), 96a (Ravina and Rav Aha b. d'Rav Avya), and 110a (Rav Sama and Ravina); Shevuot 41a (Rav Aha b. d'Rava and Rav Yemar), Avodah Zarah 71b-72a (Mar Kashisha b. d'Rav Hisda and Ravina); Menahot 21b-22a (Ravina and Rav Mordechai), 48a (Ravina and Rav Aha b. d'Rava), and 52a (Rabbanan and Rabbah Zuti); Hullin 80a (Rav Aha b. d'Rava [or b. d'Rav Avya] and Rav Hanan), 137a (Rav Aha b. d'Rava and Ravina), and 141b (Ravina and Rav Ati [*DS* het]; and possibly Baba Batra 150a-b (Rav Aha b. d'Rav Avya and Ravina [see also Baba Batra 68a]) and Menahot 6a (Rav Aha Saba and Rav Aha b. d'Rava [*DS* hei and zayin]).

[30]Berakhot 38a ("a certain rabbi" and Ravina), Eruvin 96a (Rav Papa and either Rav Mesharshya or Rav Nahman bar Yizhak) and 85b (Rav Papa and Ravina), Pesahim 69b (Rav Huna b. d'Rav Yehoshua and Rav Ada bar Ahava), Ketubot 35a-b (Rav Papa and Rav Ada bar Ahava), Nedarim 26a-b (Rav Papa, Rav Ada bar Ahava, and Ravina), Gittin 25a-26a (Ravina and Rav Mesharshya [*DS* Feldblum, notes on line 6]) and 90a (Rav Papa and Rav Mesharshya), Baba Batra 151b (Rav Mesharshya and Ravina), Makkot 8a-b ("a certain rabbi," Ravina, and possibly Rav Ada bar Ahava), Avodah Zarah 46b (Rav Papa and Rav Huna b. d'Rav Yehoshua), Menahot 67a (Rav Papa and Ravina), and Temurah 17a (Rav Papa and Rav Ada [bar Ahava]).

[31]Baba Batra 85b (Rav Huna with Rav Sheshet and Rav Nahman); Baba Kamma 106a (Rav Nahman with Rav Aha bar Manyumi and Rami bar Hama); Moed Katan 2b and Baba Kamma 66a-b (Rabbah with Rav Yosef and Abaye); and Baba Mezia 29b (Rav Yosef with Rehava and Abaye). On Bezah 21a, Rav Avya Saba's dialogue with Rav Huna is immediately followed by Rabbah bar Rav Huna's dialogue with his father, but we are told that the latter dialogue took place after Rav Avya Saba left the room.

Rav Ashi and a succession of different subordinates are relatively common, but are rare involving earlier Amoraim.

In discussing the significance of these findings,[32] it is important to note that the first two distinctions pose the same problem: What is the reason for the apparently superfluous mention of a superior sage?

Three responses are possible. First, perhaps traditions involving lesser sixth-generation Amoraim were preserved primarily to the extent to which they impinged on two dominant rabbis of the generation: Rav Ashi and Ravina. Exchanges between Rav Aha b. d'Rava and Rav Mordechai, for example, had little chance of survival, but the likelihood of survival increased dramatically when Rav Ashi's presence was also noted. So important were Rav Ashi and Ravina, either in the eyes of their contemporaries or in the eyes of subsequent generations (or both), that they were mentioned even when they served no apparent function in the discussion, even when usual rabbinic usage did not call for the explicit mention of a superior sage.

In earlier generations, a statement by Rav Yosef or Abaye, for example, had a very good chance of survival even without mention of Rabbah, their superior, since Rav Yosef and Abaye were important personalities in their own right. Rav Ashi's generation, however, possessed no counterpart to Rav Yosef or Abaye, with the possible exception of Ravina. Superior rabbis in earlier generations did not overshadow all others as did Rav Ashi and Ravina. No one challenged

---

[32]It bears mentioning that the phenomenon of dialogue chains most likely does not prove that during the later Amoraic period subordinate rabbis gathered together in larger numbers than was the case earlier on. I say this because the number of rabbis explicitly referred to by name is most likely not an accurate reflection of the number of rabbis actually present (see above). Although most interactions between Amoraim take the form of dialogues between two rabbis, therefore, lower-level rabbis and/or students are most likely also in attendance, at least occasionally.

Perhaps the strongest argument in favor of this claim is the fact, noted above, that with rare exceptions only rabbis who contribute to a discussion are mentioned in the Talmud by name. Unless we are prepared to say that students virtually never sit silently before a master, the implication is that silent, and therfore unmentioned, spectators are at least occasionally in attendance.

This claim receives further support from the fact that on several occasions, passages which begin with a report that "Rav X said to Rav Y," i.e., which seem to involve only two people, turn out to have been witnessed by others. Rav X or Rav Y, for example, says something foolish or controversial, prompting laughter or murmuring by previously unmentioned spectators. See, for example, Berakhot 19b and Gittin 55b. Very likely, many discussions which begin with a report that "Rav X said to Rav Y" and proceed smoothly as dialogues from start to finish are likewise to be understood as having been witnessed by others.

the predominant status of Rav Ashi and Ravina, and therefore no one was mentioned with any regularity apart from them. Two other explanations are also possible. First, perhaps the Talmud's record regarding the sixth Amoraic generation derives primarily from Rav Ashi and Ravina. According to this explanation, only Rav Ashi and Ravina preserved and transmitted a record of sixth-generation Amoraic activity, which accounts for their apparent omnipresence.

According to a third explanation, the "superfluous" mention of the superior sage indicates that the schools of later Amoraim are more centralized than their earlier Amoraic counterparts. The "omnipresence" of Rav Ashi and Ravina, in other words, may be an accurate reflection of historical reality. To a greater degree than in earlier generations, sixth-generation subordinates perhaps speak for "publication," i.e., for permanent preservation, only or primarily in the presence of a tiny number of superior sages. Or perhaps Rav Ashi's school, more so than earlier schools, is a meeting place where rabbis from diverse localities gather together.[33]

In any event, according to all three explanations the apparent centrality of a few superior scholars manifests itself during the later Amoraic period in ways not encountered earlier. As I noted above, earlier and later Amoraim tend to appear in the presence of and in connection with a few important rabbis in every generation.[34] The

---

[33] In *The Redaction of the Babylonian Talmud*, pp. 57-65, I concluded that the rabbinic movement in Babylonia is most likely not as centralized as the constant mention of a few sages might lead us to believe. I concluded that the activity of several Amoraim qua Amoraim takes place beyond the purview of the important sages who comprise the bulk of the Talmud, but that this independent activity for the most part did not survive. I concluded this because several sages mentioned only or primarily in conjunction with a few important rabbis are portrayed as the equals or superiors of those rabbis. It is unlikely that a superior would act as judge or halachic authority only in the presence of his inferior, or that a colleague who shows himself to be the equal of the most prominent rabbi of his generation acts as a halachic decisor only in confrontation with that prominent rabbi.

In most cases, however, rabbis mentioned only or primarily in the presence of a few important sages consistently act as the inferiors of those important sages. In most cases, therefore, the evidence indicating that Amoraic activity tends to revolve around a few important sages might be an accurate reflection of reality. In most cases, in other words, the apparent omnipresence of Rav Ashi and others might be an accurate reflection of their centrality in the rabbinic movement.

[34] By the term "in connection with," I refer to the dispute form ("Said Rabbi X...Rabbi Y said...", or "Said Rabbi X...Said Rabbi Y..."). See chapter 5, above, and chapter 10, below. See also Weiss, *Al ha-Yezira ha-Sifrutit Shel ha-Amoraim*, pp. 2-3; and Bokser, *Post Mishnaic Judaism in Transition*, pp. 327-51.

apparent omnipresence of a tiny number of important sages, however, is never greater than in the sixth generation.

7

Quotation Forms in the Babylonian Talmud

The present chapter analyzes a group of technical terms and attempts to show differences between the introductory formulae introducing statements by early, later, and middle-generation Amoraim. These differences, I argue, further support my claim regarding the presence of diverse sources in the Bavli, distinguishable along chronological lines. Earlier scholars claimed that technical terminology derived from a single source, having been added as part of the post-Amoraic editing of the Talmud.[1]

By technical terminology I refer to expressions such as *Matkif Lah* ("He objected from logic against a particular source") and *Eitivei* ("He objected from a source in the presence of another Amora"), which do not form part of an Amora's actual statement, but which serve to introduce the statement, functioning as "single word abbreviations for larger expressions," and facilitating transitions.[2]

Scholarly discussion of the provenance of Talmudic terminology has tended to base itself on only a handful of cases involving a few selected terms. Hyman Klein, for example, argues that the term *Amar* ("Said") introducing an Amora's statement is a later editorial addition.[3] He bases

---

[1]Nahum Brüll, "Die Entstehungsgeschichte der Babylonischen Talmuds als Schriftwerkes," *Jahrbücher für Jüdische Geschichte und Literatur* 2 (1876), pp. 67-68, was the first to attribute certain technical terms to post-Amoraic editors. Kaplan, *The Redaction of the Babylonian Talmud*, p. 13, pointed out that the absence of some of these terms in the Yerushalmi very likely suggested this conclusion to Brüll. Halivni, *Midrash, Mishnah, and Gemara*, pp. 98-99, goes further, suggesting that all of the Talmud's technical terminology derives from the post-Amoraic editors. Halivni was anticipated by Klein, who in "Gemara and Sebara," pp. 85-90, argues that technical terms belong to the layer of sebaric interpretation and not to the original text. In his later work, Klein explicitly dates this layer to the post-Amoraic period.
[2]See Halivni, *Midrash, Mishnah, and Gemara*, p. 98.
[3]Klein, "Gemara and Sebara," p. 87.

himself on Baba Kamma 110b, where according to one version the term *Ba'i* ("Asked") introduces Rava's statement, while in a second version the term *Amar* introduces Rava's statement. Klein writes that "The alternate versions substitute *Amar* for *Ba'i* and so indicate that the word *Amar* itself before an amoraic dictum is not the Hebrew word but the Aramaic. Accordingly, the original forms of the dicta merely had the name followed by the dictum." Klein assumes, however, that a change from Hebrew to Aramaic often indicates that the Aramaic portion of the text derives from the later, "sebaric" layer of interpretation, an assumption which has much to recommend it, but which is still the subject of scholarly debate.[4] More importantly, even if we accept Klein's Hebrew-Aramaic dichotomy, he fails to take into account the possibility that the Hebrew term *Amar* originally introduced both versions of Rava's statement. The later editors might have substituted the term *Ba'i* for the term *Amar* in the first version, while allowing the Hebrew term *Amar* to remain in the second version of Rava's statement.

The above example illustrates the slender basis upon which modern scholarly discussion of the provenance of technical terminology has tended to rest. Several technical terms, when studied in full, will very likely turn out not to derive from the final editorial layer of the Talmud. In the following pages, I examine one group of technical terms which has been subjected to only a modicum of critical scrutiny: quotation forms, introductory phrases whose primary function is to identify the author of a statement and its tradent. My goal is to evaluate whether these introductory phrases betray the existence of opposing sources, or whether they show signs of deriving from a single, later editorial source.

Before making this evaluation, however, several gaps in our understanding of the meaning and function of Talmudic quotation forms need to be filled. Unfortunately, the literature on this subject, both medieval and modern, is extremely impoverished. The classic statement on this matter is found in *Seder Tannaim ve-Amoraim*.[5] We read there: *ve-Khol Heikha de-Ika Amar R. Ploni Amar R. Ploni Rabo Hu ve-Khol Heikha de-Ika Amar R. Ploni mi-Shum R. Ploni Lo Rabo Hu*. According to *Seder Tannaim ve-Amoraim*, the quotation form: "Said Rabbi X said Rabbi Y," (which we will refer to as quotation form A) is used only when Rabbi Y is the teacher of Rabbi X. The form: "Said Rabbi X in the name of Rabbi Y," (*Amar Rabbi X mi-Shum Rabbi Y*, which we will refer to as quotation form B) is used only when Rabbi Y is not the teacher of Rabbi X. Virtually all

---

[4]Halivni, in his multi-volume commentary on the Talmud (*Mekorot u-Mesorot*), does not consider changes from Hebrew to Aramaic (or vice versa) to be helpful in identifying additions by the anonymous editors.

[5]*Seder Tannaim ve-Amoraim*, ed. Kahan, pp. 30-31. See the variants cited there.

subsequent discussion on this subject is little more than a restatement of the definitions of *Seder Tannaim ve-Amoraim*,[6] with the slight modification that form A is generally understood in later literature as representing direct transmission (i.e., the first rabbi is repeating something he heard directly from the second rabbi). Form B, as well as the related form: *Amar Rabbi X mi-Shmei de-Rabbi Y* (from here on, quotation form C[7]) is understood in later literature as representing indirect transmission (i.e., the first rabbi is repeating something he did not hear directly from the second rabbi).[8]

These definitions stood largely unchallenged until the time of Yad Malakhi, who was the first to examine large quantities of Talmudic evidence on the subject rather than merely content himself with repeating the conventional definitions.[9] He found several exceptions to both generalizations set forth in *Seder Tannaim ve-Amoraim*,[10] citing cases in which "the one who repeats the tradition [in quotation form A] never saw the one who originated the tradition," as well as cases in which form C is used even when a student is quoting his teacher.[11] Yad Malakhi

---

[6]See, for example, *Sefer ha-Keritut*, Lashon Limudim, Section 3, chapter 79. However, see Rashbam's comment on Baba Batra 114b, s.v. *mi-Shum*. Compare the discussion below.

[7]When translated into English ("Said Rabbi X in the name of Rabbi Y") forms B and C appear to be identical. Such a translation, however, conceals the fact that the phrase rendered in each case as "in the name of" is Hebrew in form B and Aramaic in form C. This slight variation suggests that the two forms are not identical, a conclusion confirmed by the differing contexts in which they appear. See the discussion below.

[8]See, for example, Rashi on Hullin 17b and 113b. Among modern commentators, see Ezra Melamed, *Eshnav ha-Talmud* (Jerusalem: Kiryat Sefer, 1976), p. 15; and Moses Mielziner, *Introduction to the Talmud* (1894; Reprint. New York: Bloch, 1968), p. 225.

[9]Malakhi Coen, *Sefer Yad Malakhi* (1852; Reprint. Jerusalem, 1976), chapters 74-75, pp. 16b-18b.

[10]For another example of modern scholarship challenging a geonic explanation of a technical term, see Epstein, *Mavo la-Nusah ha-Mishna*, pp. 814-15; and Zussman, *Sugiot Bavliot*, pp. 123-25.

[11]See Frankel, *Mavo ha-Yerushalmi*, pp. 53b-54a; and Rafael Halperin, *Atlas Ez-Hayyim* (Tel Aviv, 1980), pp. 146-50. Due to the fact that Yad Malakhi made no use of Talmudic manuscripts, several of his examples are based on scribal errors. Nevertheless, his basic point is correct, and has been confirmed by Halperin. Cases in which form A is used even though the tradent could not have come in contact with the author of the statement include Shabbat 37a, 51a, and 127a, Eruvin 78a and 88a, Pesahim 76a, Yoma 39b, Megillah 14a, Yevamot 44a, Gittin 38b, 57b, and 74a, Baba Kamma 38b, Baba Batra 91b, Hullin 20a, and possibly Ketubot 68b.

Yad Malakhi also made note of Ketubot 80b, where Rav Papa states that Yehuda Mar bar Maremar's form C quotation of Rava is not a genuine quotation

assumes, however (without evidence), that quotation form C is used when the tradent did not hear the statement directly from its author.

The problem of the meaning of quotation forms A-C in the Babylonian Talmud, therefore, has only begun to receive serious consideration. The ensuing discussion attempts to contribute to the elucidation of these terms by suggesting answers to the following questions: First, does the content of the statement being quoted have any effect on the type of quotation form employed in a particular context? Second, do purely formal considerations, such as the names of the rabbis involved in transmitting the statement, ever play a decisive role? Having suggested answers to these questions, we will return to the problem with which we opened the discussion: Do these forms derive from a single or from multiple sources?

It should be noted that we employ phraseology such as "Amora X quotes in form A, B, or C," or "during a particular generation, quotation form C is utilized," only because these are the conventional ways of describing quotation. We are not suggesting that the tradents themselves are necessarily responsible for the forms presently found in the Talmud. Although we will conclude that quotation patterns indicate the presence of early, later, and middle-Amoraic sources in the Talmud, this conclusion will not enable us to say how close to the time of a statement's original formulation its quotation form was added. To consistently convey our doubts on these matters, however, would necessitate a great many awkward and laborious locutions. The gain in ease of expression, we feel, more than compensates for the slight loss in precision.

A survey of quotations in the Babylonian Talmud reveals that the content of the statement being quoted plays no role in determining the type of quotation form employed. Nothing about the content of statements quoted in form A, for example, distinguishes them from statements quoted in forms B or C, and vice versa.

Several facts support this conclusion. Leaving aside cases in which purely formal considerations determine the quotation form (see below), we find that individual Amoraim never quote earlier Amoraim in more than one of the three forms described above.[12] That is, they consistently

---

related matter, and the inference was formulated as a statement and transmitted in Rava's name. Yad Malakhi deduces from Rav Papa's observation that when not explicitly stated otherwise, form C quotations are actual quotations of the Amora represented as the author of the statement, and are not based on inference. It should further be noted that the same observation is made about form A quotations on Eruvin 46a, Yevamot 60b, Gittin 39a-b, and Baba Kamma 20a. In this regard as well, therefore, the two forms are identical.
[12]See the Appendix, below.

quote earlier Amoraim either in form A or form C, but do not quote in a combination of the two. I find it highly unlikely that all of the sages who quote earlier Amoraim exclusively in form A, for example, should quote only one category of statement, while all those who quote earlier Amoraim in form C should quote only a second category of statement. If the content of the statement determined its quotation form, I would expect a far more random distribution of forms, with at least *some* of the hundreds of Amoraic statements quoted by figures like Rav Yehuda or Rav Huna being of the type that called for forms other than quotation form A. I would expect to find, in a survey of the entire Amoraic period, *some* Amoraim who quote earlier Amoraim in more than one type of form.

In addition, once again leaving aside formal considerations, Amoraim quote in form B only when quoting Tannaim, or when quoting transitional figures (rabbis who lived during the transitional age between the Tannaitic and Amoraic periods).[13] Here as well, if the content of the statement played a role in determining its quotation form, I would expect a far more random distribution of forms. I would not expect so direct and obvious a link between the use of form B in a particular context, and the chronology of the rabbi who authored the statement.

Finally, once again leaving aside cases in which purely formal considerations are decisive, we find that Rav is the only Amora quoted in form C by Amoraim living prior to the fourth generation, although even Rav is quoted far more frequently in form A than in form C.[14]

---

[13]See the Appendix, below, for discussion of R. Abahu, R. Elazar, R. Ilai, Rav Huna, R. Hanina, Resh Lakish, Shmuel, R. Yehoshua ben Levi, Rav Yehuda, and R. Yohanan. Other Amoraim whose statements follow the same pattern include Rav Sheshet, Rav Shizbi, Ulla, and R. Yirmiya (see Kosowsky, *Ozar ha-Shemot*, pp. 926-31, 1144-49, 1545-46, and 1761-68). See also Shabbat 64b, where Rav Anani bar Sasson quotes a Tanna in form C. Most likely, the correct reading is form B (see the previous note).

[14]See the Appendix, below, for discussion of Rav Hanina bar Kahana, Rav Malkia, Rabbah bar Shmuel, R. Yaakov bar Idi, Rav Yehuda, and R. Yohanan, and n. 20, below, with regard to Rabbah bar bar Hannah's quotation on Baba Kamma 51b. See also Eruvin 29a and *DS* mem; Pesahim 103a and *DS* samekh; and Niddah 15b and Albeck, *Mavo la-Talmudim*, p. 423, n. 428. See also Nedarim 8b and *Ozar ha-Geonim*, ed. Benjamin Lewin (Jerusalem, 1942), Interpretations, chapter 25, p. 72. On Berakhot 62b, Rav Hannah bar Adda quotes Rav Sama b. d'Rav Mari in form C, and Albeck, *Mavo la-Talmudim*, p. 287, places Rav Hannah bar Adda in the third generation because on Hullin 133a, Rava and Rav Safra go to the house of his son. However, the reading in Hullin is uncertain, for an alternate version reads bar Bizna instead of bar Adda. We have no way of determining, therefore, exactly when Rav Hannah bar Adda lived. See also Berakhot 62b and *DS* yud (and parallel), according to which Rav Hannah bar Adda's quotation of Rav Sama b. d'Rav Mari comes to explicate Rava's statement.

It is highly unlikely that for such an extended period of time only Rav should be the author of a particular kind of statement, the kind of statement that calls for form C, and that Rav should utter this kind of statement only in the company of a few selected students. It is likely, therefore, that the content of the statement being quoted has no effect whatsoever on the type of quotation form employed.

Additional support for this conclusion is provided by the fact that, at times, identical statements are reported by more than one set of tradents, and yet the quotation forms differ among the various sets of tradents. On Baba Batra 111a, for example, Rav Hinena bar Shelamya and Rav Huna each quote the same statement by Rav. Rav Hinena bar Shelamya's quotation, however, is transmitted in form C, while Rav Huna's is transmitted in form A.[15] The content of Rav's statement is the same in both instances, and yet the quotation forms are different.

If the content of the statement itself does not determine its quotation form, however, then what is the determining factor? Frequently, purely formal considerations turn out to be decisive. We find, first of all, that quotation forms are frequently determined by the presence of a few key phrases in the formula used to introduce the quote. For example, when the tradent is referred to informally, as "Huna, our colleague," rather than as Rav Huna, or as "Yehuda, my brother," rather than as Rav Yehuda, the quotation is invariably transmitted in form C.[16] Similarly,

---

[15]See also Pesahim 33b, Sotah 10b, Gittin 13b and 23a, Kiddushin 65b and 78b (see *Sheiltot*, ed. Kalman Mirsky [Jerusalem, 1966], Sheiltah 121, p. 227, and the variants cited there), Shevuot 17b and 41a-b, Hullin 74a, and Niddah 25a.

[16]See, for example, Shabbat 51b-52a and 156a, Eruvin 21a, Sukkah 43b, and Ketubot 21a and 60a.

In addition, we find that quotations are transmitted in form B or form C: (1) when the transmitters of the statement are referred to by a geographic designation, for example, "in the west they say" (see, for example, Yoma 86b, Sukkah 55a, Taanit 8b, and Megillah 5a); (2) when a third party repeats or alludes to a quotation in the presence of its tradent, or when the tradent himself repeats or alludes to his quotation (see, for example, Berakhot 8a, 33b, and 42a, and Shabbat 10b, 59b, 138b, and 146b); (3) when the tradent transmits the quotation in the context of the following story forms: *Yativ Rabbi X ve-ka-Amar* ("Rabbi X sat and said" – see the references cited in n. 22, below), and possibly *Rabbanan de-Atu mei-....Amrei Amar Rabbi X* ("the rabbis who came from...said: Said Rabbi X" – Gittin 39b [but see *DS* Feldblum, notes on line 38], Sanhedrin 30b, and Hullin 18b [but see *DS* kuf] and 57a [but see *DS* taf]; (4) when two tradents transmit the statement in the following form: "Rabbi X and Rabbi Y, and the two of them" (see, for example, Shabbat 38b and 108b, Yoma 53b, Taanit 24b, and Ketubot 7b); (5) when more than one Amora is suggested as the author of the statement (see, for example, Berakhot 20b, Shabbat 108b, Pesahim 119b, and Sotah 4b and 5a); (6) when the quotation is introduced by a verb other than some form of the verb "to say" (see, for example, Berakhot 51a, and Shabbat 22a, 48b, 75b, 101a, 146b, 147a, and 154a); (7) when the name or title of the tradent is not specified, but rather we

when the author of a statement is referred to not by his proper name, but by a descriptive substitute, for example *Rabenu* ("our rabbi"), or *Gavra Rabbah* ("a great man"), his quotation is transmitted in form B or form C.[17] This fact very likely explains why only Rav is quoted in form C by Amoraim living prior to the fourth generation (see above). The fact that he is referred to throughout the Talmud not by his real name, *Rav Abba*, but as Rav, the "master" par excellence, determined the form several Amoraim used to transmit his statements.

In several cases, in fact, a statement is quoted twice within the same discussion: once *with* one of the key expressions referred to above, and once without.[18] In each case, form C is utilized when the quotation is introduced by the key expression; when the same quotation, involving the same Amoraim, is repeated a few lines later without this expression, it is transmitted in form A.

Other factors further demonstrate the importance of purely formal considerations in determining quotation forms. For example, a quotation which is usually transmitted in forms B or C will be transmitted in form A simply because it is not the final link in a quotation chain. For example, R. Yohanan consistently quotes in form B, with the exception of four cases in which he quotes a rabbi who himself continues on to quote an earlier rabbi in form A.[19] The form *Amar... mi-Shum... Amar* is stylistically unacceptable, apparently because of its awkwardness, and the middle term in the quotation chain changes to *Amar*.[20] Similarly, quotations reported in the context of the following story form: *Yativ Rabbi*

---

are told only that "they said," or "it was said," in the name of a particular Amora (see, for example, Berakhot 45b, Eruvin 5a, Pesahim 108a, Moed Katan 24a, and Ketubot 96b). See also Ketubot 33b and Baba Kamma 71a, where the following expression: *Rabbi X ve-Rabbi Y ve-Khol Havurata* ("Rabbi X and Rabbi Y and the entire group") introduces a form C quotation.

[17]See, for example, Berakhot 22a, 25b, 30b, 33b, 34b, 38b, 44b, 49a, and 55b, Shabbat 47b, Eruvin 16b, 67a, and 80a, Pesahim 33a and 115a, Yoma 15a and 33a, and Rosh Hashana 19b.

[18]See Shabbat 52a (compare Shabbat 51b), Eruvin 12a and 21a, Ketubot 21a, Gittin 52b and 86b, Avodah Zarah 16b, Zevahim 58a, and Menahot 17a. See also Ketubot 12b, Baba Kamma 21a, Menahot 39a, and Bekhorot 22a.

[19]Shabbat 39a and 47a, Baba Batra 113a, and Hullin 34b. See *DS* alef on Hullin 34b.

[20]See also Rabbah bar bar Hannah's two form C quotations of R. Mani on Baba Kamma 51b. (Rabbah bar bar Hannah elsewhere quotes only in form A. See Kosowsky, *Ozar ha-Shemot*, pp. 1454-61.) Evidently, the form *Amar... de-Amar mi-Shmei de-...de-Amar mi-Shmei de-* was also stylistically acceptable, with the final term in the quotation chain changing to *mi-Shmei de-*, in conformity with the middle term.

X ve-ka-Amar ("Rabbi X sat and said"), or variations thereof,[21] are consistently transmitted in form C, as follows: *Yativ Rabbi X ve-ka-Amar mi-Shmei de-* ("Rabbi X sat and said in the name of").[22] When the rabbi quoted in the context of the story continues on to quote an earlier Amora in form A, however, the first quotation is likewise transmitted in form A, as follows: *Yativ Rabbi X ve-ka-Amar... Amar Rabbi Y... Amar Rabbi Z* ("Rabbi X sat and said: Rabbi Y said...Rabbi Z said").[23] The form *Yativ Rabbi X ve-ka-Amar mi-Shmei de-Rabbi Y... Amar Rabbi Z* ("Rabbi X sat and said in the name of Rabbi Y: Rabbi Z said") is stylistically unacceptable, and the phrase *mi-Shmei de-* changes to *Amar.*

Other phenomena likewise show the importance of formal considerations in determining quotation forms. Several statements are reported in forms B or C simply because the name of the Amora who originated the statement is attached to the name of the tradent. For example, Shmuel Saba, referred to in the Talmud as Shmuel Saba Hatnei d'R. Hanina (the son-in-law of R. Hanina), quotes his father-in-law, R. Hanina, in form C.[24] Only the fact that the father-in-law's name is attached to the name of the son-in-law distinguishes this quotation from the thousands of other quotations of earlier Amoraic statements by pre-fourth-generation Amoraim, all of which (with the exception of cases in which purely formal considerations are decisive) are transmitted in form A (see below). Similarly, Ephraim Safra, referred to in the Talmud as Ephraim Safra the student of Resh Lakish, quotes Resh Lakish in form B or form C.[25] Only the attachment of the teacher's name to the name of the student distinguishes this quotation from the thousands of quotations of Amoraic statements by pre-fourth generation Amoraim, all of which (if we disregard formal considerations) are transmitted in form A.[26]

---

[21]One such variation is the form: *Yativ Rabbi X kamei de-Rabbi Y ve-ka-Amar* ("Rabbi X sat before Rabbi Y and said").
[22]See, for example, Pesahim 23b, 33b, and 101b, Yoma 73a, Bezah 20a, and Moed Katan 24a. The only exception is Pesahim 72b, where we find: "R. Zeira and R. Shmuel bar Yizhak sat and said: R. Shimon ben Lakish said." However, this single exception is most likely attributable to scribal error.
[23]See Eruvin 7a, Hullin 49a, 57a, and 74a, and Niddah 26b. See also Avodah Zarah 16b and *DS* vav. The manuscript of the Jewish Theological Seminary, ed. Shraga Abramson (New York, 1957), likewise renders this as a form A quotation.
[24]Berakhot 62b.
[25]Baba Mezia 119a. See also *DS* het, and see also Yer. Baba Mezia 10:6.
[26]See also Berakhot 23a (and *DS* khaf) and 24b (and *DS* resh), Eruvin 8b, Yoma 4b, Taanit 13a, Megillah 32a, Ketubot 75a, Sotah 10b, Gittin 50a, and Baba Batra 43a. See also Baba Kamma 80b, Baba Mezia 87a, Baba Batra 7a and 151b, and Avodah Zarah 37b.

Finally, several Amoraim (but not *all* Amoraim – see below) depart from their usual quotation pattern when quoting an Amora who lacks the title "rabbi" introducing his name. Shmuel, for example, quotes regularly in form B,[27] except for several cases in which he quotes Levi in form C.[28] Similarly, R. Yohanan quotes exclusively in form B,[29] with the exception of one case in which he quotes Ilfa in form C.[30] Ulla never quotes in form C, with the exception of one quotation of Bar Peda.[31] Once again, only the absence of the title "rabbi" introducing the author's name distinguishes these quotations from the thousands of quotations of Amoraic statements by pre-fourth-generation Amoraim, all of which (if we disregard formal considerations) are transmitted in form A.[32]

Purely formal considerations, therefore, often play a critical role in determining a statement's quotation form. How can we account, however, for the numerous cases in which formal considerations do not come into play? What is the determining factor in these cases?

As a first step toward answering this question, it is important to note the correlation between the distribution of quotation forms and the chronology of the Amoraim involved in transmitting the quote. Setting aside cases in which formal considerations are decisive, we find that the first three generations of Amoraim quote earlier Amoraim only in form A, and never in form C. Second, most fourth-generation Amoraim quote earlier Amoraim only in form A, while a few fourth-generation Amoraim quote only in form C. Third, only form C is utilized after the fourth Amoraic generation, and the other two forms disappear.[33]

---

[27]See the Appendix, below.

[28]Eruvin 10a (see *DS* lamed), Sukkah 7a, Nedarim 82a, Gittin 13b, and Menahot 39b. Shmuel also quotes Saba in form C on Kiddushin 71a and Menahot 28b.

[29]See the Appendix, below.

[30]Zevahim 20a. See also Resh Lakish's quotation of Hizkiya on Baba Kamma 9b. Resh Lakish, however, however, quotes Levi Saba, Bar Kappara, Abba Cohen Bardela, and Bar Tautni in form B, the quotation form he regularly employs.

[31]Kiddushin 54b.

[32]Other form C quotations of Amoraim lacking the term "rabbi" introducing their names are found on Berakhot 8a, Shabbat 57b, 66b, and 79a, Moed Katan 5b, Ketubot 17b, 27a, 74a, and 109a, Nedarim 56a, Gittin 5b and 22a, Kiddushin 78b, Baba Kamma 55a, Baba Mezia 114a and 117b, Baba Batra 163a, Sanhedrin 26a, Avodah Zarah 37a and 48b, Zevahim 9b, and Hullin 48a.

It is important to note, however, that this latest pattern is not followed by all Amoraim. To mention only the most obvious exception, we find that Shmuel is routinely quoted in form A, even though the title "rabbi" does not introduce his name. See the discussion below.

[33]See the Appendix, below.

These findings help us answer our question regarding the provenance of Babylonian Talmudic quotation forms. We concluded above that there is no correlation between the content of the statement being quoted and the type of quotation form employed. Consequently, it is unclear what could have possibly induced later editors to distribute these forms as they are presently found in the Talmud. It is unclear why the form these editors favored for *pre*-fourth-generation quotations of earlier Amoraim (form A) should be seen as completely inappropriate for quotations by *post*-fourth-generation Amoraim. Similarly, it is unclear why a form they assigned to earlier Amoraim only when certain formal criteria were satisfied (form C) should be seen by them as appropriate for later Amoraim even when these formal criteria were not satisfied. One might wish to argue that these editors assigned a new form to later Amoraim on account of the shift from prescriptive to argumentational statements, a shift which becomes increasingly pronounced beginning in the fourth generation.[34] Or that the decrease in the number of Amoraic statements transmitted in any kind of quotation form – a decrease which reaches dramatic proportions beginning in the fourth generation – somehow figured into their editorial decision. Neither of these or other comparable explanations, however, can account for the fact that several Amoraim quote exclusively in form C when the author of the statement is referred to not by his real name, but by a descriptive substitute, but many others quote in form A under the same circumstances (see above). Or that several Amoraim quote earlier sages in form C simply because they lack the title "rabbi" introducing their names, but several others quote in form A under the same circumstances. Or that some fourth-generation Amoraim quote earlier Amoraim exclusively in form A (with the exception of cases in which formal considerations are decisive), while other fourth-generation Amoraim quote exclusively in form C.[35] Or that some Amoraim consistently quote in form B whenever they quote

---

[34]See Kraemer, *Stylistic Characteristics of Amoraic Literature*, pp. 57, 64, 69-70, 80-81, and 109; and Kalmin, *The Redaction of the Babylonian Talmud*, pp. 43-49 and 52-57.

[35]Among fourth-generation Amoraim, Abaye (see the Appendix, below), Rav Aha bar Pinhas (see Eruvin 29b and *DS* gimel, and Moed Katan 15a and *DS* samekh on 15b), Rav Papa b. d'Rav Aha bar Adda (see Eruvin 21b), and possibly Rav Avya (see Bezah 13b and Halivni, *Mekorot u-Mesorot*: Yoma-Hagigah, p. 288, n. 1; see also Hullin 50a and *DS* zadi) quote in form C. See also Albeck, *Mavo la-Talmudim*, pp. 357, 366, and 374. See also Rav Mari b. d'bat Shmuel's quotation on Baba Batra 61b, and see the Appendix, below, with regard to Rav Huna bar Yehuda and Rav Hizkiya.

Tannaim or transitional rabbis, while other Amoraim consistently quote in form A under the same circumstances.[36] In other words, according to the theory which assigns responsibility for quotation forms to a single, later editorial source, we cannot account for the fact that several of these patterns are only partial patterns, applying with total consistency to some Amoraim, but not applying at all to many others.

Most likely, therefore, quotation forms A, B, and C derive from different, chronologically distinguishable sources, and perhaps were added to the text roughly contemporary with the Amoraic statements themselves. Evidently, certain Amoraim exhibit one quotation pattern, while other Amoraim exhibit a different pattern, simply because one pattern was current in a particular locality or at a particular time, while another pattern was current in a different locality or at a different time. Perhaps the various forms are indicative of differences in the academic setting or institutional framework within which quotations were made. In any event, the differences between Amoraim on this matter were not smoothed over or edited out by later generations.[37]

It should be emphasized that even the purely formal quotation patterns described above most likely do not derive from a single, later editorial source. Most likely quotation forms were fixed already during the Amoraic period in accordance with formulaic patterns. The total consistency with which many of these formal patterns are adhered to

---

[36]For a list of Amoraim who quote in form B whenever they quote Tannaim or transitional rabbis, see the Appendix, below. Rav Hama bar Yosef (see Albeck, *Mavo la-Talmudim,* p. 182), R. Hanina Trita'ah, Rav Hiyya bar Abin, Rav Inia, R. Mani, Rav Safra, Rabbah, Rabbah bar Hannah, Rav Yosef, and Zeiri quote in form A when they quote Tannaim or transitional rabbis. See Shabbat 37a (twice) and 127a (twice), Eruvin 78a and 88a, Pesahim 46a, Yoma 39b, Megillah 14a, Yevamot 44a, Nedarim 57b (and parallel), Gittin 57b, Baba Kamma 38b and 112b, Baba Batra 91b and 124a, Avodah Zarah 44b and 51b, Hullin 75b, and Niddah 61b. Some Amoraim, in fact, consistently quote Tannaim in form B and quote transitional rabbis in form A. See the Appendix, below, for our discussion of R. Elazar, R. Ilai (see Hullin 24b), and Rav Yehuda. See also Sukkah 44b, Ketubot 54b, Kiddushin 19a and 33a, and Zevahim 103a (R. Aibo), Menahot 69b and Hullin 76a (Ulla), Berakhot 33b and Shabbat 47a (R. Hanina), Shabbat 37a and Kiddushin 30a (Rav Safra — see also Avodah Zarah 30b; the chronology of R. Yehoshua de-Roma here is uncertain [see Hyman, *Toldot Tannaim ve-Amoraim,* p. 651]).

[37]See Weiss, *Le-Heker ha-Talmud,* pp. 64-70, who theorizes that in the initial stages of a statement's transmission, its basic content was preserved with little attention paid to its exact phraseology. Only later would the statement achieve fixed literary formulation. Weiss concludes that this "literary fixing" took place, at least at times, during the Amoraic period.

throughout the Talmud (for example, when the quotation does not form the final link in a quotation chain, or when the author of the statement is referred to informally, for example as "Huna, our colleague") does not argue against an Amoraic date for their addition to the Talmud. Such consistency, at first glance, seems best explicable according to the view that later editors reviewed the sources and systematically altered them in accordance with the above-mentioned formal patterns. Examination of quotation patterns as a whole, however, yields a markedly different conclusion. Such examination forces us to ask why later editors would alter their sources in such a highly selective fashion, imposing stylistic uniformity among all Amoriam when certain formal criteria were satisfied, but failing to do so in the presence of other formal criteria (the absence of the term "rabbi" introducing the author's name, the use of a descriptive substitute instead of the author's real name), and failing to do so likewise when formal criteria were absent altogether (with marked differences between *pre*-fourth-generation, fourth-generation, and *post*-fourth-generation Amoraim when formal criteria play no role, and with some Amoraim quoting Tannaim or transitional rabbis exclusively in form B, and other Amoraim quoting them exclusively in form A). According to the theory that quotation forms A and C do not derive from the final editors, however, such partial consistency is easily explicable, with some patterns followed consistently throughout the entire Amoraic period existing alongside other patterns which changed from one generation to the next, and existing as well alongside patterns which were followed consistently by certain Amoraim living at certain times periods, but not at all by others.

To reiterate, if we set aside cases in which purely formal considerations are decisive, we find that only forms A and B are utilized during the first three Amoraic generations. After the fourth generation, however, only form C is utilized, and it is utilized even in situations where formal considerations play no role. In between these two extremes, the third and fourth generations constitute a transitional period, during which time the use of forms A and B sharply decreases. The disappearance of these forms after the fourth generation, therefore, is the continuation of a trend which began generations earlier. The fourth generation is also transitional in that only beginning with this generation do we find that some Amoraim consistently transmit earlier Amoraic statements in form C even when formal considerations play no role. In other words, with the fourth generation the role of form C begins to expand, and its use as the exclusive form after the fourth generation is the continuation of this earlier trend.

The following quotation forms frequently introduce statements by Amoraim in the Yerushalmi: *Amar Rabbi X be-Shem Rabbi Y* ("Said Rabbi X in the name of Rabbi Y"), or *Rabbi X be-Shem Rabbi Y* ("Rabbi X in the name of Rabbi Y"), or *Rabbi X Rabbi Y be-Shem Rabbi Z* ("Rabbi X Rabbi Y in the name of Rabbi Z"), and possibly *Amar Rabbi X Ba'i Rabbi Y* ("Said Rabbi X concluded [?] Rabbi Y").[38] The presence of such forms in the Yerushalmi provides a modicum of support for our view that the Bavli's quotation forms do not derive from the final editors. The Yerushalmi, apparently completed early in the fifth century C.E.,[39] contains quotation forms, and it is reasonable to assume that such forms were added to both Talmuds at approximately the same time. If this assumption is correct, then quotation forms were added to the Bavli no later than the early fifth century, and according to an emerging scholarly consensus, the final editing of the Bavli began after the conclusion of the Amoraic period in the early sixth century.

Unfortunately, this argument is less than fully conclusive. The fact that the Yerushalmi contains anonymous editorial discussions, coupled with the fact that a substantial body of scholarly opinion dates the Bavli's anonymous editorial layer to the sixth century and beyond, should guard us against drawing facile comparisons between the editing of the two Talmuds. Redaction in the Yerushalmi, whether in the form of anonymous editorial commentary or the addition of technical terms, might have begun earlier than in the Bavli.

Detailed scrutiny of the Yerushalmi's quotation forms might reveal patterns comparable to those found in the Bavli, in which case our conclusions regarding the presence of diverse sources in the Bavli would apply as well to the Yerushalmi. It is also possible, however, that the Yerushalmi's quotation patterns will reveal the hand of a later editor for whom the character of the statement, or some purely formal considerations, consistently determined the form used in a particular context. Our impression of the Yerushalmi as the less edited of the two Talmuds does not argue decisively against this second possibility, for scholars of the last several decades have found that the Yerushalmi is a much more thoroughly edited document than has ever before been imagined.[40] Further improvement in our ability to unravel the Yerushalmi's obscurities may lend further support to this scholarly

---

[38]See Frankel, *Mavo ha-Yerushalmi,* pp. 9b-10a, and see chapter 5, above. See also Yerushalmi Shabbat 3:7, where the term *mi-Shum* is used to introduce R. Yosa's quotation of D'veit R. Yannai. The word *mi-Shum,* however, is very likely a scribal error for the Yerushalmi's usual term, *be-Shem.*

[39]Bokser, "An Annotated Bibliographical Guide to the Study of the Palestinian Talmud," p. 193.

[40]*Ibid.,* pp. 191-94.

trend, and may reveal additional areas in which the Yerushalmi equals, and even surpasses, the Bavli in editorial sophistication.

Part Two

HISTORICAL STUDIES

8

Rabbinic Attitudes Toward Rabbis

Throughout Part 1, our primary focus was literary rather than historical. We argued that the Bavli contains diverse sources, and identified these sources by appeal to internal contradictions and shifts of perception and terminology within the Bavli, and by comparison with the Yerushalmi. Part 2 of this study focuses primarily on history.

The present chapter analyzes the information supplied by the Talmud regarding rabbinic attitudes toward rabbis. In both halachic and agadic contexts sages comment on each other's erudition, piety, personality, and the like.[1] This chapter argues that rabbis routinely express hostility, reverence, and other comparable attitudes toward contemporaries and near-contemporaries, but not toward their more distant predecessors.

I examine whether this difference between contemporary and non-contemporary attitudes is explicable on historical or literary grounds, and argue in favor of historical explanation. As noted in chapter 2, above, literary explanation views differences between early and later rabbis as evidence of changes in the type of literature considered worthy of preservation for posterity. Historical explanation, which accounts better for the evidence, views differences between early and later rabbis as evidence of changing rabbinic attitudes toward rabbis.

The above-mentioned difference between contemporary and non-contemporary attitudes admits of three possible historical explanations. According to two of the three explanations, this difference further supports my claim regarding diverse sources in the Talmud. According to to the third, however, this difference between contemporary and non-contemporary attitudes has no impact on the central thesis of Part 1 of this book. The present chapter, therefore, which is similar in several ways to chapter 2, above, belongs in Part 2 of this study because it makes

---

[1]See, for example, Ephraim E. Urbach, *Hazal: Pirkei Emunot ve-Deot* (1969; Reprint: Jerusalem: Magnes Press, 1986), pp. 557-64.

definite historical claims, and only possibly contributes to our understanding of the composition of the Talmud.[2]

This chapter also argues that attributed rabbis and anonymous editors react differently to the personalities of sages, providing additional evidence of diverse sources. This distinction between the anonymous and attributed sections of the Talmud supports the claims of David Halivni, Shamma Friedman, and others that by studying these sections independently, we add significantly to our understanding of the Talmud.[3]

The discussion of the anonymous and attributed sources could have been included in Part 1 as an independent chapter, since it advances my thesis regarding diverse sources. Due to its brevity, however, and to the fact that it deals with praise and criticism, I have included it in the present chapter, which systematically examines rabbinic praise and criticism of rabbis.[4]

Rabbinic Attitudes Toward Rabbis in Contemporary and Non-contemporary Commentary

Analysis of commentary found in several Talmudic tractates,[5] and of commentary attributed to several prominent sages,[6] reveals that rabbis

---

[2]See the Preface, above, for earlier published versions of this chapter. I wish to thank Professor Yeshayahu Gafni of Hebrew Univerity for his critique of my earlier arguments.

[3]See the literature cited in the Introduction, above. For another possible distinction between anonymous and attributed statements, see Appendix 1, below.

[4]See the Introduction, above, for detailed discussion of the terms "commentary," "dialogue," and "stories."

[5]I analyzed tractates Shabbat, Ketubot, Baba Mezia, Avodah Zarah, and Hullin for expressions of reverence and special respect. See below for documentation. In addition, analysis of tractates Berakhot, Eruvin, Pesahim, Yoma, Yevamot, Gittin, Baba Batra, Zevahim, and Niddah yielded 27 to 31 cases in which rabbis criticize or express hostility toward contemporaries or near-contemporaries, and only 3 to 7 cases in which they express comparable sentiments toward non-contemporaries. These 27 to 31 cases are found on Berakhot 38b (R. Zeira – R. Binyamin bar Yafet [Here and throughout this chapter, the first rabbi mentioned is the author of the commentary and the second is the subject of the commentary]); Eruvin 67b (Rava – Rav Huna bar Hinena) and 90a (Rava – Rami bar Hama); Pesahim 34a-b (R. Yirmiya – Rav Sheshet) and 70b (Abaye – Rabin); Yevamot 24b (Rav Sheshet – Rav), 55b (Rav Dimi – Rabbah bar bar Hana), 57a (R. Yirmiya – Rava or Rabbah), 64b (Abaye – Rav Yizhak bar Yosef), 91a (Rav Sheshet – Rav), and 109b (Rav Sheshet – Rav); Gittin 6b (Rav Yosef – R. Evyatar); Baba Batra 7a (Rava – Mar Zutra b. d'Rav Nahman), 9a-b (Rava or Rabbah – Rav Ahdevui bar Ami or Rav Sheshet), 22a (Rav Yosef – Rav Ada bar Ahava), 22a (Rav Dimi Minehardea – Rav Ada bar Ahava), 22a (Abaye – Rav Ada bar Ahava),

chronologically removed by more than a generation are addressed primarily as disembodied authors of authoritative pronouncements. They are addressed as sources of knowledge, that is, as abstract texts. Contemporaries, however, occasionally address one another with hostility, ambivalence, and competitiveness, or, alternatively, with praise or expressions of special respect.

This point bears restating. Commentary ascribed to rabbis more than a generation removed from their sources contains almost none of the harsh insults and ambivalences, and likewise few expressions of reverence and respect, which frequently characterize commentary ascribed to contemporaries and near-contemporaries. Commentary ascribed to rabbis more than a generation removed tends to be dispassionate, to respond to the substance of the statements and not to the statements' author.

Contemporaries and near-contemporaries express not only anger or surprise in response to specific statements or actions, but also the conviction that a particular sage is fundamentally flawed or inadequate. The accusation will be made, for example, that a rabbi's traditions are untrustworthy, that he violates the halacha, that his premature death was punishment for his failure to show proper respect toward great scholars, that he has not served as apprentice to a rabbi and is therefore not a full-fledged member of the rabbinic community, and the like. Such

---

22a (Rava – Rav Ada bar Ahava), 22a (Rav Nahman bar Yizhak – Rav Ada bar Ahava), 51b (Ravana Ukba and Ravana Nehemia, the grandsons of Rav – R. Elazar), 116a-b (Rava – Rami bar Hama), and 151b (Rava – Mar Zutra b. d'Rav Nahman); Zevahim 60b (R. Yirmiya – Abaye); Niddah 20a-b (R. Yishmael b'R. Yosi – R. Hanina), 33a-b (Rava – Rami bar Hama), and 60a (Rav Sheshet – Rav); and possibly Yevamot 75b-76a (Rav Papi – Rav Bibi bar Abaye); Baba Batra 137b (Rav Huna b. d'Rav Yehoshua – Rav Bibi bar Abaye) and 151a (Rav Huna b. d'Rav Yehoshua – Rav Bibi bar Abaye); and Zevahim 118b (Rav Yosef – Rav Dimi).

The 3 to 7 cases in which rabbis criticize or express hostility toward non-contemporaries are found on Yevamot 62b (Rav Hama bar Abba or Rav Hiyya bar Abin – the students of R. Akiba); Yevamot 62a (Rav Nahman – the students of R. Akiba); Gittin 56a (R. Yohanan – R. Zecharya ben Avkulas); and possibly Berakhot 20a (Rav Papa [in Abaye's presence. According to Pesahim 104b, Abaye was a student of Rav Yehuda. Rav Papa's commentary on a statement by Rav Yehuda, therefore, should perhaps not be considered as non-contemporary] – Rav Yehuda); Pesahim 70b (Rav Ashi – Yehuda ben Dortai [Yehuda ben Dortai appears only in this one context, and it is doubtful that he is a rabbi. See Hyman, *Toldot Tannaim ve-Amoraim*, pp. 559-60; and Zussman, "Heker Toldot ha-Halacha u-Megilot Midbar Yehuda," p. 39]), Yevamot 105b (Rav Nahman bar Yizhak – Avdan), and Gittin 7a (R. Abahu – R. Hanina ben Gamliel).

[6]Rav, Rav Sheshet, R. Yirmiya, Rav Yosef, Rami bar Hama, and Rav Ashi. See below for documentation.

accusations, which strike at the very core of a rabbi's character, appear primarily in commentary ascribed to contemporaries and near-contemporaries. Once the chronological distance between commentator and source goes beyond a single generation, such thorough denunciations are extremely scarce.

It bears repeating that by the term "commentary," I refer to remarks made by Rabbi X concerning either the statements or the character of Rabbi Y in situations where it is reasonably clear that the two rabbis are not depicted as speaking together and are not mentioned in the context of a single story. Defining the term "commentary" in this fashion enables me to confine the discussion to cases in which interaction between contemporaries approximates interaction between rabbis separated from each other by several generations. Examination of such cases reveals that negative or reverential attitudes are regularly expressed primarily in commentary by contemporaries and near-contemporaries.

I will analyze anonymous editorial commentary in greater detail below, observing that anonymous commentary is likewise largely devoid of praise or criticism of sages. For the moment, however, I confine my remarks to Amoraic commentary. As noted above, the difference between contemporary and non-contemporary commentary is more easily explicable on historical than on literary grounds. This difference is better explicable as evidence of changing rabbinic attitudes than as evidence of changing standards of literary preservation.

Literary explanation fails here because it cannot account for the fact that Amoraim who are credited with authoring positive and negative opinions about their contemporaries and near-contemporaries are not credited with authoring such opinions about their more distant predecessors. We would expect little or no praise and criticism of contemporaries and near-contemporaries if literary factors were at work, if the phenomenon were due to a change in the kind of material considered worthy of preservation for posterity. According to literary explanation, in other words, there is no satisfactory explanation for the difference between Amoraic attitudes toward contemporaries and those expressed toward non-contemporaries. Praise and criticism are either worthy of preservation or they are not; it is unlikely that criticism of contemporaries should be considered worthy of preservation and criticism of non-contemporaries should be considered unworthy.

Historical explanations, however, easily account for the evidence. One possibility is that the Talmud attests to a diminution of concern for the rabbis as people, and to a greater concern for the content of their statements, as the chronological distance between commentator and source increases. According to this explanation, feelings inspired in rabbis by the giants of their own time were more powerful than those inspired by the greats of the past, judging from the relative frequency with which these feelings receive concrete expression in the sources. This is not to suggest, for example, that Rav Yehuda did not consider R. Akiba, who preceded him by several generations, to be a great rabbi. But Yehuda praises Rav and Shmuel, his teachers, for example, more frequently than he praises Akiba because his immediate predecessors affected him more powerfully and personally than did the great rabbi of the more distant past.

According to an alternative historical explanation, the difference between contemporaries and non-contemporaries is due to increasing respect and reverence for the rabbinic heroes of past generations as the chronological gap increases. A later Amora such as Rava, for example, feels free to criticize his own contemporaries, but not an outstanding early Amora such as Rav. Similarly, Rav Yehuda does not praise R. Akiba because he feels inadequate to express any sort of opinion, even favorable, for such an extraordinary individual. *Mutatis mutandis*, we find a similar idea in the rabbinic belief that spontaneous human praise of God, whose greatness is beyond human comprehension, is actually a grievous insult. Merely human praise of God, the rabbis believe, actually limits His greatness, and only in special circumstances is it permissible to praise God.[7]

According to a third historical explanation, the phenomenon under discussion reveals the methods by which later Amoraim praise or criticize their distant predecessors. Perhaps later rabbis created the strong negative responses to earlier rabbis such as Rav, for example, and attributed them to Rav's contemporaries out of respect for the giants of the past or out of concern for their own reputations. Later rabbis perhaps hesitated to express such sentiments in their own names, but felt free to do so in the names of earlier scholars. Perhaps later rabbis, for example, did not have the audacity to openly insult or express ambivalence toward Rav, and therefore attributed such sentiments to Shmuel, Rav's contemporary. Perhaps an effective way to criticize one's contemporaries was to say nasty things about a much earlier rabbi with whom these contemporaries were closely identified. One might criticize one's contemporaries, for example, by criticizing an early rabbi whom they considered to be their spiritual progenitor or the founder of their school (see the Introduction, above).

Similarly, perhaps later rabbis refrained from praising the giants of the past in their own names, and preferred to praise them

---

[7] See b. Berakhot 33b and Yer. Berakhot 9:1.

pseudepigraphically. Perhaps later rabbis reasoned that it would be insulting to Rav, for example, to receive praise from rabbis so vastly his inferior (i.e., themselves). They therefore attributed their own expressions of reverence to much earlier sages.

According to the first two historical explanations, incidentally, the difference between contemporary and non-contemporary commentary provides further evidence of diverse sources in the Talmud. The third historical explanation, however, need not imply the existence of diverse sources. Later generations might be responsible for the distinction between contemporary and non-contemporary commentary, with later rabbis refraining from personal reactions in their own named statements, while attributing hostile and positive sentiments to the earlier rabbis most likely to have expressed them, namely to contemporaries and near-contemporaries of the sages who were targets of their praise or criticism. If Rava wants to criticize Rav, for example, it makes sense that he would attribute the criticism to Shmuel, Rav's contemporary. If he wishes to praise R. Akiba, he would be likely to do so in the name of Akiba's contemporary, R. Yishmael, and less likely to do so in the name a non-contemporary of Akiba, such as Shmuel. I am not claiming that the commentary under discussion makes sense only when viewed as an invention by later generations, but rather that the data admits of such an explanation.

It bears repeating that by the term "non-contemporaries," I refer to rabbis separated from one another by more than a single generation. By the terms "contemporaries and near-contemporaries," I refer to rabbis separated from one another by a single generation or less. According to these definitions, for example, Abaye (a fourth-generation Amora) is a near-contemporary of Rabbah and Rav Yosef (third-generation Amoraim) but not of Rav and Shmuel (first-generation Amoraim). Rav Sheshet, an early third-generation Amora, is a near-contemporary of Rav, but not of Rabbi, who lived at the end of the Tannaitic period.

We find other distinctions between contemporary and non-contemporary commentary which are likewise easily explicable on historical grounds. In the rare instances in which criticisms and hostility are found in non-contemporary commentary, both the level of hostility and the character of the criticisms are clearly motivated by specific actions or opinions found in the immediate context. This is not always the case with hostility and criticisms found in contemporary commentary. Similarly, later Amoraim praise lesser rabbis *only* when the praise is motivated by specific literary sources at our disposal. Contemporaries and near-contemporaries, in contrast, praise lesser rabbis even when not motivated by specific literary sources at our disposal.

The famous story of Kamza and Bar Kamza on Gittin 55b-56a illustrates my claim regarding hostile commentary. The story features R. Zecharya ben Avkulas' obstruction of efforts to stop Bar Kamza from informing against the Jews, and R. Yohanan, commenting on the story, claims that "the dilatoriness of R. Zecharya ben Avkulas" brought about the destruction of the Temple and the exile of the Jews from their land.[8] Yohanan's comment is clearly a negative reaction to Zecharya ben Avkulas' specific actions in this story. That is, the Talmud records Yohanan's response to a literary figure and not to a living, breathing individual. Rav Hiyya bar Abin[9] responds in the same fashion to "the students of R. Akiba," who he claims "died a bad death."[10] Hiyya bar Abin's comment is a negative reaction to their failure, explicitly criticized in a story, to show proper respect toward one another. Similarly, Rav Nahman bar Yizhak once blesses God for punishing Avdan "in this world."[11] According to one interpretation, Nahman bar Yizhak expresses satisfaction that Avdan receives his just deserts for humiliating the great scholar, R. Yishmael b'R. Yosi,[12] and responds to two traditions which view Avdan as wicked and deserving of extremely vile punishments. Elsewhere, on Pesahim 70b, Yehuda ben Dortai, a contemporary of Shemaya and Avtalion, "goes south" in protest over a temple practice which he feels is incorrect. Rav Ashi, a late Amora, criticizes Yehuda ben Dortai as a "separatist," but his criticism is clearly motivated by Yehuda's actions in this story.[13]

When we turn to hostility and criticism expressed in commentary by contemporaries and near-contemporaries, in contrast, we find a markedly different picture. Analysis of commentary found in several Talmudic tractates reveals several cases in which contemporaries or near-contemporaries harshly disparage one another and the disparagement is not clearly motivated by specific actions or opinions found in the

---

[8]For further discussion of this story, see Tosefta Shabbat 16:7 and Saul Lieberman, *Tosefta ki-Feshutah* (New York: Jewish Theological Seminary), vol. 3, pp. 268-69; David Rokeah, "Zecharya ben Avkulas: Anvetanut O Kanaut?" *Zion* 53, No. 1 (1988), pp. 53-56 and "be-Khol Zot Mishak Milim," *Zion* 53, No. 3 (1988), pp. 317-22; and Daniel Schwartz, "Od le-She'elat 'Zecharya ben Avkulas: Anvetanut O Kanaut,'" *Zion* 53, No. 3 (1988), pp. 313-16.
[9]Or Rav Hama bar Abba.
[10]Yevamot 62b.
[11]Yevamot 105b.
[12]Perhaps Nahman bar Yizhak's statement should be understood not as joy over the horrible fate suffered by Avdan, but as happiness that a rabbi suffered in this world and was therefore spared punishment in the world to come.
[13]See, however, my comments above.

immediate context. In one case, for example, R. Zeira rejects R. Binyamin bar Yafet's version of a statement by R. Yohanan, asserting that Binyamin is not a careful pupil and his traditions are unreliable.[14] In another context, Abaye disparages Rav Yizhak bar Yosef in virtually identical terms.[15] Nothing about the actions of either Amora in these contexts clearly motivates Abaye's and Zeira's comments. Similarly, Rabban Ukba and Rabban Nehemia protest against Rav Hisda's decision in favor of an opinion by R. Elazar, referring to Elazar as a "little" man.[16] Rava criticizes a statement by his contemporary, Rav Huna bar Hinena, expressing outrage that "one who does not know how to explain Tannaitic statements" objects against R. Yohanan's statement.[17] Nothing about the opinions of either Amora in these contexts clearly accounts for the hostility directed against them. In several instances, R. Yirmiya derides the "stupid Babylonians who make obscure statements because they live in a dark land," and nothing about the statements by the Babylonians accounts for the severity of Yirmiya's reaction (see below). Similarly, Rav Sheshet objects in eight contexts that Rav uttered a particular statement "while lying down drowsing,"[18] and nothing about Rav's opinions explains the hostile tone of Sheshet's responses or indicates why Sheshet objects far more cordially against comparable statements by other Amoraim.[19]

One might argue, perhaps, that the hostility expressed by Rava toward Rav Huna bar Hinena, for example, is motivated by a literary source found in some other context in the Talmud. This conjecture, however, fails to explain why non-contemporary hostility is fully understandable as a reaction to sources found in the immediate context, whereas contemporary hostility is often not. In addition, examination of Huna bar Hinena's statements elsewhere in the Talmud[20] reveals a few opinions or actions which by a stretch of the imagination might explain Rava's wrath in this context, but we search in vain for the same obvious and direct connection between objectionable action and criticism present in the cases involving non-contemporaries. Both the level of hostility and the character of the criticisms found in commentary by contemporaries

---

[14]Berakhot 38b.
[15]Yevamot 64b.
[16]Baba Batra 51b.
[17]Eruvin 67b.
[18]Yevamot 24b, 91a, and 109b, Baba Kamma 47b, 65a, and 67b, Bekhorot 23b, and Niddah 60a.
[19]See, for example, Eruvin 66a and Niddah 70a, and see the discussion below.
[20]See Kosowsky, *Ozar ha-Shemot*, pp. 391-92; Albeck, *Mavo la-Talmudim*, p. 362; and Kalmin, *The Redaction of the Babylonian Talmud*, pp. 64 and 181. See also chapter 1, above.

and near-contemporaries, therefore, are often not fully explicable as reactions to the literary sources at our disposal.

As noted above, this distinction between contemporary and non-contemporary commentary is easily explicable on historical grounds. According to this theory, later generations respond to earlier rabbis only through the medium of literary sources, whereas personal experiences not recorded in the Talmud occasionally find expression in commentary by contemporaries and near-contemporaries. These personal experiences occasionally contribute to the vehemence with which contemporaries criticize and express hostility toward one another.

According to an alternative historical explanation, later Amoraim sometimes openly criticize early rabbis when the risk to their reputations is particularly small. A later Amora, for example, openly criticizes Zecharya ben Avkulas without fear of being condemned as arrogant or disrespectful toward the greats of the distant past, because (1) in the particular story described above Zecharya's explicit actions are objectionable and clearly deserve censure, and (2) because Zecharya, at least from the standpoint of subsequent generations, is a lesser rabbi, i.e., not one of the outstanding sages of his generation. More gratuitous expressions of hostility toward important early rabbis, i.e., harsh criticisms which are not clearly motivated by particular literary sources at our disposal, tend to be expressed pseudepigraphically, i.e., in the names of contemporaries and near-contemporaries of the important early rabbis, reducing the risk of censure by one's contemporaries.

As noted above, we also find that early and later Amoraim are distinct in that later Amoraim praise lesser rabbis *only* when the praise is motivated by specific literary sources at our disposal. Contemporaries and near-contemporaries, in contrast, praise lesser rabbis even when not motivated by specific literary sources at our disposal.

Lesser rabbis such as Rav Malkio, Rav Hiyya bar Abin, Rav Hinena b. d'Rava Mipashronia,[21] and Rav Tevut or Rav Shmuel bar Zutra are praised in commentary by contemporaries and near-contemporaries, and nothing known about them anywhere in the sources motivates the praise. Nothing known about Rav Tevut or Rav Yishmael bar Zutra explains Ravina's extravagant praise of his honesty.[22] Nothing known about Rav Malkio explains why Rabbah or Rava praises him as "wise,"[23]

---

[21]With regard to this Amora, see Hyman, *Toldot Tannaim ve-Amoraim*, p. 475. Albeck, *Mavo la-Talmudim*, p. 673, places him in the fourth and fifth generations.
[22]Baba Mezia 49a-b. There were two, and possibly more, Amoraim named Ravina. The fifth-generation Ravina must be referred to because Rav Papi, who also dates from the fifth generation, states that Ravina himself reported to him the text of Rav Tevut's or Rav Yishmael bar Zutra's statement.
[23]Yevamot 113a.

and nothing known about Rav Hiyya bar Abin and Rav Hinena b. d'Rava Mipashronia explains why Rava possibly refers to the former as a "lion of the company,"[24] and to the latter as "wise."[25]

In contrast, rabbis praise lesser non-contemporaries only when motivated by specific sources which clearly depict them as extraordinary. On Ketubot 62b, for example, Rami bar Hama praises R. Oshaya, R. Hama, and R. Bisa, son, father, and grandfather respectively, as a "threefold cord that will not be broken." A striking story which describes the three rabbis as conferring with one another on a halachic matter motivates Rami's praises. The Talmud puzzles over the infrequency with which sons of rabbis become rabbis themselves.[26] It is especially noteworthy to find three successive generations of rabbis, all active in each other's lifetimes, and the specific story motivates Rami's remark.

This distinction between contemporary and non-contemporary commentary is also easily explicable on historical grounds. According to this explanation, later Amoraim have access to lesser rabbis only via their literary remains, and therefore praise them only when motivated by explicit cues supplied by the sources. Contemporary attitudes toward lesser rabbis, however, are influenced by personal experiences not always recorded in the Talmud. Lesser rabbis, therefore, are occasionally praised by contemporaries even when no clear motivation can be found in specific literary sources at our disposal.

The Specific Evidence of the Sources

1. Praise and Special Respect

It will be helpful at this juncture to further illustrate my arguments with specific examples, and to provide statistics in support of the claims advanced above.

---

[24]Shabbat 111b. See Hyman, *Toldot Tannaim ve-Amoraim*, pp. 439-41; Albeck, *Mavo la-Talmudim*, pp. 284-85; and Kosowsky, *Ozar ha-Shemot*, pp. 480-82.

[25]Hullin 112a. It is possible, however, that Rava's statement should be viewed as the concluding part of the story rather than as commentary on the story. See the discussion above.

[26]See Nedarim 81a and Yeshayahu Gafni, "'Shevet u-Mehokek': Al Defusei Manhigut Hadashim bi-Tekufat ha-Talmud be-Erez Yisrael u-ve-Bavel," in *Kehuna u-Melukha: Yahasei Dat u-Medina be-Yisrael u-va-Amim*, ed. Yeshayahu Gafni and Gabriel Motzkin (Jerusalem: Merkaz Zalman Shazar, 1987), pp. 85-88. See also Daniel Boyarin, "Literary Fat Rabbis: On the Historical Origins of the Grotesque Body," *Journal of the History of Sexuality* 1, No. 4 (1991), pp. 562-72, and the sources cited in n. 32, there.

We find positive commentary on Gittin 19b and Niddah 20b, where Ulla, a Palestinian rabbi visiting Babylonia, respectfully refers to a Palestinian sage, R. Elazar, as "the master of the land of Israel." Another example is found on Eruvin 13b, where Rabbi boasts that he is sharper than his fellows because he "saw R. Meir from the back." Had he seen R. Meir "from the front," claims Rabbi, he would have been even sharper. Along these same lines, on Baba Batra 125b R. Elazar states that a certain issue "began with great men" (i.e., Rav Huna), and "ended with small men" (i.e., himself). On Pesahim 48a, R. Yirmiya expresses surprise at R. Zeira's suggestion that Rami bar Hama's argument should not be accepted: "A matter which has been difficult for many years..., now that they explain it in the name of a great man we should not accept it?" On Baba Batra 51b, Rabban Ukba and Rabban Nehemia ask why Rav Hisda abandons the view of "the great ones" (i.e., Rav) and follows that of "the small ones" (i.e., R. Elazar). Hisda answers that he also follows "the great ones," for R. Yohanan agrees with Elazar.

In all, examination of several Talmudic tractates (see above) reveals 20 to 37 cases[27] in which Amoraic commentary contains praise or

---

[27]Shabbat 53a (the early R. Zeira respectfully refers to Shmuel as *Ariokh*. See Jastrow, *Dictionary*, p. 119; and Levy, *Wörterbuch*, vol. 1, p. 165. Compare *Arukh ha-Shalem*, ed. Kohut, vol. 1, pp. 282-83. Even if the term is negative, its usage in this context still supports the central claim of this chapter, namely that most positive and negative commentary is attributed to contemporaries and near-contemporaries); 81b (R. Natan bar Oshaya – R. Yohanan); 112b (Rav Yizhak bar Yosef interprets a mishna in a forced manner "so that R. Yohanan's words will not be broken [i.e., contradicted]"); and 112b (The early R. Zeira unfavorably compares his own generation with that of R. Yohanan, declaring that "If the early ones are angels, we are men. If they are men, we are donkeys." Our text has R. Zeira quoting another Amora, but Hyman, *Toldot Tannaim ve-Amoraim*, p. 45; Frankel, *Mavo ha-Yerushalmi*, p. 57a; and Albeck, *Mavo ha-Talmudim*, p. 314, correctly observe that the names should be reversed, according to which R. Abba bar Zevina quotes R. Zeira); Ketubot 11b (Rav Hiyya bar Abin – Rav Amram "and all the greats of the generation"); 43a (Rava – Rav Yosef); 53a (Rav Hisda – R. Elazar); and 107b (Rav Shemen bar Abba – Shmuel); Baba Mezia 16a (Rami bar Hama – Rav Sheshet) and 49a-b (Ravina, quoted by Rav Papi – Rav Tevut or Rav Yishmael bar Zutra); Avodah Zarah 16b (Rav Yehuda – Rav or Shmuel); 40a (The early Rav Ada bar Ahava respectfully refers to Rav, Shmuel, and R. Yohanan either as "three lords: [*Arukh ha-Shalem*, ed. Kohut, vol. 7, p. 185], or as "three verses," i.e., three great sages who are as authoritative as scripture [Rashi, and Jastrow, *Dictionary*, p. 1410]); and 53b (Ulla – Rav and Shmuel); Hullin 18b (Rav Yosef – Rav Yehuda); 43b-44a (Mar b. d'Ravina says he objects "against the enemies of Rava." As Rashi notes, Mar b. d'Ravina is speaking euphemistically since he actually objects against Rava. Uncomfortable about objecting against his superior, he employs this circumlocution); 54a (R. Yohanan and Resh Lakish – Rav); 68b (Ulla – Rav and Shmuel); 76a (Rav Yehuda – Shmuel); 105a (Shmuel – his father); and 137b (R. Yohanan – Rav); and possibly Shabbat 108b

expressions of special respect for contemporary or near-contemporary Amoraim.[28] In contrast, we find comparable expressions of praise in non-contemporary commentary only five or six times.[29]

Examination of Amoraic *and Tannaitic* statements in several other tractates[30] reveals similar generational contrasts. Specifically, we find 44 to 80 cases in which Amoraic and Tannaitic commentary contains praise or expressions of special respect for contemporary or near-contemporary rabbis,[31] and only 10 to 21 cases in which Amoraim or Tannaim express praise or special respect for non-contemporaries.[32]

(Mar Ukba – Shmuel); and 111b (Rava – Rav Hiyya bar Abin); Ketubot 43b (Abimi bar Papi might respectfully refer to Shmuel as *Shekod*. The text reads: "*Shekod* said it. Who is this? Shmuel...." The identification of *Shekod* as Shmuel might be a later editorial insertion, and I therefore consider this case as uncertain praise. Regarding the term *Shekod*, see *Arukh ha-Shalem*, ed. Kohut, vol. 8, p. 147; and Jastrow, *Dictionary*, p. 1621); 61a (Rav Anan bar Tahalifa – Shmuel); and 75a (Rav Hisda – Rav Shila); Baba Mezia 8a-b (Rav Yehuda – Shmuel); 15a (Rav Nahman – Shmuel); 16b (Rav Nahman – Shmuel); and 51b (Rav Anan – Shmuel); and Hullin 29b (Rabbah bar Simi – Rav Yosef); 38a (Rav Anan – Shmuel); 43b (Rav Papi – Rav Bibi bar Abaye); 76b (the early R. Zeira – Shmuel); 90b (Rav Hisda – Rav Huna); 105a (Rav Asi – Shmuel); and 112a (Rava – Rav Hinena b. d'Rava Mipashronia). See also the story of the death of Rabbah bar Nahmani on Baba Mezia 86a, reported by Rav Kahana in the name of Rav Hama the grandson of Hasa. The precise chronological relationship between the Amoraim who are credited with transmitting the story is not entirely clear.

[28]In a personal communication of June 10, 1991, Shamma Friedman pointed out to me that the term *gavra rabbah* ("great man") might not always signify high praise. The term might sometimes refer to an individual who demonstrates expertise in Bible and Mishna rather than to an outstanding sage. See, for example, Baba Mezia 84a and Sanhedrin 30b. I therefore consider usages of this term as uncertain praise unless the context establishes clearly that high praise is intended.

[29]Shabbat 110a (Contemporaries of Abaye – Rav); Ketubot 62b (Rami bar Hama – R. Oshaya, R. Hama, and R. Bisa) and 63b (Rav Nahman bar Yizhak – R. Hanina [see *DS* Herschler, notes on line 15, and n. 21]); Hullin 28a-b (Rava – R. Yohanan) and 50a (Rava – R. Yohanan); and possibly Ketubot 106a (see Appendix 2, below).

[30]Berakhot, Eruvin, Pesahim, Yoma, Yevamot, Gittin, Baba Batra, Zevahim, and Niddah.

[31]Berakhot 12a (Shmuel – Rav); 30b (R. Zeira – R. Yohanan); 33b (R. Zeira – R. Hiyya bar Abba); 38b (R. Zeira – R. Hiyya bar Abba); and 63a (R. Yosi ben Kippar and the grandson of Zechariah ben Kevutal – R. Akiba); Eruvin 11a (Rav Yosef – Rav); 12b (R. Zeira – Rav Yehuda and Rav Hiyya bar Ashi); 13b (Rabbi – R. Meir); 13b (R. Yohanan – Sumkhos); 53a (R. Yohanan – R. Oshaya); 66a (Rav Sheshet – R. Zeira); 79b (Rava or Rabbah – Rav Yehuda); and 79b-80a (Amemar – The sages of Pumbedita); Pesahim 48a (R. Yirmiya – Rami bar Hama); 51a (Rabbah bar bar Hana – R. Yohanan); 51a-b (R. Yohanan ben Elazar and R. Shimon ben Lakunia – R. Shimon bar Yohai); 53b-54a (Rav Yosef – Ulla and Rabbah bar bar Hana); and 113b (Rava or Rabbah – Rav Hananya and Rav Oshaya. See Albeck, *Mavo la-Talmudim*, p. 221); Yevamot 35a (Rav Amram – Rav Sheshet); 58a (Rav Amram –

Rav Sheshet); and 64b (Abaye – Rabin); Gittin 6b (Abaye – R. Evyatar); 19b (Ulla –
R. Elazar); 59a (Rav Aha b. d'Rava – Rav Ashi); 67a (Rabbi – R. Yosi); 67a (Isi ben
Yehuda – R. Meir, R. Yehuda, R. Tarfon, R. Yishmael, R. Akiba, R. Yohanan ben
Nuri, R. Elazar ben Azariah, R. Eliezer ben Yaakov, R. Yosi, and R. Shimon); and
79a (Rami bar Hama – Rav Hisda); Baba Batra 8b (Rav – Rav Shmuel bar Shelat);
51b (Ravana Ukba and Ravana Nehemia, grandsons of Rav – Rav; and Rav Hisda
– R. Yohanan); 53b (Rav Amram – Rav Sheshet); 82b (R. Zeira – R. Elazar); 125b
(R. Elazar – Rav Huna); 154b (R. Zeira – Rav Yosef); and 171b (Rav Yizhak bar
Yosef – Rav and Shmuel [see *DS* samekh]); Zevahim 44a (R. Yirmiya – Rav Yosef)
and 100b (R. Yirmiya – Rav Yosef); Niddah 13a (Shmuel – Rav Yehuda); 20a (R.
Hanina – Bar Kappara); 20b (R. Yohanan – R. Hanina); 20b (R. Elazar – R.
Hanina); 20b (Ulla – R. Elazar); 61b (Rava – Rav Hisda); 65a (Shmuel – Rav); and
70a (Rav Sheshet – Shmuel); and possibly Berakhot 20a (Abaye – Rav Yehuda.
The same statement is also found on Taanit 24a and Sanhedrin 105b, attributed to
different Amoraim); 39b (Rav Nahman bar Yizhak – Mar b. d'Ravina); and 49b
(Rav Nahman – Shmuel); Eruvin 6b (Rav Anan – Shmuel); 20a (Abaye – Rabbah);
22a (Rava – Rav Ada bar Matna); 30a (Rav Nahman bar Yizhak – Rav Yosef. See,
for example, Berakhot 64a, where Rav Yosef is identified as Sinai); 38b (Rabbah
bar Rav Hanan – Rabbah); 45a (Rabbah bar Rav Hanan – Rabbah); 53a (R.
Yohanan – R. Oshaya); 54b (R. Yizhak ben Elazar – R. Elazar ben Pedat); 67b
(Abaye – Rabbah); 81a (Mar Ukba – Shmuel); and 89a (Abaye – Rabbah); Pesahim
54a (Rabbah – Shmuel or Rav Papa – Rava); 101a (Abaye – Rabbah); 101a (Abaye
– Rabbah); and 108a (Abaye – Rabbah); Yoma 49a (R. Hanina – R. Yehoshua ben
Levi); Yevamot 21b (Rav Hisda – R. Ami); 92b (Resh Lakish – R. Yannai. Resh
Lakish may or may not be speaking in R. Yannai's presence); and 113a (Rava –
Rav Malkio); Gittin 44b (Rav Anan – Shmuel); 59a (R. Hillel b. d'R. Vals – Rabbi);
59a (Rav Mordechai – Rav Ashi); and 59b (Abaye – Rabbah); Baba Batra 8b
([twice] Abaye – Rabbah); 38b (Rav Anan – Shmuel); 62b (Abaye – Rabbah); 88a
(Rava – R. Zeira); 88a (Rav Oshaya – Rav Safra); 115b (Rabbah – Shmuel or Rav
Papa – Rava); and 170a (Abaye – Rabbah); Zevahim 43b (Rava – the later Rav
Yizhak bar Avdimi and R. Zeira); and Niddah 25b (Rav Ami bar Shmuel –
Shmuel).

[32]Berakhot 61b (Rav – R. Hanina ben Dosa); Eruvin 13b (R. Aha bar Hanina
– R. Meir); 53a (R. Yohanan – R. Elazar ben Shamua and possibly R. Akiba); 53a
(R. Yohanan – R. Meir); and 67b (Rava – R. Yohanan); Yoma 53b (Rav Yosef – R.
Hanina ben Dosa); 69b (R. Yehoshua ben Levi – The men of the great assembly);
and 85b (Rav Nahman bar Yizhak or Ravina – Shmuel); Gittin 18b-19a (R.
Yehoshua ben Levi – R. Shimon); Niddah 6a (Rabbi – R. Eliezer); and possibly
Eruvin 39b-40a (Amemar – Rav Sheshet [see below]); Pesahim 54a (Rava –
Shmuel); Gittin 59a (Rabbah b. d'Rava – Rabbi) and 59a (Rav Aha b. d'Rava –
Rabbi); Baba Batra 115b (Rava – Shmuel); and Zevahim 43b (Rava – the early Rav
Yizhak bar Avdimi and Zeiri). On Eruvin 39b-40a, Rav Ashi quotes Amemar's
alternative version of a story involving Rav Sheshet and Rav Nahman. The
anonymous editors correctly point out that Amemar's version implies that the
dialogue between Sheshet and Rabbah bar Shmuel never took place. This
dialogue portrays Sheshet in an unflattering light, asking Rabbah bar Shmuel to
suppress a Tannaitic source which supports his opponents. Perhaps Amemar's
version arose as a deliberate attempt to neutralize the criticism of Sheshet
contained in this source. See, however, the discussion below. See also Eruvin

2. Hostility

The Statements of Rav

Examination of statements by Rav supports my contention that hostile commentary is attributed almost exclusively to contemporaries and near-contemporaries. Rav Sheshet, separated from Rav by a full generation, responds negatively to Rav's statements and actions with relative frequency, remarking eight times that "Rav said this while lying down drowsing."[33] Later Amoraim, however, never express comparable sentiments toward Rav.[34]

In his only objection against a statement by Shmuel, Sheshet expresses surprise that a "great man like Shmuel would say such a thing."[35] I could discern no qualitative difference between Shmuel's and Rav's statements, supporting my claim that the tone of Sheshet's criticisms indicates an unfavorable opinion of Rav, and not merely disapproval of Rav's views in these specific contexts.[36]

79b, where Rav Haviva's reference to Rav Yehuda as "the elders of Pumbedita" mimics Rava's or Rabbah's earlier references to Rav Yehuda in this fashion.

In addition, on Pesahim 51a Rabbah bar bar Hana quotes praise of R. Shimon by earlier rabbis, perhaps indicating his especially high regard for a rabbi who preceded him by several generations. Similar cases are found on Berakhot 63a (R. Abahu and Rav Safra – R. Akiba); Yevamot 49b (Shimon ben Azai – the early R. Eliezer ben Yaakov); Gittin 58a (Rav and Rav Yehuda – the son and daughter of R. Yishmael ben Elisha); and Baba Batra 165b (Amemar, Rav Ashi, Mar bar Hiyya, and Ravina – R. Yirmiya). These five cases are included in the statistics as uncertain cases of non-contemporary praise.

[33]See the references cited above.

[34]On Pesahim 104a and Kiddushin 71b, either Rav Yosef or Abaye curse "with regard to it [i.e., a previously stated opinion of Rav]," perhaps meaning that they curse statements by Rav (On Moed Katan 12b, all versions agree that the author is Abaye). Even according to this interpretation, Sheshet's statements are more personal, since he explicitly directs his comments to Rav ("Rav said this while lying down drowsing"), whereas Abaye and/or Yosef direct their curses to the opinion. In addition, the expression "Rav Yosef [or Abaye] cursed with regard to it" is closely related to, and very likely synonymous with, another expression: "Rabbi X cursed one who" followed a particular view. In other words, the expression "cursed with regard to it" very likely means that Abaye and/or Yosef are not cursing Rav's opinion, but rather are cursing one who follows Rav's opinion. See, for example, Rashi on Kiddushin 33b and R. Shlomo ben ha-Yatom on Moed Katan 12b. See Masoret ha-Shas on Kiddushin 33b. Incidentally, we find no hint of animosity toward Rav attributed to either Yosef or Abaye in other contexts.

[35]Niddah 70a.

[36]See also Moed Katan 24b for Sheshet's comment on a statement by R. Yizhak, a third-generation Palestinian sage. See also Shabbat 43a-b.

Some of these eight cases may simply be the result of editorial mimicry of an Amoraic expression.[37] The expression perhaps became known as one of Sheshet's signature phrases, and later editors who bore no ill will toward Rav perhaps added it where they thought it was applicable. It is unlikely, however, that most or even the majority of these cases reflect editorial mimicry. More likely, they indicate real hostility toward Rav.

Shmuel's relationship with Rav, more fully documented than any other relationship between first-generation rabbis, will further illustrate the distinction between contemporary and non-contemporary commentary. In most cases, however, Rav's and Shmuel's opinions about one another must be considered doubtful commentary, since scribes may have mistakenly omitted a word or phrase and changed dialogue into commentary.

Rav's and Shmuel's commentary reveals a combination of harsh opposition and fierce competition between the two sages.[38] Shmuel acerbically dismisses opinions by Rav with the declaration that "if Rav said this, then he knows nothing about the laws of Shabbat,"[39] or about defects in animals which render them unfit for human consumption,[40] and the like.[41] Rav Tahalifa bar Avdimi decides a case in conformity with Shmuel's view and against Rav's, and Rav declares his actions to be "ruinous."[42] Elsewhere, Shmuel responds in the same fashion when Rav Yosef b. d'Rav Menashya Midevil decides in favor of Rav.[43] In another context, when R. Elazar reports Rav's opinion before Shmuel, Shmuel commands his attendants to "stuff Elazar with barley [animal fodder]."[44]

---

[37]See, for example, Friedman, *Perek ha-Isha Rabbah ba-Bavli,* pp. 87-99.

[38]My point is not that Talmudic accounts of Amoraic attitudes toward Rav add up to a consistent, coherent portrait. Some accounts are contradictory and may derive from diverse sources. In addition to the attitudes expressed by Rav and Shmuel toward one another documented here, for example, we also find examples of cooperation and profound respect. See Kalmin, "Saints or Sinners, Scholars or Ignoramuses? Stories About the Rabbis as Evidence for the Composite Nature of the Babylonian Talmud," pp. 187-89.

[39]Shabbat 53a.

[40]Hullin 45b.

[41]Moed Katan 12b. See also Kiddushin 44b for Rav's reaction to what he mistakenly believes is the opinion of Shmuel. See also Shmuel's sarcastic reaction on Berakhot 60b.

[42]Bezah 16b.

[43]Kiddushin 79b.

[44]Ketubot 77a.

Such reactions recede as we move later in the Amoraic period, ceasing altogether in commentary attributed to rabbis who post-date Rav Sheshet.

Rav Sheshet

Analysis of statements by Rav Sheshet, a third-generation Babylonian Amora, further illustrates the above claims. Sheshet and contemporaries and near-contemporaries occasionally criticize one another, but we find no comparable criticisms of or by non-contemporaries.

Sheshet's hostility toward Rav was mentioned above. Elsewhere, Rava might criticize Sheshet, referring either to Sheshet or to Rav Ahdevui bar Ami (also a third-generation Amora) as "a child who debased his mother."[45] In another context, Rava perhaps denies Rami bar Hama's claim that Sheshet is an extraordinary man.[46]

Rav Yosef

Analysis of statements by Rav Yosef yields patterns similar to those described above. In one context, Yosef, a third-generation Amora, questions the reliability of R. Evyatar, a second-generation Amora, and offers as proof Evyatar's violation of the halacha.[47] In another context, Yosef boastfully claims responsibility for the death of Rav Ada bar Ahava.[48]

As the chronological distance grows, however, the substance of statements by earlier rabbis becomes the exclusive concern of Yosef's commentary. Yosef twice criticizes statements by rabbis separated from him by a generation or more, but most likely he (or whoever recorded these sentiments in his name) reacts to the substance of the statement and bears no special ill-feeling toward the statement's author.

Specifically, in one context Yosef is troubled by R. Yehuda ha-Nasi's silence during Avdan's attempted humiliation of R. Yishmael b'R. Yosi, and criticizes his inaction.[49] Yosef's statement is merely criticism of Yehuda ha-Nasi's actions in one specific context, and reveals no special

---

[45]Baba Batra 9a-b.
[46]Baba Mezia 16a. Rami bar Hama exclaims, "Behold the man (i.e., Sheshet) and behold the objection!" Rava remarks, "I see the man, but I do not see the objection." Perhaps Rava shares Rami's high opinion of Sheshet, but simply denies that in this particular instance Sheshet's argument is decisive. On the other hand, perhaps Rava suggests that Sheshet is a man and nothing more, in contrast to Rami, who implies that Sheshet is an extraordinary man.
[47]Gittin 6b. See also Shabbat 142b, Eruvin 29a, Pesahim 52b, and Zevahim 118b.
[48]Baba Batra 22a.
[49]Yevamot 105b.

ill-feeling toward the patriarch. Elsewhere, Yosef criticizes a Tanna, R. Hillel,[50] exclaiming, "May his master [i.e., God] forgive R. Hillel" for claiming that "There will be no messiah for Israel, for they already enjoyed him during the days of Hezekiah." Hillel's opinion, however, is clearly at odds with the common rabbinic belief in the coming of the messiah. Yosef most likely reacts to the substance of the statement, a reaction not fueled by particular concern for the character of its author, R. Hillel.[51]

Rami bar Hama

Analysis of Amoraic commentary based on statements by Rami bar Hama, a third- and fourth-generation Babylonian Amora, yields similar results. Examination of this commentary reveals the following picture: The person, Rami bar Hama, is of intense concern to Rava, Rami's younger contemporary, but not at all to subsequent generations. Rava's attitude toward Rami, as expressed in his commentary, can best be described as ambivalent. The two Amoraim are portrayed as subordinates of Rav Hisda, and on one occasion are depicted as study partners. Both are Hisda's sons-in-law, with Rami predeceasing Rava and Rava marrying his widow. Their lives, therefore, are intimately intertwined, and supply clear motivation for a complex relationship. Psychohistory is a perilous undertaking when applied to Talmudic personalities, however, and we must be careful to avoid the anachronistic projection of modern preoccupations onto ancient personalities. I note these details because they may shed light on other aspects of their relationship (see below), but whatever biographical conclusions we draw must be considered extremely tentative. For the reasons stated above, the possibility that later generations created this material cannot be discounted.

Rava's strongest expression of disapproval toward Rami comes in response to Rami's refusal to count Rav Menashya bar Tahalifa as one of three learned men included in the preliminary invitation to say the

---

[50]Sanhedrin 99a.

[51]See also Gittin 56b, where either Yosef or R. Akiba react to Yohanan ben Zakkai's failure to respond effectively to Vespasian, the future Roman emperor, just prior to the destruction of Jerusalem. According to Yosef or Akiba, God deliberately confounds Yohanan's speech, directly intervening at this criticial juncture in Jewish history and causing Yohanan to request a scholarly refuge at Yavneh rather than an end to the Roman siege. Yosef (or Akiba) does not criticize Yohanan, but rather transforms the encounter into an act of God, eliminating Yohanan's responsibility for the final outcome. See also the discussion above, where we discuss criticisms by non-contemporaries in response to specific literary sources.

blessing after meals.[52] Rami considers Menashya to be an *am ha-arez*, a less than full-fledged member of the rabbinic elite, and therefore excludes him. A report of Rami's death follows, and Rava claims that Rami died because of his exclusion of Menashya, implying that Rami's death came as punishment for the insufficient respect he displayed toward another scholar.

Rava's ambivalent attitude toward Rami is most clearly expressed in one context in which Rami induces his superior, Hisda, to reverse roles and perform a menial task on Rami's behalf, like a student serving his teacher. In exchange for Hisda's service, Rami agrees to reveal his interpretation of a mishna. Rava reacts with amazement and very likely more than a hint of jealousy in response to Hisda's acceptance of Rami's argument, which he thinks is faulty. Someone whose master favors him can do whatever he pleases without losing his master's favor, exclaims Rava, and he proceeds to refute Rami's reasoning.[53]

Rava likewise expresses ambivalence toward Rami in three contexts in which he credits him with *harifut*, sharpness and keen discernment, but claims that this very strength led him to *shabeshta*, careless error (see above).[54] The fact that Rami is singled out for this criticism in diverse contexts is indicative of criticism of Rami the person and not merely of the substance of Rami's statements. Rava also criticizes Rami's *shabeshta* in one context[55] without accompanying praise of his *harifut*.[56]

Rava portrays Rami as a formidable but one-dimensional scholar, therefore, a portrayal also found in the story which unfavorably compares Rami to Rav Sheshet, examined in detail in the introductory chapter.

Despite some obscurities, several aspects of Rava's attitude are comprehensible, and the portrait which emerges is perfectly believable as the ambivalent reaction by one rabbi toward a contemporary. The Talmud might preserve Rava's actual attitude toward Rami (or at least remnants of this attitude, since a complete picture does not emerge from the scattered facts about their relationship provided by the Talmud), but a later editorial role cannot be excluded. Perhaps the Talmud provides direct access not to Rava's attitude, but to subsequent generations' versions of what that attitude was. We must also make allowances for a degree of editorial standardization which all Amoraic statements have

---

[52]Berakhot 47b.
[53]Baba Kamma 20b.
[54]Eruvin 90a, Baba Mezia 96a-b, and Niddah 33a-b.
[55]Baba Batra 116a-b.
[56]See, however, Halivni, *Mekorot u-Mesorot:* Eruvin-Pesahim, pp. 233-34.

undergone, and cannot presume to have Rava's original words.[57] Were we to have a more complete record of Amoraic reaction to Rami, furthermore, we might discover different versions of Rava's attitude toward Rami, as we found to be the case numerous times in chapter 1, above.

R. Yirmiya

Amoraic commentary on statements by R. Yirmiya, and Yirmiya's commentary on statements by contemporaries and predecessors, further illustrates the above claims.

Yirmiya, it is important to bear in mind, is depicted by Talmudic sources as a third-generation Amora who began his career in Babylonia and eventually moved to Palestine. With rare exceptions, Yirmiya's commentary reflects hostility toward contemporary and near-contemporary Babylonian Amoraim. For example, commenting on statements by Rav Sheshet,[58] Rabbah,[59] and Rav Nahman,[60] Yirmiya derides the "stupid Babylonians" who make "obscure statements" because they live in a dark land.

Yirmiya's Babylonian contemporaries and near-contemporaries respond to Yirmiya with comparable sentiments. Rava uses Yirmiya as illustration of his point that Babylonian scholars are superior to Palestinians. While in Babylonia, claims Rava, Yirmiya failed to understand rabbinic discourse, but upon moving to Palestine he became an esteemed scholar who ridicules his Babylonian superiors. Rava argues that the standards are lower in Palestine, allowing a scholar of Yirmiya's caliber to rise above his contemporaries and ridicule his Babylonian superiors with impunity. Elsewhere, Rava displays knowledge of, and discomfort with, one of Yirmiya's insulting references to the "stupid Babylonians." Rava rejects an argument advanced by his subordinate, Rav Papa, remarking that "up until now they have called us stupid, now they will call us the stupid among the stupid."[61] Rava accepts the logic of Yirmiya's argument, but is stung by his criticism of Babylonian scholars.[62]

---

[57]See Green, "What's in a Name? – The Problematic of Rabbinic 'Biography,'" pp. 77-96.

[58]Pesahim 34b.

[59]Yoma 57a and Menahot 52a. The printed editions read Rava in both places, but Rabbah is preferable chronologically. See chapter 10, below.

[60]Bekhorot 25b. See also Zevahim 60b. See also Sanhedrin 24a, where Yirmiya ridicules Babylonian learning.

[61]Yoma 57a.

[62]For another disapproving remark by a Babylonian rabbi directed at Yirmiya, see Rav Aha bar Yaakov's comment on Niddah 23a.

Along these same lines, Abaye once refuses to accept an opinion reported to him in Yirmiya's name, but accepts the same opinion reported to him later on in the name of R. Yohanan.[63] Abaye remarks that "if I had been worthy, I would have learned the tradition in the first place," although his meaning is not entirely clear. Perhaps he reasons as follows: The statement was first reported to him in the name of an unacceptable authority, causing him to postpone memorization of a correct opinion. According to this understanding, Abaye reasons that he was lacking in merit to begin with, and the heavenly powers hindered his learning. This passage perhaps depicts contemporary animosity toward Yirmiya missing from later commentary on his statements.

The situation changes dramatically when we turn to commentary on statements by Yirmiya by Amoraim who post-date him by a single generation or more. In contrast to Yirmiya's relationships with contemporaries, we find no hint of hostility toward him in later Amoraic commentary on his statements.

The Talmud might accurately preserve the basic tenor of Yirmiya's attitudes toward Babylonian scholars and Babylonian reaction to Yirmiya. The same reservations expressed above about the trustworthiness of biographical data, however, apply with equal force here.

Implications for Study of the Talmud's Anonymous Commentary

In the following discussion, I argue that commentary by the Talmud's anonymous editors is distinguishable from commentary by Amoraim. This conclusion further supports my claim that the Talmud is comprised of diverse, objectively identifiable sources.

First, anonymous commentary, unlike commentary by Amoraim (both contemporary and non-contemporary), occasionally neutralizes the criticisms of rabbis found in attributed sources and makes peace between sages when the sources portray conflict.[64] Anonymous commentators show their high regard for rabbis by "reinterpreting" sources which depict these rabbis in an unfavorable light. Amoraim, both contemporary and non-contemporary, do not display the same tendency to reduce conflict and neutralize criticism. Second, the anonymous editors, in contrast to attributed rabbis, both contemporary and non-

---

[63]Shabbat 21b.

[64]The anonymous editors only infrequently remove insults against earlier rabbis (see below). For the most part, they leave the offending passages untouched. Perhaps systematic study would reveal patterns to the editors' decisions to comment on certain sources and to ignore others, but I have not been able to discern any as yet.

contemporary, tend to express their high regard for individual rabbis by supplying the rationale behind all opinions in a dispute, even those rejected for halachic purposes. They use respectful epithets such as "a lion of the company" or "a fearer of heaven" in referring to rabbis only when prompted by exegetical motives, notably the need to reconcile contradictory sources. Third, anonymous commentary, unlike commentary by contemporary Amoraim, is almost totally devoid of criticism of sages and is concerned much more with the substance of a statement than with the statement's author.

The first two characteristics mentioned above, it bears emphasizing, distinguish anonymous commentary from commentary by all Amoraim, both contemporary and non-contemporary. The third characteristic distinguishes anonymous commentary from contemporary Amoraic commentary, but not from commentary by non-contemporary Amoraim.

Because the Talmud's editorial commentary is anonymous, it is frequently indistinguishable from the Amoraic sources on which it is based. Often it is only through complicated critical analysis of a discussion that the seams separating the editors from the Amoraim become visible. The methods used in this study to distinguish between anonymous commentators and attributed sources were developed, and continue to be developed, by David Halivni, Shamma Friedman, and others,[65] and these methods have found wide, but not universal, acceptance in modern Talmudic scholarship. The present study, therefore, which uses Friedman's and Halivni's methods and discovers significant distinctions between Amoraic and anonymous literature, supports the theoretical framework devised by these scholars for subdividing the Talmudic corpus. In the final analysis, the results obtained through application of a theory represent the most effective test of the validity of that theory, and the results of the present study indicate that the methods of these scholars contribute to our understanding of the various components of Talmudic literature.

To be specific, examination of several Talmudic tractates[66] reveals 5 cases in which the anonymous editors speak highly of specific individuals in response to exegetical concerns.[67] On Niddah 25b, for example, the editors resolve a contradiction between Shmuel's own

---

[65]See the references cited in the Introduction, above.
[66]Berakhot, Eruvin, Pesahim, Yoma, Yevamot, Gittin, Baba Batra, Zevahim, and Niddah.
[67]Berakhot 45b (Rav Papa), Pesahim 110a (Rava, Abaye, and Rav Nahman bar Yizhak), Yevamot 60a (R. Eliezer ben Yaakov), Baba Batra 31b (R. Yehuda, R. Elazar, and R. Shimon ben Elazar), and Niddah 25b (Shmuel) and 64b (Shmuel). See also Baba Batra 10b (R. Akiba and his fellows).

actions and his statements in other contexts by positing that Shmuel's "strength," i.e., his expertise, entitles him to judge differently than others.

In addition, examination of these tractates reveals 9 or 10 cases in which anonymous praise is motivated by stories in which a rabbi acts or appears to act immorally or in violation of the halacha. The editors insist upon the protagonist's righteousness, neutralizing the criticism contained in their sources or "reinterpreting" his actions so that they conform to the editors' standards of acceptable conduct.[68] On Yoma 84a, for example, R. Yohanan receives medical advice from "a certain [non-Jewish] matron" on condition that he not reveal it. Yohanan "swears to the God of Israel: 'I will not reveal it,'" but announces it in public the very next day. The editors wonder at Yohanan's action, and explain that Yohanan actually "swears: 'To the God of Israel I will not reveal it,'" i.e., he will not reveal it to the God of Israel, but will reveal it to the people of Israel. "But is not the name of God profaned?" the editors object, and they answer that Yohanan explained his vow to the matron and therefore was guilty of no deception. The story itself, however, supplies no indication that Yohanan explained his vow. The editors interpret Yohanan's actions in a forced manner, defending against the suggestion that he engages in unethical conduct.

A brief example of the editors' tendency to make peace where the sources portray conflict is provided by one context in which Rav's refusal to enter a building ahead of Shmuel[69] is explained by the editors as an attempt on Rav's part to make amends for his earlier curse of Shmuel. This curse consisted of a successful prayer for the death of Shmuel's male children.[70] Rav and Shmuel are not bitter enemies, the editors would have us believe. Perhaps they began as such, but were eventually reconciled, and now Rav wishes to appease his colleague by showing him special respect.

The editors' habit of giving both sides of an issue, of supplying the reasoning behind even rejected views, is perhaps further manifestation of their tendency to guide earlier portrayals of sages toward the same positive conclusion. The editors, in contrast to Amoraim, often (but by no means always) avoid refutation of earlier views, even those of Bet Shammai, whose opinions are virtually never accepted as law. They struggle to show the logic of R. Eliezer's view, even though the final

---

[68]Eruvin 39b-40a (Rav Sheshet), Yoma 84a (R. Yohanan) and 87a-b (R. Hanina), Yevamot 96b (R. Elazar and R. Yosi) and 99b (R. Elazar bar Zadok), Gittin 7a (R. Hanina ben Gamliel), Baba Batra 3b-4a (Rava ben Buti), Zevahim 102b (R. Elazar b'R. Shimon), Niddah 20b (Rav Yizhak b. d'Rav Yehuda), and possibly Niddah 20a-b (R. Hanina and R. Yishmael b'R. Yosi).
[69]Baba Kamma 80a-b.
[70]Shabbat 108a.

ruling almost always goes against him, perhaps further manifestation of their desire to protect the reputations of the greats of the past.

Further illustration[71] of the claim that anonymous editorial commentary is distinguishable from Amoraic commentary is provided by a narrative in which the patriarch, R. Yehuda ha-Nasi, grants full rabbinic authority to Rabbah bar Hana, permitting him to judge, to issue practical halachic decisions, and to determine the ritual status of first-born animals. The patriarch grants Rav, however, the former two prerogatives but denies him the third.[72]

The anonymous editors ask why Yehuda ha-Nasi treats Rav and Rabbah bar Hana differently. The editors answer by quoting Rav's own testimony that he was expert in the laws of first-born animals, and argue that Yehuda ha-Nasi was concerned lest Rav's decisions in these matters not be fully comprehended by others less knowledgeable. Rav's very expertise was potentially a source of danger, according to the editors, for others might observe him and arrive at misunderstandings about the law.

Alternatively, the editors suggest, Yehuda ha-Nasi grants fewer prerogatives to Rav because he wishes to bolster Rabbah bar Hana's reputation in the eyes of Babylonian Jews, who might otherwise not be inclined to respect him. Rav, however, will win the people's respect on his own merits, and needs no help from the patriarchate.[73]

The anonymous editors are perhaps attempting to resolve the discrepancy between this story's conception of the importance of Rav and the Talmud's dominant conception. The story perhaps considers Rav to be Rabbah bar Hana's inferior, in contrast to the dominant Talmudic conception, which views Rav as superior. The editors therefore assert that Rav's greatness, or Rabbah bar Hana's insecure position in the eyes of his contemporaries, explains Yehuda ha-Nasi's preference for the "wrong" sage.

Alternatively, however, the editors are perhaps motivated by a desire to create harmony where the sources portray conflict. This desire leads to their refusal to interpret the patriarch's actions as evidence of a

---

[71]See also Appendix 4, below.

[72]Sanhedrin 5a-b.

[73]In explaining the editors' alternative response, I have accepted the interpretation of Rashi and Yad Rama. These commentators read quite a lot into the editors' brief remark, but I have no fully satisfactory alternative to suggest. In any case, the editors' first response supports my contention here.

For manuscript variants of this story, see Rosental, "Rav Ben-Ahi R. Hiyya Gam Ben-Ahoto?", pp. 289-307. The sections of the story which Rosental identifies as late additions have not been included in my description of the narrative.

lack of complete favor toward Rav, or as a shrewd attempt on the part of a skilled politician to maintain control over an individual he perceives as a potential threat, both of which are likely interpretations of the story.[74]

According to both interpretations, it bears emphasizing, this example illustrates the unique nature of the Talmud's anonymous commentary. According to the first interpretation, the editors affirm Rav's greatness in the face of the story's presentation of an opposing view. According to the second interpretation, the editors claim that the patriarch acts out of a desire to see that the law is properly observed and the sages properly respected, smoothing over the conflict between sages implicit in the story.

Perhaps my findings have implications for the dating or authorship of the Talmud's anonymous commentary. Many scholars believe that this commentary was composed late in the Talmudic period, but as I argue in a recent study, the case can hardly be considered closed.[75] Perhaps my current findings shed light on this difficult problem, which has perplexed scholars for generations. Perhaps the distinctions between Amoraic and anonymous editorial commentary prove that the Amoraim and the anonymous editors cannot be the same people and therefore date from different time periods. Or that they operated simultaneously but independently, leaving behind different literatures composed by different groups at the same time.

The distinctions between editorial and Amoraic commentary, however, might derive from the different roles these commentaries play and tell us nothing about who authored them or when they were composed. Amoraim who polemicize against contemporaries and near-contemporaries are perhaps completely evenhanded when commenting, as editors, on statements by the same individuals. Perhaps as named Amoraim they insult and criticize, and express their dislikes and ambivalences, while as anonymous editors they refuse to do so, and struggle to make the sages seem uniformly righteous and their arguments uniformly reasonable.

To use an imperfect modern analogy, an author who signs his name to an article in a journal might be free to express negative opinions regarding a particular public figure. The editors of the same publication, however, might struggle to maintain neutrality, for example by soliciting contributions from authors representing opposing points of view. The same individual, in fact, in the same publication, might express himself

---

[74]See also Urbach, *Ha-Halacha*, pp. 192-93; and Gafni, *Yehudei Bavel bi-Tekufat ha-Talmud*, pp. 100-1.

[75]Kalmin, *The Redaction of the Babylonian Talmud*, pp. 1-11 and 51-94.

one way as an author and another way as an anonymous editor, an advocate on the one hand and a disinterested observer on the other. To be sure, the different roles of editors and authors can express themselves in a variety of ways in the modern and ancient worlds. My point is simply that the distinction suggested above between editors and Amoraim is a reasonable one, and not an arbitrary invention on my part.

The findings of the present study, therefore, provide no clear answer to the problem of the chronology of anonymous commentary or the identity of its authors.

9

Middle-Generation Amoraim as Among the Editors of the Talmud

Throughout Part 1, we repeatedly portrayed middle-generation Babylonian Amoraim as transitional. The present chapter argues that these transitional features may reveal the role of third- and fourth-generation Amoraim in the editing of earlier Amoraic statements. This chapter thus draws together the diverse source analyses of Part 1 and suggests that they reveal a historical phenomenon.

Throughout Part 1, first-, second-, and third-generation Amoraic statements and stories repeatedly followed one set of patterns, and post-third-generation Amoraim followed a different set. We found that (1) Amoraic statements decrease in number after the third generation, with the decrease especially pronounced after the fourth generation[1]; (2) Post-third-generation Amoraim respond differently to the authority and statements of Rav and Shmuel than do Amoraim of the first, second, and third generations. Post-third-generation Amoraim tend to minimize distinctions between Rav and Shmuel and to view them as a unit; (3) Babylonian Amoraim of the fourth generation and later comment on statements by R. Yohanan, a prominent Palestinian sage, as frequently as they comment on statements by Shmuel, a prominent Babylonian. Earlier Babylonian Amoraim comment much more frequently on statements by Shmuel than on statements by Yohanan; (4) Dialogue chains involving Rava and his subordinates are more prevalent than those involving early Amoraim (see chapter 6); (5) Early Palestinian Amoraic discourse and interactions differ from those of early Babylonian Amoraim. In two cases, the earliest attested Babylonian parallels involve fourth-generation Amoraim (see chapter 5); (6) Quotation forms introducing statements by post-fourth-generation Amoraim differ from those introducing statements by pre-fourth-generation Amoraim. Fourth-generation Amoraic quotations exhibit characteristics of both pre-

---

[1]See chapter 2 and Appendix 3 of chapter 8, above. See also chapter 10, below.

and post-fourth-generation materials; and (7) Fourth-generation Amoraim quote much less frequently than do earlier Amoraim, and post-fourth-generation Amoraim quote even less.[2]

We also have reason to believe that (8) relatively little non-halachic material is attributed to or involves post-third-generation Amoraim. Even taking account of the general decrease in attributed Amoraic statements after the third generation (see #1, above), the decrease in non-halachic material seems impressive, particularly in statements attributed to and stories involving post-fourth-generation Amoraim. This issue, however, is in need of further study.

The transitional character of the middle Amoraic period (i.e., the third and fourth generations) has been documented by earlier studies as well. This period, for example, is portrayed as a time during which rabbinic academic institutions become increasingly complex.[3] In addition, statements attributed to third- and fourth-generation Amoraim are frequently argumentational, in contrast to statements attributed to earlier Amoraim, which tend to be prescriptive and interpretive (see below).[4]

This lengthy list of transitions does not negate the importance of changes assigned by the Talmud to Amoraic generations other than the fourth. It also does not nullify the substantial continuities between the earlier and later Amoraic periods. The concentration of phenomena pointing to the fourth, and to a lesser extent the third, generations as transitional, however, is difficult to deny.

What is the significance of these findings? Do the changing sources attest to (1) institutional developments, (2) shifts in the role of the rabbi, or (3) a turning point in the formation of the Talmud? Perhaps they indicate that the middle-Amoraic generations began a period of extensive editing, although due to our incomplete understanding of the history of

---

[2] I refer, of course, to quotations transmitted in forms A-C described in chapter 7, above. Other forms of quotation were not included in that survey.

[3] Goodblatt, *Rabbinic Instruction in Sasanian Babylonia*, pp. 166-69 and 185-87; and Gafni, *Yehudei Bavel bi-Tekufat ha-Talmud*, pp. 190, 210-13, and 223-26.

[4] See Weiss, *Al ha-Yezira ha-Sifrutit Shel ha-Amoraim*, pp. 10-23, who argues that second-generation Palestinians, R. Yohanan and Resh Lakish, were the originators of lengthy argumentation, and that the form they developed subsequently influenced discourse in Babylonia. See also Kraemer, *Stylistic Characteristics of Amoraic Literature*, p. 138, n. 3; Kalmin, *The Redaction of the Babylonian Talmud*, pp. 51-57; Halivni, *Midrash, Mishnah, and Gemara*, p. 66; and Eliezer Diamond, *Dugma le-Mahadura Madait Im Perush le-Massekhet Taanit, Talmud Bavli, Rosh Perek Alef, be-Zeruf Mavo* (Ph.D. Dissertation, Jewish Theological Seminary, 1990), pp. 6-7.

the period and the development of Talmudic literature, this explanation is at present speculative.[5]

Traditions and schools which earlier Amoraic sources portray as separate, it will be recalled, appear to converge during the fourth generation (#3 and #4, above).[6] This convergence might indicate editorial activity, since editors would have an obvious interest in drawing together diverse strands of tradition. Editorial activity would also be facilitated by such a convergence.[7] Perhaps the increase in institutional complexity discernible in middle-Amoraic sources (see above) further facilitated this process, with larger groups of scholars from diverse localities gathering more frequently for extended periods of concentrated study, bringing with them diverse traditions. (This claim, it is important to note, does not contradict Part 2's characterization of the rabbinic movement in fourth-generation Babylonia as diverse and uncentralized. It is only to suggest that, compared to earlier generations, the middle Amoraic period was a time of *increasing* institutional complexity.)

The decrease in quotation beginning in the fourth generation, coupled with the advent of a new terminology of quotation (#6 and #7, above), might also indicate editorial activity. Quotation chains, i.e., lists of rabbis involved in transmitting statements (e.g., Said Rav X... said Rav Y... said Rav Z...), generally extend from the third to the first and from the sixth to the fourth generations. In general, in other words, a transmissional boundary separates the early from the later Amoraic periods, with little quotation of first- to third-generation Amoraim by fourth- to sixth-generation Amoraim.[8] This boundary is observable both in the terminology of quotation and in the number of statements quoted. A similar boundary, with similar characteristics, separates the Amoraic from the Tannaitic periods, periods which we know to have been separated by a major work of editing (the Mishna). Perhaps similar

---

[5]Halevy, *Dorot ha-Rishonim*, vol. 2, pp. 473 and 480-500, also views fourth-generation Amoraim as active editors. See the review and evaluation of Halevy's theory in Kaplan, *The Redaction of the Babylonian Talmud*, pp. 19-25.

[6]According to one interpretation of this phenomenon suggested in chapter 2, above, the sources attest not to the convergence of traditions but to decreasing preference for the authority and statements of particular Amoraim. According to this interpretation, no editorial activity is indicated.

[7]The two activities: convergence of traditions and editing, might have mutually reinforced each other, with the former stimulating the latter, which in turn stimulated further gathering of traditions, and so on.

[8]Rava, who quotes third-generation rabbis with relative frequency, is a notable exception. Interestingly, the terminology of quotation introducing Rava's statements is the same as that introducing statements by pre-fourth-generation Amoraim (see chapter 7, above), indicating that Rava, for some reason, is depicted as "traditional" in this regard.

changes during the later period indicate that the fourth generation was also a period of extensive editing.

Supporting this conjecture is the fact, noted by earlier scholars, that use of the term *matnei* is attributed to later Amoraim much more frequently than to earlier Amoraim. This increase is especially striking in view of the relative paucity of material deriving from the later period (see above). The term indicates that an Amora transmits or has before him versions of traditions, groupings of traditions, or even full-fledged discussions,[9] and the heavy concentration of usages of this term beginning in the middle Amoraic generations might indicate that extensive editing began during this time.

As noted above, the quantity of attributed Amoraic material decreases after the third generation, with the decrease becoming particularly sharp after the fourth generation. Certain kinds of statements and stories which were common earlier become less common (#1 and #8, above). Later Amoraim, in all likelihood, were no less productive than their predecessors, so why does the Talmud record a relatively small number of their statements? A variety of different explanations can be offered, but one possibility is that later Amoraic energies were expended on editing, leaving little time for "traditional" Amoraic activity.[10]

Perhaps also relevant is the dramatic increase in argumentation beginning in the middle Amoraic period. The Talmud's anonymous editorial commentary is heavily argumentational, meaning that the standard Talmudic give-and-take is found with particular frequency in the unattributed sections of the Talmud. Perhaps the similarity between unattributed editorial statements and statements by middle-generation (and later) Amoraim is further indication that anonymous editing began during this time.

Most likely, furthermore, early Amoraic generations also played a role in the editorial process. Several of the above-mentioned features of fourth-generation Amoraic activity are observable to a lesser extent during the earlier period. If these features indicate extensive editing during the fourth generation, they perhaps indicate less extensive editing during earlier generations.

---

[9]See Wilhelm Bacher, *Tradition und Tradenten in den Schulen Palästinas und Babyloniens* (1914. Reprint; Berlin, 1966), pp. 578-89; and Lewy, *Mavo u-Ferush le-Talmud Yerushalmi*, pp. 3-13.

[10]Alternatively, perhaps there are fewer statements in the names of later Amoraim because of a lack of interest on the part of post-Amoraic generations in preserving their statements. Perhaps post-Amoraic generations concentrated their energies on preserving statements by early Amoraim, and tended to neglect those attributed to later Amoraim.

The fact that so many diverse phenomena admit of a single historical explanation constitutes a strong *prima facie* argument in its favor, although the phenomena do not *necessarily* indicate editorial activity and my claims must therefore be regarded as tentative. We know precious little about the Talmud's editing, and the observations in this chapter are offered as stimuli for further study rather than as final statements on the subject. Systematic examination of the role of fourth-generation Amoraim in Talmudic discussions is necessary before firm conclusions can be reached.

The concluding chapter, below, explains why the Talmud's portrayal of the transitional nature of middle-generation Amoraim is most likely not an editorial invention.

10

Friends and Colleagues, or Barely Acquainted?
Relationships Between Fourth-Generation Teachers in the Babylonian Talmud

The present chapter challenges conventional notions about the unified nature of the rabbinic movement in Babylonia by examining the relationship between Abaye and Rava, two of the most important Amoraim mentioned in the Talmud. This chapter argues, contrary to popular belief, that face-to-face contact between Abaye and Rava is extremely infrequent, and the lengthy dialogues between them which supposedly fill the Talmud simply do not exist.

Before I support these claims, a few preliminary definitions are in order. As noted in chapter 5, above, the term "dispute" refers to juxtaposed, contradictory Amoraic opinions which may or may not have been uttered at the same time in the same place. For example, when the Talmud uses the common dispute form: "Says Rabbi A: X; Rabbi B says: Y," we are uncertain whether or not the Amoraim involved state their opinions in each other's presence. By contrast, the term "dialogue" describes actual communication, either when the Amoraim involved speak together in each other's presence,[1] or when they communicate indirectly, via messenger. Finally, the term "dispute dialogue" refers to dialogue between Amoraim whose contradictory opinions are juxtaposed in dispute form. Put simply, dispute dialogue is dialogue between rabbis involved in a dispute.

---

[1]For further discussion of the term "dialogue," and of some problems involved in identifying dialogue in the Talmud, see the Introduction, above.

Illusory Dialogue Between Abaye and Rava

The paucity of dispute dialogue between Abaye and Rava is one of several indications that portrayals of direct contact between them are surprisingly rare. To be specific, I found a total of 232 to 257 disputes between Abaye and Rava scattered throughout more than half of the Talmud,[2] and only two cases of dispute dialogue between them.[3] This finding is one of several indications that in sharp contrast to the conventional view, Abaye and Rava had little direct contact.[4]

According to the conventional view, Abaye and Rava were extremely close colleagues who had frequent face-to-face contact in the course of which they exchanged opposing opinions and discussed these opinions in dialogues which fill the Babylonian Talmud. Yizhak Halevy, for example, speaks of a unified Babylonian academy after the death of Rav. According to Halevy, this unified academy continued in existence until the death of Rava, at which point Rava's students, Rav Nahman bar Yizhak and Rav Papa, went their separate ways.[5] According to Halevy, all Babylonian sages gathered at this unified academy, and because of the activity of the *nehutei*, sages who travelled back and forth between Palestine and Babylonia, the sages who created the Palestinian Talmud were also well represented in the unified Babylonian academy.

In answer to the problem of Abaye's well-documented link to the city of Pumbedita and Rava's equally well-documented link to Mahoza, Aharon Hyman reconstructs the following sequence of events: Rava grew up in Mahoza and studied there with Rav Nahman. Rava eventually moved to Pumbedita, where he and Abaye studied together with Rav Yosef and became close colleagues. Sometime before Rav Yosef's death, Rava returned to Mahoza as the head of his own private yeshiva. Eventually, Abaye was chosen as head of the academy in Pumbedita, and although Rava remained in Mahoza, he and Abaye

---

[2]See Appendix 1, below.
[3]Shabbat 7b and Baba Mezia 36b.
[4]See Baruch M. Bokser, *Samuel's Commentary on the Mishnah; Its Nature, Forms, and Content* (Leiden: E.J. Brill, 1975), pp. 207-15, and *Post Mishnaic Judaism in Transition*, pp. 327-51, who demonstrates that the dispute form is not necessarily (and often cannot be) indicative of face-to-face contact. He concludes that although Rav's and Shmuel's opinions are juxtaposed in dispute form throughout the Talmud, they rarely converse directly. Mielziner, *Introduction to the Talmud*, p. 262, observes that Rav and Shmuel are "rarely mentioned as having been personally engaged in debates with each other." See also Urbach, *Ha-Halacha*, pp. 197 and 202; Kalmin, "Collegial Interaction in the Babylonian Talmud," pp. 383-84 and 396-406; and chapter 5, above, and chapter 11, below.
[5]Halevy, *Dorot ha-Rishonim*, vol. 2, pp. 480-522.

remained in close contact for the rest of their lives.[6] Upon Abaye's death, Abaye's students travelled to Mahoza and studied with Rava, who now headed the unified Babylonian academy.[7]

Mordechai Yudelowitz believes that the "*havayot de-Abaye ve-Rava*,"[8] the disputes and argumentation between Abaye and Rava which fill the Talmud (but see below), date from the period of Abaye's leadership of the academy in Pumbedita.[9] David Halivni observes that "the Babylonian Talmud is replete with discussions [between Abaye and Rava] on all aspects of rabbinic learning – so much so that 'Abaye and Rava' became in later jargon a synonym for the Talmud itself."[10]

Avraham Weiss' description of the relationship between Abaye and Rava differs from that of Halevy and Hyman.[11] Weiss theorizes that some of Abaye's teachings travelled from Abaye in Pumbedita to Rava in Mahoza, transported there by rabbis who served as disciples of both Amoraim.[12] In other words, Abaye and Rava did not always dispute against one another in face-to-face confrontation.

Weiss may prefer this description of the interaction between Abaye and Rava because the Talmud contains explicit evidence that some of Abaye's statements were transported from Pumbedita to Mahoza and repeated in Rava's presence.[13] Accordingly, Abaye's statements occasionally reached Rava through intermediaries, and not simply through face-to-face contact. Furthermore, the Talmud unambiguously depicts Abaye and Rava active in different cities, with Rava already established as head in Mahoza while Abaye was still a student of Rav Yosef in Pumbedita. This picture of Rava as a mature scholar,

---

[6]Hyman, *Toldot Tannaim ve-Amoraim*, pp. 1041-47. Compare Bacher, *Die Agada der Amoräer*, p. 115, and Yehuda Leib Maimon, *Abaye ve-Rava; Toldoteihem u-Massekhet Ma'amareihem ve-Sugyateihem ba-Halacha u-va-Agadah* (Jerusalem: Mosad ha-Rav Kuk, 1965), p. 238, who claim, without citing any evidence, that Rava founded his academy after the death of Rav Yosef, shortly after Abaye was chosen as head in Pumbedita. See also Yudelowitz, *Yeshivat Pumbedita*, p. 41, and *Mahoza*, p. 71.
[7]See also Yudelowitz, *Mahoza*, pp. 71 and 81-82, and *Encyclopaedia Hebraica* (Jerusalem: Encyclopaedia Publishing Company, 1949-1981), vol. 1, pp. 141-42, and vol. 30, p. 436.
[8]Sukkah 28a and Baba Batra 134a. See Graetz, *Geschichte der Juden*, vol. 4, pp. 330-31; Frankel, *Mavo ha-Yerushalmi*, p. 35b; Mielziner, *Introduction to the Talmud*, p. 261; Kaplan, *The Redaction of the Babylonian Talmud*, pp. 21-22; Dor, *Torat Erez Yisrael be-Bavel*, p. 11; and Halivni, *Midrash, Mishnah, and Gemara*, p. 70.
[9]See Yudelowitz, *Mahoza*, pp. 81-82, and *Yeshivat Pumbedita*, p. 40.
[10]Halivni, *Midrash, Mishnah, and Gemara*, p. 78.
[11]Weiss, *Hithavut ha-Talmud bi-Shlemuto*, pp. 14-56.
[12]*Ibid.*, p. 32.
[13]See, for example, Eruvin 63b-64a, Pesahim 11b-12a, and Nedarim 54a-b. See also Berakhot 56a-b.

functioning in a different city during the lifetime of his teacher, most likely induced Weiss to modify the conventional view of the relationship between Abaye and Rava.

The evidence of the Talmud, however, indicates that Weiss did not go far enough in rejecting the conventional view, in detaching the activity of Abaye from that of Rava. The evidence of the Talmud suggests strongly that Abaye and Rava hardly ever engage in direct discourse with one another. To be specific, having examined approximately 3500 statements scattered throughout more than half of the Babylonian Talmud,[14] I found only 10 to 17 cases in which Abaye and Rava converse with one another, and 15 to 22 cases in which they appear in each other's presence.[15]

It is undeniable that according to the printed editions and manuscripts of the Talmud, Rava and Abaye talk to one another more often than 10 to 17 times. To be specific, of the approximately 3500 appearances by Abaye and Rava examined thus far, I found 200 cases in which the printed editions or manuscripts preserve a record of Abaye and Rava conversing with one another or appearing in each other's presence.[16] That is, I found 200 cases, involving 400 appearances by Abaye and Rava, in which at least a single version recorded in *Dikdukei Soferim* preserves a record of Abaye and Rava conversing or appearing with one another.[17] It is important to note, however, that 118 of these 200 cases are uncertain, for the most part because of confusion between the names Rava and Rabbah in the manuscripts and printed editions.[18] In other words, examination of approximately 3500 appearances by Abaye and Rava yields only 82 cases in which the manuscripts unanimously portray Abaye and Rava conversing or appearing with one another. Even if we accept the testimony of the manuscripts and printed editions at face value, therefore, face-to-face contact between Abaye and Rava is

---

[14]Thus far, I have examined the following tractates: Berakhot, Shabbat, Eruvin, Pesahim, Bezah, Megillah, Moed Katan, Ketubot, Nedarim, Gittin, Kiddushin, Baba Kamma, Baba Mezia, Baba Batra, Sanhedrin, Makkot, Avodah Zarah, Hullin, and Bekhorot.

[15]See Appendix 2, below.

[16]See Appendix 3, below.

[17]In fact, the figure 200 is almost certainly too high, since it includes cases in which the surrounding context indicates that the correct reading is Rabbah rather than Rava (see below). It also includes cases in which no versions read Rava, but the surrounding context indicates that the correct reading is Rava rather than Rabbah.

[18]See Appendix 3, below, and see the references to *DS*, there. For manuscript confusion between Rabbah's name and the names of other Amoraim, see Daniel Sperber, "Ha-Im Ala Rabbah le-Erez Yisrael?" *Sinai* 71 (1972), pp. 140-45; and see the following note.

not as ubiquitous in the Talmud as is generally assumed. I contend, furthermore, that nearly all of these 200 exchanges are between Abaye and his teacher, Rabbah, and not between Abaye and his contemporary, Rava.

Given the frequency with which the names Rava and Rabbah interchange in the manuscripts, how can we be certain in any given context which name is correct? So frequently is there confusion between these two names, in fact, that even when all textual witnesses agree, we often cannot be certain which Amora is referred to.[19] When Rava or Rabbah appear in Abaye's presence, however, in all but a few instances it is possible to determine who is speaking based on the nature of their interaction. In several instances, Abaye clearly relates to Rabbah like a subordinate in the presence of his superior, approaching him for halachic guidance or the correct interpretation of a source. In such instances, and in cases where Abaye is described as "sitting before" Rabbah in language descriptive of an encounter between a subordinate and his superior,[20] we can safely conclude that his teacher, Rabbah, is referred to and not his younger contemporary, Rava.[21] Furthermore, several scholars have noted that when Rabbah or Rava states an opinion and Abaye follows with discussion of the opinion, and the surrounding context provides some basis upon which to decide who is speaking, Abaye invariably turns out to be speaking with Rabbah, his teacher.[22] Whenever the

---

[19]See Friedman, "Ketiv ha-Shemot 'Rabbah' ve-'Rava' ba-Talmud ha-Bavli," pp. 140-64. See especially Friedman's discussion of methods used by medieval commentators to determine whether Rabbah or Rava is speaking. In a personal communication on October 19, 1988, Friedman phrased his conclusions as follows: "There is evidence indicating that the standard orthographic distinction between the name Rava and Rabbah was a convention that was gradually developed in order to facilitate this distinction which originally had no graphic form." Throughout this chapter, I adhere to the convention of using the name Rabbah to refer to Abaye's teacher, and the name Rava to refer to Abaye's younger contemporary. I do so only for purposes of clarity, and not because I disagree with Friedman's conclusions regarding the original spelling of the names.

[20]See Goodblatt, *Rabbinic Instruction in Sasanian Babylonia*, pp. 199-259; Gafni, *Yehudei Bavel bi-Tekufat ha-Talmud*, pp. 274-79; Kalmin, "Collegial Interaction in the Babylonian Talmud," pp. 390-96; and chapter 5, above, and chapter 11, below.

[21]See, for example, Shabbat 46b and 153a (see below), Pesahim 120b, Eruvin 19b (four times) and 20a (twice), Bezah 36b, Moed Katan 19b, Ketubot 14a and 42a-b, Gittin 28a, Baba Kamma 7a-b and 11a, Baba Mezia 30b and 93b-94a, Avodah Zarah 50b, and possibly Shabbat 95a,

[22]See Yudelowitz, *Yeshivat Pumbedita*, p. 50. See also Halivni, *Mekorot u-Mesorot: Yoma-Hagiga*, p. 508, n. 2, and the references cited there. Compare Maimon, *Abaye ve-Rava*, pp. 611-94.

presence or arrangement of Amoraim allows a determination to be made, Abaye turns out to be speaking with Rabbah rather than with his younger contemporary, Rava. It will be helpful to document this claim in detail:

1. On Eruvin 71a-b, the discussion begins with a statement by Rabbah and continues with a dialogue between Abaye and Rabbah. Rav Yosef, Rabbah's younger contemporary and Rava's teacher, follows with an alternative to Rabbah's view. Amoraic opinions are usually arranged chronologically,[23] and therefore the first opinion – against which Abaye objects – is most likely attributed to Rabbah, the teacher, and not Rava, the contemporary. If the first opinion had been attributed to Rava, then the view of Rav Yosef, the older Amora, would most likely have been placed first. Discussions on Shabbat 23b and 42b-43a, Eruvin 67b, Bezah 2b, 5a, 7b, and 18a, Moed Katan 2b, Baba Kamma 28b-29a and 66a-b, Sanhedrin 98b, and Hullin 14a-b[24] follow the same basic pattern.[25] It is certainly possible that in some of these passages, factors other than chronology determined the order of Amoraim, according to which the arrangement of Rav Yosef after Rabbah says nothing about their relative chronology. Nevertheless, chronology is the dominant principle by which Talmudic discussions are ordered, and Abaye is most likely depicted as conversing with Rabbah in the cases cited above.

2. On Pesahim 11a (and parallel), Abaye objects in the presence of Rabbah against an interpretation by Rabbah, and Rabbah resolves the objection. Abaye follows with an opposing interpretation, against which Rava objects and follows with a third interpretation. The Amora in whose presence Abaye dialogues, the Amora whose opinion is placed before the opinions of Abaye and Rava, is most likely Rabbah, Abaye's teacher. Discussions on Shabbat 124a,[26] Pesahim 69a-b, Ketubot 14a and 42a-b, Gittin 28a-b, Baba Kamma 7a-b, 42a, and 66a-b, Baba Batra 45a-b and 135a, Avodah Zarah 76a, and Hullin 20b-21a follow the same basic pattern, with Abaye conversing with Rabbah in each instance.

3. Discussions on Eruvin 38b and 44b-45a contain dialogue between Abaye and Rabbah in response to a statement by Rabbah. Rabbah bar

---

[23]For further discussion of this issue, see Tosafot, s.v. Rabbah, on Pesahim 103a; Weiss, *Al ha-Yezira ha-Sifrutit shel ha-Amoraim*, pp. 240-41, and *Mehkarim ba-Talmud* (Jerusalem: Mosad ha-Rav Kuk, 1975), pp. 160-212.; Halivni, *Mekorot u-Mesorot: Shabbat*, pp. 1-2, and *Eruvin-Pesahim*, p. 584, n. 2; and Shamma Friedman, "Kol ha-Kazar Kodem," in *Kovez Ma'amarim be-Lashon Hazal*, ed. Moshe Bar-Asher (Jerusalem: 1980), pp. 299-326.

[24]*DS* pei.

[25]It should be noted that on Shabbat 23b, the author of the alternative view is Rav Hisda rather than Rav Yosef.

[26]See Halivni, *Mekorot u-Mesorot: Shabbat*, p. 335, n. 1.

Rav Hanan and Abaye follow with a discussion of Rabbah's view, in the course of which Rabbah bar Rav Hanan refers to Rabbah as "Mar." The Amora who dialogues with Abaye and is the subject of the subsequent dialogue between Abaye and Rabbah bar Rav Hanan is most likely Rabbah, for Rabbah's students frequently refer to their master as "Mar," and Rabbah bar Rav Hanan is portrayed in several contexts as a close disciple of Rabbah.[27] A discussion on Baba Batra 62b is structured in similar fashion, concluding with Abaye's reference to "Mar's" opinion. Another discussion on Baba Batra 62b is structured in similar fashion and most likely involves the same Amoraim, although it lacks Abaye's concluding discussion.

4. On Shabbat 153a, Abaye and Rabbah assume that Abaye and Rabbah bar Rav Hanan will be present at Rabbah's funeral. Rabbah, the third-generation Pumbeditan, is most likely referred to, since Abaye's and Rabbah bar Rav Hanan's presence at the funeral of Rava, who died after Abaye according to several Talmudic accounts, would not be expected. In addition, Abaye refers to his interlocutor as "Mar," and identifies his place of residence as Pumbedita. Rabbah is active in Pumbedita throughout the Talmud, while Rava is closely associated with the city of Mahoza. In this context, Abaye is most likely conversing with his teacher, Rabbah, and not with his contemporary, Rava.

5. On Pesahim 46b, contradictory opinions of Rav Hisda and Rabbah are arranged in dispute form. In general, such arrangement is an indication of contemporaneity, so the Amora referred to in dispute with Rav Hisda is most likely Rabbah, his younger contemporary, rather than Rava, Rav Hisda's student. In the continuation on 47b-48a, Abaye and Rabbah discuss Rabbah's view, and most likely the discussion is between Abaye and his teacher, Rabbah, who authored the opinion on which the discussion is based. We find similar arrangements involving the same Amoraim on Makkot 9a, and involving Rav Nahman in dispute with Rabbah on Baba Batra 124b. The Amora in whose presence Abaye discusses this opinion, therefore, is Rabbah, his teacher, and not Rava, his contemporary. The anonymous editorial assertion on Makkot 9a that Rabbah and Rav Hisda "are consistent with their own reasoning," i.e., that the same Amoraim express the same opinions in a different context, identifies Rabbah as the author of another statement on Makkot 9a. The Amora in whose presence Abaye discusses this opinion, therefore, is Rabbah, the teacher, and not Rava, the contemporary.

6. On Hullin 43b, the discussion opens with a report of Rabbah's halachic action, and continues with an objection by Abaye in Rabbah's presence. The anonymous editors conclude that Rabbah must have been

---

[27] DS lamed and Albeck, *Mavo la-Talmudim*, p. 376.

aware of the difficulty raised by Abaye, and performed this action only in order to sharpen the mind of his student. The anonymous, editorial interpretation is highly dubious, but informs us nevertheless that the editors understand Abaye to be objecting in the presence of his teacher, Rabbah, and not his contemporary, Rava. Abaye's interaction with Rabbah on Gittin 37b is likewise that of a student in the presence of his teacher. Here as well, Abaye's dialogue is with Rabbah, his teacher, and not with Rava, his contemporary.

7. On Baba Batra 31a, Rabbah states an opinion and Abaye objects in his presence. Rabbah is most likely referred to, since Rava expresses a contradictory opinion on Baba Batra 33b.[28] Similarly, according to some versions of Pesahim 63a, Abaye objects against the opinion of Rabbah, in Rabbah's presence.[29] Rabbah is most likely referred to, since his statement on Pesahim 63a contradicts the opinion of Rava on Menahot 16b.[30] Sometimes the Talmud attributes contradictory views to the same Amora, but these cases are the exception rather than the rule.

8. On Shabbat 122b-123a, the discussion begins with a statement by Rav Yehuda, against which Rabbah objects, presumably in Rav Yehuda's presence. Rabbah follows with an alternative view, and Abaye and Rabbah discuss this opinion. Most likely, the Amora to whom the alternative view is attributed is the same Amora who objected against Yehuda, and it is questionable whether or not Rava is ever portrayed as appearing in Rav Yehuda's presence.[31] The author of the alternative view, therefore, i.e., the Amora who dialogues with Abaye, is most likely Rabbah. Discussions involving Rav Huna, Ulla, and Rav Hamnuna in the presence of Ulla on Eruvin 104a, Nedarim 29a, Baba Batra 172b, Sanhedrin 65a, and Hullin 9b[32] follow the same basic pattern.

In all, having examined more than half of the Talmud, I found 38 to 46 cases where the surrounding context indicates that Abaye is objecting in the presence of Rabbah, his superior,[33] and only three uncertain cases

---

[28]See Rashba, Ritba, and Ran on Baba Batra 31a, and see Tosafot Rid on Baba Batra 33b. The statement is certainly attributed to Rava on 33b, as the introductory formula ("Abaye and Rava, the two of them said...") makes clear.

[29]See Halivni, *Mekorot u-Mesorot:* Eruvin-Pesahim, pp. 459-60.

[30]Rabbah and Rav Simi bar Ashi (a fifth-generation Amora) most likely had no direct contact. The statement in Simi's presence on Menahot 16b, therefore, is most likely attributed to Rava.

[31]See Albeck, *Mavo la-Talmudim*, pp. 374-75.

[32]*DS* zadi.

[33]See Shabbat 23b, 42b-43a, 124a, and 153a, Eruvin 38b, 44b-45a, 67b, and 71a-b, Pesahim 11a (and parallel), 47b-48a (see also 46b), and 69a-b, Bezah 2b, 5a, 7b, and 18a, Moed Katan 2b, Ketubot 14a and 42a-b, Gittin 28a-b and 37a-b, Baba Kamma 7a-b, 28b-29a, 42a, and 66a-b, Baba Batra 31a (see Rashba, Ritba, and Ran; see also Baba Batra 33b and Tosafot Rid, there), 45a-b, 62b (twice), 124b, and 135a,

in which the context suggests that Abaye is objecting against Rava.[34] Most likely, we should interpret the uncertain cases in line with the more certain cases, and conclude that Abaye routinely converses with his teacher, Rabbah, and rarely converses with his contemporary, Rava.

Further proof of the claim that Abaye and Rava communicate with one another only rarely is the fact that a substantial number of supposed dialogues between them are formulated as follows: a statement by Abaye will be followed by Rava's objection against Abaye's view in Abaye's presence. Abaye will offer no response and Rava will follow with his own opinion. Having examined more than half of the Talmud, I found 32 to 47 cases in which the discussion follows this pattern, and in none of them does Abaye respond to Rava's objection.[35] It can hardly be maintained that Abaye never responds because in every instance he has no answer to Rava's objection. More likely, Abaye fails to respond because the dialogue is no dialogue and Rava is not objecting in the

---

Sanhedrin 98b, Makkot 9a (twice), Avodah Zarah 76a, Hullin 14a-b (*DS* pei), 20b-21a, and 43b, and possibly Shabbat 74b (see Halivni, *Mekorot u-Mesorot:* Shabbat, pp. 217-18) and 122b-123a, Eruvin 104a, Pesahim 63a (see Halivni, *Mekorot u-Mesorot:* Eruvin-Pesahim, pp. 459-60), Nedarim 29a, Baba Batra 172b, Sanhedrin 65a, and Hullin 9b (*DS* zadi).

[34]See Eruvin 37b-38a (compare Halivni, *Mekorot u-Mesorot:* Eruvin-Pesahim, pp. 109-10), Baba Kamma 113b, and Baba Batra 29a (see Appendix 2, below). With regard to Baba Mezia 60a, see Tosafot, s.v. Rava, and Friedman, "Ketiv ha-Shemot 'Rabbah' ve-'Rava' ba-Talmud ha-Bavli," pp. 158-64.

[35]Berakhot 20b, Shabbat 14a, 107b, 122b, and 123b (see Halivni, *Mekorot u-Mesorot:* Shabbat, pp. 334-35), Eruvin 8b and 24b, Pesahim 6a, Ketubot 12a and 80a, Gittin 50a, Baba Kamma 66b (see Tosafot, s.v. Rava, on Baba Kamma 67b) and 117a, Baba Mezia 31a, 62b, 70b, and 72a-b, Baba Batra 4a, 19a, 20b, 24a, 140b, 143b, and 171b, Sanhedrin 46b and 74b, Makkot 23a, Avodah Zarah 76a, Hullin 41b, 101b, 108a, and 111b, Bekhorot 4a and 16b, and possibly Shabbat 74b (see Halivni, *Mekorot u-Mesorot:* Shabbat, pp. 217-18), Pesahim 40a (*DS* yud), 58b (*DS* bet), and 68a (*DS* lamed), Ketubot 6b (*DS* Herschler, nn. on line 7, and n. 19) and 108b (*ibid.,* nn. on line 8), Nedarim 24b (the Vatican manuscript lacks the word *lei*), Gittin 8b (twice) (*DS* Feldblum, notes on lines 19 and 22. One could understand this discussion as follows: Abaye responds to the introductory question and Rava objects in his presence. Abaye is unable to respond, and changes his mind on the strength of Rava's argument, offering an alternative response. Rava again objects in Abaye's presence, and Abaye is once again unable to respond. Rava follows with his own answer to the question, which he and Rav Ada bar Matna discuss. Alternatively, however, Abaye [or later editors on his behalf] originally answered the question in one fashion, then changed his mind and offered an alternative response. Both of these responses came before Rava at some later date, and he [or later editors on his behalf] objected against both, thereby explaining why his response was preferable), Baba Kamma 8b (*DS*), Baba Mezia 52a (*DS* ayin) and 89b (*DS* bet), Baba Batra 111b (*DS* samekh) and 143b (*DS* kuf), Hullin 10b (*DS* nun), and Bekhorot 13b (see the parallel on Avodah Zarah 71b).

presence of Abaye. Later scribes (but see below) mistakenly added the word *lei* ("to him") to the phrase "Rava said," yielding the reading *Amar lei Rava* ("Rava said to him"), or they added *lei...le-Abaye*, yielding the reading *Amar lei Rava le-Abaye* ("Rava said to Abaye") and creating the impression that Abaye and Rava were speaking in each other's presence. It is no accident that the manuscripts often disagree about whether the words *lei* and *lei...le-Abaye* belong in the text.[36] Abaye and Rava, we see once again, rarely dialogue with one another.

Authentic Dialogue Between Abaye and Rava, for the Most Part, Has Not Been "Rigged"

Perhaps, it might be argued, dialogues between Abaye and Rava are more frequent, and the separation between Talmudic centers less extreme, than I claim above. Perhaps the 32 to 47 cases in which Rava objects against Abaye's view, Abaye fails to respond, and Rava follows with his own opinion are to be understood as actual face-to-face encounters, preserved, however, from the point of view of Rava and his students or of later editors, reflecting their perception of Rava as the greatest scholar of his generation. Abaye never responds to Rava's objections, Rava's students or the later editors would perhaps like us to believe, because Abaye was helpless in the face of Rava's superior learning and dialectical skill.

As we observed in chapter 1, above, in fact, there is evidence that such an attitude was held by, or attributed to, at least one of Rava's students. We found stories, for example, which describe legal cases brought before Abaye for judgment, whereupon Abaye procrastinates and fails to deliver a prompt verdict. The litigants are told by a student of Rava to go before Rava, whose "knife is sharp," and Rava delivers a prompt, and correct, decision.[37] In such cases, we concluded, the story was very likely orchestrated to portray Rava as the greater of the two scholars.

Nevertheless, the cases in which Abaye's statements are objected against by Rava with no response should most likely not be viewed as evidence of actual face-to-face contact. I say this in part because of the rarity with which Abaye and Rava speak together in other Talmudic contexts (see above). This fact reduces the likelihood that we should trust the fragile evidence of face-to-face contact provided by the 32 to 47 cases under consideration.

---

[36]See the references cited in the previous note. See also the secondary literature cited in n. 37 of the Introduction, above.
[37]Yevamot 122a (see *DS* yud, on Hullin 77a) and Hullin 77a.

It is likely, in other words, that in most of these cases either *Talmudic* students or editors or *post-Talmudic* scribes[38] created the impression that Rava and Abaye were communicating directly. *Talmudic* students or editors, or *post-Talmudic* scribes are responsible for adding the word *lei* ("to him"), or the phrase *lei...le-Abaye* ("to Abaye"), to the introduction to Rava's objection, either (1) out of carelessness, (2) because of their mistaken belief that the objection was uttered in Abaye's presence, or (3) in order to increase the effectiveness of their polemic against Abaye.

The polemic is more effective if the contact is direct because Abaye looks particularly bad if he is consistently unable to respond to Rava's direct challenges. The students, editors, or scribes, in their effort to make Abaye look bad, are perhaps not bothered by the historical fact that Abaye and Rava rarely interact. They wish to portray Abaye negatively, and are perhaps willing to play fast and loose with the facts in order to acheive their goal.

I referred above to the evidence of face-to-face contact supplied by these 32 to 47 cases as "fragile." I consider it such for two reasons. First, as noted above, in several cases the manuscripts disagree about whether the words *lei* or *lei...le-Abaye* belong in the text. As Shamma Friedman has noted, manuscript variation is one important indicator of a late editorial or post-Talmudic addition to the text.[39]

Second, these cases are suspect because a mere word or phrase is fragile evidence of direct contact. Scribes often emended texts in subtle (or not so subtle) ways, and minor adjustments to the text were made at many points during the long and often less than perfect history of the Talmud's transmission.[40] That scribes would sometimes invent dialogue between Abaye and Rava when none existed is extremely likely, given the popular belief that they converse together throughout the Talmud.

To repeat, given the huge number of statements by Abaye and Rava preserved in the Talmud, and the paucity of firm evidence of direct contact between them (such as is provided, for example, by their rare appearances together in stories), it is likely that most or all of the 32 to 47 "dialogues" under discussion are not real dialogues. They are not trustworthy evidence of actual, albeit doctored, contact between Abaye and Rava.

---

[38]Or oral transmitters. See the discussion of scribes versus oral transmitters in n. 37 of the Introduction, above.

[39]Friedman, "Al Derekh Heker ha-Sugya," pp. 30-31. See also Goodblatt, "The Babylonian Talmud," p. 163.

[40]See the references cited in n. 35, above.

Further supporting this conclusion is the fact that there is no fixed pattern regarding who has the final word or silences the other in debate when Abaye and Rava are definitely portrayed as speaking in each other's presence. There is no fixed pattern regarding who wins the debate when Abaye and Rava appear together in a story which most likely depicts face-to-face contact between them. At times, Rava defeats Abaye in argument, but almost as often Abaye defeats Rava. Abaye defeats Rava, for example, in one case in which Abaye, Rava, Rav Zeira, and Rabbah bar Matna are described as "needing a leader."[41] They decide that the honor will fall to whoever makes a statement which withstands his colleagues' criticism. Abaye's opinion prevails and he wins the right to open the discussion. In another context, Abaye suggests how an impoverished scholar can legally improve his financial situation.[42] Rava follows with an objection, in Abaye's presence; Abaye responds, and Abaye's view prevails. In a third context, in fact, Rava himself is portrayed as recounting a conversation he had with Abaye in which Abaye "surrounded [him] with proofs."[43] Rava quotes Abaye's objection, his own response, and Abaye's refutation of his response.[44] If, in the 32 to 47 cases referred to above, Abaye and Rava actually conversed together but Abaye's responses were intentionally deleted by Rava and his school, or by later editors, we would not expect such selective consistency. We would not expect Rava to consistently have the last word only when the discussion was structured in one fashion, and in a fashion which makes it doubtful that Abaye and Rava were speaking in each other's presence. We would expect Rava to consistently have the last word in other circumstances as well, namely when he and Abaye were undoubtedly portrayed as conversing in each other's presence.

When Abaye and Rava are depicted as directly conversing with one another, Abaye is able to respond on his own behalf, and not surprisingly, he occasionally defeats Rava in argument. The numerous cases in which Abaye's statements are objected to with no response, and Rava gets the last word, should most likely not be viewed as doctored accounts of actual face-to-face contact.

Having rejected the possibility that the 32 to 47 cases under consideration are doctored accounts of actual contact, three possible understandings remain. Either (1) students or editors arranged Rava's objection and opinion after Abaye's view in order to make Rava appear

---

[41]Horayot 14a. The phrase literally means they "needed a head."
[42]Baba Batra 174b.
[43]Avodah Zarah 57b-58a.
[44]See also Shabbat 7b, Eruvin 57b (twice), Ketubot 39a and 81a-b (see Halivni, *Mekorot u-Mesorot: Nashim*, pp. 45-46), and possibly Hullin 125b.

superior, but post-Talmudic scribes are responsible for the word *lei*; (2) Talmudic students or editors added the word *lei*, creating dialogue where none existed in order to depict Abaye as helpless in the face of Rava's superior dialectical skill; or (3) the placement of Rava's objection and opinion after Abaye's comment is not a deliberate polemic. It indicates nothing more than their chronological relationship.

The first two alternatives bear restating, since the nature of the polemic is subtly different in each case. According to the first alternative, there was originally no hint of dialogue between Abaye and Rava in the 32 to 47 cases under discussion until post-Talmudic scribes added to the discussion. During the Talmudic period, students or editors who wished to portray Rava's as the more reasonable view placed his objections and opinions after those of Abaye, enabling Rava to have the last word. To maintain the possibility of such limited manipulation, however, is not the same as saying that *Talmudic* students or editors invented dialogue between Abaye and Rava in order to depict Abaye as unable to respond to Rava's arguments (alternative #2). It is also not the same as saying that Rava and his school, or later editors *active during the Talmudic period*, preserved a distorted account of actual face-to-face contact between Rava and Abaye, that they deliberately suppressed Abaye's side of the dialogue. It is simply to say that the structure of these discussions (with Rava objecting against Abaye's view, and following with an opposing opinion) might reflect a deliberate attempt on the part of Rava's students, or later editors, at presenting Rava's view as the more reasonable alternative. Perhaps such discussions would look different if they reached us from the point of view of editors favoring Abaye. For example, perhaps Rava's objections against Abaye would not have been preserved, or perhaps Rava's opinions would have been omitted altogether if the discussions came to us from Abaye's point of view.

According to the second alternative, students or editors *active during the Talmudic period* invented the notion that Abaye and Rava conversed together in these contexts. The words *lei* and *lei...le-Abaye* are a Talmudic rather than a post-Talmudic contribution to the text, creating the impression that Abaye was unable to respond to Rava's direct objections. He was helpless in the face of Rava's superior learning and dialectical skill.

According to the third alternative, cases in which Rava objects to Abaye with no response are not evidence of an editorial attempt at favoring Rava's view. Perhaps such discussions indicate nothing more than the movement of traditions from Abaye in Pumbedita to Rava in Mahoza, from the earlier Amora to the later.

While absolute certainty on this question is beyond our grasp, one argument favors the latter alternative, namely that the placement of Rava's objections and opinions after Abaye's comments reflects chronology rather than polemics. Arguing in favor of this alternative is the fact that on several occasions, obscure fourth-generation Amoraim such as Rav Dimi Minehardea, Rabbah bar Ulla, Rav Ada bar Ahava, and the Nehardeans[45] have the last word vis-à-vis Abaye and Rava. Their statements are juxtaposed to and explicitly object against opposing statements by Abaye or Rava, both with and without dialogue between them.[46] I noted in chapter 1, above, that statements by the overwhelming majority of fourth-generation Amoraim are preserved in the Talmud primarily to the extent to which they impinge upon a tiny number of important Amoraim (for example, Abaye and Rava).[47] In other words, fourth-generation Amoraim depend on Abaye and Rava for the preservation of their statements in the Talmud. Considering their dependence on Abaye and Rava, it is difficult to view cases in which Rav Dimi Minehardea, Rabbah bar Ulla, Rav Ada bar Ahava, or the Nehardeans are given the last word vis-à-vis Abaye or Rava as attempts by disciples or later editors at portraying their views as authoritative. Very likely, therefore, identically formulated cases in which Rava is given the last word vis-à-vis Abaye should likewise not be understood as attempts at favoring Rava's view. The placement of objections and contradictory opinions by Rav Dimi Minehardea (and others) after statements by Abaye and Rava most likely reflects their chronological relationship rather than an attempt at making the author of the second opinion seem superior, and the same is true of the placement of Rava's statements and objections after those of Abaye.[48]

Once we remove the "dialogues" described above from consideration, the dialogues that were actually with Rabbah and the "created" dialogues with Rava, and remove as well cases in which Abaye clearly relates to Rabbah like a student in the presence of his teacher, we are left with 10 to 17 cases, scattered throughout more than half of the Talmud, in which Abaye and Rava converse. In sharp contrast to the

---

[45]See Goodblatt, "Local Traditions in the Babylonian Talmud," pp. 187-94.
[46]Shabbat 129a, Pesahim 58b, Bezah 6a, Ketubot 71b, Gittin 75a-b, Baba Kamma 6a and 42a, Baba Batra 21a (twice), Avodah Zarah 12a, 30a-b (the Munich manuscript reads Rav Papa instead of Rava), and 44b, Zevahim 96b, Menahot 35a (twice), Arakhin 22b, Niddah 24b, and possibly Yoma 72b.
[47]For further details, see Kalmin, *The Redaction of the Babylonian Talmud*, pp. 51-65. See also Neusner, *A History of the Jews in Babylonia*, vol. 4, p. 74, n. 1, and pp. 287-89.
[48]See the discussion of the theory of Avraham Weiss, above.

conventional view, therefore, the Talmud actually portrays Abaye and Rava as active in separate Talmudic centers functioning at a distant remove from one another, with little direct contact.

Further proof of this conclusion is found in the fact that throughout the Talmud, Rava frequently betrays awareness of the opinions of Abaye, but Abaye only rarely betrays awareness of Rava's views.[49] Were their disputes depicted as face-to-face, we would not expect so extreme a disparity. We find, for example, a small but important corpus of disputes between Rav and his younger contemporary, Rav Asi.[50] Their disputes are formulated in exactly the same manner as are Abaye's disputes with Rava, with Rav's opinion consistently placed first and followed by Rav Asi's opposing opinion. And yet more often than not, both Rav and Rav Asi demonstrate knowledge of one another's positions,[51] suggesting that Rav and Rav Asi, in contrast to Abaye and Rava, are depicted as disputing in each other's presence. Second, on several occasions we find discussions involving Abaye and Rava arranged as follows: a statement by Abaye will be followed by an alternate opinion by Rava, which will in turn be followed by discussion of the issue by Rava and a student, or Abaye and a student. Why is it that Abaye never participates in dialogues between Rava and his students, and Rava never participates in dialogues between Abaye and his students? Or we find one of the disputants, Abaye or Rava, supporting his own view, or resolving an unattributed objection against the opposing view, and the like. Argumentation concerning Abaye's and Rava's juxtaposed opinions, even argumentation attributed to Abaye or Rava themselves, is quite routine.[52] What is exceptional is dispute dialogue, face-to-face argumentation between Abaye and Rava together in each other's presence. Again, the example of Rav and Rav Asi is instructive, for Rav and Rav Asi, in each other's presence, are portrayed

---

[49]See Appendix 4, below.

[50]Shabbat 50a, Megillah 5a, Ketubot 48b, Kiddushin 45b, 46a, and 63b (twice), and Sanhedrin 29b.

[51]Rav demonstrates knowledge of Rav Asi's position on Megillah 5a, Ketubot 48b, Kiddushin 45b and 46a, and Sanhedrin 29b.

[52]Berakhot 20b and 25a, Shabbat 11b (and parallel), 33a, 66a, 74a, 123a, and 154b-155a, Eruvin 9a and 63b-64a, Pesahim 11a (and parallel), 11b-12a, 12b, 45b-46a, 51b-52a (*DS* vav), 69a-b, and 71a, Ketubot 6b, 11a, 14a, 30a-b, 35a-b, 40a-b, 42a-b, and 81b-82a, Nedarim 5b, 19a-b, 39b, 54a-b, and 84b, Gittin 8b, 25a-26a, 28a, 34a, and 61a-b, Kiddushin 51a and 55a-b, Baba Kamma 43a-b and 94a, Baba Mezia 12a-b, 21a-22a, 28a, 48b, 62b, 63a-b, 80a-b, and 109a, Baba Batra 19a, 24a, and 173a, Sanhedrin 61b (twice), 75b, 77b, and 86a, Makkot 6a, Avodah Zarah 66a and 66b, Hullin 10b, 20b-21a, 77a, 100a-b, 106a, 111b, and 125b, Bekhorot 4a, 15a, 31b, and 54a-b, and possibly Shabbat 72b and Eruvin 99a-b.

as discussing their juxtaposed opinions in a relatively high percentage of cases.[53]

Further proof for my claim that contact between Abaye and Rava is portrayed as irregular and infrequent is found in the fact that a significant portion of their real dialogue is via messenger, or begins with face-to-face contact but continues via messenger, or is introduced by language indicative of a chance encounter or a brief visit.[54] In these contexts, Abaye and Rava are depicted as occasional visitors from different cities.

Summary and Conclusions

We have seen that the Talmud rarely depicts direct contact between Abaye and Rava. The lengthy arguments between them which supposedly fill the Babylonian Talmud do not exist,[55] indicating that the rabbinic movement in Amoraic Babylonia, at least during the fourth generation,[56] was much less organized and unified than earlier scholars believed.

According to my findings, the terms *havayot de-Rav u-Shmuel* and *havayot de-Abaye ve-Rava* most likely do not refer to the large amount of argumentation engaged in by Rav together with Shmuel and Abaye together with Rava.[57] The problematic nature of the term as applied to Rav and Shmuel has already been noted by David Halivni, since the Talmud preserves relatively little argumentation between them. Halivni claims that argumentation between Rav and Shmuel once existed, but was lost over time since it was not systematically and officially preserved, in contrast to the *havayot de-Abaye ve-Rava*, far more of which survived.[58]

Halivni argues that this "lost" early argumentation supports his theory regarding the pivotal role played by late, anonymous editors in

---

[53]Ketubot 48b and Kiddushin 46a.
[54]Eruvin 92a-93a, Moed Katan 16a, Ketubot 81a-b, and Avodah Zarah 57b-58a. On Moed Katan 16a, Abaye and Rava excommunicate a butcher who acted disrespectfully toward Rav Tuvi bar Matna. The continuation makes it clear that the rabbis responsible for the excommunication were eager to leave and that it would be difficult to gather them together again. See Ritba and *Perush Rashi le-Massekhet Moed Katan* (Jerusalem: Mekizei Nirdamim, 1961), ed. Efraim Kupfer.
[55]Compare Green, "Storytelling and Holy Man, The Case of Ancient Judaism," pp. 34-42.
[56]See the following chapter with regard to the question of whether a similar picture emerges from scrutiny of other Amoraic generations.
[57]See Levy, *Wörterbuch*, vol. 1, p. 458; *Arukh ha-Shalem*, ed. Kohut, vol. 3, p. 194; and Jastrow, *Dictionary*, p. 338.
[58]Halivni, *Midrash, Mishnah, and Gemara*, p. 70.

the preservation and reconstruction of Amoraic argumentation. Why did argumentation between Rav and Shmuel perish, while that between Abaye and Rava survived to a far greater extent? The answer, according to Halivni, is to be found in the greater chronological distance separating the earliest Amoraim from the anonymous editors, who for the first time systematically preserved and reconstructed Amoraic argumentation. In reconstructing the deliberations between Rav and Shmuel – claims Halivni – the late, anonymous editors had very little material to work with. Most of these deliberations were lost during the Amoraic period, a period characterized by lack of interest in the systematic preservation of argumentation. The editors' sources for the middle Amoraic generations, substantially closer to them in time, were far more complete. Less was forgotten because less time separated the editors from their middle-Amoraic sources.[59]

According to the findings of the present study, however, dialogues between Abaye and Rava are extremely rare, in relative terms no more prevalent than dialogues between Rav and Shmuel. Argumentation between Abaye and Rava, no less than that between Rav and Shmuel, did not survive for the simple reason that a necessary precondition for its existence, frequent face-to-face contact between the Amoraim involved, did not exist. Halivni's argument based on his understanding of the terms *havayot de-Rav u-Shmuel* and *havayot de-Abaye ve-Rava*, therefore, disappears.[60]

What, then, is the meaning of the term *havayot de-Abaye ve-Rava*? Examination of its usage throughout the Talmud shows that it refers to the discussions, arguments, or investigations of Abaye and Rava.[61] Nothing about the term, however, implies that the discussions, arguments, or investigations of Abaye and Rava were authored by Abaye and Rava together in each other's presence. Nothing precludes the discussions' having been authored by Abaye and Rava individually or in dialogue with their students. In fact, examination of the term's usage throughout the Talmud reveals that it usually introduces argumentational statements by individual Amoraim, and only rarely introduces dialogue between Amoraim.[62]

---

[59]*Ibid.*, pp. 66-87.
[60]It is important to note, however, that other arguments by Halivni on behalf of his position are not affected by my findings.
[61]See the references cited in Kosowsky, *Ozar Lashon ha-Talmud*, vol. 11, pp. 562-63, 572, and 605. See also Rashbam, Ritba, and Meyuhas le-R. Gershom on Baba Batra 134a.
[62]Kosowsky, *op. cit.*, vol. 11, p. 572. On Niddah 65b the term appears to refer to argumentation between R. Yohanan and Resh Lakish.

Most likely, the discussions of Abaye and Rava are paired together in the phrase *havayot de-Abaye ve-Rava* because Abaye and Rava are considered by whoever coined the term to be the most important rabbis of their generation, perhaps of the entire Amoraic period, and not because they routinely dialogue in each other's presence. We find other cases where Abaye and Rava are grouped together because of their preeminent status and not because of their appearance together in one another's presence. In one context, for example, we find an account of an extraordinary event that took place on the day that Abaye and Rava died.[63] Most likely, we are not to infer that Abaye and Rava died on the same day, for the tradition is well-established elsewhere in the Talmud that Abaye predeceased Rava.[64] Rather, the two sages are linked together in death because they were considered by whoever transmitted this account to be the most important scholars of their generation. Mention of the one outstanding sage conjured up the name of his outstanding contemporary.

A significant amount of argumentation survives even from the time of Rav and Shmuel between rabbis who regularly come in contact with one another. Much of the demonstrably face-to-face interaction between Rav and his students and Shmuel and his students, for example, takes the form of argumentation. The same is true of later Amoraic generations, where most of the face-to-face interaction between students and teachers takes the form of argumentation. Furthermore, on the rare occasions when Rav and Shmuel do come in contact with one another, argumentation is the most frequent result, and the same is true of argumentation between later Amoraic masters. The appropriate question to pose regarding the early Amoraic generations, therefore, is not simply why the argumentation which survived from this period is so brief when compared to that from the third and fourth generations,[65] but also why so little interaction between students and teachers survived from this early period. The increase in the amount of argumentation as we move later in the Amoraic period, therefore, may reflect a change in the master-disciple relationship and not simply a change in rabbinic attitudes toward argumentation.

---

[63]Moed Katan 25b.
[64]See Berakhot 56a-b, Ketubot 65a and 106a (*DS* Herschler, notes on line 17, and n. 38), and Gittin 60b.
[65]See Kraemer, *Stylistic Characteristics of Amoraic Literature*, pp. 47-136.

11

Collegial Interaction in the Babylonian Talmud

The present chapter further supports my claim that the Babylonian rabbinic movement is portrayed throughout the Talmud as decentralized. According to the Talmudic portrayal, Babylonian Amoraim did not create institutions which facilitated regular interaction between the most prominent rabbinic leaders, even when these leaders lived in close proximity to one another.

To argue this thesis, it is necessary to enter the scholarly debate regarding the Sitz im Leben of rabbinic interactions in Amoraic Babylonia. Discussion of this issue has focused on whether or not Amoraim interact in the context of academies or disciple circles.[1] The academy model posits a high level of organization and unity in Amoraic Babylonia,[2] whereas the disciple circle model (which envisions groups of students gathered around a single master within no larger institutional context) posits extreme decentralization. The present chapter suggests a compromise between these two extremes, arguing that the phenomenon of personal contacts between teachers of widely different status has not received sufficient attention in earlier scholarly discussion.

According to the present chapter, in other words, David Goodblatt's cogent arguments in favor of the existence of disciple circles in Amoraic Babylonia should not lead to an overemphasis on the master-disciple relationship as the paradigm of rabbinic interactions throughout the Talmud. At the same time, the likelihood that teachers of widely different status interact frequently in accordance with strict hierarchical rules does not imply that the locus of their interaction is an academy. There is no evidence that interactions between teachers take place within a larger institutional framework which transcends the personalities of the

---

[1]See the references to Goodblatt's and Gafni's arguments in the Introduction, above.

[2]See, for example, the previous chapter for a description of the theories of Halevy and Hyman.

rabbis involved in the relationship. These interactions take place in formal settings and are governed by strict, objectively definable rules, but there is no evidence that these formal settings are academies.

Interactions Between Babylonian Amoraim: Two Diverse Kinds of Inferior-Superior Interaction

The discussion below presupposes a distinction between two very common relationships between Babylonian Amoraim, between (1) rabbis of near-equal status, and (2) rabbis of widely different status.[3] It will be helpful to describe the salient features of these relationships.

Babylonian Amoraim of near-equal status tend to express opinions in the form of declarative statements in opposition to one another, but hierarchical distinctions between them are nevertheless maintained. The relationships between Rav and Shmuel and other well-known Amoraic pairs come immediately to mind.[4] When contact between Rav and Shmuel is direct, Rav is depicted as the superior sage.[5] On several occasions, for example, Shmuel's role in the discussion is confined to asking questions or making objections against legal judgments or statements by Rav.[6] On one occasion, when Rav Shila performs a legal action which Rav considers incorrect, he invites Shmuel to join him in excommunicating Shila,[7] the only unambiguous example of coordinated action on their part recorded in the Talmud, and even here Rav is the initiating party. Only once does Shmuel initiate action in Rav's presence, and Rav "turns his face" as a sign of displeasure.[8] The uncharacteristic nature of Shmuel's action in this context, furthermore, induces the anonymous editors to conjecture that the encounter takes place "in the locality of Shmuel."

---

[3]For a brief discussion of hierarchical relationships in Sasanian Persia, see James R. Russell, "Sages and Scribes at the Courts of Ancient Iran," in *The Sage in Israel and the Ancient Near East*, pp. 142-43.

[4]See chapters 5 and 10, above. Rav's and Shmuel's opposing opinions are frequently juxtaposed, but only in four cases is there proof, in the form of dialogues between them, that the opposing opinions were stated in each other's presence. See Baba Kamma 52b-53a and 75a, Avodah Zarah 35b-36a, and Niddah 64a. See also Shabbat 140a. See Bokser, *Samuel's Commentary on the Mishna*, pp. 207-15; and *Post-Mishnaic Judaism in Transition*, pp. 26-32, 36-38, and chapters 7 and 10, there; and Urbach, *Ha-Halacha*, pp. 197-202.

[5]See also Halevy, *Dorot ha-Rishonim*, vol. 3, pp. 400-4; and Hyman, *Toldot Tannaim ve-Amoraim*, pp. 28-29 and 1124-25.

[6]Berakhot 47a and 53b, Ketubot 22a-b, Baba Mezia 15b, and Hullin 59a and 107a. See also Eruvin 12b.

[7]Yevamot 121a.

[8]Eruvin 94a.

The relationship between Abaye and Rava is depicted in strikingly similar fashion. Confining the discussion to cases in which face-to-face contact between Abaye and Rava is reasonably certain (see chapter 10, above), we find that Abaye is depicted as the superior sage. On several occasions, Rava asks questions or makes objections based on statements by Abaye, or engages in other forms of activity indicative of subordinate status.[9] Only once do we find cooperation between them on a matter of communal or internally rabbinic importance, and Abaye is the dominant rabbi.[10] Strikingly, here too excommunication is involved, indicating that excommunication, more than other forms of activity, necessitated cooperation among the leaders of the rabbinic movement. With rare exceptions, rabbis are not depicted as working together. Rather, action appears to be initiated by a single dominant rabbi surrounded by figures of lesser status who typically do no more than register their support or express their opposition.[11]

Relationships between rabbis of more widely different status (the second type of relationship referred to above) are characterized by the inferior party's inability, in the superior's presence, to express himself in the form of declarative statements in opposition to the views of the superior. Abaye in the presence of Yosef, for example, never states his opinions in the form of declarative statements in contradiction to Yosef's views. Instead, Abaye registers his disagreement by (1) rejecting Yosef's opinions and arguments, presumably in his presence,[12] (2) objecting

---

[9]Eruvin 57b (twice) and 92a-93a, Yevamot 21b, Ketubot 39a, Baba Batra 174b, Shevuot 35a-b, and possibly Shabbat 35a, Eruvin 46a (see *DS* hei), Taanit 12a, and Gittin 8b. See also Hyman, *Toldot Tannaim ve-Amoraim*, p. 250.

[10]Moed Katan 16a. I base this claim on the fact that Abaye leads the deliberations after the butcher changes his conduct. *Sefer Yuhasin ha-Shalem*, ed. Zvi Philipovsky and Avraham Freiman (Jerusalem, 1963), p. 145, reads Abaye and Rabbanan.

[11]On Sotah 22b, Abaye and Rava might give instructions to a Tanna, a professional repeater of early rabbinic traditions, regarding the correct reading of a Tannaitic source. The unparalleled nature of this joint effort, however, makes it likely that the version without their names is correct. See *DS* Liss, notes on line 8.

[12]Shabbat 42a, 42b, 51a, 108a, 131a, and 145b, Ketubot 6b, Nedarim 77a and 84a-b, Sotah 45a, Gittin 23b, Kiddushin 46a, Baba Kamma 60a, Baba Mezia 16a, Baba Batra 14b, Sanhedrin 47a-b, Avodah Zarah 26a (three times), and Hullin 8a. For similar interactions involving Abaye and Rabbah, see especially Ketubot 27b (and parallels) and Baba Kamma 114a. See also Berakhot 61b, Eruvin 71a and 93b, Sukkah 44a, Taanit 4b, Yevamot 69b-70a, Gittin 24b, Kiddushin 5b, Baba Kamma 113b, Baba Mezia 90b and 116b, Baba Batra 16a, Shevuot 38b, Hullin 29a and 120a, and Arakhin 15b. With regard to Rabbah bar Rav Hanan and Rav Yosef, see Baba Batra 26a. With regard to Amemar and Rav Ashi, see Berakhot 12a and Baba Kamma 79a. See also Halevy, *Dorot ha-Rishonim*, vol. 2, p. 516.

against his statements, and (3) exhorting Yosef not to disagree with a particular Amora, superior to them both, and explaining his reasoning.[13]

In one important context, Abaye's objection is treated by contemporaries as a viable halachic position in opposition to the view of Yosef.[14] Yosef states his opinion and Abaye follows with an objection in his presence. The issue is sent before R. Hanina bar Papi, who sends back in support of Yosef. Abaye refuses to retract, however, on the grounds that Hanina bar Papi fails to supply arguments on behalf of his position.[15] The issue is then sent to Rav Manyumi b. d'Rav Nihumi, who sends back in support of Abaye. Abaye is not free to express himself in declarative form, as a near-equal of Yosef. Instead, he opposes Yosef in ways which maintain a strict distinction between them.

The relationship between Rav Papa and Rav Huna b. d'Rav Yehoshua conforms to the same pattern. Papa's views are regularly expressed in the form of declarative statements, either that such-and-such is the law or that such-and-such is the correct interpretation, while Huna b. d'Rav Yehoshua expresses opposing opinions in the form of rejections of Papa's reasoning[16] and objections against Papa's views,[17] but never in the form of declarative statements. Two of Huna b. d'Rav Yehoshua's objections[18] are likewise treated as viable halachic positions in opposition to views expressed declaratively by Papa.[19]

---

[13]Baba Batra 82b.
[14]Ketubot 81b.
[15]See Meiri on Baba Batra 130b.
[16]Berakhot 22a and Ketubot 84b-85a, and possibly Yoma 49a (*DS* zadi) and Yoma 57b (*DS* mem).
[17]Yevamot 85a and 91b, Gittin 58b, Baba Mezia 66b, Makkot 7a, Shevuot 48b, Niddah 39a-b and 54b, and possibly Shevuot 48b. On Gittin 58b (see also Sanhedrin 26b and *DS* zayin), Shevuot 37b, and possibly Arakhin 31b (R. Gershom and the London manuscript both lack Huna b. d'Rav Yehoshua's name), Huna objects against Papa's opinion and follows with his own view. There is no dialogue between them in any of these cases, however, and consequently no proof that Huna b. d'Rav Yehoshua expresses opinions contrary to Papa's, in Papa's presence, in the form of declarative statements.
[18]Avodah Zarah 72a and Niddah 39a-b.
[19]Rav Nahman bar Yizhak likewise never expresses opinions in the form of declarative statements in opposition to the opinions of Rava. Another form of authoritative expression, however, is apparently open to him. On Hullin 88b, Nahman bar Yizhak challenges Rava to explain why he rejects opinions publicly proclaimed by Rav Nahman bar Rav Hisda. Nahman bar Yizhak claims to have originated the opinion himself, deriving it from a mishna. Nahman bar Yizhak authors an original interpretation which he expresses in the form of an abstract halacha, and instructs Nahman bar Rav Hisda.
Similarly, Rav Ashi is clearly portrayed as Rav Mordechai's superior throughout the Talmud (see Kalmin, *The Redaction of the Babylonian Talmud*, pp. 103-22), but Mordechai is also depicted as independent of Ashi to a limited extent

Some Amoraim express themselves in the form of objections and questions while in the presence of superiors, but in the form of declarative statements when apart from these superiors. In several cases, for example, a middle-level sage states an opinion following which an inferior rabbi objects in his presence. The matter is brought before a third Amora, superior to them both, who repeats the objection almost word-for-word in the form of a declarative statement.[20] The middle-level sage who expressed himself in declarative form in the presence of the inferior sage confines himself to objections and questions once he enters the presence of his superior.

As noted above, forms of disagreement other than declarative contradiction are available to such inferiors in the presence of superiors. Rav Hisda and Rav Nahman, for example, reject Rav Huna's views in his presence, occasionally in extremely blunt and peremptory fashion. "By God!" exclaims Hisda. "If R. Yohanan said this to me himself I would not listen to him."[21] Or: "Do not retract [in the latter case], urges Hisda, "for if [you do], you have lost the former [argument] as well."[22] "Why are you stealing?" says Nahman to Huna on three occasions. "If you agree with the opinion of Rav X then say the halacha follows Rav X!"[23] Or: "Why do you answer with a tradition that has been hammered with one hundred hammer blows.... Instead, answer him with this...."[24] Or: "Do not disagree with Shmuel, for a Tannaitic tradition supports him."[25] Such cases indicate the occasionally surprising freedom of expression permitted to inferiors in the presence of superiors, but fall short of contradiction as near-equals in the form of declarative statements.

These few examples illustrate the claim that relationships between "near-equals" and "rabbis of widely different status" are objectively distinguishable. Relationships between Amoraim vary depending on the relative status of the Amoraim involved.

---

in that he twice contrasts his own version of an earlier source with Ashi's version (Menahot 42b and Bekhorot 5b), and once states his own, apparently original, interpretation of a mishna in Ashi's presence (Baba Kamma 62a).

[20]See, for example, Eruvin 40a, Gittin 73a, and Baba Batra 26a.

[21]Berakhot 24b.

[22]Hullin 19a-b. The evidence of face-to-face contact depends on the word *lei*, "to him," which might be a scribal error. See the Introduction, and chapters 2 and 10, above. On Hullin 19a-b, Hisda's use of the second person in addressing Huna might further indicate that their contact is direct.

[23]Yevamot 91a, Ketubot 19a, and Baba Batra 133a.

[24]Baba Batra 85b.

[25]Eruvin 42a.

Collegial Interaction in the Babylonian Talmud: Relationships Between Contemporary Teachers

As noted above, the present chapter attempts to describe the decentralized character of the Babylonian rabbinic movement as portrayed by the Talmud. The following discussion, therefore, focuses on the nature and frequency of collegial interactions, i.e., interactions between teachers with students of their own (as opposed to interactions between teachers and simple students, i.e., rabbis with no students of their own). I argue that many, very likely most interactions between rabbis involve colleagues (i.e., teachers) of widely different status. Colleagues of approximately equal status, particularly the most important leaders of their generation, rarely interact, supporting my claim that the Bavli depicts a decentralized rabbinic movement.

To accomplish these goals, we need to determine whether interactions involve colleagues of different status, or teachers and simple students. This seemingly simple task is actually quite difficult, however. It is often impossible to tell the difference between simple students (disciples with no students of their own) and inferior teachers, since both simple students and inferior teachers often relate to superior sages in the same hierarchical fashion.[26] Objective criteria distinguish some relationships, however, as involving teachers of different rank rather than teachers and simple disciples.

One such criterion is the juxtaposition of opposing opinions in dispute form ("Says Rav X... Rav Y says..."), generally viewed as a reliable indicator of collegial status. As noted in chapters 5 and 10 above, however, this criterion is surprisingly disappointing as evidence of collegial interaction between Babylonian Amoraim. Juxtaposed opinions are almost never accompanied by dialogue, according to which there is surprisingly little evidence that the paired Amoraim interacted together as colleagues. Furthermore, in general, there is little firm evidence of direct contact of any sort between Babylonian Amoraim whose opposing opinions are frequently juxtaposed in dispute form, with Rav and Shmuel and Abaye and Rava, to name only the most famous, interacting together only rarely. We must look, therefore, to other forms of relationship to find the most frequently encountered varieties of collegial interaction.

In the following pages, analysis of a technical term describing the seating arrangement of three rabbis will be a first step toward discovery of some of these other forms. The technical term under examination at least occasionally describes a formal encounter between two contemporary teachers of different rank.

---

[26]See Appendix 2, below.

This technical formula, found twelve times throughout the Talmud, describes Rav X sitting behind Rav Y while Rav Y sits facing Rav Z.[27] In such situations, Rav Z is the superior sage, Rav Y is below him in rank, and Rav X is the inferior of the three.[28]

Very likely, this technical term describes, at least occasionally, an encounter between two contemporary teachers of different rank.[29] First, the formula typically introduces teaching activity by superior and middle-level sages. The superior Amora instructs the middle-level sage, and the middle-level sage instructs the inferior sage, resolving his objections, answering his questions, and interpreting statements which he fails to understand. Second, on two occasions analysis of interactions between the superior and middle-level sages throughout the Talmud indicates that the Talmud consistently depicts them as teachers of different rank. Most likely, the encounter described by this technical

---

[27]*Yativ Rav X Ahorei Rav Y ve-Yativ Rav Y Kamei de-Rav Z.* Analysis of this formula indicates, incidentally, that a change in social setting at least sometimes produces a change in the rules of conduct required of inferiors in the presence of superiors. Rav X, the inferior sage, is not permitted to speak directly to the highest-ranking sage. His queries and objections are directed instead to the middle-level sage (Eruvin 43b-44a [see Gafni, *Yehudei Bavel bi-Tekufat ha-Talmud,* p. 275, n. 1], Pesahim 37b, Baba Kamma 116b, Baba Batra 152a-b, and Hullin 16a [see Yudelowitz, *Yeshivat Pumbedita,* p. 20, n. 9]). At times the inferior clearly takes pains to insure that the superior sage cannot hear him, either by whispering questions to the middle-level sage, or by refraining from speaking until the superior leaves the room (Pesahim 37b, Baba Kamma 116b, and Baba Batra 152a-b). To my knowledge, in no other circumstances do we find a prohibition of direct contact between an inferior and a superior, indicating that the term under discussion describes a unique encounter with its own special rule of conduct. Standards of appropriate behavior, therefore, sometimes change along with the contexts in which the behavior takes place.

On Niddah 27a, Rav Papa sits behind Rav Bibi while Bibi faces Rav Hamnuna. Papa speaks directly "to them," apparently to Bibi and Hamnuna. Papa is laughed at, however, very likely (in part) because of his breach of etiquette.

[28]Gafni, *Yehudei Bavel bi-Tekufat ha-Talmud,* pp. 274-79, lists the cases, provides variants, and discusses the relationships between the rabbis mentioned. See also Moshe Beer, "Mi-Ba'ayot Hithavutah Shel ha-Metivta be-Bavel," *Proceedings of the Fourth World Congress of Jewish Studies* 1 (1967), pp. 99-101; Moshe Kosowsky, "Ha-Yeshiva ba-'Yeshiva,'" in *S.K. Mirsky Jubilee Volume* (New York, 1958), pp. 312-27; Albeck, *Mavo la-Talmudim,* pp. 17-18; Moshe Gewirtsmann, "Ha-Munah 'Yetiv' u-Mashmauto," *Sinai* 65 (1969), pp. 9-20; and Goodblatt, *Rabbinic Instruction in Sasanian Babylonia,* pp. 221-38.

[29]See also Goodblatt, "Local Traditions in the Babylonian Talmud," pp. 204-16, especially pp. 206 and 210-16, who speculates that the term "(the) Nehardeans say..." might refer to "a circle or association of masters," or even to "a kind of guild of rabbis" perhaps closely resembling "the masters of Caesarea" described by Lee Levine in *Caesaria Under Roman Rule* (Leiden: E.J. Brill, 1975), pp. 93-97.

term is to be understood in light of this consistent pattern, namely, as an encounter between teachers of different rank.

Specifically, analysis of the relationships between Rav Huna and Rav Yehuda, and Rabbi and R. Hiyya, superior and middle-level sages according to the formula under discussion, most likely indicates that they should be viewed as contemporary teachers of different rank.[30] Yehuda is once clearly described as an independent but inferior teacher appearing in the presence of Huna, his superior.[31] Yehuda, described as head in Pumbedita, "goes before" Huna and asks him a question, and Huna responds like a teacher instructing his student. Elsewhere, Huna expresses a halachic opinion and word reaches Yehuda, who is angered by Huna's contradiction of his (Yehuda's) view.[32] On several occasions, subordinates ask questions of Huna and subsequently bring the same question before Yehuda,[33] very likely further indication that they are portrayed throughout the Talmud as contemporary teachers.[34]

A passage[35] in which "Rav Kahana sits behind Rav Yehuda, and Rav Yehuda sits before Rav Huna,"[36] therefore, should most likely be understood as another encounter between contemporary teachers, with the seating arrangement reflecting Huna's character as the superior of the two colleagues.[37] The fact that Yehuda "sits before" Huna is no obstacle

---

[30]See also *Igeret Rav Sherira Gaon*, ed. Lewin, p. 84; Weiss, *Dor Dor ve-Dorshav*, vol. 3, p. 160, n. 14, and pp. 167 and 178.

[31]Kiddushin 70a-b.

[32]Hullin 19a. See also Bekhorot 44a, where there is no reason to assume that the two Amoraim are in each other's presence.

[33]Berakhot 39a, Eruvin 17a, 40b (twice), and 93b, and possibly Shabbat 47a (*DS* gimel). See also *Seder Tannaim ve-Amoraim*, ed. Kahan, p. 20; *Sefer ha-Kabalah*, ed. Gerson D. Cohen (Philadelphia: Jewish Publication Society, 1967), p. 25; and *Sefer ha-Keritut*, Yemot Olam, Part 3, chapter 20.

[34]It is possible, although unlikely, that the stories depict each one of these questions as having been brought before Yehuda after Huna's death.

[35]Hullin 111b. See *DS* shin, and see *Igeret Rav Sherira Gaon*, ed. Lewin, p. 84; Hyman, *Toldot Tannaim ve-Amoraim*, p. 545; and Florsheim, "Ha-Yahasim Bein Hakhmei ha-Dor ha-Sheni Shel Amoraei Bavel," pp. 283-84.

[36]See Gafni, *Yehudei Bavel bi-Tekufat ha-Talmud*, p. 278.

[37]Hyman, *Toldot Tannaim ve-Amoraim*, pp. 339 and 545, and Albeck, *Mavo la-Talmudim*, p. 200, assume that the encounter takes place after Yehuda attained scholarly maturity and established himself in Pumbedita. Halperin, *Atlas Ez-Hayyim*, vol. 3, pp. 164-65, claims that the seating arrangement under discussion occasionally depicts two masters of different rank and a single student, but he is confident that the arrangement usually portrays two students in the presence of a teacher. See also p. 179, there. See also Bacher, *Die Agada der Babylonischen Amoräer*, p. 133; Jawetz, *Toldot Yisrael*, vol. 8, p. 72; Yudelowitz, *Yeshivat Pumbedita*, p. 9; and Goodblatt, *Rabbinic Instruction in Sasanian Babylonia*, pp. 233-34 and 274-76, who assume that this seating arrangement depicts two students before a common teacher.

whatsoever to viewing Yehuda as a teacher in his own right, for the term does not consistently describe simple students in the presence of their teachers.[38]

A similar account involving Rabbi, R. Hiyya, and Rav further supports this conclusion.[39] This account describes interaction between rabbis in Palestine, but uses the same terminology described above, and very likely describes substantially the same hierarchical relationship between sages.[40]

That Rabbi and R. Hiyya are portrayed throughout the Talmud as contemporary teachers of different rank is indicated by one source in which "Rabbi decreed that one should not teach students in the marketplace," whereupon Hiyya "went out and taught his two nephews, Rav and Rabbah bar Hana, in the marketplace." Rabbi is angry when he learns of Hiyya's action, and places him under a ban for thirty days.[41] This story is the most explicit of several portrayals of Hiyya teaching Rav while simultaneously a subordinate of Rabbi.[42]

In another context, Rav "sits behind R. Hiyya and R. Hiyya sits before Rabbi." Rav questions Hiyya concerning a statement by Rabbi, and Hiyya responds with an explanation.[43] The fixed seating arrangement described here portrays Hiyya instructing Rav at the time of the encounter, and at least in some instances the technical formula describes interaction between contemporary teachers of different rank.

Very likely, at least some of the other usages of the term depict the same relationship between Amoraim. In no cases can we state with comparable certainty that the middle-level sage is portrayed as a simple student at the time of the encounter.

These few cases, furthermore, portray colleagues interacting in formal settings and not merely as a result of chance encounters, a conclusion supported by the discussion of third-generation Pumbedita which follows. The exact nature of these formal gatherings is not evident

---

[38]See Gafni, *Yehudei Bavel bi-Tekufat ha-Talmud*, pp. 200-1, especially p. 200, n. 100.
[39]See also Kosowsky, "Ha-Yeshiva ba-'Yeshiva,'" pp. 323-24, who claims that some students sat behind the teacher. Kosowsky visualizes a single teacher facing one group of students while another group of students sits facing his back.
[40]See also Gafni, *Yehudei Bavel bi-Tekufat ha-Talmud*, pp. 278-79. With regard to the relationships between Rabbi, R. Hiyya, and Rav, see also *Yihusei Tannaim ve-Amoraim*, ed. Yehuda Leib Maimon (Jerusalem: Mosad ha-Rav Kuk, 1963), pp. 249-53.
[41]Moed Katan 16a-b.
[42]See Berakhot 43a (and parallel), Shabbat 3a-b, Yoma 87a-b, and Sanhedrin 5a-b. See also Yerushalmi Hagigah 1:4 (and Urbach, *Ha-Halacha*, p. 192-93) and Kilayim 9:3. See also Eruvin 73a; *Sefer ha-Keritut*, Yemot Olam, Part 2, chapter 1; and *Sefer Yuhasin ha-Shalem*, ed. Philipovsky and Freiman, p. 138.
[43]Hullin 16a.

from the skeletal descriptions of seating arrangement provided by the formula discussed above. While this term most likely does not describe a disciple circle, there is no compelling evidence that it describes three Amoraim interacting together in the context of an academy. Very likely, we should accept the explicit evidence at face value, according to which the term depicts personal encounters between teachers, perhaps in the presence of simple students, perhaps in the presence of other teachers of different rank.

Collegial Interaction Throughout the Talmud: The Case of Third-Generation Pumbedita

Having described typical forms of collegial interaction, we examine relationships between prominent third-generation Pumbeditan colleagues for further evidence of Amoraic decentralization. We noted above that Rav and Shmuel and Abaye and Rava, important Amoraim of the first and fourth generations respectively, rarely interact, and that dispute dialogue between Babylonian Amoraim in every generation is extremely rare. How frequently do colleagues interact in third-generation Pumbedita, apparently the most richly documented time and place in the entire Bavli?

Analysis of relationships between Rabbah, Rav Yosef, and Abaye reveals a picture of three contemporary Pumbeditan teachers. Rabbah is portrayed as the superior and Yosef his near-equal, and face-to-face contact between them is relatively rare. Abaye, on the other hand, is portrayed as Rabbah's and Yosef's inferior colleague, and face-to-face contact between them (i.e., between Abaye and Rabbah, and Abaye and Yosef) is routine.[44]

Examining first Yosef's relationship with Rabbah, one source depicts Rabbah as head in Pumbedita, with Yosef ruling in his stead after his death.[45] This narrative portrays the two Amoraim as candidates for the same position of authority. Rabbah wins the appointment, and dies after twenty-two years of rule, following which Yosef assumes control.[46] This source, however, says nothing about their relationship during the period of Rabbah's rule. What is the nature of that relationship?

---

[44]See also the discussion of Rabbah bar Rav Hanan, below.
[45]Berakhot 64a and parallel. Compare Neusner, *A History of the Jews in Babylonia*, vol. 4, pp. 91-102; and Beer, *Rashut ha-Golah*, pp. 100-6.
[46]See chapter 1, above, for further discussion of this story. See also the discussion of Baba Mezia 86a, which contradicts, in part for polemical reasons, several aspects of the dominant Talmudic portrayal of the relationship between Rabbah and Yosef.

Two sources[47] most likely depict Yosef as a teacher in his own right, inferior to Rabbah, during the period of Rabbah's rule. According to these sources, objections posed to Rabbah by Abaye and Rabbah bar Rav Hanan "were difficult for Rabbah and Rav Yosef for twenty-two years." These sources allude to the twenty-two years that Rabbah ruled prior to Yosef, and imply that all through Rabbah's reign Yosef responds to objections posed by inferiors,[48] and presumably does so successfully at times. We cannot interpret that Yosef knows the answers to these difficulties already during Rabbah's rule, but lacks authority to state them publicly until after Rabbah's death, for the sources state explicitly that the issues were "difficult for Yosef," and not that he lacked authority to respond.[49]

Other sources similarly portray Yosef as a teacher in his own right during the period of Rabbah's rule. One source, for example, depicts a lower-level rabbi asking Yosef a halachic question during Rabbah's lifetime (see below).[50] According to another source, Rabbah states an opinion, Abaye objects in his presence, and Rabbah responds. "I wanted to object against the master [Rabbah]," continues Abaye, "but Rav Yosef did not let me," since he considers it inappropriate to object when a superior is about to decide a question which impinges on biblical law. Later on, in Rabbah's absence, Yosef asks Abaye to state his objection against Rabbah. Abaye obliges, and Yosef resolves the objection.[51] Yosef, therefore, is shown teaching Abaye at the same time that he is Rabbah's subordinate.

Further indication that Yosef is depicted as a teacher of students during Rabbah's rule is perhaps provided by the hundreds of dialogues between Yosef and Abaye recorded throughout the Talmud. According to one story referred to above, Yosef lived a very short time following Rabbah's death,[52] and it is unlikely that the hundreds of dialogues between Abaye and Yosef scattered throughout the Talmud date from the approximately two years that Yosef lived following Rabbah's death.

---

[47]For further discussion of these sources, see chapter 1, above.

[48]Ketubot 42b (*DS* Herschler, notes on line 13, and n. 20) and Baba Kamma 66b (*DS* ayin). This inference is corroborated by several other sources. See, for example, Kiddushin 58a, and see the discussion below.

[49]Very likely, the same background is presupposed by several cases in which Abaye and Rabbah dialogue together, and Abaye subsequently goes before Yosef. See Pesahim 108a, Yevamot 110a-b, and Zevahim 75b-76a, and see the discussion below.

[50]Niddah 42a.

[51]Eruvin 67b.

[52]Berakhot 64a (and parallel). See *DS* khaf, according to which the versions are divided as to whether Yosef lived two or two-and-one-half years after Rabbah's death.

To my knowledge, Yosef and Abaye dialogue together more frequently than any other pair of Amoraim, and if we deny that Yosef taught students during Rabbah's lifetime, we must assign all of this activity to a tiny period at the end of his life.[53]

It is possible, of course, that this story is fictional, in which case the argument of the previous paragraph is not probative. A storyteller perhaps invented the detail of Yosef's brief rule, and the hundreds of dialogues between Abaye and Yosef need not be assigned to a tiny period at the end of Yosef's life.

Another argument depends on accepting the sources' historicity, and I likewise offer it tentatively. One source refers to Yosef's sickness, which causes him to "forget his learning."[54] On several occasions, Abaye jogs Yosef's memory by repeating statements he made earlier to students.[55] Unless we wish to assign all of this activity (Yosef's teaching, his forgetting, and Abaye's reminding) to the final two years of Yosef's life (an extremely unlikely proposition), then it follows that Yosef taught students throughout Rabbah's lifetime. If this story is fictional, however, it is useless as evidence regarding Yosef's status during Rabbah's rule.

In any event, several of the sources examined above unambiguously depict Yosef as a teacher of students during Rabbah's lifetime. The frequency with which Yosef and Rabbah interact, however, is a separate question, and evidence of direct contact between them is surprisingly rare. In all, they appear in each other's presence only 23 times,[56] quite a small number given their geographical and chronological proximity and the frequency with which they appear throughout the Talmud.

Rabbah's and Yosef's contradictory opinions are often juxtaposed, but only on four occasions is there proof, in the form of dialogue, that they state their opinions in each other's presence.[57] They are referred to as "the Amoraim of Pumbedita,"[58] but this designation need not imply a collegial relationship or even direct contact between them. They might simply be grouped together on account of their geographical and

---

[53]See also Hyman, *Toldot Tannaim ve-Amoraim*, p. 747.

[54]Nedarim 41a. See also Shabbat 22a, Eruvin 75b, Ketubot 2a, and Baba Batra 134b, and see the references cited in the following note.

[55]Eruvin 10a, 41a, 66b, 73a, and 89b, Makkot 4a, and Niddah 39a and 63b.

[56]Shabbat 18a, Eruvin 51a, 65b, 67b, 78a-b, and 78b, Pesahim 28a and 37b, Moed Katan 2b, Yevamot 66b, Nedarim 46a-b, Kiddushin 58a, Baba Kamma 56b-57b and 66a-b, Baba Batra 32b (twice), Zevahim 14b, Menahot 39a (twice), Hullin 46a and 123a, Bekhorot 31a, and Meilah 2b-3a. See also Berakhot 64a, Shabbat 40a and 99b, Pesahim 108a, Bezah 7b, Moed Katan 25b and 27b, Yevamot 110a-b, Ketubot 42a-b and 106a, Gittin 60b, Sanhedrin 17b, Zevahim 75b-76a, and Niddah 42a.

[57]Moed Katan 2b, Baba Kamma 56b-57b and 66a-b, and Meilah 2b-3a.

[58]Sanhedrin 17b.

chronological proximity.[59] The same is true of another account which speaks of four hundred rabbis who remain throughout the year when part-time students leave "the house of Rabbah and Rav Yosef."[60] At first glance, this account appears to imply that the two Amoraim preside together over a single academic institution. However, the phrase could simply be a shorthand reference to "the house of Rabbah and the house of Rav Yosef," i.e., to both of their independent schools, which are mentioned together because of their geographical and chronological proximity.

Turning now to the relationship between Abaye and Rabbah, they are portrayed as contemporary teachers of different rank in one story in which Rav Shmuel bar Bisna asks Abaye a question, travels next to Rabbah and asks the same question, and from there goes before Yosef and repeats the question again, receiving the same response each time. Ultimately, Shmuel bar Bisna returns to Abaye for further discussion of the issue.[61] Clearly, this encounter purports to take place during the lifetime of Rabbah and portrays Abaye as a teacher of students while Rabbah is still alive.

Abaye and Rabbah are depicted as contemporary teachers in another story as well. Rav Mordechai asks a halachic question first of Rabbah, then of Yosef, and finally of Abaye.[62] In the end, Mordechai objects against "them," apparently addressing all three of his superiors, suggesting that Abaye taught Mordechai during Rabbah's lifetime.[63]

Abaye and Rabbah, furthermore, are portrayed by the Bavli as close throughout their entire lives, and a clear hierarchical distinction between them is consistently maintained. Abaye is identified by a geonic source

---

[59]See also chapter 10, above.
[60]Ketubot 106a.
[61]Niddah 42a.
[62]Shabbat 99b. The printed edition reads Rava (see, however, Masoret ha-Shas), but the placement of his statement prior to Yosef's and Abaye's indicates that Rabbah is referred to. See *DS* ayin, and chapter 10, above.
[63]Although the word "them" is found in all versions, it might be a scribal addition or a later expansion of an abbreviated text. The text at one time perhaps read *alef-lamed*, which later scribes expanded to *amar lehu* ("he said to them"). The text could just as easily have been expanded to *amar lei* ("he said to him"), namely to Abaye alone. Mordechai, therefore, should perhaps be understood as objecting in the presence of Abaye alone.

Even according to this understanding, however, the source very likely depicts Abaye, Yosef, and Rabbah as contemporary teachers, particularly in view of the strikingly similar story involving Shmuel bar Bisna discussed immediately above. The possibility that Mordechai went before Abaye after Rabbah's and Yosef's death, however, cannot be entirely dismissed. See the discussion of Huna and Yehuda, above.

as Rabbah's nephew,[64] a tradition perhaps confirmed by, perhaps based on, the unusually large number of cases in which Abaye interacts with Rabbah as a child and has intimate encounters with Rabbah and his family.[65] In any event, Abaye and Rabbah purportedly had a close relationship, which according to two stories lasted until Rabbah's death. According to one source, Rabbah expresses certainty that Abaye will be present at his funeral and will loudly mourn his death.[66] Elsewhere, Abaye is portrayed as Rabbah's loyal disciple at the time of his death, most prominent among those who attend to his body.[67]

Turning now to the relationship between Abaye and Yosef, they are also depicted as contemporary teachers of different rank, and they likewise interact frequently throughout the Talmud. In addition to Abaye's resolution of a halachic question by Rav Shmuel bar Bisna during the lifetime of Yosef, and his contact with Yosef as teacher of Rav Mordechai (see above), Abaye's status as Yosef's colleague is indicated by a story which recounts Rav Ada bar Ahava's premature death. According to this story, Yosef claims that "I punished him [i.e., brought about his death], for I cursed him." Abaye insists that "I punished him, for [Ada bar Ahava] would say to the rabbis, 'Instead of gnawing bones in the house of Abaye, come and eat choice meat in the house of Rava.'"[68] That is, Ada bar Ahava died according to this passage during Yosef's lifetime, and Abaye, prior to Ada's death, is an independent teacher, head of his own "house," i.e., his own academic institution.[69]

Very likely, contact between Abaye and Yosef as colleagues of different rank is observable in one case in which Abaye's objection in the presence of Yosef is treated by contemporaries as a viable halachic position in opposition to Yosef's view.[70] When R. Hanina bar Papi sends back in agreement with Yosef, Abaye refuses to retract. The issue is then sent before Rav Manyumi b. d'Rav Nihumi, who sends back in support of Abaye. It is difficult to view Abaye's actions as those of a simple student in the presence of his teacher, and this case very likely portrays contact between them as colleagues.

---

[64]See *Arukh ha-Shalem*, ed. Kohut, vol. 1, p. 9, quoting Rav Sherira Gaon.
[65]Berakhot 48a, Shabbat 154b, Pesahim 101a, 108a, and 115b, and Sukkah 53a.
[66]Shabbat 153a.
[67]Baba Mezia 86a. Obviously we are not compelled to accept most of the story as historical evidence in order to take seriously the story's conception of the relationship between Abaye and Rabbah.
[68]Baba Batra 22a. For further discussion of this story, see the Introduction, above.
[69]See *Sefer Yuhasin ha-Shalem*, ed. Philipovsky and Freiman, p. 170; and Jehiel Heilprin, *Seder ha-Dorot* (1769; rpt. Warsaw, 1883), vol. 2, pp. 23-24. Regarding the term *Bei* ("house of") as a reference to an academic institution, see Goodblatt, *Rabbinic Instruction in Sasanian Babylonia*, pp. 108-54.
[70]Ketubot 81b. See also the discussion above.

In addition, Abaye's and Yosef's initial interaction in this context (i.e., Abaye's objection in Yosef's presence) is typical of their interaction throughout the Talmud. Only the continuation of the story distinguishes their relationship here from their relationship in numerous other contexts. Very likely, many other cases in which Abaye objects in Yosef's presence are to be understood as contact not between a simple student and his teacher, but between superior and inferior colleagues. Further supporting this claim is the fact that Abaye's frequently blunt rejections of Yosef's opinions and arguments[71] sound like the words of a mature scholar rather than of a simple disciple.[72]

It is also worth noting that Rava, Abaye's younger contemporary, appears in several stories as an independent teacher in Mahoza while Abaye objects in Yosef's presence as an inferior in Pumbedita.[73] It is unlikely that Abaye, Rava's senior, is to be viewed as no more than a simple student of Yosef in stories which depict Rava as an independent teacher. Many of Abaye's objections in Yosef's presence, therefore, should likewise be viewed as those of an inferior teacher in the presence of his superior.

This conclusion is strengthened by one source which depicts Abaye objecting in Yosef's presence at the time of his (i.e., Yosef's) sixtieth birthday.[74] Their interaction here is typical of their interaction elsewhere, further indication that in all likelihood, Abaye and Yosef are depicted throughout the Talmud as colleagues of different rank, even when the text supplies no explicit evidence of a collegial relationship between them.

Even Rabbah bar Rav Hanan (Rabbah's,[75] Abaye's,[76] and to a lesser extent Yosef's[77] inferior throughout the Talmud) is described by one story as an independent teacher during Rabbah's and Abaye's lifetime. According to this narrative,[78] Rabbah bar Rav Hanan has authority to

---

[71]See the references cited above. In addition, Yosef objects and Abaye resolves the objection, presumably in Yosef's presence, on Berakhot 21a, Shabbat 62b, 108a, and 108b, Pesahim 71a, Ketubot 6b, Kiddushin 25b, Shevuot 26a, Hullin 36b and 123b, and Arakhin 6a.

[72]See *Sefer Yuhasin ha-Shalem*, ed. Philipovsky and Freiman, pp. 104 and 107; Seder ha-Dorot vol. 2, pp. 23-24; Yudelowitz, *Yeshivat Pumbedita*, p. 48; and Halperin, *Atlas Ez-Hayyim*, vol. 3, pp. 181-82, who refer to Abaye as Yosef's colleague or student-colleague.

[73]Nedarim 55a, Baba Batra 22a, and Hullin 133a.

[74]Moed Katan 28a.

[75]See Kalmin, *The Redaction of the Babylonian Talmud*, pp. 126-33. See especially Berakhot 48a (*DS* vav) and Shabbat 153a.

[76]Kalmin, *The Redaction of the Babylonian Talmud*, pp. 126-33.

[77]See Hyman, *Toldot Tannaim ve-Amoraim*, p. 1059.

[78]Bezah 12b.

render practical halachic decisions (*Hora'ah*) during Rabbah's lifetime, very likely revealing his status as an independent teacher.[79]

According to the admittedly meager information concerning this Amora, he remains close with Rabbah and Abaye throughout his lifetime. He has an intimate encounter with Rabbah and Abaye as a child in Rabbah's household,[80] and elsewhere Rabbah expresses confidence that Rabbah bar Rav Hanan, together with Abaye, will be present at his funeral and will loudly mourn his death.[81]

Abaye, furthermore, is depicted as Rabbah's subordinate in the story featuring Rabbah bar Rav Hanan's practical halachic decision. Abaye objects as an inferior in the presence of Rabbah (in conformity with their relationship throughout the Talmud), at a time when Abaye's inferior, Rabbah bar Rav Hanan, exercises authority as an independent teacher. We have further indication, therefore, that many of Abaye's objections and questions to Rabbah throughout the Talmud should be viewed as those of an inferior colleague rather than those of a simple student to his teacher.

Perhaps the rarity of the Talmudic term *Talmid-Haver* (student-colleague), which describes a student who is also a teacher in his own right,[82] argues against the above conclusions. That the term describes an inferior colleague is shown, for example, by a case in which the early Ravina, during Rav Ashi's lifetime, examines a butcher's knife to determine its acceptability. Ravina refers to his action as *Hora'ah*, and as noted above, authority to engage in *Hora'ah* very likely implies possession of independent authority as a teacher. When attacked by Ashi for overstepping his bounds, Ravina defends himself by claiming status as Rav Ashi's student-colleague. As the term implies, therefore, a student-colleague is an independent, but inferior, teacher.

Since the term appears only rarely throughout the Talmud, perhaps the implication is that the inferior colleague, the student who teaches students of his own, is an extremely uncommon rabbinic type. However, other Talmudic terms of relationship (*Talmid*, "student", *Rav*, "teacher," and *Haver*, "colleague"), also refer at least occasionally to inferior and superior colleagues. A relationship between teachers of different rank is sometimes described in the Talmud as a relationship between a *Talmid* and a *Rav*,[83] two *Haverim*, or a *Talmid-Haver* and his superior. A rabbi can

---

[79]See Appendix 1, below.
[80]Berakhot 48a (*DS* vav).
[81]Shabbat 153a.
[82]For more on the term *Talmid-Haver*, see Halperin, *Atlas Ez-Hayyim*, vol. 3, pp. 178-88.
[83]See, for example, Halperin, *Atlas Ez-Hayyim*, vol. 3, pp. 123-31 and 179.

be a *Talmid* and simultaneously instruct students of his own. Some Amoraim, for example, are called "students of [the Amora named] Rav," even in contexts where they act as teachers.[84] Similarly, an Amora can be a *Rav* and simultaneously be subordinate to other Amoraim.

Rav Ada bar Ahava, for example, meets Rav Dimi Minehardea for the first time when Dimi arrives in Mahoza with produce to sell.[85] Ada confronts him with several difficult halachic questions to determine whether he merits market privileges reserved for sages. When Dimi is unable to respond, Ada announces that "I am your *Rav*, and Rava is the *Rav* of your *Rav*." Ada, in referring to himself as Dimi's *Rav*, claims superiority over Dimi in the hierarchy of sages while simultaneously admitting his inferiority to Rava.

Similarly, in two cases Rav Ada bar Matna objects in Rava's presence and Ravina resolves the objection, also in Rava's presence. Rava commands Ada bar Matna to "listen to what your *Rav* [i.e., Ravina] says."[86] The term *Rav* expresses Ravina's superiority to Ada in the hierarchy of sages, and Ravina is obviously Rava's inferior.

The rarity of the term *Talmid-Haver*, therefore, says nothing about the importance or frequency of the phenomenon of the inferior who is a teacher in his own right.

Summary and Conclusions

The sources under consideration either (1) accurately describe Amoraic relationships in third-generation Pumbedita, or (2) reflect later conceptions regarding these relationships. Irrespective of their provenance, the sources describe rabbis whose near-equality discourages frequent contact between them, either because of the intensity of competition between them, or because of societal norms which call for rabbis who have achieved special prominence to establish their own fully independent schools. In either case, the sources depict a paucity of contact between Rabbah and Yosef, two of the most important rabbis of

---

[84]Pesahim 103a-b and 105a. See also Shabbat 19b. See also Yevamot 16a, with regard to Tannaim. In a related phenomenon, R Hiyya's sons are referred to simply as "the sons of R. Hiyya" on Bezah 9b, even though they act as independent teachers. See also Baba Kamma 117a-b, where R. Yohanan, clearly an independent teacher, refers to himself as Rav Kahana's *Talmid*. See also Shabbat 51a and Eruvin 13a with regard to Tannaim. See also Berakhot 32a, where Moshe is referred to as a *Talmid* and God as his *Rav*, and Moshe is the teacher of Israel, instructing them in the laws of the Torah.
[85]Baba Batra 22a.
[86]Shevuot 18b and Zevahim 100b. Compare Hyman, *Toldot Tannaim ve-Amoraim*, p. 1088.

their generation, and support my claim regarding the decentralized character of the Babylonian rabbinic movement.

The issue merits further study, but by way of preliminary observation it should be noted that one narrative attests to competition either between Yosef and Rabbah, or between subsequent generations of rabbis who viewed themselves as Yosef's and Rabbah's disciples. This narrative, it will be recalled, portrays Yosef's scholarship as superior to Rabbah's, and seeks to explain why Rabbah was nevertheless chosen before Yosef as head in Pumbedita. This story provides some support for my suggestion that Yosef and Rabbah are depicted as deliberately avoiding contact with one another because of the intensity of competition between them.[87]

Interaction between Abaye and Rabbah, and Abaye and Yosef, however, is portrayed as routine, apparently because the hierarchical distinction between them was substantially clearer and competition between them less intense. We find no narratives, for example, depicting attempts by Abaye to place himself above Rabbah or Yosef, or efforts by Rabbah or Yosef to remind Abaye of his inferior status. Interaction between Abaye and Rabbah, and Abaye and Yosef, is typical of interaction between rabbis throughout the Talmud, suggesting that the relationship between colleagues of different rank rather than the master-disciple relationship is the most commonly observed form of interaction recorded in the Talmud.

Obviously, conclusions based on several diverse sources are more firmly established than are conclusions based on fewer sources. The present study of third-generation Pumbedita must be augmented by similar studies of other localities and time periods.

The findings of the present chapter, furthermore, increase the likelihood that the Babylonian rabbinic movement was much larger than a simple count of the number of Amoraim mentioned in the Talmud would suggest. According to the conclusions above, most of the sages mentioned in the Talmud are among the leaders of the rabbinic movement, and under most circumstances the ordinary rank and file are not cited or named.

This conclusion has possible implications for study of the role of Babylonian rabbis in Jewish society. The extent of rabbinic influence on the general Jewish population is disputed by scholars, with some positing a great deal of influence and others positing much less.[88] The

---

[87]Berakhot 64a (and parallel). See also Baba Mezia 86a and the discussion above.
[88]See Gafni, *Yehudei Bavel bi-Tekufat ha-Talmud*, pp. 204-32 and 235-36. Compare Jacob Neusner, "Rabbis and Community in Third Century Babylonia," in

findings of this chapter support the former view, since it is unlikely (although possible) that a large rabbinic movement had little impact on the general Jewish population.

A large rabbinic movement, however, need not imply the existence of academies during the Amoraic period in Babylonia. The likelihood that contacts between teachers were witnessed by large numbers of students does not imply that the locus of their interaction was an academy. Even disciple circles can consist of large numbers of students. As Goodblatt observes, the fundamental difference between his view and the traditional conception is the difference between (1) a temporary entity that does not survive the death of the individual master who heads the disciple circle, and (2) a permanent institution with a corporate identity that transcends the personality of the individual master.[89]

The conclusions of the present chapter also challenge conventional descriptions of the division between Amoraic generations and the roles of students and teachers. According to conventional descriptions, a particular master is stationed in a particular locality, holding sway over an entire generation of scholars or perhaps sharing power with a small number of contemporaries who rule in different cities. When this master dies, one of his students rules in his place, perhaps moving the school to a neighboring city. When this new master dies, his student in turn takes control, or perhaps two students form competing schools in different localities, and so on until the conclusion of the Amoraic period. Occasionally there may be a brief interregnum following the death of a master, or competition between several of his students over who should rule in his place. Occasionally, a student graduates from the school of his master during the master's lifetime and forms a school of his own, usually in a different city, but for the most part the younger generation politely waits for the older generation to relinquish power before attempting to assert independent authority.

This overly schematic and orderly portrayal finds its earliest expression in geonic and later medieval literature,[90] but these early commentators are concerned with chronicling the history of the leadership of the academy, which passes in their view in orderly fashion from one generation to the next. With rare exceptions, they are not concerned with authorities that exist contemporary with, but

---

Religions in Antiquity: Essays in Memory of E.R. Goodenough, ed. Jacob Neusner (Leiden: E.J. Brill, 1968), pp. 438-59.
[89]Goodblatt, "Hitpathuyot Hadashot be-Heker Yeshivot Bavel," p. 38.
[90]See, for example, *Seder Tannaim ve-Amoraim,* ed. Kahan, pp. 4-6 and 9-10; *Igeret Rav Sherira Gaon,* ed Lewin, pp. 78-97; and *Sefer ha-Kabalah,* ed. Cohen, pp. 24-27 and 31-32 (Hebrew text).

independent of, the heads of academies. The geonic preoccupation is reflected in numerous modern scholarly treatments of the subject.

A recent description of the Amoraic period by Avraham Goldberg, based entirely on geonic sources, will serve as an excellent illustration of this point.[91] Goldberg writes:

> Shmuel died in 254 C.E. and his chief pupil, *Rav Yehuda*, reestablished the academy in Pumbeditha following the destruction of Nehardea. Rav was succeeded, following his decease in 247, by his pupil *Rav Huna*....
>
> The hegemony of Sura was eclipsed for a long period following the demise of *Rav Hisda* (flor. 299-309), Rav Huna's successor....
>
> The third-generation heads in Pumbeditha were *Rabba bar Nahmani* (309-330) and *Rav Yosef bar Hiya* (330-333).
>
> Their chief pupils were *Abaye* and *Rava*.... Abaye (333-338) carried on the strong Babylonian tradition in Pumbeditha. Yet when Rava acceded to headship, he removed the academy to Mahoza where he taught for a longer period (338-352)....
>
> Rava's pupils were the leading figures of the next generation. One, *Rav Nahman bar Yizhak* (352-356) moved back to Pumbeditha.... Another, *Rav Pappa* (359-371) established a rival academy at Naresh, not far South from Sura.
>
> *Rav Ashi* succeeded Rav Pappa and returned the academy to Sura.

Throughout this chapter, however, we found repeatedly that the picture reflected by the Talmudic sources is substantially less tidy than the above description implies. The boundaries separating the generations and the distinctions between masters and disciples were found to be far less rigid than modern scholarly accounts based on geonic sources lead us to believe.

---

[91]Goldberg, "The Babylonian Talmud," pp. 326-27.

Conclusion

Part 1 of this study concluded that the Talmud contains diverse sources. Briefly summarizing, we found that (1) some Talmudic stories reflect diverse polemical perspectives (chapter 1); (2) early Amoraim tend to distinguish between the authority and statements of Rav and Shmuel, but later Amoraim tend to view them as a unit (chapter 2); (3) (Palestinian) Tannaim and (Babylonian) Amoraim differ on the subject of dreams and dream interpreters. (Palestinian) Tannaim, for example, interpret the symbolic dreams of non-rabbis, and (Babylonian) Amoraim interpret the message dreams of fellow rabbis (chapter 3); (4) statements by early Amoraim presuppose distinct judicial and academic hierarchies, but statements by later Amoraim do not (chapter 4); (5) both the Bavli and Yerushalmi agree that several features of the discourse, activity, and relationships of Palestinian Amoraim set them apart from Babylonian Amoraim (chapter 5); (6) early and later Amoraic discourse differs. Later Amoraim, for example, tend to listen silently while subordinates speak, but early Amoraim do not (chapter 6); (7) quotation forms vary according to the chronology of the Amoraim who transmit the quote, with early and later Amoraic statements introduced by different quotation forms. Some middle-generation Amoriam follow the early pattern and others follow the later pattern (chapter 7); and (8) anonymous commentary responds differently to the personalities of rabbis than does attributed commentary (chapter 8).[1]

Part 2 of this study concluded that the Talmud depicts the Babylonian rabbinic movement as decentralized. The most important rabbinic leaders in each generation had surprisingly little direct contact, and colleagues of approximately equal status interacted much less frequently than did colleagues of more widely different status.

The two parts of this book, therefore, reinforce one another, since Part 2's conclusion that the Babylonian rabbinic movement lacked unity and centralization confirms Part 1's conclusion regarding diverse

---

[1] In addition, contemporaries and near-contemporaries regularly praise and criticize one another, but non-contemporaries do so only rarely (chapter 8). We observed that this distinction between contemporary and non-contemporary commentary provides evidence of diverse sources according to two of three possible historical explanations of the phenomenon.

sources, and Part 1's conclusions argue in favor of the historicity of the Bavli's portrayals of a decentralized rabbinic movement responsible for producing and transmitting these sources. A unified movement would most likely not have produced, for example, the stories reflecting diverse polemical perspectives analyzed in chapter 1, nor would a unified movement have introduced statements by contemporary rabbis (for example, Abaye and Rava, or diverse students of Rav) with different quotation forms (chapter 7),[2] or Babylonianized most, but not all, Palestinian sources (chapter 5).

The two parts of this study independently confirm one another, with diverse, even totally unrelated sources repeatedly yielding the same conclusions. Analyses of (1) relationships in third-generation Pumbedita (chapter 11), (2) of the polemical intent of stories involving second-generation Palestinian sages (chapter 1), (3) of relationships between prominent fourth-generation rabbis (chapter 10), and (4) of quotation forms introducing Amoraic statements (chapter 7), to cite only a few examples, all showed the diversity of the Amoraic movement and the corresponding diversity of the literature produced by this movement.

Part 2's tentative conclusion that middle-generation Amoraim, in addition to later, post-Amoraic generations,[3] were among the editors of the Talmud, also supports the conclusions of Part 1. Diverse editors active in different time periods are likely to have produced the variegated, "thick" document posited by this book, with Amoraim of the first two or three generations repeatedly acting in one fashion and Amoraim of later generations conforming to different patterns. Editors active during a single time period, however, would have more likely produced the "thin," relatively undifferentiated document hypothesized by Jacob Neusner.

I am well aware that any historical conclusions based on ancient texts are open to challenge, and that an obvious objection can be raised against the above contentions. As noted in the introductory chapter, Neusner believes that the bulk of the Talmud reflects a single, late editorial voice. Later editors, claims Neusner, very likely had access to sources from different time periods, but reworked them so extensively that at present it is generally impossible to differentiate the contribution of the Amoraim from that of the editors. One might object, therefore, that the patterns

---

[2]For example, statements by Abaye are introduced by one form, and statements by Rava are introduced by a different form. Some students of Rav consistently quote statements by Rav by means of one form, and other students of Rav consistently use a different form. Some Amoraim quote rabbis whose names lack the honorific title "Rabbi" by means of one type of form, and others use a different form.

[3]See the studies cited in the Preface, above.

described throughout this book should be viewed as the invention of later editors. The editors who composed the bulk of the Talmud (according to Neusner) perhaps invented the distinctions between early and later, Palestinian and Babylonian, and anonymous and attributed statements described throughout this book. Perhaps these editors created the correspondence between the two parts of this study, between the source analyses of Part 1 and the examination of relationships and institutions of Part 2, repeatedly depicting middle-generation Amoraim as transitional, inventing distinctions between chronologically and geographically diverse rabbis, and fabricating a disorganized rabbinic movement likely to have produced and preserved an accurate record of Amoraic diversity. The editors' motive might have been to create a convincing portrait of early rabbis to lend credence to their claim to be accurately reporting the opinions and actions of the great sages of the distant past.[4]

Virtually anything is possible when speculating about the activity of ancient editors, and mathematical certainty on this issue is simply beyond our grasp. The best one can achieve is a convincing demonstration of a theory's usefulness, or lack thereof, in accounting for the extant data, and the studies which comprise this book show the problematic nature of Neusner's portrayal of the Talmud's editors. Neusner's theory requires us to posit an editor of unbelievable sophistication and thoroughness. In the absence of ancient models for such an editor, I prefer to view the diversity attested to in both parts of this study, and the transitional character of middle-generation Amoraim documented throughout Part 1, as the product of genuine historical processes rather than as the work of a genius centuries ahead of his time.[5]

If correct, the conclusions of this book increase the likelihood that Talmudic sources other than those specifically analyzed derive from the periods and places they purport to derive from, and contain usable historical information about pre-redactional centuries. If ancient Jewish literature is a rich source regarding pre-redactional centuries, furthermore, it is unlikely that other ancient literatures are useless in this regard. New techniques need to be developed to improve our ability to identify and describe diverse sources, since the findings of this study are directly applicable to certain features of the texts but not at all to others.

---

[4]In a personal communication of November 30, 1992, Neusner accused me of "confusing truth with verisimilitude."

[5]For a similar argument advanced in a critique of Neusner's work on the Mishna, see Shaye J.D. Cohen, "Jacob Neusner, Mishnah, and Counter-Rabbinics," *Conservative Judaism* 37, No. 1 (1983), pp. 48-63.

If successful, this book has demonstrated that the effort is worth making, that the sources are susceptible to this kind of inquiry, and that if the proper methodologies can be developed the rewards are likely to be substantial.

APPENDICES

Appendices to the Introduction

Appendix One: The Story of Mar bar Rav Ashi's Accession to Power in Mata Mehasia

The story of Mar bar Rav Ashi's accession to power,[1] analyzed briefly above, has been the subject of much scholarly attention for the light it sheds on the rabbinic movement and its institutions during the final Amoraic period.[2] It is particularly important because information about this period is so scarce.

Avinoam Cohen provides the most recent, comprehensive, and sophisticated treatment of this story. In this appendix, I review his arguments in detail, since my interpretation of the story and my evaluation of its use as historical evidence differ from Cohen's in several important respects.

Cohen claims that the story lacks signs of having been invented or doctored to reflect a particular point of view, and is therefore most likely reliable historically. It is not consistently sympathetic or hostile to either of the story's major protagonists. Certain aspects of the story, Cohen argues, portray Mar bar Rav Ashi in negative terms, demonstrating the unworthy means he used to wrest power out of the hands of his rival, while other aspects portray him positively, describing his actions as fulfillment of a divine prophecy.[3]

More fundamentally, argues Cohen, if one insists on understanding the story as a consistent polemic against Mar bar Rav Ashi, one acknowledges the existence of tension between late Amoraim and affirms the story's basic historicity. According to this argument, the story's reliability as a historical source is affirmed whether we understand it as a consistent polemic or not.

I argued above, however, that the story very likely reflects a consistent point of view, not against, but in favor of Mar bar Rav Ashi. I

---

[1]Baba Batra 12b.
[2]See above for a partial bibliography.
[3]Cohen, *Mar Bar Rav Ashi,* p. 56, n. 12.

claimed that the story derives from sources sympathetic to Mar bar Rav Ashi and legitimates his claim to the office of head of the *metivta*.

Cohen also argues that the story is most likely accurate because it depicts the late Amoraic period in conformity with its portrayal elsewhere in the Babylonian Talmud.[4] The story's portrayal of Aha Midifti as the leading scholar of his generation is consistent with his portrayal elsewhere, which according to Cohen demonstrates his superior qualifications for the office of head of the *metivta*. The story's characterization of Mar bar Rav Ashi as resolute, audacious, and daring, claims Cohen, is also consistent with his portrayal elsewhere. Mar bar Rav Ashi's "social isolation," his tendency throughout the Talmud to appear by himself, is understandable as a response by Mar bar Rav Ashi's contemporaries to his elevation against their will. Finally, the story's portrayal of opposition to Mar bar Rav Ashi is consistent with the opposition to him expressed elsewhere in the Talmud, indicated by the frequency with which his opinions are rejected.

These arguments also fail upon closer examination. First, the consistency between Mar bar Rav Ashi's portrayal here and his portrayal elsewhere in the Talmud is no proof that the story is true. Even if the story is sheer fabrication, is it surprising that its authors portray Mar bar Rav Ashi as forceful and daring given the fact that these aspects of his personality (according to Cohen) are well-known from elsewhere in the Talmud?

Second, while Mar bar Rav Ashi's *tendency* to appear in isolation is an undeniable fact, his "social isolation" is by no means total, for he several times appears in the presence of Ravina. Cohen's claim that encounters between Mar bar Rav Ashi and Ravina are unique in that they take place "outside the yeshiva" rests on the assumption that yeshivot, academies, existed during the final Amoraic generations, an assumption which has been seriously called into question by recent scholarship.[5] It also rests on the assumption that most Amoraic interaction takes place "inside the academy," even though Amoraic dialogues typically lack all specification of social context and provide no indication of where they take place. Mar bar Rav Ashi's dialogues with Ravina, therefore, need not be unique, and Mar's "isolation" is not as extreme as Cohen maintains.

It is also doubtful that the literary fact of Mar's relative isolation translates into social reality. In general, Amoraim speak in groups of two, and very infrequently in groups of three or four. Medieval commentators observe that as a rule, only those Amoraim who actively

---

[4]Cohen, *Mar Bar Rav Ashi*, pp. 57-58.
[5]See the references cited above, and see chapter 11, below.

participate in a discussion are mentioned in the Talmud by name.[6] Very likely, dialogues and individual statements take place in the presence of other rabbis, and Mar's "isolation" is a literary but not a social fact. At most, Cohen can point to the paucity of contact between Mar and several of his most important contemporaries, who very likely would have interacted with him at least occasionally had they been present when he uttered his statements. Geographical factors, however, and not opposition, may have been the determining factor in this peculiar feature of Mar bar Rav Ashi's discourse.

Cohen's other arguments in favor of the story's historicity likewise fail to convince. He claims, it will be recalled, that the story's portrayal of contemporary opposition to Mar bar Rav Ashi is consistent with the opposition to him expressed elsewhere in the Talmud. It is not at all clear, however, that the story depicts contemporary opposition to Mar bar Rav Ashi. True, Aha Midifti is initially chosen as head of the *metivta* in Mata Mehasia, but Mar bar Rav Ashi is in a different city (Mahoza) at the time. Geographical proximity rather than opposition may have induced Mar bar Rav Ashi's contemporaries to choose a different rabbi. In addition, the story nowhere alludes to opposition toward Mar bar Rav Ashi on account of his treatment of Aha Midifti. On the contrary, Aha alone reacts in the story, acknowledging defeat without the slightest trace of bitterness toward his rival.

Cohen's claim regarding Aha's superior qualifications for the office of head of the *metivta* is also debatable at best. Aha's contribution to the Talmud consists almost exclusively of objections and questions in the presence of his superior, Ravina,[7] and it is by no means clear why such activity uniquely qualifies him for the office of head of the *metivta*.

Perhaps it will be argued that several of the story's historical details are reliable, for it is unlikely that sources sympathetic to Mar bar Rav Ashi would fabricate a story in which he acts unethically. Perhaps the transmitters of this story cannot omit mention of well-known details about the event even though they reflect poorly on the hero of the tale. They cannot suppress the details, but can provide a narrative context which makes them seem more palatable.

It is likely, however, that Mar bar Rav Ashi's actions do not appear objectionable in the slightest to the story's authors and transmitters. Very likely, his actions are viewed as no more unethical than those of the biblical matriarch, Rebekkah. Rebekkah, it will be recalled, receives a prophecy concerning her sons, Jacob and Esau. She knows in advance that Jacob, the younger sibling, will be blessed in place of his older

---

[6]See Gafni, "He'arot le-Ma'amaro Shel D. Goodblatt," pp. 53-54.
[7]Kalmin, *The Redaction of the Babylonian Talmud,* pp. 103-22.

brother, Esau. At times with cunning and deceit, Rebekkah sees to it that God's plan is put into effect.[8] Very likely, Mar bar Rav Ashi's actions as well are not viewed as morally objectionable, and even circles sympathetic to Mar bar Rav Ashi would not hesitate to invent a story in which he seizes power from a rival. On the contrary, Mar bar Rav Ashi's effort in bringing about the fulfillment of the prophecy, bending the actions of men to conform to the contrary will of God, is very likely seen as the only legitimate course of action given the prophetic insight which only he possesses.

---

[8]Genesis 25:19-28:9.

Appendices to the Introduction

Appendix Two: The Unit of Sources Describing Rav Ada bar Ahava's Death: Do They Derive from Diverse Polemical Perspectives?

As noted above, the stories and statements collected on Baba Batra 22a describe Rav Ada bar Ahava's death as deserved punishment for his humiliating treatment of Dimi Minehardea, and orchestrate events to cast Ada in an unfavorable light. This unit of stories and statements, we concluded, attest either to contemporary hatred of Ada bar Ahava, or to later hostility between competing schools.

The final story in the unit, that involving Rav Nahman bar Yizhak, perhaps reflects a different polemical perspective. The story perhaps derives from sources sympathetic to Ada or the school he founded. It portrays Ada as an extremely important and knowledgeable sage, whose learning is indispensible to Nahman bar Yizhak and sought after by Rav Papa and Rav Huna b. d'Rav Yehoshua.

The story is prefaced by Nahman bar Yizhak's assertion of responsibility for Ada's death, as follows: "I punished him, for Rav Nahman bar Yizhak[1] was head of the *kallah* (a gathering of rabbis and

---

[1]Nahman bar Yizhak, incidentally, certainly did not say: "I punished him, for Rav Nahman bar Yizhak was head of the *kallah*...." (See especially the Hamburg manuscript, which reads "Rav Nahman bar Yizhak said: 'I punished him.' And it is reasonable to conclude that Rav Nahman bar Yizhak punished him....") Clearly the introductory assertion and accompanying explanation were not uttered simultaneously. Very likely, the editor had at his disposal a story and a separate assertion of responsibility. Perhaps the editor had only the story, and composed the assertion of responsibility himself as an introduction to the story.

In addition, in all likelihood the assertions and explanations attributed to the Amoraim who precede Nahman bar Yizhak were also authored independently. Yosef's and Dimi's explanations are absent from the Munich manuscript, and Yosef's explanation is found only in the margin of the Florence manuscript (see *DS* bet and gimel). As Friedman observes in "Al Derekh Heker ha-Sugya," pp.

223

non-rabbis for a period of concentrated study)."[2] According to the story, Nahman was in the habit of reviewing his lecture with Ada before entering the *kallah*. One day, however, Rav Papa and Rav Huna b. d'Rav Yehoshua request Ada to review with them Rava's recent halachic lecture. Ada obliges them, the hour grows late,[3] and Nahman's audience grows impatient for his lecture to begin. Nahman explains that he awaits the bier of Rav Ada bar Ahava, whereupon word arrives that Ada is dead.[4]

Perhaps Nahman's comment about Ada's bier should be interpreted as anger, perhaps not. Perhaps Nahman assumes that Ada missed his appointment because he is dead. In other words, when Nahman says, "I am waiting for the bier of Rav Ada bar Ahava," he is either angrily pronouncing Ada's death sentence, or calmly assuming that only Ada's death would explain his uncharacteristic tardiness, delaying Nahman's lecture to the assembled crowd. Perhaps by announcing what he assumes is already Ada's fate, Nahman unwittingly puts it into effect. Such is the power of the spoken word, the story perhaps claims, even when uttered in error and without malice.

Understood in this fashion, the story is strikingly similar to another story which relates the death of Yehuda, son of R. Hiyya.[5] According to this story, Yehuda returns home from the study house each week prior to Shabbat. One week, Yehuda is absorbed in his studies and fails to arrive at the usual time. His father-in-law, R. Yannai, assumes that Yehuda must be dead, and orders his bed overturned as a sign of mourning. "It was like an error which issued forth from a ruler,"[6] the story concludes, and Yannai unwittingly brings about his son-in-law's death.

The Yehuda-Yannai story revolves around the tension between two crucially important commandments, study of Torah and responsibility to one's family, which frequently place conflicting demands upon an

---

30-31, manuscript variation is an important indicator of later scribal or editorial activity.

[2]See Goodblatt, *Rabbinic Instruction in Sasanian Babylonia*, pp. 155-70.

[3]See the commentary of R. Hananel in *Shitat Kadmonim Al Shalosh Bavot*, ed. Moshe Blau. It is unclear whether Hananel is summarizing part of the story or quoting in full the version before him.

[4]An anonymous statement at the conclusion of the unit decides in favor of the final story's version of the circumstances leading to Ada's death, concluding that "it is likely that Rav Nahman bar Yizhak punished him." The anonymous conclusion, which endorses the view that Nahman bar Yizhak punished Ada bar Ahava, is missing from several manuscripts and is found in different contexts in different manuscripts. Both facts suggest that the statement is a late addition to the Talmud.

[5]Ketubot 62b.

[6]Kohelet 10:5.

individual. Yehuda engages in Torah study at the expense of his commitment to family, causing Yannai to misinterpret his son-in-law's failure to arrive at the appointed time. Similarly, Ada instructs two scholars instead of helping Nahman instruct a large crowd of people, perhaps causing Nahman to misinterpret Ada's failure to arrive at the appointed time. Neither Ada nor Yehuda, therefore, are totally blameless, although it is unclear whether the story views Ada's fate as disproportionate to his actual wrongdoing. Both rabbis choose incorrectly between two competing responsibilities, neglecting obligations which demand immediate attention in favor of other, less pressing obligations. In the story of Ada's death, Nahman, like Yannai, might act unwittingly, and Ada's death, like Yehuda's, is perhaps "like an error which issued forth from a ruler."

Certainty on this issue, however, is not possible, for the expression "like an error which issued forth from a ruler" is used to describe Yehuda's death but not Ada's. Perhaps the parallel between the two stories is not exact, and while Yehuda's death was not intended, Ada's death perhaps was.

The editors preface the story of Ada's death with Nahman's assertion of responsibility, and thereby reveal their interpretation of Nahman's actions. The term "punish" implies intentionality on Nahman's part.[7] Nahman punishes Ada and deliberately brings about his death, claim the editors, and Ada's death is not "like an error which issued forth from a ruler."[8] The editors may be incorrect, however, and the unit of stories

---

[7]See *Ozar Lashon ha-Talmud,* ed. Haim Kosowsky and Benjamin Kosowsky (Jerusalem: Ministry of Education and Culture, Government of Israel, and Jewish Theological Seminary, 1973), vol. 30, pp. 891-96. Nahman would most likely not have said "I punished him" unless he actually *intended* to punish Ada.

[8]In interpreting the Nahman-Ada story, a second version needs to be considered. According to this version (see *DS* vav), Nahman encounters Ada and asks him to attend his lecture. Ada agrees, but fails to appear, and Nahman lectures unsuccessfully. Humiliated, Nahman prays for Ada's death and his prayer is answered. The second version makes no mention of Papa and Huna b. d'Rav Yehoshua, and the guilt falls squarely on Ada for failing to attend Nahman's lecture. According to this version, the connection between the story of Ada's death and Nahman's claim to have punished him is clear, perhaps indicating that the second version is original.

More likely, however, the first version is original, and the second version arose as an attempt to solve the problem of the lack of congruity between Nahman's use of the term "punish" and the first version's account of Ada's death. Later scribes radically altered the story in an attempt to "clarify" exactly how and why Nahman punished Ada. The second version might have also arisen as an attempt to eliminate the first version's positive attitude toward Ada, to conform the final story to the other Amoraic evaluations of Ada's character.

about Ada's death perhaps contains material which derives from diverse polemical perspectives.

The possibility that two early, i.e., Talmudic, recensions of the story have survived cannot be rejected, however. One recension perhaps reflects the perspective of sources hostile to Ada bar Ahava or his school, and the other reflects the opposing perspective.

Appendix to Chapter 1

Earlier Scholarly Discussion of the Geniva Stories

The story of Geniva's conflict with Mar Ukba has been the subject of scholarly concern for the light it sheds on the relationship between the exilarch, the rabbis, and the Persian government. In general, the Talmud provides little information about the exilarchate and the Persian government, and is interested in both institutions only to the extent to which they impinge on the rabbis.[1] The story of the altercation between Geniva and Mar Ukba is extremely valuable historically, for it is one of the few instances in which the rabbis, the exilarch, and the Persian government converge in a single story. The dramatic end to the tale: a prominent sage taken out, imprisoned, and executed,[2] has further stimulated the interest of scholars.

How much do we actually know, however, about the reasons for Geniva's conflict with Mar Ukba? Jacob Neusner claims that the story of Geniva's encounter with Rav Huna and Rav Hisda (the second story surveyed above) provides the answer to this question.

According to Neusner, this second story supplies the motivation behind Mar Ukba's anger and the source of his conflict with Geniva. Geniva believes that the rabbis are kings, claims Neusner. Geniva rejects the exilarch's authority, declaring false his claims of Davidic descent. The true descendants of David are the rabbis who alone have the right to rule the Jewish people based on their knowledge of Torah.[3] Given this background, Ukba's anger is easily understandable, as is Huna's or Hisda's reference to Geniva as a man of division. The rabbis themselves,

---

[1]See Neusner, *A History of the Jews in Babylonia*, vol. 3, pp. 202-13; vol. 4, pp. 125-31; and vol. 5, pp. 321-29; Beer, *Rashut ha-Golah*, p. 2; and Yeshayahu Gafni, "Al Mazav ha-Mehkar: Sekira Al ha-Mehkar ha-Histori Shel Bavel ha-Talmudit be-Dorot ha-Aharonim," *Yidion ha-Igud ha-Olami le-Madaei ha-Yahadut* 21 (1982), pp. 5, 9, and 12.

[2]Yer. Gittin 6:5 and b. Gittin 65b-66a.

[3]See also Solomon Funk, *Die Juden in Babylonien 200-500*, Part 1 (Berlin, 1902), pp. 108-9, n. 5.

claims Neusner, were divided on the issue of the exilarch's authority. Some actively supported Geniva while others were sympathetic to him but uncomfortable with his tactics. Undeniably a man of learning, he was also a troublemaker. In the opinion of many rabbis, argues Neusner, close association with Geniva was to be avoided because of his dangerous challenge to the exilarch.

Neusner concludes that both stories outlined above "derive from exilarchic circles."[4] The first story clearly favors the exilarch, reporting Geniva's imprisonment as God's reward for Ukba's restraint. The second story, argues Neusner, likewise supports the exilarch. It "seems to stress that Geniva's meddling and divisiveness did not win the support of the great men of the generation," that these great men did not pay Geniva the respect due a man of his learning. The story serves the exilarch's cause by teaching that despite his learning, Geniva was a man of division, avoided by the most prominent rabbis of his day.

Moshe Beer, like Neusner, uses the Huna-Hisda narratives to shed light on the story of Mar Ukba and Elazar. He points out the antagonism between Huna and Geniva reflected in the Huna-Hisda narratives, combines this with the claim of a post-Talmudic commentator that Huna was "of the family of the patriarch," and concludes that Geniva's problems with Huna and Mar Ukba stem from Geniva's opposition to exilarchic interference in the internal affairs of the rabbis. Specifically, Geniva opposed the exilarch's role in the selection of Huna as head of the rabbinic academy.[5] Beer explains Geniva's reference to Huna and Hisda as "kings" as a mocking reference to Huna's close connection to the exilarch, who derives his power from the Persian government.

The attempt by both scholars to use the Huna-Hisda narratives to explain the conflict between Geniva and Mar Ukba is unsuccessful, however. As noted above, the stories most likely reflect different perspectives on the merits of Geniva and derive from diverse sources. Neusner's claim that all three stories reflect a common pro-exilarchic standpoint, that they derive from a common source and can be used to shed light on one another, is especially unconvincing. Neusner is most likely correct about the anti-Geniva stance of the Mar Ukba tale. The Huna-Hisda stories, however, are sympathetic to Geniva and hostile to Huna and Hisda.

---

[4]Neusner, *A History of the Jews in Babylonia*, vol. 2, p. 80.
[5]Beer, "Rivo Shel Geniva," pp. 284-86. See also *Rashut ha-Golah*, pp. 94-98, where Beer slightly modifies his theory. The post-Talmudic commentator is Rav Sherira Gaon. See also the references cited in the Introduction, above, and chapter 11, below, with regard to the organization of rabbinic education in Amoraic Babylonia.

It is also impossible to accept Neusner's claim that Geniva's reference to the rabbis as kings was viewed by his contemporaries as subversive. It is odd that neither Huna nor Hisda are put off by Geniva's subversive claims. On the contrary, they respond to Geniva's shocking statement by inviting him to dinner![6]

The stories about Geniva share in common the view that he was a controversial figure. His designation as a man of division in the Huna-Hisda narrative may or may not be an allusion to his conflict with Mar Ukba. Even assuming it is, however, the Huna-Hisda narrative provides no help in determining the cause of that conflict.[7] More importantly, even if the Huna-Hisda narrative did give us insight into this difficult question, it would be insight deriving from sources sympathetic to Geniva. The authors of the Mar Ukba-Elazar tale, hostile to Geniva and sympathetic to Mar Ukba, would very likely have explained the matter differently.

---

[6]See also Yoel Florsheim, "Yisudan ve-Reshit Hitpathutan Shel Yeshivot Bavel – Sura ve-Pumbedita," *Zion* 39 (1974), p. 186, n. 10.
[7]See also Bacher, *Die Agada der Babylonischen Amoräer*, p. 72.

Appendix to Chapter 2

Amoraic Quotation of and Commentary on Statements by Rav and Shmuel

I argued above that analysis of Amoraic quotation of and commentary on statements by Rav and Shmuel yields further evidence of differences between early and later Amoraim. I claimed that several early Amoraim quote and comment on statements by Rav to the virtual exclusion of statements by Shmuel, and vice versa, whereas later Amoraim quote and comment on Rav's and Shmuel's statements to approximately the same degree.

To establish these claims, I surveyed tractates Shabbat, Ketubot, and Baba Mezia to determine which Amoraim exhibit a clear preference for or familiarity with statements by Rav to the virtual exclusion of statements by Shmuel, and vice versa. If an Amora quotes or comments on statements by Rav at least four times more frequently than on statements by Shmuel, or vice versa, the Amora exhibits a *clear preference* for or *clear familiarity* with the statements of Rav (or Shmuel). If the ratio is 2 to 1 or less, the Amora exhibits no preference for or special familiarity with the statements of either Rav or Shmuel.

As a glance at the chart on the following page reveals, the basic trend of the evidence is clear: only early Amoraim prefer or are familiar with statements by Rav to the virtual exclusion of statements by Shmuel, or vice versa. The tendency is strongest among second-generation Amoraim, weaker in the third generation, and virtually absent after the third generation.

Immediately following the chart below, I list the names of Amoraim who quote and comment on statements by Rav and/or Shmuel at least four times, together with their chronology and the number of quotations and comments. It will be recalled that second- and third-generation rabbis are considered early, and post-third-generation rabbis are considered late. Page references to relevant Talmudic passages are provided in accompanying footnotes, and the following chart summarizes the data.

Chart

	Number of Amoraim Exhibiting Clear Preference for or Clear Familiarity with Statements by Rav or Shmuel	Number of Amoraim Exhibiting Preference for or Familiarity with Statements by Rav or Shmuel	Number of Amoriam Exhibiting no Preference for Statements by Rav or Shmuel
2nd Generation	14	1	2
3rd Generation	2	5-6	6-7
4th Generation	0	0	3
5th Generation	0	1	1
6th Generation	0	0	3
7th Generation	0	0	0

Clear Preference for or Clear Familiarity with Statements by Rav

2nd gen.	Rav Abba bar Zavda	6 Rav;[1] 0 Shmuel.
2nd gen.	Rav Ada bar Ahava	5 Rav;[2] 0 Shmuel.
2nd gen.	R. Elazar	4 or 5 Rav;[3] 0 Shmuel.
2nd gen.	Rav Gidul	5 Rav;[4] 0 Shmuel.
2nd gen.	Rav Huna	19 to 22 Rav;[5] 1 Shmuel.[6]
2nd gen.	Rav Hiyya bar Ashi	19 or 20 Rav;[7] 0 Shmuel.

---

[1]Shabbat 111a and 120a, Ketubot 6b and 7a, and Baba Mezia 25b (twice).
[2]Shabbat 22a-b and 135a, and Ketubot 24a, 40a, and 62b.
[3]Shabbat 20a, 44b, and 140a, Ketubot 104a-b, and possibly Shabbat 124b.
[4]Shabbat 7a, 24a, and 30b, and Ketubot 102b and 106a.
[5]Shabbat 41a, 138b (three times), 139b, 140a, and 142b; Ketubot 7a, 18a, 21b (twice), 22a, 40b, 58b, 89a-b, and 104b; Baba Mezia 16b, 63a, and 107a; and possibly Shabbat 5a (see Halivni, *Mekorot u-Mesorot: Shabbat*, p. 273, n. 2) and 113b and Ketubot 21b.
[6]Baba Mezia 14b.
[7]Shabbat 23a, 34a, 52a, 53a, 99b, 107a, 111a-b, 113a, 118b, 124b, 139b, 140b, 142a (see *DS* hei), 142b, and 145a (twice); Ketubot 6a, 15a-b, and 112b; and possibly Shabbat 50b.

Clear Preference for or Clear Familiarity with Statements by Rav (continued)

2nd gen.	Rav Hama bar Gurya	12 Rav;[8] 0 Shmuel.
2nd gen.	Rav Yehuda b. d'Rav Shmuel bar Shelat	4 Rav;[9] 0 Shmuel.
2nd gen.	Rav Matna	5 Rav;[10] 0 Shmuel.
2nd gen.	Rabbah bar Abuha	8 Rav;[11] 2 Shmuel.[12]
2nd gen.	Rava bar Mehasya	11 Rav;[13] 0 Shmuel.
3rd gen.	Rav Abba	10 to 13 Rav;[14] 2 Shmuel.[15]

Preference for or Familiarity with Statements by Rav

3rd gen.	Rav Dimi	3 Rav;[16] 1 Shmuel.[17]

Clear Preference for or Clear Familiarity with Statements by Shmuel

2nd gen.	Rav Hanan bar Ami	0 Rav; 4 Shmuel.[18]
2nd gen.	Mar bar Hamduri or Bar Hamduri	0 Rav; 4 Shmuel.[19]
2nd gen.	Mar Ukba	0 Rav; 4 Shmuel.[20]
2nd gen.	Rav Anan	1 Rav;[21] 5 Shmuel.[22]

---

[8]Shabbat 9a (twice), 10b (four times), 11a (five times), and 37a.
[9]Shabbat 30b, 118b, 119b (*DS* lamed), and 153a (*DS* ayin).
[10]Shabbat 24a and 29a, Ketubot 44b and 86b-87a, and Baba Mezia 37a-b.
[11]Shabbat 129b (three times) and 130b, and Baba Mezia 41a, 48a, 76a-b, and 99a.
[12]Ketubot 93a-b and 93b-94a.
[13]Shabbat 10b (six times) and 11a (five times).
[14]Shabbat 34a, 41a, 107a, 113a, and 124b; Ketubot 21b (twice) and 104b; Baba Mezia 107a (twice); and possibly Shabbat 5a (*DS* nun) and 50b and Ketubot 21b.
[15]Shabbat 143b and Ketubot 76a-b.
[16]Shabbat 134b and 145a and Ketubot 106b-107a.
[17]Ketubot 106b-107b (It is likely that Rav Dimi is to be understood as having reported the entire discussion based on the decisions of Rabbi and R. Yishmael, including the statement by Shmuel).
[18]Shabbat 13a and 111b, Ketubot 6a-b, and Baba Mezia 82b.
[19]Shabbat 107b (twice) and 125a (twice).
[20]Shabbat 108b (twice) and 109a (twice).
[21]Shabbat 12b.
[22]Ketubot 54a and 89a, and Baba Mezia 51a-b and 70a (twice).

Preference for or Familiarity with Statements by Shmuel

2nd gen.	Rami bar Yehezkel	1 Rav;[23] 3 Shmuel.[24]
3rd gen.	Rav Huna bar Hiyya	1 Rav;[25] 3 Shmuel.[26]
3rd gen. *(possible)*	Rav Hiyya bar Abin	3-5 Rav;[27] 7 Shmuel.[28]
3rd gen.	Rav Yosef	14 or 15 Rav;[29] 34 or 35 Shmuel.[30]
3rd gen.	Rav Shmuel bar Yehuda	1 or 2 Rav;[31] 4 Shmuel.[32]
5th gen.	Rav Huna b. d'Rav Yehoshua	3 Rav;[33] 8 Shmuel.[34]

---

[23]Shabbat 138b.
[24]Ketubot 21a, 60a, and 76a-b.
[25]Shabbat 156a.
[26]Shabbat 51b-52a and Ketubot 79b and 101a.
[27]Shabbat 111b and 140a and Ketubot 54a, and possibly Shabbat 111a-b (twice – The identification of Rav Hiyya bar Abin as the "lion of the company" referred to by Rava is an explanatory addition to Rava's statement, and is perhaps incorrect).
[28]Shabbat 52a, 111b, and 129a, Ketubot 54a and 85b, and Baba Mezia 15a and 100a.
[29]Shabbat 11a, 24a, 40a, 51a, 52a, 59b, 101a, 134b, and 146b, Ketubot 6a-b, 60b, 79b, and 89a-b, Baba Mezia 110b, and possibly Shabbat 22a.
[30]Shabbat 22a, 34b (twice), 37b, 51a (twice), 52a, 57b, 62b, 66a, 97a-b, 106b, 113a, 147b, and 147b-148a, Ketubot 2a, 6a-b, 9b, 12b, 14a, 15b, 56b-57a, 59a, 60b, 89a, and 111a, and Baba Mezia 8a-b (twice), 15a (twice), 29b, 34b-35a, 55b-56a, and 113a, and possibly Baba Mezia 8a-b.
[31]Shabbat 37b, and possibly Shabbat 5a (see Halivni, *Mekorot u-Mesorot*: Shabbat, p. 273, n. 2).
[32]Shabbat 37b (twice), Ketubot 12b, and Baba Mezia 36b.
[33]Shabbat 22a-b and 120a and Ketubot 84b-85a.
[34]Shabbat 22a-b and 128b-129a, Ketubot 59a (twice), 60b, 84b-85a, and 86a, and Baba Mezia 99b.

No Preference for or Special Familiarity with Statements by Rav or Shmuel

2nd gen.	Rav Yehuda	70-76 Rav;[35] 106-108 Shmuel.[36]
2nd gen.	Rav Yirmiya bar Abba	4 Rav;[37] 2 Shmuel.[38]
3rd gen.	Rav Oshaya	2 Rav;[39] 2 Shmuel.[40]
3rd gen.	R. Zeira	7 or 8 Rav;[41] 6 Shmuel.[42]
3rd gen.	Rav Hisda	8 Rav;[43] 5 or 6 Shmuel.[44]
3rd gen. (possible)	Rav Hiyya bar Abin[45]	3-5 Rav; 7 Shmuel.
3rd gen.	R. Yirmiya	4 Rav;[46] 2 Shmuel.[47]

---

[35]Shabbat 9a, 13b, 16b, 25b, 29a, 30a (twice), 44a, 47a, 48a-b, 48b, 56b (twice), 62b-63a, 64b, 77b (twice), 80b, 83b, 87b, 100a (twice), 101a, 105b, 107b, 118b (twice), 119b (twice), 120a, 127a, 128b, 129a, 133a (twice), 146b, 147b, 149b (four times), 149b-150a, 156a (twice), and 157a; Ketubot 14b-15a, 15b, 21a, 29a, 36a, 43a, 66b, 86b-87a, 94b, 104a-b, 108b, and 109b; Baba Mezia 30a-b, 30b, 33a (twice), 37a-b, 75a, 75b, 85a, 85b, 86b (twice), 102a, and 108a, and possibly Shabbat 22a, 54b, and 92b, Ketubot 11b, and Baba Mezia 85a and 87a.
[36]Shabbat 4b, 12a, 14b (twice), 34b (four times), 35a, 35b, 37b, 40b (twice), 43b, 45a, 47a, 51a (twice), 51b, 52a (twice), 56b (three times), 57b, 60b, 62b, 77b, 91a, 96b, 97a-b, 106b, 108b, 113a (twice), 124b (twice), 125a, 128b-129a (three times), 129a (twice), 136a, 143b (twice), 144b-145a, 146b, 147b, 147b-148a, 149a, 149b, 150a, 150b, and 151a; Ketubot 2a, 2b, 9b, 12b (twice), 15b, 21a (three times), 26a, 27a, 28b, 44a, 51b, 54a, 56b-57a, 60a, 62b, 69b, 71b, 72a (three times), 72b (four times), 76a-b, 77a, 100b, 106a, and 111a; Baba Mezia 8a-b (three times), 11a, 19b-20a, 23b, 23b-24a, 29b (twice), 36b (twice), 38b, 39a, 43b, 59b, 75a (three times), and 112b, and possibly Shabbat 54a and 59b (*DS* dalet).
[37]Shabbat 52a, 137b, and 156a, and Ketubot 60a.
[38]Shabbat 52a and 106b.
[39]Ketubot 11b and Baba Mezia 23b (Regarding the third-generation Rav Oshaya, see Hyman, *Toldot Tannaim ve-Amoraim*, pp. 116-17).
[40]Ketubot 11b and Baba Mezia 43b.
[41]Shabbat 53a, 125a, 130b, and 145a, Ketubot 77a and 106a, Baba Mezia 23b, and possibly Shabbat 21b.
[42]Shabbat 53a, Ketubot 77a and 96a, and Baba Mezia 12b, 16b, and 112b.
[43]Shabbat 10b (twice), 11a, 62b-63a, and 144b-145a, Ketubot 6a-b, 72b-73a, and 86b, and Baba Mezia 36a.
[44]Shabbat 144b-145a and 146b, Ketubot 6a-b, 72b-73b, and 86b, and possibly Shabbat 97a-b (see *DS* het and yud).
[45]See the references cited above, nn. 27-28.
[46]Shabbat 21b and 145a and Ketubot 15a-b (twice).
[47]Shabbat 143b and Ketubot 15a-b.

No Preference for or Special Familiarity with Statements
by Rav or Shmuel (continued)

3rd gen.	Rav Nahman	20 Rav;[48] 29-31 Shmuel.[49]
3rd gen.	Rabbah	10 Rav;[50] 14 Shmuel.[51]
3rd gen.	Rav Sheshet	8 Rav;[52] 5 Shmuel.[53]
4th gen.	Abaye	36 Rav;[54] 36 Shmuel.[55]
4th gen.	Rav Nahman bar Yizhak	5 Rav;[56] 5 Shmuel.[57]
4th gen.	Rava	14 or 15 Rav;[58] 17-18 Shmuel.[59]

---

[48]Shabbat 129b (three times) and 130b; Ketubot 8a, 14b-15a, 54a (twice), 89a-b, 94a-b, 104a-b, and 106a; and Baba Mezia 10a, 41a, 48a, 51a, 76a-b, 94a, 99a, and 108a.

[49]Shabbat 53a, 57b, 108b, 113a, 124b, and 135a; Ketubot 10a, 54a (three times), 56b-57a, 77a, 79a, 87a, 89b, 93a-b, 93b-94a, 100a, and 108b, and Baba Mezia 14b-15a (twice), 15a, 16b, 39a, 55b-56a, 70a, 75a, 110b, and 112b, and possibly Ketubot 79b (see DS Herschler, notes on line 8) and Baba Mezia 28b (DS lamed).

[50]Shabbat 22a-b (three times), 25b, and 40a, and Ketubot 6a-b, 19a, 60a, and 72b-73a (twice). On Shabbat 25b and Ketubot 6a-b and 60a, the printed edition reads Rava, but see chapter 10, below.

[51]Shabbat 22a-b (three times), 34b (twice), and 146b, Ketubot 6a-b (twice), 72b-73b (twice), 93a-b, and 111a, and Baba Mezia 19b-20a, and 34b-35a. On Ketubot 6a-b and Baba Mezia 19b-20a and 34b-35a, the printed edition reads Rava, but see chapter 10, below.

[52]Shabbat 22a-b, Ketubot 94a-b, 104a-b, and 106b-107a, and Baba Mezia 38b, 41a (twice), and 69b.

[53]Shabbat 22a-b, Ketubot 106b-107a, and Baba Mezia 38b, 55b-56a, and 106a.

[54]Shabbat 7a-b, 16b, 21b, 22a-b (three times), 24a, 40a, 52a (twice), 57b, 90b, 99a, 101a, 109b-110a, 130b, 134b, 138b, 145a, and 156a; Ketubot 6a-b (twice), 13a, 17b, 19a, 21a, 24a, 60b, 62a, and 72b-73b (twice), and Baba Mezia 23b, 36a-b, 49a, 51a-b, and 59a.

[55]Shabbat 22a-b (three times), 45b, 51a, 52a, 54a, 57b, 62b, 106b, 113a, 128b-129a (twice), 145a (twice), 146b, and 147b; Ketubot 6a-b (twice), 12b, 14a, 56b-57a, 59a, 60b, 65a, 72b-73b (twice), and 79a; and Baba Mezia 8a-b, 15a (twice), 19b-20a, 29b (twice), 51a-b, and 55b-56a.

[56]Shabbat 57b, Ketubot 6a-b, and Baba Mezia 77a-b (twice) and 94a.

[57]Shabbat 57b and 143b, and Ketubot 6a-b, 68a, and 76a-b.

[58]Shabbat 16b, 22a-b, 52a, 99a, and 111a-b (twice); Ketubot 6a-b (twice), 54a, and 72b-73a; Baba Mezia 10a, 15b, 36a-b, 64b-65a; and possibly Baba Mezia 64a.

[59]Shabbat 22a-b, 107b, 113a, 124b, 125a, 128b-129a, and 133b; Ketubot 6a-b (twice), 21a, 54a, 72b-73a, 79a, and 85b; Baba Mezia 14b, 15a, 15b, and 51a-b; and possibly Ketubot 79b.

No Preference for or Special Familiarity with Statements by Rav or Shmuel (continued)

5th gen.	Rav Papa	15-17 Rav;[60] 13 Shmuel.[61]
6th gen.	Rav Ashi	15-17 Rav;[62] 15-17 Shmuel.[63]
6th gen.	Mar Zutra	2 Rav;[64] 3-5 Shmuel.[65]
6th gen.	Ravina	1-2 Rav;[66] 2-3 Shmuel.[67]

---

[60]Shabbat 20a, 22a-b, 53a, 54b, 79b, 118b, and 119a; Ketubot 13a, 17b, 58b, 84b-85a, and 106b-107a; Baba Mezia 59a, 69b, and 101a; and possibly Baba Mezia 45b (twice).

[61]Shabbat 22a-b, 53a, and 119a, Ketubot 58b, 60b, 84b-85a, 89b, 101a, and 106b-107a (twice), and Baba Mezia 57b, 91a, and 101a.

[62]Shabbat 9a, 11a (twice), 59b, 107a, 116b, and 130b-131a; Ketubot 19a, 33a-b, 86b-87a, and 102b; Baba Mezia 15b, 76a-b, 92a, and 99a, and possibly Shabbat 120b and Baba Mezia 45b.

[63]Shabbat 59b, 97a-b, 107a-b, 107b, 116b, 128b-129a, 136a, and 146b; Ketubot 21a-b, 60a, and 72a; Baba Mezia 14b-15a, 34b-35a, 93a, and 110b; and possibly Shabbat 50b and 59b (*DS* dalet).

[64]Shabbat 140a and Baba Mezia 15b.

[65]Shabbat 128b-129a and 140a, Baba Mezia 23b-24a, and possibly Shabbat 50b and 124b (see *DS* het).

[66]Ketubot 102b and possibly Shabbat 120b.

[67]Shabbat 97a-b and Baba Mezia 110b, and possibly Shabbat 59b (*DS* dalet).

Appendices to Chapter 3

Appendix One: The Purpose of b. Berakhot 56b-57b

As noted above, some of the material found on b. Berakhot 56b-57b (translated in Appendix 2, below) might have originally been intended for use by professional dream interpreters. By including it in the Talmud, however, the rabbis perhaps deliberately made the esoteric knowledge of professionals available for use by non-professionals. In other words, perhaps this material originally aided interpreters, but in its present context it undercuts the interpreter's role and makes it easier for non-specialists to function without him.

The story of Bar Hedya on Berakhot 56b, examined in detail above, supports this contention. According to this story, a dream manual which originally aids the corrupt dream interpreter performs a much different function once it become public knowledge. Rava, it will be recalled, is ignorant of at least one crucial passage from Bar Hedya's manual until it accidentally drops out of his pocket. Rava is powerless against Bar Hedya until his accidental discovery enables him to gain the upper hand. Perhaps portions of b. Berakhot 56b-57b are the product of a similar struggle between rabbis and professional dream interpreters.

It is worthwhile noting that another Talmudic story, preserved in both Talmuds, depicts a rabbi publicizing the technical knowledge of a professional and thereby endangering her livelihood.[1] Other stories depict a rabbi threatening craftsmen and merchants with loss of income. Unless they lower their prices, the rabbi warns, he will issue a halachic ruling that will force prices down without their consent.[2]

---

[1]See b. Yoma 84a and parallel, and Yer. Shabbat 14:4 (14d) and parallel (involving R. Yohanan).
[2]b. Pesahim 30a and Sukkah 34b.

Appendices to Chapter 3

Appendix Two: Translation of b. Berakhot 56b-57b[1]

1.   R. Hanina said: One who sees a well in a dream will see peace, as it is said, "But when Isaac's servants, digging in the wadi, found there a well of spring water, the herdsmen of Gerar quarreled with Isaac's herdsmen.... He moved from there and dug yet another well, and they did not quarrel over it" (Gen. 26:19-22).

2.   R. Natan says: He will find Torah, as it is said, "For he who finds me finds life" (Prov. 8:35), and it is written here "a well of living water"[2] (Gen. 26:19).

   a.   Rava said: [It means], literally, life.

3.   R. Hanan said: There are three [dream-images which mean] peace: A river, a bird, and a pot. A river, as it is written: "I will extend to you peace like a river" (Is. 66:12). A bird, as it is written: "Like the birds that fly, even so will the Lord of Hosts shield Jerusalem, shielding and saving, protecting and rescuing" (Is. 31:5). A pot, as it is written: "O Lord, may you establish [*Tishpot*, which also means 'to set a cooking pot over fire'] peace for us" (Is. 26:12).

   a.   R. Hanina said: [This refers to] a pot that has no meat in it, as it is said,[3] "You have devoured My people's flesh.... You have cut it up as into a pot, like meat in a cauldron" (Micah 3:3).

4. A.   R. Yehoshua ben Levi said: One who sees a river in a dream should get up early and say, "I will extend to you peace like

---

[1]The translation is based on that of Maurice Simon, *Berakoth* (London: The Soncino Press, 1948), and Jacob Neusner, *Tractate Berakhot* (Chico, California: Scholars Press, 1984). I do not indicate every point at which I follow their translations.
[2]The phrase actually means "a spring."
[3]See *DS* ayin.

a river" (Is. 66:12) before another verse precedes it: "For distress will come in like a river" (Is. 59:19).

B.   One who sees a bird in a dream should get up early and say, "Like the birds that fly, even so will the Lord of Hosts shield Jerusalem, shielding and saving, protecting and rescuing" (Is. 31:5), before another verse precedes it: "Like a sparrow wandering from its nest is a man who wanders from his home" (Prov. 27:8).

C.   One who sees a pot in a dream should get up early and say, "O Lord, may you establish peace for us" (Is. 26:12), before another verse precedes it: "Put the caldron [on the fire].... Assuredly, thus said the Lord God: Woe to the city of blood, a caldron whose scum is in it, whose scum has not been cleaned out..." (Ez. 24:3-6).

D.   One who sees grapes in a dream should get up early and say, "I found Israel [as pleasing] as grapes in the wilderness" (Hosea 9:10), before another verse precedes it: "The grapes for them are poison" (Deut. 32:32).

E.   One who sees a mountain in a dream should get up early and say, "How welcome on the mountain are the footsteps of the herald, announcing happiness" (Is. 52:7), before another verse precedes it: "For the mountains I take up weeping and wailing" (Jer. 9:9).

F.   One who sees a horn in a dream should get up early and say, "And in that day, a great ram's horn shall be sounded, and the strayed who are in the land of Assyria and the expelled who are in the land of Egypt shall come and worship the Lord on the holy mount, in Jerusalem" (Is. 27:13), before another verse precedes it: "Sound a ram's horn in Gibeah, a trumpet in Ramah; Give the alarm in Beth-aven; After you, Benjamin! Ephraim is stricken with horror on the day of chastisement" (Hosea 5:8-9).

G.   One who sees a dog in a dream should get up early and say, "But not a dog shall snarl at any of the Israelites" (Ex. 11:7), before another verse precedes it: "And the dogs are greedy" (Is. 56:11).

H.   One who sees a lion in a dream should get up early and say, "A lion has roared, who can but fear? My Lord God has spoken, who can but prophesy?" (Amos 3:8), before another verse precedes it: "The lion has come up from his thicket, the destroyer of nations has set out" (Jer. 4:7).

I.   One who sees hair-cutting in a dream should get up early and say, "He had his hair cut and changed his clothes and he

	appeared before Pharoah" (Gen. 41:14),[4] before another verse precedes it: "If my hair were cut, my strength would leave me" (Judges 16:16).
J.	One who sees a well in a dream should get up early and say, "A well of fresh water" (Song of Songs 4:15), before another verse precedes it: "As a well flows with water, so she flows with wickedness" (Jer. 6:7).
K.	One who sees a reed in a dream should get up early and say, "He shall not break even a bruised reed" (Is. 42:3), before another verse precedes it: "You are relying on Egypt, that splintered reed of a staff" (Is. 36:6).
5.	Our rabbis taught [in a Tannaitic tradition]: One who sees a reed in a dream should expect wisdom, as it is said, "Acquire [*Kana*, which also means 'reed'] wisdom" (Prov. 4:5). [One who sees] reeds should expect discernment, as it is said, "With all your acquisitions, acquire discernment" (Prov. 4:7).
6.	R. Zeira said: A gourd, a palm-heart, wax, and a reed are all good for dreams.
7.	It is taught [in a Tannaitic tradition]: Gourds are shown only to one who fears heaven with all of his strength.
L.	One who sees an ox in a dream should get up early and say, "Like a firstling ox in his majesty" (Deut. 33:17), before a different verse precedes it: "When an ox gores a man" (Ex. 21:28).
8.	Our rabbis taught [in a Tannaitic tradition]: Five things were said regarding an ox: (1) One who eats of his flesh becomes rich, (2) [If he] attacked him, his children will attack their Torah studies, (3) [If he] bit him, sufferings will come upon him, (4) [If he] kicked him, a long journey has been prepared for him, (5) [If he] rode him, he will rise to greatness.
a.	But [on the contrary] it is taught [in a Tannaitic tradition]: [If he] rode him, he will die.
b.	There is no difficulty, one case refers to him riding the ox, the other case refers to the ox riding him.
9. A.	One who sees an ass in a dream should expect salvation, as it is said, "Lo, your king is coming to you. He is victorious, triumphant, yet humble, riding on an ass" (Zech. 9:9).
B.	One who sees a cat in a dream, in a place where they call it *shunra*, a pleasant song (*shira na'ah*) will be made for him. [In

---

[4]Joseph is removed from prison and brought before Pharoah. He interprets Pharoah's dreams, and is appointed his chief adviser.

a place where they call it] *shinra,* a bad change (*shinui ra*) will be made for him.

C. One who sees grapes in a dream, if white, both in season and not in season they are beneficial. If black, in season they are beneficial, not in season, they are harmful.

D. One who sees a white horse in a dream, whether walking slowly or quickly, it is good for him. If red, if it walks slowly it is good, if quickly it is bad.

E. One who sees Yishmael in a dream, his prayer is answered.

    a. This refers only to Yishmael son of Avraham, but an ordinary Arab, no.

F. One who sees a camel in a dream, his death was decreed from heaven but he was spared.

    a. R. Hama b'R. Hanina said: What verse [proves this]? "I Myself will go down with you to Egypt, and I Myself will also bring you back [*Gam aloh,* similar to *Gamal,* camel]" (Gen. 46:4).

    b. Rav Nahman bar Yizhak said: From here: "Also [*Gam*], the Lord has remitted your sin; you shall not die" (2 Sam. 12:13).

G. One who sees Pinhas in a dream, a wonder will be done for him.

H. One who sees an elephant (*pil*) in a dream, wonders (*pelaot*) will be done for him. [If one sees] elephants (*pilim*), great wonders will be done for him.

    a. But [on the contrary] it is taught [in a Tannaitic tradition]: All kinds of animals are good for dreams except for the elephant and the ape.

    b. There is no difficulty [Berakhot 57a], one case refers to a saddled [elephant], the other to an unsaddled [elephant].

I. One who sees Huna in a dream, a miracle will be done for him. Hanina, Hananya, Yohanan, great miracles will be done for him.

J. One who sees a eulogy in a dream, heaven will care for him and redeem him.[5]

    a. Provided that the [eulogy] is in writing.

K. One who responds, "May His great name be blessed" is assured of membership in the world to come.

---

[5]The Hebrew word for eulogy (*Hesped*) is interpreted as care (*Hus*) and redemption (*pdh*).

L. One who recites the Shema[6] deserves to have the divine presence rest upon him, but his generation is not deserving of it.

M. One who puts on tefillin in a dream should expect greatness, as it is said, "And all the peoples of the earth shall see that the Lord's name is proclaimed over you" (Deut. 28:10), and it is taught [in a Tannaitic tradition]: R. Eliezer the great says, This [refers to] the tefillin [placed on] the head.

N. One who prays in a dream, it is a good sign for him.
  a. Provided that he does not finish.

O. One who has sex with his mother in a dream should expect discernment, as it is said, "You shall call discernment 'mother'" (Prov. 2:3).[7]

P. One who has sex with a betrothed girl should expect Torah, as it is said, "Moshe charged us with Torah as the heritage of the congregation of Jacob" (Deut. 33:4). Do not read "heritage" [*Morasha*], but "betrothed" [*Meorasa*].

Q. One who has sex with his sister in a dream should expect wisdom, as it is said, "Say to wisdom: 'You are my sister'" (Prov. 7:4).

R. One who has sex with a married woman in a dream is assured of membership in the world to come.
  a. Provided that he does not know her and did not fantasize about her in the evening.[8]

10. A. R. Hiyya bar Abba said: One who sees wheat in a dream will see peace, as it is said, "He endows your realm with peace, and satisfies you with choice wheat" (Ps. 147:14).

B. One who sees barley (*Se'orim*) in a dream, his sins have departed (*Saru*), as it is said, "Your sin shall depart" (Is. 6:7).
  a. R. Zeira said: I did not leave Babylonia for the land of Israel until I saw barley in a dream.

C. One who sees a laden vine in a dream, his wife will not miscarry, as it is said, "Your wife shall be like a fruitful vine" (Ps. 128:3). [One who sees] a choice vine should expect the messiah, as it is said, "He [the messiah] tethers his ass to a vine, his ass's foal to a choice vine" (Gen. 49:11).

---

[6]The Shema is one of the centerpieces of Jewish liturgy. It consists of three paragraphs (Deuteronomy 6:4-9; 11:13-21; and Numbers 15:37-41) and takes its name from the first word in the opening paragraph.
[7]The verse, according to our present versions, should actually be translated "If (*Im*) you call to understanding...." The Hebrew word for mother is *Eim* or *Ima*.
[8]See Afik, *Tefisat he-Halom Ezel Hazal*, p. 101.

D.   One who sees a fig tree in a dream retains his learning, as it is said, "He who tends a fig tree will enjoy its fruit" (Prov. 27:18).

E.   One who sees pomegranates in a dream, [if he sees] small ones, his business will be as fruitful as a pomegranate. [If he sees] big ones, his business will grow like a pomegranate. [If it is] divided, if he is a sage, he should expect Torah, as it is said, "Of her who taught me – I would let you drink of the spiced wine, of my pomegranate juice" (Song of Songs 8:2). If he is unlearned, he should expect to [fulfill] commandments, as it is said, "Your brow (*Rakatekh*) is like a pomegranate split open" (Song of Songs 4:3). What is *Rakatekh*? Even the empty (*Reik*) among you will be as full of commandments as a pomegranate.

F.   One who sees olives in a dream, [if he sees] small ones, his business will be fruitful and grow and endure like olives.

a.   This refers to fruit, but trees, he will have many children, as it is said, "Your children, like olive saplings..." (Ps. 128:3).

G.   Others say: One who sees an olive in a dream will acquire a good reputation, as it is said, "The Lord called your name 'verdant olive tree, fair, with choice fruit'" (Jer. 11:16).

H.   One who sees olive oil in a dream should expect the light of Torah, as it is said, "They should bring you clear oil of beaten olives for light" (Ex. 27:20).

I.   One who sees dates [*Tamarim*] in a dream, his sins will come to an end [*Tamu*], as it is said, "Your iniquity is at an end, Fair Zion" (Lam. 4:22).

11. A. Rav Yosef said: One who sees a goat in a dream, the year will be blessed for him. [If he sees] goats, years will be blessed for him, as it is said: "The goats' milk will suffice for your food" (Prov. 27:27).

B.   One who sees a myrtle in a dream, his property will prosper. And if he has no property, an inheritance will fall to him from an unexpected place.

a.   Ulla said, and others say: it is taught in a Tannaitic tradition: Provided he saw [the myrtle] on its stem.

C.   One who sees a citron in a dream, he is splendid to his Creator, as it is said, "The fruit of splendid trees" (Lev. 23:40).[9]

---

[9]According to rabbinic interpretation, the fruit referred to is a citron. The word *hadar* is understood in this context to mean "splendid."

D. One who sees a palm branch (*lulav*) in a dream is single-minded (*lev*) [in his devotion] to his Father in heaven.

E. One who sees a goose in a dream should expect wisdom, as it is said, "Wisdom cries aloud in the street" (Prov. 1:20). And one who has sex with it will become head of the yeshiva.[10]

    a. Rav Ashi said: I saw it and had sex with it and rose to greatness.

F. One who sees a chicken in a dream should expect a male child. [If he sees] chickens, he should expect male children. [If he sees] a hen (*Tarnegolet*), he should expect a fine courtyard and joy (*Tarbiza na'ah ve-gilah*).

G. One who sees eggs in a dream, his request is left undecided. [If] they were broken, his request is carried out. The same [is true] of nuts, and cucumbers, and glass vessels, and all other breakable things like these.

H. One who enters a city, his desires will be carried out, as it is said, "And He brought them to the port they desired" (Ps. 107:30).

I. One who shaves his head in a dream, it is a good sign for him. [If he shaves] his head and his beard, [it is a good sign] for him and his entire family.

J. One who sits in a small boat will acquire a good reputation. [If he sits] in a large boat, he and his entire family [will acquire a good reputation].

    a. Provided that he is raised up high.

K. One who moves his bowels in a dream, it is a good sign for him, as it is said, "Quickly the crouching one is freed" (Is. 51:14).[11]

    a. Provided that he does not wipe himself.

L. One who goes up to a roof in a dream will rise to greatness. If he goes down, he will fall from greatness.

    a. Abaye and Rava both said: Once he goes up, he stays up.

M. One who tears his clothes in a dream, his writ of judgment will be torn.

N. One who stands naked in a dream, [if he is] in Babylonia, he stands without sin. [If he is] in the land of Israel, he is naked without the [performance of] commandments.

O. One who is seized by soldiers will be protected. If they put him in a neck-chain, he will be better protected.

---

[10]See the discussion of this term, above.
[11]The rabbis understand *zo'eh* ("crouching") as related to the word *zo'ah* ("feces").

    a.   This refers to a neck-chain, but a mere rope, no.

P.   One who enters a marsh in a dream will become head of the yeshiva.[12] [If he enters] a forest, he will become head of those who attend the bi-annual study session.[13]

    a.   Rav Papa and Rav Huna b. d'Rav Yehoshua [each] saw a dream. Rav Papa, who entered a marsh, became head of the yeshiva. Rav Huna b. d'Rav Yehoshua, who entered a forest, became head of those who attend the biannual study session. Some say they both entered a marsh, but Rav Papa, who carried a drum,[14] became head of the yeshiva. Rav Huna b. d'Rav Yehoshua, who did not carry a drum, became head of those who attend the bi-annual study session.

    b.   Said Rav Ashi: I entered a marsh and carried a drum and made a loud noise with it.

12.   A Tanna [who memorizes and repeats rabbinic traditions] recited a Tannaitic tradition in the presence of Rav Nahman bar Yizhak: One who lets blood in a dream, his sins are forgiven him.

    a.   But [on the contrary] it is taught [in a Tannaitic tradition]: His sins are laid out for him.

    b.   What does "laid out" mean? "Laid out" in order to be forgiven.

13.   A Tanna recited a Tannaitic tradition in the presence of Rav Sheshet: One who sees a snake in a dream, his means of support will be prepared for him. If he bit him, [his means of support] will be doubled. If he killed him, he will lose his means of support.

    a.   Rav Sheshet said to him: If he killed him, how much the more so will his means of support be doubled!

    b.   This isn't the case. Rav Sheshet himself saw a snake in a dream and killed it.

14.   A Tanna recited a Tannaitic tradition in the presence of R. Yohanan: All kinds of liquids are good for dreams except wine. One drinks it and it is good for him, another drinks it and it is bad for him. One drinks it and it is good for him, as it is said, "Wine cheers the hearts of men" (Ps. 104:15). Another drinks it and it is bad for him, as it is said, "Give

---

[12]See the note above.

[13]With regard to the Hebrew term *kallah* (translated here as "study session"), see Goodblatt, *Rabbinic Instruction in Sasanian Babylonia,* pp. 155-70.

[14]See *Arukh-ha-Shalem,* vol. 4, pp. 8-9; and Jastrow, *Dictionary,* p. 518.

strong drink to the lost and wine to the embittered" (Prov. 31:6).

a. R. Yohanan said to the Tanna: Teach [thus]: It is always good for a sage, as it is said, "Come, eat my food and drink the wine that I have mixed [*Masakhti*, which is understood as related to the word *Masekhet*, Talmudic discourse]" (Prov. 9:5).[15]

15. [Berakhot 57b] R. Yohanan said: If one got up early and a biblical verse fell into his mouth, it is a minor prophecy.

16 A. Our rabbis taught [in a Tannaitic tradition]: There are three kings: One who sees David in a dream should expect piety. [One who sees] Shlomo should expect wisdom. [One who sees] Ahav should worry about punishment.

B. There are three prophets: One who sees the book of Kings should expect greatness. [One who sees] Yehezkel should expect wisdom. [One who sees] Yeshayahu should expect consolation. [One who sees] Yirmiya should worry about punishment.

C. There are three larger writings: One who sees the book of Psalms should expect piety. [One who sees] Proverbs should expect wisdom. One who sees Job should worry about punishment.

D. There are three smaller writings: One who sees the Song of Songs in a dream should expect piety. [One who sees] Kohelet should expect wisdom. [One who sees] Lamentations should worry about punishment.

E. One who sees the scroll of Esther, a miracle will happen to him.

F. There are three sages. One who sees Rabbi in a dream should expect wisdom. [One who sees] R. Elazar ben Azariah should expect riches. [One who sees] R. Yishmael ben Elisha should worry about punishment.

G. There are three disciples of sages: One who sees Ben Azai in a dream should expect piety. [One who sees] Ben Zoma should expect wisdom. [One who sees] "The Other"[16] should worry about punishment.

---

[15]The verse should actually be translated "and drink the wine that I have mixed." The rabbis understand *masakhti* ("mixed') as *masekhti* ("my Talmudic discussion").

[16]The Talmud refers to Elisha ben Abuya, a famous heretic, in this fashion to avoid having to refer to him by name.

H.   All kinds of animals are good for dreams except for the elephant, the ape, and the long-tailed ape.

  a. But [on the contrary] the master said: One who sees an elephant in a dream, a miracle will happen to him.

  b. There is no difficulty. One case refers to a saddled [elephant], the other case refers to an unsaddled [elephant].

I.   All kinds of metal are good for dreams except for a shovel, a mattock, and a spade.

  a. This applies when he saw them with their handles.

J.   All kinds of fruits are good for dreams except for unripe dates.

K.   All kinds of vegetables are good for dreams except for turnip-heads.

  a. But [on the contrary] Rav said: I did not become rich until I saw turnip-heads.

  b. He saw them with their stalk.

L.   All kinds of colors are good for dreams except for blue.

M.   [All kinds of creeping things are good for dreams except for] the mole.[17]

M.   All kinds of birds are good for dreams except for the owl and the horned-owl.[18]

N.   Five things are one-sixtieth: Fire, honey, Shabbat, sleep, and dreams.... Dreams are one-sixtieth of prophecy....

O.   Six things are a good sign for a sick person: sneezing, sweat, a bowel movement, semen, sleep, and dreams.... Dreams, as it is written "You have made me dream and revived me"[19] (Isa. 38:16)....

17.   Our rabbis taught [in a Tannaitic tradition]:[20] If a dead person is in a house, there will be peace in the house. If he eats or drinks in a house it is a good sign for the house. If he removed vessels from the house it is a bad sign for the house.

  a. Rav Papa interpreted it [as referring to] shoes and sandals. Anything that the dead takes away is good except for shoes and sandals. Anything that the dead gives is good except for ashes and mustard.

---

[17]See *DS* het; *Arukh ha-Shalem,* vol. 2, p. 27, and vol. 7, pp. 210-11; and Jastrow, *Dictionary,* p. 1343.

[18]See *Arukh ha-Shalem,* vol. 7, pp. 66 and 166-67; Levy, *Wörterbuch,* vol. 4, p. 246; and Jastrow, *Dictionary,* pp. 1315 and 1366.

[19]The verse actually means "You have restored me to health and revived me."

[20]It is not clear whether this statement deals with dreams.

Appendices to Chapter 5

Appendix One: R. Yohanan Comments on Statements by Rabbis Well Below Him in Status: The Evidence of the Yerushalmi

As noted above, the Yerushalmi also preserves cases in which R. Yohanan comments on statements by rabbis well below him in status. The cases are as follows: (1) Elazar states his opinion on a non-halachic matter and Yohanan rejects his view (Yer. Berakhot 8d). (2) Resh Lakish states his opinion and Yohanan explains the conditions under which Resh Lakish's view applies ("provided that") (Yer. Kilayim 28d). (3) Resh Lakish derives a law from a mishna and Yohanan states that the two cases are different and explains why Resh Lakish's reasoning is faulty (Yer. Hallah 59b). (4) and (5) Yohanan objects against a statement by Resh Lakish and follows with an alternative view (Yer. Shabbat 13d[1] and Yer. Gittin 44b). (6) Elazar states his opinion and Yohanan praises him, saying "R. Elazar taught us well" (Yer. Megillah 72c). (7) and (8) Elazar states his opinion and Yohanan asserts that "R. Elazar heard it from me" and repeated it without attribution (Yer. Yevamot 11b and 15a).

---

[1]See also the parallel on Yer. Gittin 44b.

Appendices to Chapter 5

Appendix Two: Palestinian Inferiors Observe Halachic Violations in Outlying Areas and Report Back to Superior Sages Translation of Texts

1) b. Yevamot 46a (b. Avodah Zarah 59a)[1]

R. Hiyya bar Abba visited Gabla. He saw Israelite women were pregnant by converts who were circumcized but not ritually immersed; and he saw idolaters were mixing Israelite wine and Israelites were drinking it; and he saw idolaters were cooking lupines and Israelites were eating them, but he said nothing to them. He came before R. Yohanan. He said to him, "Go and declare their children to be illegitimate, and their wine to be wine poured out to idols, and their lupines to be cooked by idolaters, because they are not people of Torah."

2) b. Sanhedrin 26a[2]

R. Hiyya bar Zarnoki and R. Shimon ben Yehozedek went to intercalate the year in Assia. Resh Lakish met and joined them. He said, "I will see what they do." He saw a man ploughing. He said to them, "A priest and he plows." They said to him, "He can say, 'I am an imperial employee.'" He then saw a man pruning a vineyard. He said to them, "A priest and he prunes." They said to him, "He can say, 'I need to make

---

[1]The following translation is based on that of A. Cohen, *Avodah Zarah* (London: The Soncino Press, 1935), p. 292; and Israel W. Slotki, *Yevamot* (London: The Soncino Press, 1936), p. 301.
[2]The following translation is based on that of Jacob Schachter, *Sanhedrin* (London: The Soncino Press, 1935), pp. 151-53; and Jacob Neusner, *Sanhedrin* (Chico, California: Scholars Press, 1984), pp. 161-62.

a bale for the wine-press.'" He said to them, "The heart knows whether it is a bale (*akkel*) or perversity (*akalkalut*)." ...

They said, "This one is bothersome." When they arrived there, they went up to the roof and removed the ladder from underneath him. He went before R. Yohanan. He said to him, "People who are suspect regarding the Sabbatical year are fit to intercalate the year?" ... Said R. Yohanan, "This is sad."

When they came before R. Yohanan, they said to him, "He called us cattle herders and the master said nothing to him." He said to them, "And if he called you sheep herders what would I say to him?"

3) b. Avodah Zarah 58b-59a[3]

R. Shimon ben Lakish visited Bozrah. He saw Israelites eating untithed fruit and prohibited them. He saw Israelites drinking water which had been worshipped by idolators and prohibited them. He came before R. Yohanan. He said to him, "While your cloak is still upon you, return. Bezer is not Bozrah, and water belonging to the public cannot become prohibited."

4) b. Rosh Hashana 21a[4]

R. Aibo bar Nagri and R. Hiyya bar Abba visited a certain locality which had been reached by messengers [sent out in] Nisan but not by messengers [sent out in] Tishrei. They observed one day [of Passover] but [Aibo and Hiyya] said nothing to them. R. Yohanan heard and became angry. He said to them, "Have I not said to you, 'When messengers [sent in] Nisan arrived but messengers [sent in] Tishrei did not arrive, observe two days [of Passover], Nisan being included so that there should be no mistake in Tishrei.'"

5) Yer. Shevi'it 8:11 (38b-c)[5]

R. Shimon ben Lakish was in Bozrah. He saw them sprinkling [on themselves in the bathhouse of] Aphrodite.[6] He said to them: "Is this not forbidden?" He went and asked R. Yohanan. R. Yohanan said to him in

---

[3]The following translation is based on that of Cohen, *Avodah Zarah*, pp. 291-92; and Gerald J. Blidstein, "R. Yohanan, Idolatry, and Public Privilege," *Journal for the Study of Judaism* 5, No. 2 (1974), p. 155.

[4]The following translation is based on that of Maurice Simon, *Rosh Hashanah* (London: The Soncino Press, 1938), p. 87.

[5]The following translation is based on that of Blidstein, "R. Yohanan, Idolatry, and Public Privilege," p. 155; and Alan J. Avery-Peck, *Shebi'it* (Chicago: University of Chicago Press, 1991), p. 293.

[6]See Michael Sokoloff, *A Dictionary of Jewish Palestinian Aramaic of the Byzantine Period* (Ramat Gan, Israel: Bar Ilan University Press, 1990), p. 178.

the name of R. Shimon ben Yehozedek, "That which is public cannot become forbidden."

6) Yer. Kiddushin 64d

R. Hiyya bar Ba went to Tyre. He went to R. Yohanan. He said to him, "What case came your way?" He said to him, "A convert who was circumcized but did not immerse." He said to him, "And why did you not attack him?"[7] R. Yehoshua ben Levi said to him, "Let him alone. He did well not to attack him."

7) Yer. Avodah Zarah 42a[8]

R. Hiyya bar Ba went to Tyre and found that R. Mana bar Tanhum had permitted their lupines. He came to R. Yohanan. He said, "What case came your way?" He said to him, "I found that R. Mana bar Tanhum had permitted their lupines." He said to him, "And you didn't attack him?" He said to him, "He is a great man and he knows how to sweeten the Mediterranean Sea." He said to him, "No, my son. He knows the behavior of the water. When the water praises its creator, it turns sweet."

---

[7]See Sokoloff, *A Dictionary of Jewish Palestinian Aramaic*, p. 424.
[8]The following translation is based on that of Jacob Neusner, *Avodah Zarah* (Chicago: University of Chicago Press, 1982), pp. 101-2.

Appendix to Chapter 7

Quotation Forms in the Babylonian Talmud

In the following pages, we discuss Amoraim who, according to the printed editions of the Talmud, quote earlier Amoraim in more than one form. All but a handful of these quotations will be shown, by reference to the manuscripts and medieval commentators, to be scribal errors. The handful of exceptions does not invalidate our basic premise regarding Amoraic quotation patterns. On the contrary, given the large number of Amoraim mentioned in the Talmud, and the far greater number of quotations by these Amoraim, it is only natural to find a small number of exceptions. Given the fact that the Talmud has undergone centuries of less than perfect transmission, it would be astonishing if every single case conformed to the general pattern.

Before beginning this discussion, it is important to note that for the most part, manuscripts of the Bavli confirm the quotation patterns described in this chapter. With the exception of the cases noted below, a review of *Dikdukei Soferim* yielded variation between forms A, B, and C only on Berakhot 7a (*DS* het), Shabbat 17b (*DS* pei), 94b, and 136b (*DS* zadi), Eruvin 102a, Pesahim 79a and 103a (*DS* zayin), Yoma 50a (*DS* nun), Rosh Hashana 10a (*DS* hei) and 12b (*DS* kuf), Taanit 14a (*DS* shin), 29b (*DS* pei and kuf), and 30a (*DS* tet), Megillah 12b (*DS* taf), and 32a (*DS* zayin), Moed Katan 18a (*DS* shin), Hagigah 3a (*DS* ayin) and 8b (*DS* bet), Yevamot 64b (*DS* Liss, notes on line 4), Ketubot 6a (*DS* Herschler, notes on line 6), 44a (*DS* Herschler, notes on line 14, and n. 48), 71b (*DS* Herschler, notes on line 13), 80b (*DS* Herschler, notes on line 2), 86a (*DS* Herschler, notes on line 9, and n. 31), and 93b (*DS* Herschler, notes on line 14, and n. 21), Nedarim 32b (*DS* Herschler, notes on line 12), Sotah 7b (*DS* Liss, notes on line 18), 10b (*DS* Liss, notes on line 17), and 20a (*DS* Liss, notes on line 19, and n. 93), Gittin 9a (*DS* Feldblum, notes on lines 3 and 9) and 52b (*DS* Feldblum, notes on line 20), Baba Kamma 96b (*DS* zadi), Baba Mezia 67b (*DS* bet), Baba Batra 75b (*DS* pei), 127a, and 150b (*DS* kuf), Avodah Zarah 31b, Menahot 17a (*DS* nun) and 40b

(*DS* resh), and Hullin 9a (*DS* khaf), 37b (*DS* vav), 53a, 53b (*DS* kuf), 56a (*DS* yud), 82a (*DS* khaf), 101b (*DS* gimel), and 137b (*DS* mem).

These few cases represent only a tiny proportion of the total number of quotations found in the Bavli. In addition, most of them involve a variant preserved in only one version, or involve confusion between form B and form C. Occasional scribal confusion between forms B and C is easily understandable.

Abaye only quotes in form C (see Kosowsky, *Ozar ha-Shemot*, pp. 82-90). On Yevamot 101a and Kiddushin 72a, the correct reading is most likely R. Abahu instead of Abaye, which is preserved in the Munich and Oxford manuscripts of Kiddushin and Hidushei Mahari Berav. It is appropriate both chronologically and geographically that R. Aha bar Hanina should quote R. Abahu, and that R. Abahu should quote R. Asi, but problematic that Abaye should do so. See also Shabbat 57b and *DS* zadi.

Rava quotes consistently in form A, with the exception of Shabbat 129a, Eruvin 3b, and Baba Mezia 36b, where he quotes in form C. In these three cases, however, Rava's quotation contradicts Abaye's version of the same quote (see R. Hananel, and *DS* mem on Shabbat 129a), and we noted above that Abaye consistently quotes in form C. It is likely that in these three cases, Rava's quotation form was altered under the influence of Abaye's.

With regard to Rav Nahman bar Yizhak, see Shabbat 57a (*DS* bet), Shevuot 40a (*DS* mem), Avodah Zarah 63a (*DS* shin), and Hullin 5b (*DS* lamed).

With regard to fifth-generation Amoraim, see Shabbat 151b (*DS* bet), Bezah 31a (*DS* shin), Baba Batra 75b (*DS* pei), Avodah Zarah 14a (*DS* gimel), and Niddah 25b (see Albeck, *Mavo la-Talmudim*, p. 230).

With regard to sixth-generation Amoraim, see Berakhot 44a (*DS* het), Baba Kamma 112b (*DS* bet), and Niddah 63a (see Albeck, *Mavo la-Talmudim*, p. 329). The name Rav Ashi on Zevahim 55b should be emended to R. Asi (see Albeck, *ibid.*, p. 250).

With regard to seventh-generation Amoraim, see Kalmin, *The Post-Rav Ashi Amoraim: Transition or Continuity?*, pp. 110-19, where I document in detail the quotation forms attributed to post-Rav Ashi Amoraim.

R. Abahu quotes regularly in form A, with the exception of several quotations of a Tanna, R. Hanina ben Gamliel, in form B (Kosowsky, *Ozar ha-Shemot*, pp. 25-39). Our printed editions of Kiddushin 40a have him quoting R. Hanina in form B, but the Munich manuscript reads R. Hanina ben Gamliel in this context as well, which is most likely correct. See also Hullin 122b and *DS* resh, and the parallel on Pesahim 46a.

With regard to R. Aha, a fourth-generation Palestinian Amora who quotes several times in form A (Kosowsky, *Ozar ha-Shemot*, p. 130), see Berakhot 60b (and *DS* shin).

R. Asi quotes often in form A (Kosowsky, *Ozar ha-Shemot*, pp. 270-78), and quotes a Tanna in form B on Taanit 14a (*DS* shin). See, however, the discussion of the quotation form on Tamid 31b (and on Baba Batra 19b and 25b) in chapter 5, above.

R. Elazar quotes regularly in form A, except for his form B quotations of Tannaim (Berakhot 31b [twice] and Pesahim 6b [and parallel]), and possibly his form C quotations of Rav (Gittin 73a [*DS* Feldblum, notes on line 5], Baba Kamma 15b [*DS* zadi] and 75b [*DS* het], and Keritut 3a [the Florence, Munich, and London manuscripts all read Rava]). With regard to his quotations of Rav, see the discussion below. See also Yoma 46a (and *DS* shin), Zevahim 65b (and *DS* zayin), Hullin 7a, and Bekhorot 52b.

Rav Huna consistently quotes in form A (Kosowsky, *Ozar ha-Shemot*, pp. 376-89), with the exception of a quotation of a Tanna, R. Yishmael b'R. Yosi, in form B on Hullin 134a (see also Shevuot 18a and Halivni, *Mekorot u-Mesorot:* Eruvin-Pesahim, p. 220, n. 1). It is strange, however, that Rav Huna should quote R. Yishmael b'R. Yosi in form B, and yet quote Rabbi (R. Yehuda ha-Nasi), Yishmael b'R. Yosi's contemporary, in form A (see Halivni, *Mekorot u-Mesorot:* Shabbat, p. 150, n. 1). Nevertheless, R. Hanina, Shmuel, and R. Yannai also depart from their usual quotation patterns and quote Rabbi in form A (Kosowsky, *Ozar ha-Shemot*, pp. 1604-25; see also Berakhot 33b and Sanhedrin 11a). In fact, Rabbi is never quoted in any form other than form A (Kosowsky, *Ozar ha-Shemot*, pp. 1489-500). See also Shabbat 130b and *DS* nun, and Zevahim 25b and *DS* pei. It is not completely clear why quotations of Rabbi should be so consistently exceptional in this regard. Perhaps the fact that he is referred to throughout the Talmud by a special honorific, "Rabbi," the "rabbi" par excellence, helps explain this curious phenomenon. We saw above that several Amoraim exhibit unique quotation patterns when the author of the statement is referred to not by his proper name, but by a descriptive substitute, for example Rav, the "master" par excellence. It is not completely clear why the title "Rav" leads (on several occasions) to quotation in form C, while the title "Rabbi" leads to quotation in form A, although the fact that Rabbi is a Palestinian Tanna, while Rav is a Babylonian Amora, is very likely a contributing factor.

With regard to Rav Huna bar Yehuda, who quotes several Amoraim in form A (Kosowsky, *Ozar ha-Shemot*, pp. 392-93), see Berakhot 48a and 48b, and *DS* taf, on Berakhot 48a. Too many variants of the names have been preserved in this context for any exact determination to be made.

With regard to Rav Hama bar Gurya, who quotes regularly in form
A (Kosowsky, *Ozar ha-Shemot*, pp. 494-95), see Avodah Zarah 16b, and n.
23, above.

Rav Hanina bar Kahana quotes several times in form A (Kosowsky,
Ozar ha-Shemot, p. 519). See also Shabbat 96a and *DS* bet, and R. Hananel
on Shabbat 97a, Taanit 30a and *DS* tet, and Sanhedrin 70a and *DS* taf.

Rav Hiyya bar Ashi quotes only in form A. See also Bekhorot 25a
and *DS* Herschler, on Ketubot 6a, notes on line 4.

R. Ilai quotes several times in form A (Kosowsky, *Ozar ha-Shemot*,
pp. 159-61), and quotes a Tanna in form B on Yevamot 65b (three
times). See also Baba Mezia 117a and *DS* zayin. In addition, he quotes
R. Yehuda bar Misparta in form B on Sanhedrin 44a (twice), and
quotes R. Yehuda ben Safra in form B on Pesahim 70b. Hyman, *Toldot
Tannaim ve-Amoraim*, p. 564, concludes that R. Yehuda ben Safra was a
second-generation Amora because on Yer. Hagigah 1:6, R. Yehuda ben
Safra quotes the latter statement in the name of R. Oshaya. If Hyman is
correct, then R. Ilai quotes earlier Amoraim in both form A and form B.
See, however, our discussion of R. Levi immediately following,
according to which it is extremely risky to draw conclusions regarding
the chronology of a rabbi mentioned in the Bavli solely on the basis of his
appearances in the Yerushalmi. Despite the parallel in the Yerushalmi,
R. Ilai may be quoting a Tanna or a transitional rabbi according to the
Bavli.

On Baba Batra 75b, R. Levi quotes R. Papi in form A, and R. Papi in
turn quotes R. Yehoshua de-Sikhnin in form B. (See also Shabbat 151b
and *DS* bet.) Judging from the contexts in which he appears in the
Yerushalmi, R. Yehoshua de-Sikhnin is a fourth-generation Palestinian
Amora, and it fits none of the quotation patterns described below for
such a relatively late Amora to be quoted in form B. Albeck, *Mavo la-
Talmudim*, p. 331, however, points out the difficulty of reconciling the
Bavli's quotation chain with the picture of the chronology of these
Amoraim which emerges from the Yerushalmi. Most likely, the
Yerushalmi and the Bavli should not be reconciled, and according to the
Bavli R. Yehoshua de-Sikhnin is a Tanna or a transitional rabbi.

Rav Malkia twice quotes Rav Ada bar Ahava in form A (Makkot 21a
and Avodah Zarah 29a; see also Bezah 29b and Ketubot 61b). See also
Avodah Zarah 35b (and *DS* resh, the Paris manuscript, and that of the
Jewish Theological Seminary, ed. Abramson).

Mar Yehuda quotes Abimi in form C on Shabbat 57b (*DS* mem) and
Hullin 48a, but quotes him in form A on Eruvin 24a (*DS* zayin). I am
unable to account for this variation in quotation forms, and must
attribute it to scribal error. Compare Shabbat 59b and *DS* daled.

Rav Menashya bar Tahalifa quotes in form C (Pesahim 6b). See also Berakhot 49b and *DS* daled. With regard to Yoma 78a, where Rav Menashya bar Tahalifa's name is the first link in a quotation chain of three elements, see the discussion above.

Rav Nahman quotes only in form A (Kosowsky, *Ozar ha-Shemot*, pp. 1084-103). According to the printed editions of Bekhorot 23b, he quotes Rav in form C, but Ramban (Halachot Bekhorot), the London manuscript, and Shita Mekubezet, n. vav, all read *Amar Rav* ("Said Rav") without Rav Nahman's name, and the Florence and Vatican manuscripts read only Rav Nahman's name.

Rabbah bar Shmuel quotes consistently in form A (Kosowsky, *Ozar ha-Shemot*, p. 1468), with the exception of three quotations of R. Hiyya on Berakhot 40a, two in form B and one in form C. However, Hyman, *Toldot Tannaim ve-Amoraim*, p. 1061, observes that there were most likely two sages named Rabbah bar Shmuel, one a third-generation Amora and the other a fifth-generation Amora. It is likely that the correct reading in all three cases on Berakhot 40a is R. Hiyya bar Abba rather than R. Hiyya (*DS* shin and Hyman, *op. cit.*, pp. 436-37 and 1085), and that R. Hiyya bar Abba is being quoted three times in form C by a fifth-generation Amora. *Ozar ha-Geonim*, ed. Lewin, Interpretations, chapter 172, p. 56, records only one of the statements, and transmits it in form C; Piskei Rid records only two of the statements, and transmits both in form C; and the Munich manuscript records two of the statements in form C.

With regard to Rabbah bar Simi, see Pesahim 6b, and compare Hullin 102a.

Rabbah bar Tahalifa quotes Rav in form C on Shabbat 120b. See also Hullin 49a (and parallel) and *DS* pei.

Rav quotes regularly in form B (Kosowsky, *Ozar ha-Shemot*, pp. 1273-1311; with regard to his quotation of Mavug in form C on Zevahim 6b, see above; with regard to Baba Kamma 115a, see *DS* bet and khaf), with the exception of five cases in which he might quote R. Hiyya in form A. See Shabbat 100a (twice) and *DS* nun (the Vatican manuscript reads Rav Yehuda quoting R. Hiyya both times); Taanit 10b and *DS* zayin; Taanit 11a and *DS* tet; and Hullin 76a and *DS* zayin and khaf. It is interesting that Rav Yehuda is involved in all five quotations. Perhaps the correct reading in each case is Rav Yehuda quoting R. Hiyya in form A, and the scribes added Rav's name to the quotation chain since Rav Yehuda so frequently quotes Rav. Rav Yehuda quotes only in form A (Kosowsky, *Ozar ha-Shemot*, pp. 631-56), with the exception of Hullin 27b (*DS* ayin), where he quotes a Tanna in form B. See also Shabbat 57b and *DS* mem, Eruvin 28a and *DS* shin, and Avodah Zarah 40a and *DS* lamed.

Ravanai quotes in form A (Kosowsky, *Ozar ha-Shemot*, p. 1526). His quotation of Abaye on Berakhot 38b is a chronological impossibility, and the name Ravanai there should most likely be emended to Ravina.

Resh Lakish quotes regularly in form B (with regard to Baba Kamma 9b, see above). See, however, Pesahim 34b and *DS* shin; Yevamot 74a (the Vatican manuscript lacks the words *Amar R. Samia*, and reads the quote in form B); Temurah 12b (see Hyman, *Toldot Tannaim ve-Amoraim*, p. 1153), and Meilah 18b (the Vatican manuscript and Meyuhas le-Rashi lack R. Yannai's name).

R. Shabtai quotes Hizkiya twice, once (Gittin 26b) in form A, and once (Baba Batra 163a) in form C. I have no explanation for this variation and must attribute it to scribal error.

Rav Shmuel bar Unia quotes Rav several times in form C (Kosowsky, *Ozar ha-Shemot*, p. 1630). See also Yevamot 105a and the parallel on Rosh Hashana 18a. The Munich and Vatican manuscripts of Yevamot likewise read the quote in form C.

Rav Shmuel bar Yizhak quotes regularly in form A. See Yevamot 46a and *DS* Liss, notes on lines 32 and 35.

R. Yaakov bar Idi quotes only in form A. See Menahot 17a and *DS* bet.

R. Yehoshua ben Levi quotes Bar Kappara several times in form B (Kosowsky, *Ozar ha-Shemot*, pp. 694-97). See Yoma 10a and *DS* ayin; Yoma 69a and *DS* resh; and Bezah 14b and 27a.

R. Yizhak quotes regularly in form A (Kosowsky, *Ozar ha-Shemot*, pp. 906-9). On Ketubot 60a, his quotation is recorded twice, the first time in form A and the second time in form B. I have no explanation for this variation and must attribute it to scribal error.

R. Yohanan consistently quotes in form B (Kosowsky, *Ozar ha-Shemot*, pp. 743-81). See Berakhot 10b and *DS* zadi; Shabbat 15b and *DS* het; Pesahim 114a and *DS* taf; Ketubot 96a and *DS* Herschler, notes on line 21; Baba Kamma 115a and *DS* bet and tet; Baba Mezia 40a and *DS* alef; Baba Batra 14b and *DS* ayin; and Niddah 61a (the Munich and Vatican manuscripts read this quotation in form B). See below with regard to Sanhedrin 83b and Zevahim 20a.

Appendices to Chapter 8

Appendix One: Anonymous and Attributed Sources in the Bavli Regarding Arabs

In this appendix, I attempt to show differences between anonymous and attributed portrayals of Arabs, and I argue that these differences decrease the likelihood that attributed portrayals of Arabs are anonymous editorial inventions. The anonymous editors would be unlikely to attribute to earlier rabbis portrayals of Arabs which differ significantly from their own, which increases the likelihood that the Amoraic portrayals derive from the Amoraim themselves. In other words, we have further evidence for the existence of diverse sources in the Talmud, some attributed and others anonymous. This conclusion must be considered tentative because the sources preserve only one or two anonymous editorial portrayals of Arabs, and firm conclusions must be based on a much larger body of evidence.

Scholars have frequently attempted to reconstruct the history of Arabic peoples before the advent of Islam. These scholars have generally concentrated on Arabic, Greco-Roman, Persian, and Syriac literature,[1] and ancient rabbinic evidence has often been ignored. Krauss surveyed rabbinic sources approximately seventy-five years ago,[2] but he did not distinguish between Palestinian and Babylonian sources or between anonymous and attributed statements. Szadzunski briefly supplemented Krauss's discussion,[3] but he sees hostility between the rabbis and Arabs even when the sources are neutral or even favorable, perhaps giving the

---

[1]See, most recently, J.B. Segal, "Arabs in Syriac Literature Before the Rise of Islam," *Jerusalem Studies in Arabic and Islam* 4 (1984), pp. 89-128.
[2]Samuel Krauss, "Talmudische Nachrichten über Arabien," *Zeitschrift der Deutschen Morgenländischen Gesellschaft* 70 (1916), pp. 321-53.
[3]E.I. Szadzunski, "Addenda to Krauss," *The American Journal of Semitic Languages and Literatures* 49, No. 4 (1933), pp. 336-38.

ancient material a modern slant. A fresh look at the evidence is therefore desirable.[4]

A glance at the rabbinic sources reveals a variety of terms designating either (1) Arabs in general, (2) particular Arabic peoples or tribes, or (3) inhabitants of Arab-controlled localities. In the following discussion, we will analyze the term most frequently encountered in Babylonian Talmudic sources (Tayaya [plural, Tayaye]), in an effort to describe rabbinic conceptions of the people referred to by this term. I hope to show that Talmudic sources (1) differentiate between Pumbeditan Tayaye and Tayaye who roam the Arabian and Sinai deserts, and (2) that Amoraim use the term Tayaye differently than do the Talmud's anonymous editors.

Tayaye

A. *Geographical Location: Pumbedita and Its Environs*

In Syriac and Persian sources, the term Tayaye originally referred to a particular tribe living on the western border of the Persian empire. Eventually the term came to designate Arabs in general.[5]

In ancient rabbinic sources, the term is found only in the Babylonian Talmud. It also has a dual meaning here, although Talmudic sources contain details about the Tayaye which are either missing from or have not yet been noticed in non-Jewish sources. The latter need to be reexamined in light of the rabbinic materials to determine whether Jewish and non-Jewish sources really differ on this issue.

In Amoraic sources, the term Tayaya designates (1) semi-nomadic traders living in the vicinity of Pumbedita, and (2) desert-dwelling warriors and guides who roamed the northern Arabian and Sinai peninsulas.

Confining ourselves to Amoraic sources which (1) depict contact between Amoraim and Tayaye *in Babylonia,* and (2) connect Tayaye to specific localities *in Babylonia,* we find that Tayaye are consistently located in Pumbedita. Abaye[6] and Ulla[7] have contact with Tayaye in Pumbedita. Rav Yehuda, head in Pumbedita, permits two students to sell wheat "on the festival of the Tayaye."[8] Shazrak the Tayaya donates a

---

[4]See also Salo Baron, *A Social and Religious History of the Jews* (1957; Reprint. Philadelphia: Jewish Publication Society, 1960), vol. 3, pp. 60-74 and 256-61.
[5]*Pauly's Real-Encyclopädie der Classischen Altertumswissenschaft,* 2nd series, ed. G. Wissowa (Stuttgart: J.B. Metzler, 1932), vol. 4a, pt. 2, columns 2025-26.
[6]Yoma 84a (and parallel) and Gittin 45b.
[7]Niddah 20a.
[8]Avodah Zarah 11b.

lamp to the synagogue of Rav Yehuda,[9] and third-generation Pumbeditan rabbis, Rehava and Rabbah,[10] disagree about proper use of the lamp. In the miraculous story of the death of Rabbah bar Nahmani,[11] a third-generation Pumbeditan rabbi, a Tayaya is thrown from one side of the Papa River to the other. As Obermeyer notes, the Papa River flowed through Pumbedita.[12] In another context, we find a description of a case involving Tayaye who arrive in Zikunia.[13] This locality is unknown to us from elsewhere, but Rav Tuvi bar Matna, a third-generation rabbi closely associated with Pumbedita,[14] remands the case to Rav Yosef, also a Pumbeditan.

In sources purporting to derive from the second to the fourth Amoraic generations, therefore, Tayaye are clearly located in and around Pumbedita. Our sources for the post-fourth-generation Amoraic period are comparatively sparse, particularly regarding Pumbedita, and stories about post-fourth-generation rabbis are comparatively brief. We find only a handful of relevant sources involving later Amoraim, and the geographical link between Tayaye and Pumbedita is neither corroborated nor contradicted by sources attributed to or dealing with later Amoraim.[15]

---

[9]Arakhin 6b.

[10]The printed text reads Rava, but see chapter 10, below. The third-generation Amora, Rabbah, is a contemporary of Rehava and is often associated with Pumbedita, whereas the fourth-generation Amora, Rava, is typically associated with Mahoza. Rabbah is almost certainly the correct reading.

An alternate reading has Rehava and Rabbah disagreeing with the "sextons of Pumbedita" regarding proper use of the lamp.

[11]Baba Mezia 86a.

[12]Jacob Obermeyer, *Die Landschaft Babylonien im Zeitalter des Talmuds und des Gaonats* (Frankfurt am Main: I. Kauffmann, 1929), p. 242.

[13]Hullin 39b.

[14]Hyman, *Toldot Tannaim ve-Amoraim*, p. 523, concludes that Tuvi was "a judge in his city close to Pumbedita, the locality of Rav Yosef." See, for example, Baba Batra 58a, which might imply that he was buried in or around Pumbedita.

[15]The sources involving later Amoraim are as follows: (1) On Avodah Zarah 29a, Rav Papa reports a remedy told to him by "a certain Tayaya"; (2) Baba Kamma 98a depicts contact between Agardamis Tayaya and Rav Papa and Rav Huna b. d'Rav Yehoshua; (3) On Shabbat 82a and 155b Rav Yirmiya Midifti ("of the city Difti"), a fifth- and sixth-generation Amora, tells of his encounters with a Tayaya.

No geographical conclusions are possible from the above evidence. The location of Difti has not yet been determined (see Oppenheimer, *Babylonia Judaica in the Talmudic Period,* pp. 112-14), and the designation "of Difti" might imply that Yirmiya was born in Difti but say nothing about where he spent his adult life. Rav Papa and Rav Huna b. d'Rav Yehoshua were both students of Abaye in Pumbedita but also of Rava in Mahoza. They are also frequently connected with Nersh. We have no way of knowing, therefore, where their encounters with Tayaye took place.

B. Characteristics of the Tayaye

Pumbeditan Tayaye

What are the characteristics of Pumbeditan Tayaye according to the Talmud? They are never depicted as military men, guards, or robbers, but as a peaceful group of itinerant[16] merchants.[17]

Amoraim consistently acknowledge the expertise of Tayaye in extra-halachic matters such as health and medicine. In two separate accounts, for example, Abaye and Rav Papa report that they tried several remedies suggested by earlier rabbis, but were not cured until they tried remedies suggested to them by "a certain Tayaya."[18]

In addition, several Amoraic sources sympathetically portray the religious beliefs and practices of the Pumbeditan Tayaye.[19] One source,[20]

---

[16]Baba Mezia 86a depicts a Tayaya riding a camel. Several statements by Babylonian Amoraim, which may or may not refer to Pumbeditan Tayaye, also indicate that Tayaye are itinerant. Yoma 23a presupposes that they carry whips, Pesahim 65b that they carry things on their backs, and Baba Kamma 55a mentions a breed of camel named after the Tayaye. Hullin 39b depicts them as arriving in Zikonia, and according to the anonymous editors on Arakhin 6b the Tayaye are irregular visitors to Rav Yehuda's synagogue.

[17]See Gittin 45b (Perhaps the Arab woman came upon the tefillin by chance, however, and is not a merchant), Baba Kamma 98a (see Rashi, Tosafot R. Perez, and E.Z. Melamed, Talmud Bavli, Massekhet Baba Kamma [Jerusalem, 1952], p. 163), Avodah Zarah 11b, and Hullin 39b. See also the discussion below.

Jastrow, Dictionary, p. 531, who defines Tayaya as a "traveler, esp. Arabian caravan merchant," has this kind of Tayaya in mind. See also Levy, Wörterbuch, vol. 2, p. 156; and Arukh ha-Shalem, ed. Kohut, vol. 4, p. 29.

[18]Yoma 84a (and parallel) (Abaye) and Avodah Zarah 29a (Rav Papa). See also Shabbat 82a, where Rav Yirmiya Midifti reports that a certain Tayaya effectively cured his constipation. We also find several stories in which Tayaye are portrayed as knowledgeable about non-halachic matters, but it is unclear whether the context is Pumbedita or the desert.

[19]In addition to the sources discussed below, see also Berakhot 6b (and DS tet) and Arakhin 6b. According to Berakhot 6b, a Tayaya (not Eliyahu disguised as a Tayaya, as in the printed edition) draws his sword and kills "a certain man [i.e., a Jew]," for praying behind a synagogue and not facing the synagogue. That is, the Tayaya is offended at the Jew's position in prayer, and his sentiments therefore conform to those of Rav Huna as modified by Abaye. We thus might find further proof of a link between Tayaye and Pumbedita (as exemplified by Abaye), and further indication of conformity between Jewish and Tayaya religious practices.

The story of the Tayaya's killing of the Jew, however, was very likely emended to conform to one or more of the Amoraic statements which precede, and earlier versions of the story may have lacked the reference to Abaye's view. The context of the story need not be Babylonia, since Rav Huna's opinion was known in Palestine (see Yer. Berakhot 5:1), and is quoted in the Bavli by R. Helbo (see DS zayin), a Palestinian Amora. As we will see below, the Tayaye who come in contact with Babylonian rabbis in Babylonia are not military men and are not

for example, depicts a Tayaya praying to God, whom he addresses as *Ribono Shel Olam*, master of the world, an epithet used frequently by the rabbis themselves. In the Tayaya's prayer, he acknowledges God's dominion over the world ("the world is Yours"), and his prayer is answered.[21]

In another context, Rav Yehuda permits students to sell to (or buy from) Tayaye on their festivals (*hagta*).[22] Despite the anonymous editors' attempt to soften the force of Yehuda's surprisingly lenient view,[23] Yehuda perhaps disagrees with other Talmudic sources which clearly view the Tayaye as idolaters.[24] In addition, Yehuda uses the neutral term *hagta* to refer to the Tayayan festivals, and avoids the pejorative term *eidam* (their calamity) commonly used by the rabbis to denote non-Jewish festivals.[25] Even if the anonymous editors are correct that Yehuda's view is reconcilable with the belief that Tayaye are idolaters, Yehuda evidently considers their festivals to be comparatively inoffensive.[26]

Desert Tayaye

Amoraic sources paint a much different picture of Tayaye who inhabit the desert regions of the Arabian and Sinai peninsulas. These Tayaye, whom I will refer to as desert Tayaye, are depicted in Amoraic sources as military men and desert guides.

---

depicted as sword-bearers, whereas the situation in the Sinai and the Arabian peninsulas is markedly different. The context of the story, therefore, is very likely the latter. As we will see below, the desert Tayaye are also depicted as favorably disposed toward the Jewish tradition.

[20]Baba Mezia 86a.

[21]The Talmud, like other ancient sources, attests to monotheistic tendencies on the part of pre-Islamic Arabs (see below). See Baron, *A Social and Religious History*, pp. 65-66 and 258-59.

[22]Avodah Zarah 11b.

[23]Shmuel, also surprisingly lenient, rules that a Jew is forbidden to do business with idolaters "only on the day of their festival" (literally, "their calamity." See below). Krauss, "Talmudische Nachrichten über Arabien," p. 350, accepts the anonymous editorial comment as an accurate interpretation of Yehuda's action. Compare also Obermeyer, *Die Landschaft Babylonien*, p. 234.

[24]Avodah Zarah 34a-b and Hullin 39b. The anonymous editorial comment based on Rav Yehuda's statement also reflects the view that Tayaye are idolaters.

[25]See *Ozar Lashon ha-Talmud*, ed. Haim Kosowsky (Jerusalem: Ministry of Education and Culture, Government of Israel, and Jewish Theological Seminary, 1964), vol. 13, pp. 54-57.

[26]Very likely, the term *hagta* is used partly because Arab holidays, like Jewish holidays, were pilgrimage festivals (hence the name *hag*, pilgrimage). Nevertheless, Yehuda's choice of a neutral term is significant.

Only Amoraim who travel the Sinai desert and the desert regions separating Babylonia and Palestine come in contact with or describe the desert Tayaye. For example, Rabbah bar bar Hana, a third-generation Amora who travelled between Palestine and Babylonia,[27] travels in the vicinity of Palestine and observes a Tayaya riding a camel and carrying a spear in his hand.[28] According to this story, a particular landmark is so high off the ground that the Tayaya looks like a tiny insect when viewed from below. Evidently the rabbis consider Tayaye to be physically imposing, which makes them an especially appropriate illustration of this point.[29]

In another context, Rabbah bar bar Hana observes a Tayaya slice up his camel with a sword.[30] In a separate passage, Rav tells R. Hiyya that he also witnessed a Tayaya slice up his camel, and that afterward he brought it back to life.[31] Talmudic sources consistently maintain that Rav was born in Babylonia but spent his early years in Palestine, where he studied with his uncle, R. Hiyya, and with the patriarch, R. Yehuda ha-Nasi.[32] In another story, Rabbah bar Rav Huna and Rav Hamnuna, third-generation Babylonian Amoraim, are transported from Babylonia for burial in Israel. Along the way, evidently in the Arabian desert, they encounter a Tayaya.[33] In another story,[34] a Tayaya accompanies R. Pinhas ben Yair, a Palestinian sage, who is journeying through the desert to redeem captives.

Elsewhere, Rabbah bar bar Hana tells a series of stories about his encounters with desert Tayaye.[35] One story takes place in the Sinai peninsula. A Tayaya accompanies Rabbah bar bar Hana in the desert and knows by smell where the road leads and how far they are from

---

[27]See Hyman, *Toldot Tannaim ve-Amoraim*, p. 1077.

[28]Taanit 22b (see *DS* het). The Tayaya passes a landmark which, according to a Baraita cited in the same context (see the discussion between R. Eliezer and his students) was well-known in Palestine.

[29]See also Rosh Hashana 26b, according to which Rabbah bar bar Hana walks with, or is accompanied by, a Tayaya (see *DS* alef). The Tayaya notices the rabbi carrying a burden and offers to carry it himself, perhaps with the expectation of receiving payment.

See also *DS* kuf, on Megillah 18a, according to which Rabbah bar bar Hannah might be quoting a story told to him by Rav, which would not affect my claim. See the discussion below.

[30]Yevamot 120b.

[31]Sanhedrin 67b.

[32]See also Yevamot 102a, where Rav, speaking to R. Hiyya, refers to a Tayayan sandal as a well-known type of footwear. In a parallel on Yer. Yevamot 12:1 there is no mention of a Tayaya.

[33]Moed Katan 25a-b.

[34]Hullin 7a.

[35]Baba Batra 73b-74a.

water. He guides the rabbi to the remains of the Israelites who died in the desert on their way to Canaan, and also shows him Mt. Sinai, the place where the earth swallowed Korah, and the spot where "heaven and earth kiss."

The Tayaya who accompanies Rabbah bar bar Hana through the Sinai desert rides a camel and holds a spear, images familiar to us from the sources above. He is knowledgeable about biblical traditions, familiar with several of the major events of Israel's Sinai experience, and believes in the existence of *Gehinom*, the netherworld. He informs Rabbah bar bar Hana that every thirty days Korah and his fellow rebels are turned over like meat in a pot and confess that "Moshe and his Torah are truthful and we are liars."

Elsewhere, Bar Adda the Tayaya has dealings with Rav Yizhak bar Yosef, another Amora who travels regularly between Israel and Babylonia.[36] Bar Adda forcibly seizes wineskins from the rabbi and returns them filled with wine.[37] That Bar Adda is referred to by name very likely indicates his important status. He is probably a chieftain who needs the wineskins to supply his army. The fact that he returns them full indicates that we are not dealing with simple thievery but with the momentary needs of an army at war.[38]

Tayaye According to the Anonymous Editors

In the following discussion, I attempt to show that the anonymous editors depict Tayaye differently than do the Amoraim, and tentatively explore the implications of this finding for study of the dating and authorship of Amoraic sources.

On Baba Batra 36a, the anonymous editors resolve a contradiction between statements by Abuha de-Shmuel and Resh Lakish. Abuha de-Shmuel implies that possession of animals is a valid and sufficient claim of ownership of the animals, whereas Resh Lakish asserts that it is not. The anonymous editors resolve the contradiction by claiming that Abuha de-Shmuel refers to his own locality, Nehardea. There are many Tayaye in Nehardea, the editors claim, and therefore shepherds return animals directly to their owners to avoid Tayayan thievery. At no time are animals left out in the open with the expectation that they will travel home by themselves. Anyone who has possession of an animal in

---

[36]Albeck, *Mavo la-Talmudim,* pp. 366-67.
[37]Avodah Zarah 33a.
[38]For another story involving Bar Adda the Tayaya, see Menahot 69b and *DS* pei.

Nehardea has a valid claim of ownership since it is unlikely that the animal was seized as it was wandering home to its owner.[39]

This discussion reveals two major distinctions between Amoraic and anonymous editorial depictions of Tayaye. According to the editors, Tayaye frequent Nehardea, while Amoraic sources place them either in and around Pumbedita or in the Arabian or Sinai desert. In addition, the editors view the Tayaye as thieves, while Amoraim portray them either as semi-nomadic traders or as nomadic warriors and desert guides.

Further evidence of a distinction between the Amoraim and the editors may be provided by the anonymous discussion of a Baraita in another context.[40] This Baraita states that "One who sees Yishmael (or *a* Yishmael) in a dream, his prayer is heard," and the anonymous editors comment that "this refers to Yishmael the son of Abraham, but a mere Tayaya, no." In the opinion of the editors, therefore, the terms Tayaya and Yishmael partially overlap, and Amoraic sources lack this idea. Not all versions have the term Tayaya, however,[41] indicating that it might be a post-Talmudic addition reflecting later usage.

Differences between anonymous and attributed portrayals of Arabs are most likely not attributable to the editors' preoccupation with resolving difficulties and clarifying obscurities in Tannaitic and Amoraic sources. One might argue, for example, that the overriding concern of the anonymous editors in commenting on the above story is to reconcile the contradictory Amoraic opinions. As a result, one might argue, the editors' claim that Tayaye are thieves who frequent Nehardea is an exegetical invention. It is useless as evidence of differences between attributed and anonymous conceptions of Tayaye.

This argument fails, however, because the editors presumably intend their arguments to be convincing. An assertion which is nothing but an ad hoc invention, which has no basis in reality or even runs counter to firmly entrenched prejudices and misconceptions, convinces no one, and hardly furthers the editors' interpretive goals. Most likely, their claims about Tayaye correspond to reality, at least as the editors conceive it, and should not be dismissed as exegetical fantasy.

The differences between attributed and anonymous portrayals of Tayaye increase the likelihood that the editors, at least in this one case,

---

[39] According to geonic accounts, Nehardea was destroyed by Palmyran Arabs in the mid-third century C.E. See Gafni, *Yehudei Bavel bi-Tekufat ha-Talmud*, pp. 263-64. It is unlikely that the anonymous editors have these Arabs in mind, however, since the usual term for Palmyra in rabbinic literature is Tadmor.

[40] Berakhot 56b.

[41] See *DS* zayin.

did not change Amoraic sources to conform to reality as they understood it. This conclusion is tentative, however, for we find only one or two cases in which the anonymous editors clearly reveal their understanding of the term "Tayaye." We cannot rule out the possibility that these one or two cases are post-Talmudic additions to the text or scribal errors, and say nothing about Talmudic understandings of the term.

Postscript
Babylonian Talmudic Portrayals Of Arvi'im

In the following pages, I analyze the term Aravi (pl. Arvi'im), which also commonly denotes Arabs in the Bavli but differs from the term "Tayaya" in several respects.

In contrast to Tayaye, Arvi'im are singled out by the rabbis as practitioners of sinful and repugnant sexual practices. Rav Yirmiya Midifti reports that "I saw an Aravi buy a thigh from the market and cut a hole in it in order to copulate with it, and he copulated with it."[42] Rabbah bar bar Hana reports that he saw a certain Aravit (Arab woman) conduct herself indecently in the marketplace, making sexual advances toward a rabbi.[43] R. Dosa, a Tanna, uses an Aravi as an example of a captor who sexually mistreats his captives. According to R. Dosa, the Aravi can be presumed to fondle, but not rape, his victims.[44] In another context, Rav Sheshet delivers his maidservants to an Aravi, telling them to "be careful [not to consort] with a Jew." The Aravi serves as the maidservant's sexual partner, helping to insure that she keeps away from Jews.[45] Elsewhere, a Tannaitic tradition maintains that "ten measures of licentiousness fell to the world, and Aravia took nine of them."[46] Here the locality rather than the people is designated, but presumably Arvi'im dwell in Aravia and are criticized by the tradition.

The Arvi'im, in contrast to the Tayaye, are viewed by the rabbis as lowly or despised. In one story,[47] Rabban Yohanan ben Zakkai spies the daughter of Nakdimon ben Gurion picking barley out of the dung of the beasts of Arvi'im. Mention of Arvi'im in this context is intended to increase our sympathy for the poor woman, formerly one of the wealthiest in Jerusalem. Lest we miss the point, Yohanan states explicitly at the conclusion of the story that when Israel performs the

---

[42]Avodah Zarah 22b.
[43]Ketubot 72b. The phrase employed literally means "spinning and weaving red against her face." The exact connotation of this phrase is not clear, although the context demands that sexual misconduct is referred to. See Rashi and Tosafot.
[44]Ketubot 36b (and parallel).
[45]Niddah 47a.
[46]Kiddushin 49b.
[47]Ketubot 66b.

will of God, no nation rules over it, but when Israel does not perform the will of God, He hands them over to a "lowly people."

Another passage, which discusses Abraham's encounter with the angels at Mamre,[48] reflects the same conception of the lowly status of Arvi'im. R. Yehoshua believes it is appropriate for Rabban Gamliel, the patriarch, to serve drinks to the assembled rabbis, and cites as proof Abraham's hospitality toward the angels. "And did they appear to him like ministering angels?" he asks rhetorically. "They appeared to him like none other than Arvi'im." The greater the contrast between Arvi'im and angels the greater the force of Yehoshua's argument, and this passage as well indicates the low esteem in which Arvi'im were held by the rabbis.

Tayaye and Arvi'im are distinguishable in other respects as well. The majority (but not all) of Talmudic references to Arvi'im involve Palestinian Tannaim. Only one source portrays contact between Arvi'im and a Pumbeditan Amora.[49] Tayaye, it will be recalled, come in contact almost exclusively with (1) Pumbeditans, and (2) Amoraim who travel in the Arabian and Sinai deserts.

The one source which portrays contact between Pumbeditan Amoraim and Arvi'im depicts the latter as thieves who seize tracts of land from their rightful Jewish owners. Tayaye, it will be recalled, are portrayed in Amoraic sources not as thieves, but as law-abiding traders, military men, and desert guides.

Finally, the Talmud contains no hint of respect for the religious practices or beliefs of the Arvi'im, nor of their expertise in non-halachic matters. The admittedly meager Talmudic sources on the subject of religious practices of Arvi'im depict them as idolaters,[50] and identify Aravia as a center of idolatry.[51]

---

[48]Kiddushin 32b.
[49]Baba Batra 168b.
[50]Yoma 47a and Yevamot 71a (and Avodah Zarah 27a).
[51]Avodah Zarah 11b.

Appendices to Chapter 8

Appendix Two: A Possible Example of Non-Contemporary Praise

A story on Ketubot 106a describes the relatively large numbers of rabbis who study with Rav, and the increasingly smaller numbers of rabbis who study with outstanding scholars of subsequent generations: Rav Huna, Rabbah, and Rav Yosef, and, according to some versions, Abaye, Rav Papa, and Rav Ashi.[1] This story favorably contrasts Rav with outstanding rabbis of subsequent generations, since large numbers of students enable a rabbi to pray effectively for rain in times of drought.

The absence of Abaye's, Papa's, and Ashi's names from some versions indicates that the story originally ended with mention of Rabbah and Rav Yosef, and that the section dealing with Abaye, Papa, and Ashi is a later addition, an attempt to bring the story up to date.[2] Perhaps, therefore, the original story was composed during the third generation,[3] in which case the story is another example of Amoraic praise of near-contemporaries, in this case praise of Rav by third-generation composers.

The updating of the story by later generations, however, very likely implies active endorsement, by at least some later rabbis, of the story's view that Rav is an extraordinary man. As the number of students decreases from generation to generation, Rav's relative greatness increases, and those who added the sections dealing with Abaye, Rav Papa, and Rav Ashi believe that Rav was substantially more powerful than the greatest late Amoraim. I therefore include this story in the statistics above as a possible example of non-contemporary praise.

---

[1]Ketubot 106a.
[2]For further discussion of this story, see chapter 1, above.
[3]See Goodblatt, *Rabbinic Instruction in Sasanian Babylonia*, pp. 54-57.

Appendices to Chapter 8

Appendix Three: The Relationship Between the Quantity of Commentary Preserved and the Quantity of Praise and Criticism

In the present Appendix, I attempt to determine the quantity of praise and criticism attributed to various Amoraim, and compare it to the amount of commentary preserved in their names. This exercise is necessary because the significance of the above findings would be greatly reduced if the quantity of praise and criticism attributed to Amoraim is a function of the amount of commentary preserved in their names. It would no longer be surprising that contemporary reactions to personality are more abundant than non-contemporary reactions, since the number of reactions to personality would vary in direct relation to the amount of commentary preserved.

Examination of statements by Shmuel and R. Yohanan in tractate Shabbat shows that the amount of praise and criticism is not a function of the amount of commentary preserved. Contemporaries and near-contemporaries praise and criticize these Amoraim much more frequently than do non-contemporaries, but at the same time contemporaries and non-contemporaries comment on their statements to roughly the same degree. Contemporary reactions to the personalities of Shmuel and Yohanan are substantially more abundant than non-contemporary reactions despite the fact that contemporary commentary is not more abundant.

The exact figures are as follows:

Chart[1]

	Contemporary and Near- Contemporary Commentary	Non-Contemporary Commentary
Shmuel (1st-generation Babylonian)	33-36[2]	27-28[3]

---

[1]In compiling the statistics regarding Shmuel and R. Yohanan, I assign rabbis who straddle the boundary between two generations to the earlier of the two generations. Rav Nahman, for example, is placed by some scholars in the second and third generations, and I assign him to the second generation. This simplifies the statistics by enabling me to assign each Amora to one generation only, eliminating confusing designations such as second- and third-generation Amoraim. My conclusion that contemporaries and near-contemporaries comment on early Amoraic statements no more frequently than do non-contemporaries would be made no less convincingly were I to assign Amoraim who straddle the boundary between two generations to the later generation.

In dealing with Rav Ashi, however, I assign such rabbis to the later generation. My conclusion that Ashi comments on statements by contemporaries and near-contemporaries less frequently than he comments on statements by non-contemporaries would be made even more convincingly were I to assign uncertain Amoraim to the earlier generation.

[2]Second-generation commentary (8 statements): Rav Nahman (Shabbat 51a, 53a, 108b, and 113a); Rav Yehuda (22a, 47a, and 113a); Mar Ukba (108b). Third-generation commentary (25 to 28 statements): Rav Yosef (22a, 45b, 51a, 52a [three times], 54a, 62b, 66a, 97a-b, 97b, and 106b); Rabbah (22a-b, 97b, and possibly 17a-b); Rav Huna bar Hiyya (52a); Rabbah bar Rav Huna (51b and 107a); R Ami (60b [see *DS* het]); R. Huna (60b); R. Zeira (53a); Rav Hisda (97a-b); Rav Yizhak b. d'Rav Yehuda (91a); Rav Safra (59b); Rehava (40b); Rav Shmuel bar Yehuda (37b); and possibly the later Rav Hamnuna (19b; See Halivni, *Mekorot u-Mesorot: Shabbat*, pp. 58-60) and Rav Hanina (17a-b).

[3]Fourth-generation commentary (15 or 16 statements): Abaye (Shabbat 22a-b, 45b, 51a, 52a [three times], 54a, 57b, 62b, and 106b); Rava (12a, 78a, 107b, 113a, and possibly 17a-b), and Rav Avya (22a-b). Fifth-generation commentary (4 statements): Rav Huna b. d'Rav Yehoshua (22a-b); Rav Nahman bar Yizhak (57b); and Rav Papa (53a and 119a). Sixth-generation commentary (8 statements): Rav Ashi (52a [see *DS* zadi]), 59b, 97b, 107b, and 116b; Rav Ashi or Mar Zutra (50b); the early Ravina (59b and 97b).

Undetermined chronology: Rav Aha bar Yosef (110b); Rav Kahana (110b); Rava bar Shira (66a [twice]); and Ravina (42a).

Chart (*continued*)

	Contemporary and Near- Contemporary Commentary	Non-Contemporary Commentary
R. Yohanan (Shmuel's younger contemporary)	33-36[4]	32-37[5]

---

[4]It should be noted that R. Yohanan is usually considered to be a second-generation Palestinian Amora, slightly younger than Shmuel. To facilitate comparison between the distribution of commentary on statements by both Amoraim, however, I assign Yohanan, like Shmuel, to the first generation.

First-generation commentary (1 statement): Eifa (Shabbat 60b [see *DS* zayin]). Second-generation commentary (11 statements): R. Huna (60b and 63b [twice; See Albeck, *Mavo-la-Talmudim*, p. 232]); the early R. Zeira (47a and 112b [see Hyman, *Toldot Tannaim ve-Amoraim*, p. 45, and the discussion above]); Rabbah bar bar Hana (39b and 60b); R. Ami (60b [see *DS* het]); R. Asi (47a); R. Natan bar Oshaya (81b); and Ulla (99b). Third-generation commentary (21 to 24 statements): Rav Yosef (20b, 39b [twice], 45b [three times], 49b, 61a, 76a, and 112a); Rabin (63b [twice] and 72a); Rav Dimi (63b and 72a); R. Yirmiya (63b [twice]); Rabbah (45b and possibly 31b, 37b, and 81b); Rav Yizhak bar Yosef (112b); Rami bar Abba (20b); and Rav Shmuel bar Yehuda (37b).

R. Ami and R. Huna (the Palestinian sage) are considered third-generation Amoraim in the present note and second-generation Amoraim in n. 2, above. This difference is due to the fact that while Shmuel's and Yohanan's lives overlapped, their chronology is not identical. Ami and Huna lived in the generation immediately following Yohanan, but a full generation separates Shmuel from Ami and Huna. As observed above, in cases of doubt I assign Amoraim to the later generation, and therefore place Huna and Ami in the third generati278on.

[5]Fourth-generation commentary (19 to 23 statements): Abaye (Shabbat 7b, 21b, 45b [twice], 47a [twice], 49b, 63b, 69a, 69b, 72a, 76a, 112a. and possibly 61a [see *DS* kuf]); and Rava (7b, 47a [twice], 69b, 75a, 94a, and possibly 31b, 37b, and 81b). Fifth-generation commentary (4 or 5 statements): Rav Papa (5b-6a and possibly 53a); Rav Aha b. d'Rav Ika (5b-6a); Rav Bibi bar Abaye (91b); and Rav Hiyya b. d'Rav Huna (5a). Sixth-generation commentary (7 statements): Rav Ashi (7a, 37b, 67a, and 71b); Rav Aha b. d'Rava (67a); Rav Ukba Mimeshan (37b); and the early Ravina (71b). Seventh-generation commentary (2 statements): Maremar (100a-b) and the later Ravina (71b).

Undetermined chronology: R. Zeira (5a, 46a, 53a, 91b, and 118b); Rav Ada bar Ahava (5a); Rav Kahana (85b); and R. Tanhum de-min Noy (30a).

Chart *(continued)*

	Contemporary and Near- Contemporary Commentary	Non-Contemporary Commentary
Rav Ashi[6] (6th-generation Babylonian)	14-17[7]	58-62[8]

---

[6]When one rabbi (A) comments on a statement by an earlier rabbi (B), and this earlier rabbi (B) in turn comments on a statement by a still earlier rabbi (C), the comment by the latest rabbi (A) occasionally alters our understanding of both earlier statements (B and C). In such instances, I consider the remark by the latest rabbi (A) as commentary on two statements (B and C). Similarly, when the comment by the latest rabbi (A) alters our understanding of three earlier statements (B, C, and D), I consider A's remark as commentary on three statements, and so on. Some comments by Ashi, therefore, figure in the statistics as both contemporary and non-contemporary commentary.

[7]Commentary on statements by fourth-generation Amoraim (8 to 11 statements): Abaye (Shabbat 36a, 66b, 101a, 107b, and 114b); Rava (8a, 42a, 70b, and possibly 109a); Abaye and Rava (possibly 120b); and Rabbah bar Shila (possibly 7a [see Halivni, *Mekorot u-Mesorot:* Shabbat, p. 17]). Commentary on statements by fifth-generation Amoraim (5 or 6 statements): Rav Papa (2b and 73b); Rav Kahana (37b [see *DS* pei] and possibly 109a); Rav Bibi bar Abaye (4a); and Rav Huna b. d'Rav Yehoshua (42a). Commentary on statements by sixth-generation Amoraim (1 or 2 statements): the early Ravina (4a [see *DS* alef and bet]); and Rav Hillel (possibly 109a).

Commentary on statements by Amoraim of undetermined chronology: Rav Ada bar Ahava (62b); R. Zeira (117b); and Rabbanan (82a).

[8]Commentary on statements by first-generation Amoraim (11 to 13 statements): Rav (Shabbat 11a [three times], 101a [see *DS* nun], 107b, and possibly 120b); Shmuel (59b, 97b, 107b, 116b, and possibly 50b); Rav Asi (50a); and Rav and Shmuel (37b). Commentary on statements by second-generation Amoraim (16 or 17 statements): R. Yohanan (6b-7a, 37b, 85b, 94a, and 110b); Rav Yehuda (37b, 59b, and 97b); Rav Hama bar Gurya (11a [twice]); Resh Lakish (16b and 94a); Rav Huna (110a); Rav Tavla (101a); Rav Kahana (85b); Mar Ukba (116b); and possibly Hiyya bar Rav (7a [see Halivni, *Mekorot u-Mesorot:* Shabbat, p. 17]). Commentary on statements by third-generation Amoraim (31 or 32 statements): Rav Yosef (11a, 37b, 97b, 101a, and 107b); Rabbah bar Rav Huna (34a, 75b, 104b, 107a-b, and 115b); Rav Sheshet (50b, 85b [twice; R. Hananel, Ri Migash, Ritba, and Sefer ha-Yashar, chapter 267, read Ashi instead of Asi], and 93b-94a); Rav Hisda (11a, 93a-b, 97a-b [see *DS* yud], and possibly 7a [see Halivni, *Mekorot u-Mesorot:* Shabbat, p. 17]); Rav Hisda or the later Rav Hamnuna (93b [twice]); Ulla (6b-7a and 85b); Rava bar Mehasya (11a [twice]); R. Elazar or Rabbah (83a); the later Rav Hamnuna (115b); the early R. Zeira (114b); R. Yizhak (43a-b); Rav Menashe (74b); Rav Nahman (101a); Rabbah (110b; The printed text reads Rava, but Abaye comments on it, indicating that Rabbah is referred to); and Rav Shmuel bar Yehuda (37b).

Accompanying footnotes further subdivide the statistics recorded in the above chart. These footnotes list the number of comments in each generation and specify the rabbis who author the comments.[9] A peculiar feature of Amoraic commentary revealed by these statistics warrants explanation in the present context, although it in no way affects my central thesis. I refer to the fact that commentary on statements by Shmuel and Yohanan increases from the first to the third generations, decreases in the fourth and fifth generations, increases again in the sixth, and decreases again in the seventh generation.

This apparently random distribution of commentary is attributable to several factors. First, the paucity of commentary by first-generation Amoraim is attributable to the tendency of rabbis not to comment on statements by their immediate contemporaries. Second, the paucity of commentary by second-generation Amoraim is attributable to the transmissional character of this generation, i.e., to the tendency of

---

[9]It will be helpful to briefly discuss three classificatory decisions made in the course of compiling the data recorded above. (1) Quotations of statements by Yohanan and Shmuel, as well as quotations by Ashi, have not been included in the statistics unless the quotations are accompanied by or constitute commentary on the statements quoted. When Rav Yehuda quotes Shmuel in the following form, for example: "Said Rav Yehuda: said Shmuel: 'It is forbidden to mix meat and milk,'" Rav Yehuda is not considered as commenting on Shmuel's statement, but rather is viewed as a tradent and nothing more. Amoraim occasionally quote statements or report actions and accompany these quotations with interpretations, or cite statements in the course of an argument, and the mere citation, given the larger context of the discussion, reveals something about the statement's meaning. In such instances, quotation has been considered commentary. Simple quotation, however, with no explicit or implicit interpretation, is not included.

(2) When Rabbi X comments on a statement by Rabbi Y, and the statement by Rabbi Y is quoted by Rabbi Z, Rabbi X's statement is counted as commentary on two discrete statements. Rabbi X presumably knows the earlier statement together with its author and tradent (At times, however, this is most likely not the case. See, for example, Halivni, *Mekorot u-Mesorot:* Eruvin-Pesahim, pp. 406-7), and might have praised or expressed respect for the author and tradent had he so desired. Since my goal is to investigate the relationship between frequency of commentary and frequency of praise, and the statement by Rabbi X might have contained two discrete instances of praise, it seems reasonable to consider his statement as two discrete instances of commentary as well.

(3) When Rabbi X comments on a statement by Rabbi Y, and the commentary by Rabbi X is quoted by Rabbi Z, the tradent is excluded from the statistics and his contribution is not considered to be commentary. For example, if Rav Nahman comments on a statement by Shmuel, and Nahman's comment is quoted by Rava in the following form: "Said Rava: said Rav Nahman: 'When Shmuel said X, he meant Y,'" Rava is not considered as the author of commentary on Shmuel's statement, but rather is viewed as a tradent and nothing more.

second-generation Amoraim to do little besides quote statements by first-generation Amoraim.

The relative frequency with which Amoraim appear in the Talmud explains other aspects of these charts. Fifth-generation Amoraim, for example, appear less frequently than sixth-generation Amoraim,[10] which accounts for the slight rise in sixth-generation commentary after decreases in fourth- and fifth-generation commentary. Seventh-generation Amoraim are mentioned only rarely in the Talmud,[11] which accounts for their almost total absence from the statistics. The third and fourth Amoraic generations are more prominently represented in the Talmud than the fifth, sixth, and seventh generations, which explains the greater amount of third- and fourth-generation commentary.

It is not completely clear why the third generation is more prominently represented in the statistics than the fourth generation. Frequency of appearance, however, is very likely the determining factor here as well. Further study of this question is necessary, for at present we lack precise statistics regarding the relative frequency with which third- and fourth-generation Amoraim are mentioned in the Talmud. By way of preliminary observation, however, it should be recalled that many dialogues conventionally assumed to involve Abaye and his fourth-generation contemporary, Rava, actually involve Abaye and his third-generation teacher, Rabbah.[12] In addition, we observed above that all but a handful of the supposed dialogues between Abaye and Rava scattered throughout the Talmud are in fact not dialogues at all, but later anonymous commentary based on their juxtaposed, contradictory opinions.[13] Conventional views regarding the amount of fourth-generation material found in the Talmud, therefore, are inaccurate due to misconceptions regarding the amount of material recorded in the names of the most prominent fourth-generation Amoraim. The peculiar zig-zag pattern described above, therefore, is very likely attributable almost entirely to frequency of appearance.

The striking difference between Rav Ashi's commentary and commentary based on statements by Shmuel and R. Yohanan is explicable along these same lines. Ashi, it will be recalled, comments on statements by non-contemporaries much more frequently than on statements by contemporaries and near-contemporaries, whereas contemporaries and non-contemporaries comment on statements by Shmuel and Yohanan to roughly the same degree. The relative

---

[10]See Kraemer, *The Mind of the Talmud*, pp. 30-41, especially pp. 39-40.
[11]Kalmin, *The Redaction of the Babylonian Talmud*, p. 156, n. 26.
[12]See chapter 10, below.
[13]*Ibid.*

infrequency with which fifth- and sixth-generation Amoraim appear throughout the Talmud explains this distinction, which is not indicative of any fundamental differences between Ashi and the other rabbis. That is, fifth- and sixth-generation Amoraim are Ashi's near-contemporaries. Since they appear so infrequently throughout the Talmud, Ashi comments on statements by near-contemporaries with relative infrequency. Fifth- and sixth-generation Amoraim are Shmuel's and Yohanan's non-contemporaries, however, and therefore their statistics look substantially different from those of Ashi.

Appendices to Chapter 8

Appendix Four: Anonymous Editorial Commentary Based on Amoraic Statements

As noted above, the Talmud's anonymous editors virtually never criticize sages. In this appendix, I examine a small number of passages and argue that there is no evidence that they run counter to the general pattern.

A comment based on a statement by Rav Yosef could perhaps be construed as editorial criticism of an earlier rabbi. The comment comes at the conclusion of a story which recounts Rav Safra's and Rava's opposing halachic actions in the house of Mar Yuhna.[1] Safra hears a disturbing biblical verse in a dream, which he fears is a sign of heavenly disapproval of his contradiction of Yosef. Yosef assures him that he has no cause for worry, implying that Rava rather than Safra acted contrary to Yosef. Safra or the anonymous editors ask why he (i.e., Safra) heard this disturbing verse, and Yosef or the editors respond that it was actually intended for Rava. Why, then, was it not sent to Rava, Safra or the editors ask, to which Yosef or the editors respond that Rava was in disfavor, literally, "rebuked," and the heavenly powers refrained from direct communication with him.

As noted above, it is unclear at first glance who speaks after Yosef assures Safra that he committed no offense. Do Yosef and Safra continue their dialogue, or have the anonymous editors intervened?[2] Both understandings are possible, and this story therefore does not provide clear evidence of anonymous editorial criticism of attributed rabbis.

It should also be noted that the criticism of Rava expressed in the conclusion of the story is consistent with disapproval of Rava attributed

---

[1]Hullin 133a. For discussion of a different aspect of this story, see chapter 3, above.
[2]The absence of the term "he said" indicating Amoraic dialogue does not decide the issue. See the discussion above, and see chapter 10, below.

to Yosef in several other contexts.[3] Quite plausibly, the same critical
sentiment is attributed to Yosef here as well.

We also find no clear evidence of hostility toward R. Yirmiya or Rav
Ashi[4] in anonymous editorial commentary on their statements. The
editors twice inform us that a certain tradition "escaped Yirmiya,"[5] and
once bluntly reject his view with the words "And it isn't so."[6] There is no
proof, however, that these expressions imply hostility or disapproval of
the author of the rejected opinion.

In seven instances, Ashi's opinions are rejected by the anonymous
editors with the expression "*beruta hi*," or "*beduta hi*."[7] The exact
significance of this expression is not clear, but it apparently means
"outside, rejected, unofficial," or "false, forged, fictional, or untrue."[8]
Whatever its actual meaning, there is no evidence that it indicates
criticism of Ashi.[9]

---

[3]See chapter 1, above.
[4]In addition to the sources cited below, see Baba Mezia 104b and Hullin 56b,
where Ashi's opinions are rejected by the anonymous editors with the words
"And it isn't so." See also the discussion above.
[5]Ketubot 15a-b and Hullin 45a.
[6]Zevahim 50b-51a.
[7]Pesahim 11a (and parallel), Yevamot 21a and 82a, Baba Mezia 71b, Baba Batra
145a, Zevahim 110b, and Menahot 95b.
[8]See, for example, *Arukh ha-Shalem*, ed. Kohut, vol. 1, Part 2, p. 15; and Jastrow,
Dictionary, pp. 139 and 191.
[9]See also Berakhot 47b, where according to some versions of the story of Rami bar
Hama's death the anonymous editors claim that Menashya was a full-fledged
rabbi, but Rami "did not examine him adequately." According to these versions,
the anonymous editors add to the criticism of Rami by injecting an element of
negligence not explicitly present in Rava's statement. The majority of versions,
however, contain no explicit criticism of Rami. See *DS* lamed and following.

Appendices to Chapter 10

Appendix One: Disputes Between Abaye and Rava

The 232 to 257 disputes between Abaye and Rava are found on Berakhot 17a, 22b, 25a, 25b, 29a, 31a, 44b, 47b, 59a, and 62a; Shabbat 8a, 11b, 13a, 23a, 24b, 26a-b, 27a, 47a, 49a, 52a, 58b-59a, 66a, 74a, 78a, 78b, 78b-79a, 80a, 92a, 99a, 111a, 118b-119a, 122a, 125a, 129a, 133a, 133b, 136a, 144b, and 154b-155a; Eruvin 3b, 9a, 15a (twice), 16b, 19a, 28b, 53a, 65a, 66b, 89b, 95a, 99a, and 101a; Pesahim 5b, 9b, 11a (and parallel), 12b, 14a, 25b, 28a, 30b, 33b, 40a, 45b-46a, 49a, 51b, 55b, 58a, 64b, 75b, 83b (and parallel), 84b, 94b, and 103a (and parallel); Bezah 11a, 13b, 14a-b, 18b (and parallel), and 38b; Moed Katan 2b, 7b, 8a, 14b, and 23a; Ketubot 22b, 24a, 30a-b, 35a, 38b, 39b (twice), 40b (and parallels), 51b-52a, 56b, 61a, 71a, 75a, 80b, and 83a; Nedarim 5b (and parallel), 14a, 16b, 22a, 23b, 39b, and 64a-b; Gittin 10b, 20b-21a, 21b-22a, 22a, 28a-b, 29a, 34a, 36b, 37b, 46b, 54b, 61a, 73b, 75a, and 84a; Kiddushin 5a, 10a, 24a, 33a, 34a-b, 36a, 39b, 45b, 48b, 51a, 66a, 69b, 78a, and 81a; Baba Kamma 6a, 23b, 40b-41a, 45b, 46b, 60a, 69b, 72b (and parallel), 84a, 86a (twice), 89a, 93b (twice), 108a, 108b, and 115a; Baba Mezia 10a, 12a-b, 21a-b, 27a, 35b (and parallels), 39b (twice), 48b, 51b, 52b, 56a, 65a (twice), 80a, 80b, 91a, 95b, 102a, 109a, 109b, 111a, and 116a; Baba Batra 12a, 12b, 17b, 22a, 29a, 56a (and parallel), 80a-b, 99a, 128b, 137a, 140b, 142a, and 173a; Sanhedrin 10a, 10b, 27a, 29a-b, 40b (and parallel), 53b, 55a, 61b (twice), 64b, 74b, 75b, 76a (three times), 76b (and parallel), and 90a; Makkot 5a, Avodah Zarah 6b (three times), 12a, 13b, 28b, 42a, 43a, 62a-b, 65a, 66a (three times), and 66b; Hullin 3a, 62b, 94a, 94b, 98b-99a, 100a-b, 103a, 106a, and 125b; Bekhorot 31b, 41a, 52a, and 54b; and possibly Berakhot 6b (*DS* daled) and 32a (*DS* gimel); Shabbat 70b-73b (six times. The usual order of opinions is reversed in all six cases, with Abaye's opinion placed after Rava's. It is therefore possible that the Amora referred to is Rabbah, Abaye's teacher, rather than Rava, his contemporary), 92a (the usual order of opinions is reversed), and 141a; Pesahim 40a (*DS* yud), 41a-b (the usual order of opinions is reversed), 41b (the usual order of opinions is reversed), 58b (*DS* bet), and 68a (*DS* lamed); Moed Katan 19b (*DS* resh); Ketubot 6b (*DS*

Herschler, notes on line 7, and n. 19); Nedarim 24b (according to the Vatican manuscript, Rava's objection was not made in Abaye's presence); Gittin 8b (*DS* Feldblum, notes on lines 19 and 22) and 49b (the usual order of opinions is reversed); Baba Kamma 53b (*DS* bet); Baba Mezia 52a (*DS* ayin) and 89b (*DS* bet); Baba Batra 111b (*DS* samekh); and Avodah Zarah 71b (and parallel). See also Berakhot 25b (twice) (*DS* khaf), 25b-26a, 27b (*DS* lamed), 35b, and 61b (*DS* taf); Shabbat 8a, 46b, 60a, and 74a; Eruvin 63b-64a and 103a; Pesahim 11b, 34b, and 71a; Moed Katan 25b; Ketubot 6b, 11a, 14a, 65a, 105b, and 106a (*DS* Herschler, notes on line 17, and nn. 37 and 38); Nedarim 54a-b (and parallel) and 55a; Kiddushin 65a (Aminoah, *Arikhat Massekhet Kiddushin*, p. 380); Baba Kamma 23a and 94a; Baba Mezia 28a, 36a-b, and 52a; Baba Batra 135a-b (*DS* zayin); Sanhedrin 86a and 99b-100a; Makkot 6a; Avodah Zarah 58a; Hullin 50a-b, 77a, 129a, and 133a (twice); and Bekhorot 4b, 12b, and 15a.

See also Berakhot 25b, 25b-26a, and 35b; Shabbat 8a, 46b, 60a, and 77a; Eruvin 103a; Pesahim 34b and 71a; Moed Katan 14b; Ketubot 11a and 14a; Gittin 25a; Kiddushin 53a; Baba Kamma 23a and 94a; Baba Mezia 28a and 52a; Sanhedrin 86a; Makkot 6a; Bekhorot 4b, 12b, and 15a; and possibly Kiddushin 64b-65a (Aminoah, *Arikhat Massekhet Kiddushin*, p. 380), where Rava comments on statements by Abaye or on dialogues in which Abaye is involved. In none of these cases do we find dialogue between Abaye and Rava. See also Sanhedrin 8a-b and Appendix 5, below.

Appendices to Chapter 10

Appendix Two: Dialogues Between Abaye and Rava and Appearances in Each Other's Presence

Abaye and Rava are depicted as conversing with one another only on Shabbat 7b; Eruvin 57b (twice) and 92a-93a; Ketubot 39a and 81a-b; Baba Mezia 36b; Baba Batra 174b; Sanhedrin 47a-b; Avodah Zarah 58a; Horayot 14a; and possibly Shabbat 35a; Eruvin 46a; Gittin 8b-9a; Baba Mezia 90b; and Baba Batra 29a and 46a-b (see below).

Abaye and Rava are portrayed in each other's presence only in the following contexts (but see below): Berakhot 56a-b; Shabbat 7b and 142b; Eruvin 57b (twice) and 92a-93a; Moed Katan 16a; Ketubot 39a and 81a-b; Baba Mezia 36b; Baba Batra 174b; Sanhedrin 47a-b; Avodah Zarah 58a; Horayot 14a; and possibly Berakhot 61b (*DS* taf); Shabbat 35a and 123a; Eruvin 46a (*DS* hei, and R. Hananel); Gittin 8b-9a (*DS* Feldblum, notes on lines 19 and 22); Baba Kamma 113b; Baba Mezia 90b (*DS* ayin); and Baba Batra 29a and 46a-b. On Baba Kamma 113b and Baba Batra 29a, Abaye is very likely conversing with Rabbah, although the arrangement of Rabbah's comment after Rav Yosef's is achronological. The arrangement of Rabbah's statements after Rav Yosef's might be due to the fact that Rav Yosef's opinions in both contexts are rejected and Rabbah's are not.

I found 24 to 26 cases in which statements by Abaye and Rava are introduced by the following formula: "Abaye and Rava, the two of them said...." See Berakhot 34b (and parallel) and 57a; Shabbat 7a, 12a, 73b, and 140a; Eruvin 35a and 78a; Pesahim 110a; Bezah 30b and 36a (and parallels); Megillah 15b; Ketubot 6a and 52b; Kiddushin 12b; Baba Kamma 42a; Baba Batra 5a-b, 33b, 40a, and 76b (and parallel); Sanhedrin 29b and 32b; Makkot 7a; Hullin 77b (and parallel); and possibly Shabbat 49b and Hullin 50a (*DS* het). However, we cannot assume that this formula indicates face-to-face contact. In view of the infrequency with which Abaye and Rava converse with one another, it seems more likely that the formula indicates that statements by Abaye were brought before Rava, and Rava expressed his agreement. See Urbach, *Ha-Halacha*, p. 310,

n. 79, who makes the same point with regard to the formula: "Rav and Shmuel, the two of them said...." See also Bacher, *Tradition und Tradinten in den Schulen Palastinas und Babyloniens*, pp. 556-60; and Bokser, *Post Mishnaic Judaism in Transition*, pp. 424-26. See also Berakhot 34b (and parallel).

See also Shabbat 47a and 123b (see Halivni, *Mekorot u-Mesorot: Shabbat*, pp. 139-40 and 334-35); Eruvin 37b-38a (see Halivni, *Mekorot u-Mesorot:* Eruvin-Pesahim, pp. 109-10); Baba Kamma 58b (It is unusual to find Abaye and Rava together in the presence of Rav Nahman. Very likely, Rabbah is providing an alternative to Rav Nahman's view, perhaps not in Nahman's presence [*DS* mem], and Abaye is objecting against Rabbah's opinion) and 84a (*DS* shin. Abaye nowhere else comes in contact with Rav Papa bar Shmuel); Baba Mezia 60a (see Tosafot, s.v. Rava, and Friedman, "Ketiv ha-Shemot 'Rabbah' ve-'Rava' ba-Talmud ha-Bavli," pp. 158-64) and 86a (The printed editions read Abaye and Rava together in the story of the death of Rabbah bar Nahmani. However, Rabbinovicz, *DS* daled, correctly decides in favor of the versions which omit Rava's name. See the discussion below); Baba Batra 139a-b (see Appendix 5, below); Hullin 31b (This passage contains a dialogue between Rava and Rav Nahman which concludes with Rava's quote of a Tannaitic tradition. A dialogue between Abaye and Rav Yosef ensues, and Abaye cites the same Tannaitic tradition cited by Rava and comments on the same sources commented on by Rava. If the story depicted direct contact between Rava, Rav Nahman, Abaye, and Rav Yosef, why would Abaye direct his comments to Rav Yosef and not to Rava and Rav Nahman who had been speaking previously? In the continuation, Rav Simi bar Ashi objects, and the anonymous editors and Rava follow with responses, which seems to indicate that Rava has been present throughout the entire discussion. However, it is strange that Rava would respond to a statement by his student, Rav Simi bar Ashi. More likely, Rava's comment is based directly on the Tannaitic tradition); and Hullin 133a (A story involving Rava and Rav Yosef concludes with dialogue between Abaye and Rav Yosef [*DS* pei]. The story depicts no direct contact between Abaye and Rava, however).

Appendices to Chapter 10

Appendix Three: Evidence of Direct Contact Between Abaye and Rava

The printed editions or manuscripts preserve a record of Abaye and Rava conversing with one another or appearing in each other's presence in the 38 to 46 cases listed in n. 33, above, and on Berakhot 36b, 48a (*DS* vav), and 56a-b; Shabbat 7b, 23b (*DS* khaf), 25b (*DS* yud), 34a (*DS* resh), 34a-b, 35a (*DS* het), 42b (*DS* kuf), 46b (*DS* mem), 74b (*DS* alef, bet, and gimel), 76b-77a, 95a (*DS* samekh), 117a (*DS* kuf), 122b-123a (*DS* mem and nun), 123a, 123b, 129a (*DS* alef), 135a-b (*DS* resh), 142b, 146b (*DS* zayin), 153a (*DS* zadi), and 154b (*DS* daled); Eruvin 19b (*DS* hei), 19b (*DS* tet), 20a (*DS* samekh), 67b (*DS* het), 92a-b (*DS* ayin and resh), 93a, and 98a (*DS* vav); Pesahim 11a (and parallel) (*DS* gimel), 20b (*DS* zayin), 33b, 63a (*DS* yud and mem), 74a (*DS* mem), 96b (*DS* nun), and 120b (*DS* pei); Bezah 12b, 22a, and 36b (*DS* khaf); Megillah 7b (*DS* daled), 8b, 8b-9a, 19a (*DS* alef), and 27a (*DS* vav); Moed Katan 10b (*DS* khaf), 11a, 16a, 18a-b, and 19b (*DS* zayin); Ketubot 6b (*DS* Herschler, notes on line 2, and n. 3), 6b (*DS* Herschler, notes on line 14, and n. 31), 14a (*DS* Herschler, notes on line 7, and n. 25), 36b (*DS* Herschler, notes on line 22, and n. 80), 37a (and parallel) (*DS* Herschler, notes on line 10, and n. 13, and notes on line 14, and n. 23), 39a, 42a (*DS* Herschler, notes on line 10, and n. 17), 62a (*DS* Herschler, notes on line 16, and n. 29), 73b (*DS* Herschler, notes on line 11, and n. 19, and notes on line 12, and n. 23), 75b (*DS* Herschler, notes on line 12, and n. 34), and 81a-b; Nedarim 29a and 73b (the Munich manuscript reads Rava); Gittin 24b (*DS* Feldblum, notes on line 29), 28a (*DS* Feldblum, notes on line 14), 37a (*DS* Feldblum, notes on line 58), and 37b (*DS* Feldblum, notes on line 3); Kiddushin 5b, 7a, 18a, 18a (see Aminoah, *Arikhat Massekhet Kiddushin*, p. 379), 20a (Aminoah, *ibid.*), 50b (Aminoah, *ibid.*, p. 380), 60a, and 64a; Baba Kamma 7a, 11a, 34a (*DS*), 39b (*DS* khaf), 42a (*DS* zadi), 43a (*DS* nun), 46a (*DS* nun), 58b (*DS* mem and nun), 66b (*DS* khaf), 84a (*DS* kuf), 84a (*DS* shin), 113b (*DS* taf), 113b (*DS* zayin), 114a (*DS* daled and hei), 117b (*DS* ayin), 117b (*DS* zadi), 117b (*DS* kuf), and 119a (*DS* kuf); Baba Mezia 30b (*DS* resh), 36b, 37b (*DS* bet), 40a (*DS* nun), 60a (*DS* het), 67a (*DS* kuf), 81b (and parallels), 86a (*DS* daled),

90b (*DS* ayin), 93a-b (*DS* kuf), 93b-94a, and 116b (*DS* tet); Baba Batra 8a (*DS* zadi), 11b-12a (and parallel) (*DS* taf and alef), 16a (*DS* gimel), 28b-29a (*DS* taf, alef, and bet), 31a (*DS* kuf), 45a-b (*DS* tet), 46a, 62b (*DS* taf), 62b (*DS* taf), 130a (*DS* daled), 135a (*DS* taf), 139a-b, 153b (*DS* gimel and hei), 154a (*DS* samekh), 171b (see Halachot Gedolot, Warsaw ed., p. 218), 172b (*DS* shin), and 174b (and parallel), Sanhedrin 21b, 47a-b, 65a (*DS*), 68b-69a (*DS* tet, on Sanhedrin 68b), and 98b (*DS* mem and nun); Makkot 7b (and parallel) (see M. Friedmann, *Babylonischer Talmud: Traktat Makkoth* [1888; Reprint. Jerusalem, 1970], p. 16, n. 10), 9a (Friedmann, *ibid.*, p. 21, n. 11), and 21b (and parallel) (Friedmann, *ibid.*, p. 55, n. 17), Avodah Zarah 15b (*DS* bet), 50b, 58a, and 76a; Hullin 9b, 10b (*DS* nun), 20b (*DS* bet), 29a (*DS* kuf), 43b (*DS* pei), 102b (twice), 120a, 120a (*DS* taf), 134a (*DS* shin), and 136a-b (*DS* daled and hei); and Bekhorot 4a, 10b (see Shita Mekubezet, n. gimel), and 45a.

Appendices to Chapter 10

Appendix Four: Abaye is Aware of Rava's Opinions, and Vice Versa

For cases in which Rava demonstrates awareness of the opinions of Abaye, see, for example, Berakhot 25b; Shabbat 11b (and parallel), 13a, 33a, 74a, and 123a; Eruvin 15a and 63b-64a; Pesahim 11b-12a, 69b, and 71a; Moed Katan 14b; Ketubot 6b, 14a, 42a-b, and 81b-82a; Nedarim 54a-b; Kiddushin 53a; Baba Kamma 23a and 94a; Baba Mezia 21a-22a, 52a, and 72a-b; Baba Batra 24a and 171b; Sanhedrin 74b and 86a; Makkot 6a; Avodah Zarah 58a; Hullin 10b, 20b-21a, 77a, 100a-b, and 108a; Bekhorot 15a; and possibly Shabbat 11b (The statement by Rava which ostensibly responds to Abaye's view is also attributed to Rav Sheshet, and Rav Sheshet most likely did not base his opinion on Abaye's attempted proof. Perhaps, therefore, Rava's statement likewise originated independent of Abaye's); Pesahim 25b-26a (According to the printed edition, Abaye's interpretation is followed by an opposing interpretation by Rava. Abaye then supports his interpretation and Rava rejects his support. The latter statement by Rava, however, is perhaps by the anonymous editors speaking on Rava's behalf, and the phrase "Rava said," should perhaps be understood as "Rava could say to you." See DS taf, on Pesahim 26a, according to which several versions lack the word "said" after Rava's name); Nedarim 19b and 47a; Baba Batra 173a (see the discussion of Pesahim 25b-26a, above. The alternate version on Baba Batra 173a lacks the word "said" after Abaye's name); and Makkot 12a (Friedmann, *Traktat Makkoth*, p. 31, n. 19). Rava responds to statements by Abaye in many other contexts (see, for example, n. 33, above), but the role of later editors in formulating Rava's statements makes it impossible to pinpoint the exact number. On several occasions, for example, the anonymous editors added a clause to Rava's statement informing us why he rejected Abaye's view and followed with an alternative.

Other than cases in which Abaye and Rava are definitely portrayed as speaking in each other's presence, Abaye demonstrates awareness of the views of Rava only in: Shabbat 123a; Eruvin 15a; Pesahim 12b; Gittin 61a-b; Baba Mezia 109a; Bekhorot 4a; and possibly Shabbat 66a (see the discussion of Pesahim 25b-26a, above. See also *DS* mem, on Shabbat 66a, according to which several versions lack the word "said" after Abaye's name); Moed Katan 13a (Halivni, *Mekorot u-Mesorot:* Yoma-Hagigah, p. 542, n. 3); and Hullin 125b (see the discussion of Pesahim 25b-26a, above). On Hullin 133a, Abaye comments on a statement apparently made first by Rava. See, however, *DS* vav, and Michael Higger, *Ozar ha-Baraitot* (New York: Devei Rabbanan, 1948), vol. 10, p. 115, according to which Rava is quoting a Tannaitic statement. Similarly, on Hullin 50a-b, there is no need to assume that Abaye's source for the opinion of Rav Nahman is Rava, who quoted it previously. Abaye could easily have independent knowledge of Rav Nahman's view.

Appendices to Chapter 10

Appendix Five: Analysis of Talmudic Passages Which Appear to Depict Direct Contact Between Abaye and Rava

In the textual analyses which follow, I attempt to show that two Talmudic passages which appear to depict face-to-face contact between Abaye and Rava actually do not. In both cases, originally independent discussions, one mentioning Abaye and the other mentioning Rava, have been combined together, creating the impression that they conversed together.

Baba Batra 139a-b

On Baba Batra 139a-b, the discussion begins with Abuha bar Geneva's question to Rava about the nature of a husband's ownership of his wife's property. Is the husband considered a buyer, such that any oral debts his wife incurs prior to the marriage cannot be collected after the marriage, or is he considered an heir, such that her oral debts can be collected after the marriage? Rava (or the anonymous editors on behalf of Rava) responds that the husband is considered an heir, but Rava's (or the anonymous editors') argument is rejected. Rav Papa, in the presence of Rava,[1] suggests that the tradition sent by Rabin from Palestine to Babylonia provides an answer to the question. According to Rabin, a widow continues to receive support from her dead husband's estate even after their daughter gets married. According to Rav Papa, this law is understandable only if the husband is considered an heir, and Abuha's question is answered. Abaye follows,[2] objecting that Rabin's view was already contained within a mishna which states that property inherited

---

[1] The Hamburg and Munich manuscripts have Rav Papa conversing with Abaye rather than with Rava. All other versions, including all of the Rishonim, read the names like the printed edition. See the discussion below.
[2] See *DS* kuf.

by a husband upon the death of his wife need not be returned during the Jubilee year.[3] According to Abaye, this mishna implies that the husband is an heir (even during his wife's lifetime), and Rabin's tradition is unnecessary. Rava objects against Rav Papa and Abaye, quoting the statement of R. Yosi b'R. Hanina, according to which a husband can void his wife's sale of "plucked property,"property that came to the wife from her father's estate but which was not registered in her marriage contract. According to Yosi b'R. Hanina, the husband can seize the property sold by his wife, which implies that he himself is considered a buyer. Thus, argues Rava, the sources contradict one another on the question of the husband's status, and Abuha bar Geneva's question cannot be answered. Rav Ashi, two generations later, resolves the contradiction, explaining that the husband is viewed as a buyer and an heir, depending on the circumstances. The various sources – the mishna, Rabin, and Yosi b'R. Hanina – each have unique features which affect the husband's status.

According to the discussion as it presently stands, Abaye participates along with Rava and his students. This discussion, at first glance, runs counter to my claim that contact between Abaye and Rava is extremely rare, that the Talmud portrays them as active in separate rabbinic centers. However, the discussion as it stands is problematic. First, Rav Ashi's concluding comment resolves the contradiction between sources, but totally ignores the introductory question which gives rise to the entire discussion. We expect Rav Ashi to explain how the sources impinge on the discussion's opening question, but he neglects to do so. In addition, Rava initially responds[4] that the husband is considered an heir. Although Rava's argument is rejected, the implication is clear that Rava initially thinks that Abuha's question can be answered. And yet later,[5] in response to Abaye's claim that the husband is an heir, Rava quotes a source which suggests that the husband is a buyer, and no answer to the question is possible. Since Rava apparently knows this source all along, his initial response to Abuha's question is incomprehensible. This second difficulty, however, can be resolved by positing that Rava's initial response is the work of the anonymous editors, and does not reflect Rava's own opinion.

In my view, two discrete discussions, dealing with common issues and sources but deriving from separate Talmudic centers, have been placed back to back. Originally, Abuha bar Geneva sends Rava a question, Rava or the anonymous editors respond, the response is rejected, and Rav Papa, in the presence of Rava, concludes with a quote

---

[3]Mishna Bekhorot 8:10.
[4]Baba Batra 139a.
[5]Baba Batra 139b.

of Rabin. A second discussion, involving Abaye in dialogue with his teacher, Rabbah, begins with Abaye's objection against the tradition of Rabin, which Abaye claims is unnecessary. Rabbah responds that the issue is more complicated than Abaye thinks, since a third source contradicts Rabin and the mishna. Rav Ashi concludes this second discussion by resolving the contradictory sources cited by Abaye and Rabbah. Rav Ashi ignores Abahu's question because he has no knowledge of it, because the discussion before him consisted only of the dialogue between Abaye and Rabbah. Two discussions, originating in two distinct Talmudic centers, have been placed back to back sometime after Rav Ashi's statement which concludes the second discussion.

Sanhedrin 8a-9b

According to the discussion as it presently stands, Ulla and Rabbah offer opposing interpretations of Mishna Sanhedrin 1:1; Rava and Rav Hiyya bar Abin resolve an objection against Ulla; and Abaye follows with an alternative interpretation of the mishna which explicitly refers to, and rejects, the interpretations of Rabbah and Ulla. Additional interpretations by Rav Papa, Rav Ashi, Ravina, and the anonymous editors follow on 8b-9b. As Hidushei ha-Ran notes, however, the discussion divides into two discrete sections distinguished by opposing interpretations of the mishna.[6] For my purposes, Ran's comment is significant because Rava's comment is the conclusion of one section and Abaye's comment is the beginning of the other section. The two statements could not have been uttered in the same place at the same time.

According to R. Meir in the mishna, the case of the defaming husband is tried with three judges, while according to the sages it is tried with twenty-three judges "because it involves a capital case." The opinion of the sages is problematic. If the case is monetary, it should be decided by three judges; if capital, it should be decided by a court of twenty-three. What is the meaning of the phrase "because it involves (literally, 'because it has') a capital case," and why should this affect the adjudication of a monetary case?

The first section, which contains statements by Ulla, Rabbah, Rav Hiyya bar Abin, and Rava, interprets the mishna as dealing with a case where the husband claimed that the woman to whom he was betrothed had committed adultery and brought witnesses who supported his claim. The father, following his daughter's conviction, brings witnesses of his own who render the husband's witnesses "lying witnesses." If the

---

[6]Hidushei ha-Ran on Sanhedrin 8a.

testimony of the father's witnesses is accepted, then the husband must pay a fine, and the husband's witnesses must be put to death. However, the father is at present only claiming the fine from the husband, and the lives of the witnesses are not at stake. According to Ulla, the sages in the mishna are concerned with slander to the court, meaning that even though the father's claim is only monetary, it could appear to the outside world that the court is trying a capital case with only three judges, since a capital crime is potentially at issue.

Rabbah, who provides an alternative to Ulla's interpretation of the view of the sages, and Rava, who resolves the objection against Ulla, likewise interpret the mishna in terms of the father's claim against the husband.

The second section, however, which begins with Abaye's interpretation and concludes with the anonymous editors' interpretations on 9b, presupposes a different understanding of the mishna. According to this section, the mishna is referring to the husband's claim against his betrothed and not to the father's counterclaim against the husband. We know from other sources that the father has no counterclaim against the husband unless his daughter had been convicted of adultery on the basis of testimony by witnesses brought by the husband.[7] Yet according to the second section, i.e., from Abaye until the conclusion on 9b, R. Meir deals with testimony which could not have resulted in the daughter's execution. Why, therefore, does R. Meir require any witnesses at all, since the father has no claim at all against the husband? According to Abaye, for example, R. Meir and the sages disagree in a case where the witnesses warned the betrothed woman not to commit adultery. These witnesses explained to her that she was about to commit a capital crime but neglected to inform her which form of execution she would receive. According to R. Meir, such a warning was incomplete and therefore the daughter could not receive the death penalty. Three judges were therefore sufficient to decide a monetary case, the husband's claim that his betrothed should not receive her ketubah. According to the sages, however, the warning was adequate and the woman therefore deserved death. Twenty-three judges were therefore needed to decide her case.

We have seen that the two sections are contradictory discussions placed back to back. The first section, which Rava's statement concludes, explains the mishna in terms of the father's claim against the husband and the husband's witnesses. The second section, which opens with Abaye's interpretation, explains the mishna in terms of the husband's

---

[7]See Yer. Sanhedrin 1:1 and b. Ketubot 44b. See Hidushei ha-Ran on Sanhedrin 8a and 8b.

claim against his betrothed. The same two interpretations are represented in the Yerushalmi.[8] The phrase "all are concerned about slander to the court and about the honor of the original judges" is a later insertion into Abaye's statement. This anonymous insertion attempts to form a bridge between the two discussions. It creates the impression that the two discussions form a coherent and continuous whole.

---

[8]Yer. Sanhedrin 1:1.

Appendices to Chapter 11

Appendix One: *Hora'ah* by Inferior Rabbis

I claimed above that rabbis who engage in practical halachic decision-making (*Hora'ah*) very likely have the status of independent teachers. In the following discussion, I lend weight to this claim by attempting to show that practical halachic decision-making requires greater authority than does the expression of abstract halachic opinions. I do so by analyzing sources which restrict *Hora'ah* by inferiors in ways not encountered in the abstract halachic realm.

Amoraim in virtually every generation debate the question of whether *Hora'ah* is permitted to an inferior during the lifetime of his superior. Some Amoraim permit *Hora'ah* by an inferior as long as the decision is rendered outside the locality of the superior. Others forbid it during the lifetime of the superior, while others forbid it until the inferior turns forty.[1] We find no comparable attempts to limit the expression of abstract halachic opinions in the locality of or during the lifetime of a superior.[2] Outside of the practical halachic realm, the sources are preoccupied with eliminating face-to-face contradiction of the views of a superior, and even here the prohibition is not uniform.[3]

The issue of the permissibility of *Hora'ah* by an inferior is raised, for example, in a story involving the second- and third-generation Suran rabbis, Rav Huna and Rav Hisda. According to the story of their tragic

[1]See Eruvin 62b-63a and Ketubot 60b. See the discussion of Baba Mezia 33a, below. See also Sotah 22a-b and Urbach, *Ha-Halacha*, p. 193; and Shabbat 19b and Halivni, *Mekorot u-Mesorot: Shabbat*, pp. 58-60. For further discussion of the term *Hora'ah*, see Jastrow, *Dictionary*, p. 596; *Arukh ha-Shalem*, ed. Kohut, vol. 2, p. 195, and vol. 3, p. 160; *Enzyklopedia Talmudit*, ed. Zevin, vol. 8, pp. 491-94 and 499-504; Mordechai Fogelman, "Din ve-Hora'ah," in *Sinai*, Jubilee Volume (Jerusalem: Mosad ha-Rav Kuk, 1958), pp. 301-7; and Halivni, *Midrash, Mishnah, and Gemara*, pp. 67-68, 139, and 140, n. 1.
[2]We also find no prohibition of judicial activity by inferiors.
[3]See Kalmin, "Collegial Interaction in the Babylonian Talmud," p. 390, for a discussion of Rav Yehuda's contradiction of Shmuel's opinion on Berakhot 36a (and parallel).

break,[4] Hisda asks Huna about a student who must choose between returning the lost article of his father and returning the lost article of his teacher. According to the Mishna, students must return the lost article of their teacher, but Hisda inquires about the case of a student whom the teacher "needs." Can such a student return the lost article of the father before returning that of the teacher?[5] Huna's response to Hisda should be carefully noted. "I don't need you," says Huna, "[rather,] you need me until you turn forty," alluding to a statement quoted by Huna in another context[6] forbidding "disciples of the sages" to render practical decisions prior to the age of forty.[7] Hisda, it is important to note, is depicted elsewhere as rendering practical halachic decisions in Kafri during Huna's lifetime.[8] Huna's response indicates that he understands Hisda to be claiming a substantial amount of independence while at the same time acknowledging his status as Huna's student. Hisda may be innocently asking about a student who supplies traditions that the master is unaware of, or whose objections and questions help the master see things in a new light, but Huna clearly does not understand him in this fashion. Huna is most likely claiming that by prematurely engaging in *Hora'ah*, i.e., by engaging in *Hora'ah* in a different locality prior to the age of forty, Hisda oversteps the bounds of his authority.

The issue of *Hora'ah* by an inferior is also raised in a story which depicts Ravina, a sixth-generation Amora, examining a butcher's knife "in [the city of] Babylonia." His contemporary, Rav Ashi, disputes his right to do so, claiming that Ravina lacks authority to render practical halachic decisions during the lifetime of his superior. Ravina notes that Rav Hamnuna, Rav Hisda's younger contemporary, gave practical halachic instruction outside of Hisda's jurisdiction during Hisda's lifetime. Hamnuna was Hisda's student-colleague, argues Ravina, and he, Ravina, possesses the same relationship to Ashi.[9] According to Ashi, however, Hamnuna refrained from *Hora'ah* altogether during the lifetime of his superior, and Ravina should therefore do likewise.

According to these sources, superior sages attempt to limit practical halachic decision-making by their inferiors in ways not encountered in the abstract halachic realm. I infer from this fact that authority to engage in the former implies authority to engage in the latter, and that an

---

[4]Baba Mezia 33a.
[5]See Rashi, R. Hananel, and Meiri. See also M.B. Lerner, "Mehkerei Talmud (Ba'a Minei Rav Hisda mei-Rav Huna – B.M. 33a)," *Sinai* 59 (1966), pp. 15-16, n. 4.
[6]Sotah 22a-b.
[7]Compare Lerner, "Mehkerei Talmud," pp. 17-18.
[8]Eruvin 62b.
[9]Eruvin 63a.

inferior rabbi who engages in *Hora'ah* during the lifetime of a superior engages in independent teaching activity as well.

Appendices to Chapter 11

Appendix Two: Simple Disciples or Colleagues of Different Rank?

In general, attempts by scholars to describe the characteristic features of collegial and master-disciple interaction have been marred by guesswork and self-contradiction. Frequently, Amoraim who consistently make objections or ask questions in the presence of superior Amoraim, or who support the opinions of these superior Amoraim, are assumed to be the students of the superior Amoraim. See, for example, Halevy, *Dorot ha-Rishonim*, vol. 2, pp. 515-16 and 539-45; and vol. 3, pp. 68-72; and Hyman, *Toldot Tannaim ve-Amoraim*, pp. 18, 21, 31-39, 75-77, 85-86, 233-34, 244-47, 255-57, 340-42, 511-13, 515-17, 546-49, 742-44, 747-49, 930-31, 937-38, 942-45, 1019-20, 1023-24, 1040-44, 1051-54, 1063-64, 1086, 1090-94, and 1126-29. Elsewhere, the same interaction is viewed by the same scholars as no obstacle to viewing a relationship as collegial in nature. See, for example, Halevy, *Dorot ha-Rishonim*, vol. 2, pp. 222, 228-30, 247, 417-21, 436, and 481; and Hyman, *Toldot Tannaim ve-Amoraim*, pp. 19-20, 29-30, 77, 232, 249-50, 253-55, 338-40, 425-29, 743, 747, 916, 934-36, 942-43, 976, 1021, 1023, 1059, 1089, and 1128-29.

Quotations are also assumed by some scholars to be firm indication of a student-teacher relationship, particularly when they take the following forms: "Rav X said Rav Y said," or "Said Rav X said Rav Y," which are traditionally understood as indicative of direct contact between the tradent and the statement's original author. See Rosh Hashana 19a-b and Yoma 43b, and *Sefer ha-Keritut*, Lashon Limudim, Section 3, chapters 79-80 (compare *Seder Tannaim ve-Amoraim*, ed. Kahan, pp. 30-31). See, however, chapter 7, above.

Following the Talmud's anonymous editors on Berakhot 27b, medieval and modern scholars routinely assume that reference by one Amora to another Amora as *Mar* is proof of a student-teacher relationship between them. See, for example, *Sefer Yuhasin ha-Shalem*, ed. Philipovsky and Freiman, p. 104. This assumption, however, has little textual support. See Cohen, *Mar Bar Rav Ashi*, p. 127, n. 29; Yudelowitz, *Mahoza*, p. 70, and Gewirtsman, "Ha-Munah 'Yetiv' u-Mashmauto," p. 9.

303

For further discussion of the criteria (or the lack thereof) by which to distinguish between collegial and master-disciple relationships, see Halperin, *Atlas Ez-Hayyim*, vol. 3, pp. 28, 30-31, 36-37, and 119-214; and Cohen, *Mar Bar Rav Ashi*, pp. 6, 16-22, 37 (especially n. 35), 125-42, 218-19, and 261-63. See also Frankel, *Mavo ha-Yerushalmi*, p. 54a, for discussion of criteria by which to distinguish between collegial and master-disciple relationships in the Yerushalmi.

By far the most careful effort at describing student-teacher interaction has been that of David Goodblatt, who discusses several terms which consistently introduce dialogues between students and teachers. Goodblatt, *Rabbinic Instruction in Sasanian Babylonia*, pp. 199-238, convincingly demonstrates that phrases such as "to sit before," and "to be found frequently before" consistently introduce interactions between students and teachers, between Amoraim of different status in an instructional context, in which a superior Amora teaches an inferior. Granting the validity of this conclusion, this chapter examines the status of the student who sits before his teacher and asks whether it is possible to determine the place of this student within the rabbinic hierarchy. In general, scholars do not consider the possibility that the inferior Amoraim who receive instruction while "sitting before" superior Amoriam are teachers of different rank rather than simple disciples. In this chapter, we have argued that on several occasions it is possible to conclude with a fair degree of certainty that the student who receives instruction before his teacher is a teacher in his own right with students of his own.

Bibliography

I. Studies, Translations, Dictionaries, and Concordances

Afik, Isaac. *Tefisat he-Halom Ezel Hazal.* Ph.D. Dissertation: Bar-Ilan University, 1990.

Albeck, Hanokh. *Mavo la-Mishna.* 1959. Reprint, Tel Aviv: Devir, 1967.

_____. *Mavo la-Talmudim.* Tel Aviv: Devir, 1969.

Albeck, Shalom. "Sof ha-Hora'ah ve-Aharonei ha-Amoraim." In *Sinai, Jubilee Volume.* Jerusalem: Mosad ha-Rav Kuk, 1958, pp. 57-60.

_____. "Ha-Dayanim bi-Yemei ha-Talmud." In *Manhigut Ruhanit be-Yisrael.* Ed. Ella Belfer. Tel Aviv: Devir, 1982.

Alexander, Philip S. "Quid Athenis Et Hierosolymis? Rabbinic Midrash and Hermeneutics in the Graeco-Roman World." In *A Tribute to Geza Vermes: Essays on Jewish and Christian Literature and History.* Ed. Philip R. Davies and Richard T. White. Sheffield, England: Journal for the Study of the Old Testament Press, 1990.

Aminoah, Noah. *Arikhat Massekhet Kiddushin.* Tel Aviv: E. Levin-Epstein, 1977.

_____. *Arikhat Massekhtot Bezah, Rosh Hashana, ve-Taanit ba-Talmud Bavli.* Tel Aviv: University of Tel Aviv, 1986.

_____. *Arikhat Massekhtot Sukkah u-Moed Katan ba-Talmud Bavli.* Tel Aviv: University of Tel Aviv, 1988.

Avery-Peck, Alan J. *Shebi'it.* Chicago: University of Chicago Press, 1991.

Bacher, Wilhelm. *Die Agada der Babylonischen Amoräer.* Frankfurt am Main, 1913.

_____. *Tradition und Tradenten in den Schulen Palästinas und Babyloniens.* 1914. Reprint, Berlin, 1966.

Baron, Salo. *A Social and Religious History of the Jews.* Vol. 3. 1957. Reprint, Philadelphia: Jewish Publication Society, 1960.

Baumgarten, Albert I. "Rabbi Judah I and His Opponents." *Journal for the Study of Judaism* 12, No. 2 (1981), pp. 135-72.

Beer, Moshe. "Rivo Shel Geniva be-Mar Ukba." *Tarbiz* 31 (1962), pp. 281-86.

_____. "Mi-Ba'ayot Hithavutah Shel ha-Metivta be-Bavel." *Proceedings of the Fourth World Congress of Jewish Studies* 1 (1967), pp. 99-101.

_____. *Rashut ha-Golah be-Bavel bi-Yemei ha-Mishna ve-ha-Talmud.* Tel Aviv: Devir, 1976.

Berman, Saul J. "Adam Hashub: New Light on the History of Babylonian Amoraic Academies." *Dinei Yisrael* 13-14 (1986-1988), pp. 123-54.

Blidstein, Gerald J. "R. Yohanan, Idolatry, and Public Privilege." *Journal for the Study of Judaism* 5, No. 2 (1974), pp. 154-61.

Bokser, Baruch M. *Samuel's Commentary on the Mishna: Its Nature, Forms, and Content.* Leiden: E.J. Brill, 1975.

_____. *Post Mishnaic Judaism in Transition.* Chico, California: Scholars Press, 1980.

_____. "An Annotated Bibliographical Guide to the Study of the Palestinian Talmud." In *The Study of Ancient Judaism II: The Palestinian and Babylonian Talmuds.* Ed. Jacob Neusner. New York: Ktav, 1981, pp. 187-94.

_____. "Wonder-Working and the Rabbinic Tradition: The Case of Hanina ben Dosa." *Journal for the Study of Judaism* 16, No. 1 (1985), pp. 42-92.

_____. "Rabbah bar Nahmani." In *The Encyclopedia of Religion.* Vol. 12. Ed. Mircea Eliade. New York: Macmillan, 1987, p. 181.

_____. "Talmudic Studies." In *The State of Jewish Studies.* Ed. Shaye J.D. Cohen and Edward L. Greenstein. New York: Jewish Theological Seminary, 1990, pp. 89-95 and 98-101.

Boyarin, Daniel. "Literary Fat Rabbis. On the Historical Origins of the Grotesque Body." *Journal of the History of Sexuality* 1, No. 4 (1991), pp. 562-72.

_____. *Carnal Israel: Reading Sex in Talmudic Culture.* Berkeley, California: University of California Press, 1993.

Brody, Yerahmiel. "Sifrut ha-Geonim ve-ha-Text ha-Talmudi." In *Mehkerei Talmud*. Ed. Yaakov Zussman and David Rosental. Jerusalem: Magnes Press, 1990, pp. 237-303.

Brüll, Nahum. "Die Entstehungsgeschichte der Babylonischen Talmuds als Schriftwerkes." *Jahrbücher für Jüdische Geschichte und Literatur* 2 (1876), pp. 67-68.

Cashdan, Eli. *Hullin*. London: Soncino Press, 1935.

Chernick, Michael. *Le-Heker ha-Midot "Kelal u-Ferat u-Kelal" ve-"Ribui u-Miut" ba-Midrashim u-va-Talmudim*. Lud: Makhon Haberman le-Mehkerei Sifrut, 1984.

Coen, Malakhi. *Sefer Yad Malakhi*. 1852. Reprint, Jerusalem, 1976.

Cohen, A. *Avodah Zarah*. London: Soncino Press, 1935.

Cohen, Avinoam. *Mar Bar Rav Ashi ve-Terumato ha-Sifrutit*. Ph.D. Dissertation: Yeshiva University, 1980.

_____. "Bikoret Hilkhatit Leumat Bikoret Sifrutit be-Sugiot ha-Talmud." *Asufot: Sefer Shanah le-Madaei ha-Yahadut* 3 (1989), pp. 331-46.

Cohen, Shaye J.D. "Patriarchs and Scholarchs." *Proceedings of the American Academy for Jewish Research* 48 (1981), pp. 57-87.

_____. "Jacob Neusner, Mishnah, and Counter-Rabbinics." *Conservative Judaism* 37, No. 1 (1983), pp. 48-63.

_____. *From the Maccabees to the Mishna*. Philadelphia: The Westminster Press, 1987.

_____. "The Modern Study of Ancient Judaism." In *The State of Jewish Studies*. Ed. Shaye J.D. Cohen and Edward L. Greenstein. New York: Jewish Theological Seminary, 1990, pp. 63-64.

Cox, Patricia. *Biography in Late Antiquity*. Berkeley, California: University of California Press, 1983.

Diamond, Eliezer. *Dugma le-Mahadura Madait Im Perush le-Massekhet Taanit, Talmud Bavli, Rosh Perek Alef, be-Zeruf Mavo*. Ph.D. Dissertation: Jewish Theological Seminary, 1990.

Dodds, E.R. *The Greeks and the Irrational*. Berkeley, California: University of California Press, 1951.

Dor, Zvi Moshe. "Ha-Mekorot ha-Erez-Yisraeli'im be-Veit Midrasho Shel Rava." *Sinai* 52 (1962), pp. 128-43; *Sinai* 53 (1963), pp. 31-49; *Sinai* 55 (1964), pp. 306-16.

_____. "He'arah le-Ma'amaro Shel A. Goldberg." *Tarbiz* 34 (1964), p. 98.

_____. *Torat Erez Yisrael be-Bavel.* Tel Aviv: Devir, 1971.

Downing, F. Gerald. "Compositional Conventions and the Synoptic Problem." *Journal of Biblical Literature* 107, No. 1 (1988), pp. 69-85.

Efrati, Yaakov. *Tekufat ha-Saboraim ve-Sifrutah.* Petah-Tikva, Israel: Agudat Benei Asher, 1973.

Ehrlich, Ernst Ludwig. "Der Traum im Talmud." *Zeitschrift für die Neutestamentliche Wissenschaft* (1956), p. 143.

Elman, Yaakov. "Righteousness as its own Reward: An Inquiry into the Theologies of the Stam." *Proceedings of the American Academy for Jewish Research* 57 (1991), pp. 35-67.

Encyclopaedia Hebraica. Jerusalem: Encyclopaedia Publishing Company, 1949-1981. Vol. 1, pp. 141-42, and Vol. 30, p. 436.

Epstein, Y.N. *Mevo'ot le-Sifrut ha-Amoraim.* Tel Aviv: Devir, 1962.

_____. *Mavo la-Nusah ha-Mishna.* Jerusalem, 1964.

Eshel, Ben-Zion. *Yishuvei ha-Yehudim be-Bavel bi-Tekufat ha-Talmud: Onomastikon Talmudi.* Jerusalem: Magnes Press, 1979.

Feldblum, Meir. "The Impact of the 'Anonymous Sugya' on Halakic Concepts." *Proceedings of the American Academy for Jewish Research* 37 (1969), pp. 19-28.

Feliks, Yehuda. *Talmud Yerushalmi Massekhet Sheviit.* Jerusalem: Rubin Mass, 1986.

Florsheim, Yoel. "Yisudan ve-Reshit Hitpathutan Shel Yeshivot Bavel-- Sura ve-Pumbedita." *Zion* 39 (1974), p. 186, n. 10.

_____. "Ha-Yahasim bein Hakhmei ha-Dor ha-Sheni Shel Amoraei Bavel." *Zion* 51 (1986), pp. 282-93.

Fogelman, Mordechai. "Din ve-Hora'ah." In *Sinai,* Jubilee Volume. Jerusalem: Mosad ha-Rav Kuk, 1958.

Fraade, Steven D. "The Early Rabbinic Sage." In *The Sage in Israel and the Ancient Near East.* Ed. John G. Gammie and Leo G. Perdue. Winona Lake, Indiana: Eisenbrauns, 1990.

Fraenkel, Yonah. "Bible Verses Quoted in Tales of the Sages." *Scripta Hierosolymitana* 22 (1971), p. 89, n. 23, and pp. 94-98.

_____. "She'elot Hermeneutiot be-Heker Sipur ha-Agadah." *Tarbiz* 47 (1978), pp. 139-72.

_____. "Teshuva." *Tarbiz* 49 (1980), p. 429.

_____. *Iyunim ba-Olamo ha-Ruhani Shel Sipur ha-Agadah.* Tel Aviv: Ha-Kibbuz ha-Meuhad, 1981.

_____. *Darkhei ha-Agadah ve-ha-Midrash.* Givatayim, Israel: Yad la-Talmud, 1991.

Francus, Yisrael. *Talmud Yerushalmi Massekhet Bezah, Im Perush Ehad ha-Kadmonim Rabenu Elazar Azkari Baal Sefer Haredim.* New York: Jewish Theological Seminary, 1967.

Frankel, Zechariah. *Mavo ha-Yerushalmi.* 1870. Reprint, Jerusalem, 1967.

Frieden, Ken. *Freud's Dream of Interpretation.* Albany: State University of New York Press, 1990.

Friedman, Shamma. *Perek ha-Isha Rabbah ba-Bavli.* Jerusalem: Jewish Theological Seminary, 1978.

_____. "Kol ha-Kazar Kodem." In *Kovez Ma'amarim be-Lashon Hazal.* Ed. Moshe Bar-Asher. Jerusalem, 1980, pp. 299-326.

_____. "La-Agadah ha-Historit ba-Talmud ha-Bavli." In *Sefer ha-Zikaron le-R. Shaul Lieberman.* Jerusalem: Saul Lieberman Institute for Talmudic Research, 1989, pp. 28-42.

_____. *Talmud Arukh: Perek ha-Sokher et ha-Umanim ba-Bavli.* Jerusalem: Jewish Theological Seminary, 1991.

_____. "Le-Hithavut Shinuyei ha-Girsaot ba-Talmud ha-Bavli." *Sidra* 7 (1991), pp. 67-102.

_____. "Ketiv ha-Shemot 'Rabbah' ve-'Rava' ba-Talmud ha-Bavli." *Sinai* 55 (1992), pp. 140-64.

Funk, Solomon. *Die Juden in Babylonien 200-500.* Part 1. Berlin, 1902.

Gafni, Yeshayahu. *Yahadut Bavel u-Mosdoteha bi-Tekufat ha-Talmud.* Jerusalem: Merkaz Zalman Shazar, 1976.

_____. "'Yeshiva' u-'Metivta.'" *Zion* 43 (1978), pp. 12-37.

_____. "Ha-Yeshiva ha-Bavlit la-Or Sugyat B.K. 117a." *Tarbiz* 49 (1980), pp. 292-301.

_____. "He'arot le-Ma'amaro Shel D. Goodblatt." _Zion_ 46 (1981), pp. 52-56.

_____. "Hiburim Nestorianim ke-Makor le-Toldot Yeshivot Bavel." _Tarbiz_ 51 (1982), pp. 567-76.

_____. "Al Mazav ha-Mehkar; Skira Al ha-Mehkar ha-Histori Shel Bavel ha-Talmudit be-Dorot ha-Aharonim." _Yidion ha-Igud ha-Olami le-Madaei ha-Yahadut_ 21 (1982), pp. 5, 9, and 12.

_____. "Ma'asei Bet-Din ba-Talmud ha-Bavli." _Proceedings of the American Academy for Jewish Research_ 49 (1982), pp. 23-40.

_____. "'Shevet u-Mehokek': Al Defusei Manhigut Hadashim bi-Tekufat ha-Talmud be-Erez Yisrael u-ve-Bavel." In _Kehuna u-Melukha: Yahasei Dat u-Medina be-Yisrael u-va-Amim._ Ed. Yeshayahu Gafni and Gabriel Motzkin. Jerusalem: Merkaz Zalman Shazar, 1987, pp. 85-88.

_____. "Le-Heker ha-Khronologia be-Igeret Rav Sherira Gaon." _Zion_ 52 (1987), pp. 1-24.

_____. "Expressions and Types of 'Local Patriotism' Among the Jews of Sasanian Babylonia." In _Irano-Judaica II._ Ed. Shaul Shaked and Amnon Netzer. Jerusalem: Ben-Zvi Institute, 1990, pp. 63-71.

_____. _Yehudei Bavel bi-Tekufat ha-Talmud._ Jerusalem: Merkaz Zalman Shazar le-Toldot Yisrael, 1991.

Gewirtsmann, Moshe. "Ha-Munah 'Yativ' u-Mashmauto." _Sinai_ 65 (1969), pp. 9-20.

Ginzberg, Louis. _Perushim ve-Hidushim ba-Yerushalmi._ 1941. Reprint, New York: Ktav, 1971.

Gnuse, Robert Karl. _The Dream Theophany of Samuel._ Lanham, Maryland: University Press of America, 1984.

Goldberg, Avraham. "Hadirat ha-Halacha Shel Erez Yisrael le-Tokh Masoret Bavel ke-Fi she-Hi Mishtakefet mi-Tokh Perek Arvei Pesahim." _Tarbiz_ 33, No. 4 (1964), pp. 337-48.

_____. "R. Zeira u-Minhag Bavel be-Erez Yisrael." _Tarbiz_ 36 (1965), pp. 319-41.

_____. "The Babylonian Talmud." In _The Literature of the Sages._ Part 1. Ed. Shmuel Safrai. Compendia Rerum Iudaricum ad Novum Testamentum, Section 2, Vol. 3. Philadelphia: Fortress Press, 1987, pp. 323-45.

_____. "Derakhim Shel Zimzum Mahlokot Ezel Amoraei Bavel." In *Mehkerei Talmud.* Ed. Yaakov Zussman and David Rosental. Jerusalem: Magnes Press, 1990, pp. 135-53.

Goldenberg, Robert. *The Sabbath-Law of Rabbi Meir.* Missoula, Montana: Scholars Press, 1978.

Goodblatt, David. *Rabbinic Instruction in Sasanian Babylonia.* Leiden: E.J. Brill, 1975.

_____. "Local Traditions in the Babylonian Talmud." *Hebrew Union College Annual* 48 (1977), pp. 187-94 and 204-16.

_____. "Hitpathuyot Hadashot be-Heker Yeshivot Bavel." *Zion* 43 (1978), pp. 14-38.

_____. "Towards the Rehabilitation of Talmudic History." In *History of Judaism: The Next Ten Years.* Ed. Baruch M. Bokser. Chico, California: Scholars Press, 1980, pp. 33-38.

_____. "The Babylonian Talmud." In *The Study of Ancient Judaism II: The Palestinian and Babylonian Talmuds.* Ed. Jacob Neusner. New York: Ktav, 1981, pp. 148-60 and 165.

Goodman, Martin. *State and Society in Roman Palestine, A.D. 132-212.* Totowa, New Jersey: Rowman and Allanheld, 1983.

Goshen-Gottstein, Alon. "R. Elazar ben Arakh: Semel u-Meziut." In *Yehudim ve-Yahadut bi-Yemei Bayit Sheni, ha-Mishna, ve-ha-Talmud.* Ed. Aharon Oppenheimer, Yeshayahu Gafni, and Menahem Stern. Jerusalem: Yad Yizhak ben Zvi, 1993, pp. 173-97.

Graetz, Heinrich. *Geschichte der Juden.* 1853-1875. Reprint, Leipzig: O. Leiner, 1873-1900.

Green, William Scott. "What's in a Name – The Problematic of Rabbinic 'Biography.'" In *Approaches to Ancient Judaism: Theory and Practice.* Ed. William Scott Green. Chico, California: Scholars Press, 1978, pp. 77- 96.

_____. "Palestinian Holy Men: Charismatic Leadership and Rabbinic Tradition." *Aufstieg und Niedergang der Römische Welt* 2: 19/2 (1979), pp. 642-44.

_____. "Context and Meaning in Rabbinic 'Biography.'" In *Approaches to Ancient Judaism.* Vol. 2. Ed. William Scott Green. Chico, California: Scholars Press, 1980, pp. 97-111.

_____. "Storytelling and Holy Man: The Case of Ancient Judaism."
In *Take Judaism for Example*. Ed. Jacob Neusner. Chicago: University
of Chicago, 1983, pp. 29-43.

Greenwald, Leopold. *Ha-Ra'u Mesadrei ha-Bavli et ha-Yerushalmi?* New
York: Ha-Makhon le-Mehkar u-le-Mada ha-Yerushalmi, 1954.

Halevi, E.E. "Od Al Genre Hadash ba-Sipurei ha-Agadah." *Tarbiz* 49
(1980), pp. 424-28.

Halevy, Yizhak. *Dorot ha-Rishonim*. 1897-1939. Reprint, Berlin: Benjamin
Harz, 1923.

Halivni, David. *Mekorot u-Mesorot:* Nashim. Tel Aviv: Devir, 1968.

_____. *Mekorot u-Mesorot:* Yoma-Hagigah. Jerusalem: Jewish
Theological Seminary, 1975.

_____. *Mekorot u-Mesorot:* Shabbat. Jerusalem: Jewish Theological
Seminary, 1982.

_____. *Mekorot u-Mesorot:* Eruvin-Pesahim. Jerusalem: Jewish
Theological Seminary, 1982.

_____. *Midrash, Mishnah, and Gemara: The Jewish Predilection For
Justified Law*. Cambridge: Harvard University Press, 1986.

Halperin, Rafael. *Atlas Ez-Hayyim*. Vols. 3-4. Tel Aviv, 1980.

Harris, Monford. "Dreams in Sefer Hasidim." *Proceedings of the American
Academy for Jewish Research* 31 (1963), pp. 68-71.

Hauptman, Judith. *Development of the Talmudic Sugya: Relationship
Between Tannaitic and Amoraic Sources*. Lanham, Maryland:
University Press of America, 1988.

Hayes, Christine. *Between the Babylonian and Palestinian Talmuds:
Accounting for Halakhic Difference in Selected Sugyot from Tractate
Avodah Zarah*. Ph.D. Dissertation: University of California at
Berkeley, 1993.

Hayman, Pinhas. *Hitpathut ve-Shinuyim be-Torat R. Yohanan ben Napha be-
Ha'avaratah me-Erez Yisrael le-Bavel*. Ph.D. Dissertation: Yeshiva
University, 1990. Ann Arbor: University Microfilms International,
1991.

Heinemann, Yizhak. *Darkhei ha-Agadah*. Jerusalem: Masada, 1949-1950.

Herr, Moshe D. "The Historical Significance of the Dialogues Between Jewish Sages and Roman Dignitaries." *Scripta Hierosolymitana* 22 (1971), pp. 123-50.

Hezser, Catherine. *Form, Function, and Historical Significance of the Rabbinic Story in Yerushalmi Neziqin.* Ph.D. Dissertation: Jewish Theological Seminary, 1992.

Higger, Michael. *Ozar ha-Baraitot.* Vol. 10. New York: Devei Rabbanan, 1948.

Hirshman, Menahem. "Li-Demuto Shel Shmuel ha-Katan." In *Yehudim ve-Yahadut bi-Yemei Bayit Sheni, ha-Mishna, ve-ha-Talmud.* Ed. Aharon Oppenheimer, Yeshayahu Gafni, and Menahem Stern. Jerusalem: Yad Yizhak Ben-Zvi, 1993, pp. 165-72.

Hornblower, J. *Hieronymus of Cardia.* London: Oxford Univerity Press, 1981.

Horowitz, Haim Shaul. "Die Komposition des Talmuds." *Monatschrift für Geschichte und Wissenschaft des Judentums* 63 (1919), pp. 122-30.

Hyman, Aharon. *Toldot Tannaim ve-Amoraim.* 1910. Reprint, Jerusalem, 1987.

Jacobs, Louis. "How Much of the Babylonian Talmud is Pseudepigraphic?" *Journal of Jewish Studies* 28, No. 1 (1977), pp. 46-59.

_____. *Structure and Form in the Babylonian Talmud.* Cambridge, England: Cambridge University Press, 1991.

Jaffee, Martin. "The Babylonian Appropriation of the Talmud Yerushalmi: Redactional Studies in the Horayot Tractates." In *New Perspectives on Ancient Judaism: The Literature of Early Rabbinic Judaism: Issues in Talmudic Redaction and Interpretation.* Vol. 4. Ed. Alan J. Avery-Peck. Lanham, Maryland: University Press of America, 1989, pp. 3-27.

Jastrow, Marcus. *A Dictionary of the Targumim, Talmud Babli, Yerushalmi, and Midrashic Literature.* 1886-1903. Reprint, New York: The Judaica Press, 1971.

Jawetz, Wolf. *Sefer Toldot Yisrael.* Vols. 7-8. 1933-1936. Reprint, Tel Aviv, 1963.

Kagan, Zipporah. "Divergent Tendencies and Their Literary Moulding in the Aggadah." *Scripta Hierosolymitana* 22 (1971), pp. 151-70.

Kalmin, Richard. *The Post-Rav Ashi Amoraim: Transition or Continuity? A Study of the Role of the Final Generations of Amoraim in the Redaction of the Talmud.* Ph.D. Dissertation: Jewish Theological Seminary, 1985. Ann Arbor: University Microfilms International, 1985.

_____. "Quotation Forms in the Babylonian Talmud." *Hebrew Union College Annual* 59 (1988), pp. 167-87.

_____. *The Redaction of the Babylonian Talmud: Amoraic or Saboraic?* Cincinnati: Hebrew Union College, 1989.

_____. "Saints or Sinners, Scholars or Ignoramuses? Stories About the Rabbis as Evidence for the Composite Nature of the Babylonian Talmud." *Association for Jewish Studies Review* 15, No. 2 (1990), pp. 179-205.

_____. "Friends and Colleagues, or Barely Acquainted? Relations Between Fourth-Generation Masters in the Babylonian Talmud." *Hebrew Union College Annual* 61 (1990), pp. 125-58.

_____. "The Talmudic Story: Aggada as History." *Proceedings of the Tenth World Congress of Jewish Studies* 1 (1990), pp. 9-16.

_____. "Collegial Interaction in the Babylonian Talmud." *Jewish Quarterly Review* 82, Nos. 3-4 (1992), pp. 383-415.

_____. "Talmudic Portrayals of Relationships Between Rabbis: Amoraic or Pseudepigraphic?" *Association for Jewish Studies Review* 17, No. 2 (1992), pp. 165-97.

_____. "Rabbinic Attitudes Toward Rabbis as a Key to the Dating of Talmudic Sources." *Jewish Quarterly Review* 84, No. 1 (1993), pp. 1-27.

_____. "Changing Amoraic Attitudes Toward the Authority and Statements of Rav and Shmuel: A Study of the Talmud as a Historical Source." *Hebrew Union College Annual* 63 (1992), pp. 83-106.

Kaplan, Julius. *The Redaction of the Babylonian Talmud.* New York: Bloch, 1933.

Kilborne, Benjamin. "Dreams." In *The Encyclopedia of Religion.* Vol. 4. Ed. Mircea Eliade. New York: Macmillan, 1987, p. 487.

Kimelman, Ronald Revuen. *Rabbi Yohanan of Tiberias: Aspects of the Social and Religious History of Third Century Palestine.* Ph.D. Dissertation: Yale University, 1977.

Klein, Hyman. "Gemara and Sebara." *Jewish Quarterly Review* 38 (1947), pp. 67-91.

Klein, Shmuel. *Sefer ha-Yishuv.* Vol. 1. Jerusalem: Mosad Bialik, 1939.

Kohut, Alexander. *Arukh ha-Shalem.* 8 Vols. 1878-1892. Reprint, Vienna, 1926.

Kosowsky, Binyamin. *Ozar ha-Shemot le-Talmud Bavli.* Jerusalem: The Ministry of Education and Culture, Government of Israel, and The Jewish Theological Seminary, 1976-1983.

Kosowsky, Haim. *Ozar Lashon ha-Talmud.* Vol. 13. Jerusalem: The Ministry of Education and Culture, Government of Israel, and The Jewish Theological Seminary, 1964.

Kosowsky, Haim and Binyamin. *Ozar Lashon ha-Talmud.* Vols. 27 and 30. Jerusalem: The Ministry of Education and Culture, Government of Israel, and The Jewish Theological Seminary, 1971 and 1973.

Kosowsky, Moshe. *Ozar Lashon Talmud Yerushalmi.* Jerusalem: Israel Academy of Sciences and Humanities, Government of Israel, and Jewish Theological Seminary, 1985.

_____. "Ha-Yeshiva ba-'Yeshiva,'" In *S.K. Mirsky Jubilee Volume.* New York, 1958, pp. 312-27.

Kraemer, David C. *Stylistic Characteristics of Amoraic Literature.* Ph.D. Dissertation: Jewish Theological Seminary, 1984. Ann Arbor: University Microfilms International, 1985.

_____. "On the Reliability of Attributions in the Babylonian Talmud." *Hebrew Union College Annual* 60 (1989), pp. 175-90.

_____. *The Mind of the Talmud: An Intellectual History of the Bavli.* New York: Oxford University Press, 1990.

Krauss, Samuel. "Talmudische Nachrichten über Arabien." *Zeitschrift der Deutschen Morgenländischen Gesellschaft* 70 (1916), pp. 321-53.

Kristianpoller, Alexander. "Traum und Traumdeutung." In *Monumenta Talmudica.* Vol. 4, part 2. Ed. Karl Albrecht et al. Vienna: Benjamin Harz, 1923.

Leon, Harry J. *The Jews of Ancient Rome.* Philadelphia: Jewish Publication Society, 1960.

Lerner, M.B. "Mehkerei Talmud (Ba'a Minei Rav Hisda mei-Rav Huna-- B.M. 3a." *Sinai* 59 (1966), pp. 15-18.

Levine, Lee. *Caesaria Under Roman Rule.* Leiden: E.J. Brill, 1975.

_____. *Ma'amad ha-Hakhamim be-Erez Yisrael.* Jerusalem: Yad Yizhak Ben-Zvi, 1985.

_____. *The Rabbinic Class of Roman Palestine in Late Antiquity* Jerusalem: Yad Izhak Ben-Zvi, 1989.

Levy, Jacob. *Neuhebräisches und Chaldäisches Wörterbuch über die Talmudim und Midraschim.* 2nd edition, revised by Lazarus Goldschmidt. Berlin: Benjamin Harz, 1924.

Lewin, Benjamin. *Rabbanan Saboraei ve-Talmudam.* Jerusalem: Ahiavar, 1937.

Lewy, Yisrael. *Mavo u-Ferush le-Talmud Yerushalmi.* 1895-1914. Reprint, Jerusalem, 1970.

Libson, Gideon. "Al Mah Menadin." *Shanaton ha-Mishpat ha-Ivri* 2 (1975), pp. 298-342.

_____. "Nidui u-Menudeh." *Shanaton ha-Mishpat ha-Ivri* 6-7 (1979-1980), pp. 177-202.

Lieberman, Saul. "Martyrs of Caesarea." *Annuaire de L'Institut de Philologie et d'Histoire Orientalis et Slaves* 7 (1939-1940), pp. 395-446.

_____. *Hellenism in Jewish Palestine.* New York: Jewish Theological Seminary, 1950.

_____. *Tosefta ki-Feshutah.* Vol. 3. New York: Jewish Theological Seminary, 1962.

Liebeschuetz, J.H.W. *Continuity and Change in Roman Religion.* Oxford: Clarendon Press, 1979.

Maimon, Yehuda Leib. *Abaye ve-Rava: Toldoteihem u-Massekhet Ma'amareihem ve-Sugyateihem ba-Halacha u-va-Agadah.* Jerusalem: Mosad ha-Rav Kuk, 1965.

Meier, John P. *A Marginal Jew: Rethinking the Historical Jesus.* New York: Doubleday, 1991.

Melamed, Ezra. *Eshnav ha-Talmud.* Jerusalem: Kiryat Sefer, 1976.

Mielziner, Moses. *Introduction to the Talmud.* 1894. Reprint, New York: Bloch, 1968.

Neusner, Jacob. *A History of the Jews in Babylonia.* 5 Vols. Leiden: E.J. Brill, 1965-70.

_____. "Rabbis and Community in Third Century Babylonia." In *Religions in Antiquity: Essays in Memory of E.R. Goodenough.* Ed. Jacob Neusner. Leiden: E.J. Brill, 1968, pp. 438-59.

_____. *The Rabbinic Traditions About the Pharisees Before 70.* Leiden: E.J. Brill, 1979.

_____. *Judaism: The Evidence of the Mishna.* Chicago: University of Chicago, 1981.

_____. *Avodah Zarah.* Chicago: University of Chicago, 1982.

_____. *In Search of Talmudic Biography: The Problem of the Attributed Saying.* Chico, California: Scholars Press, 1984.

_____. *Sanhedrin.* Chico, California: Scholars Press, 1984.

_____. *Berakhot.* Chico, California: Scholars Press, 1984.

_____. *Judaism: The Classical Statement.* Chicago: University of Chicago, 1986.

_____. *The Bavli and Its Sources: The Question of Tradition in the Case of Tractate Sukkah.* Atlanta: Scholars Press, 1987.

_____. *Making the Classics in Judaism.* Atlanta: Scholars Press, 1989.

_____. *Sources and Traditions: Types of Compositions in the Talmud of Babylonia.* Atlanta: Scholars Press, 1992.

Niehoff, Maren. "A Dream Which is Not Interpreted is Like a Letter Which is Not Read." *Journal of Jewish Studies* 43, No. 1 (1992), pp. 58-84.

Oberhelman, Steven M. *The Oneirocriticon of Achmet: A Medieval Greek and Arabic Treatise on the Interpretation of Dreams.* Lubbock, Texas: Texas Tech University Press, 1991.

Obermeyer, Jacob. *Die Landschaft Babylonien im Zeitalter des Talmuds und des Gaonats.* Frankfurt am Main: I. Kauffmann, 1929.

Oppenheim, A. Leo. "The Interpretation of Dreams in the Ancient Near East with a Translation of an Assyrian Dream-Book." *Transactions of the American Philosophical Society.* New Series, 46, Part 3 (1956), p. 218.

_____. "Mantic Dreams in the Ancient Near East." In *The Dream and Human Societies.* Ed. G.E. Von Grunebaum and Roger Caillois. Berkeley, California: University of California Press, 1966.

Oppenheimer, Aharon. "Batei Midrash be-Erez Yisrael be-Reshit Tekufat ha-Amoraim." *Katedra* 8 (1978), pp. 80-89.

_____. *Babylonia Judaica in the Talmudic Period.* Wiesbaden: Ludwig Reichert, 1983.

Pauly's Real-Encyclopädie der Classischen Altertumswissenschaft. Ed. G. Wissowa et al. Stuttgart: J.B. Metzler, 1932. 1st Series, Vol. 18, columns 448-59. 2nd Series, Vol. 4a, pt. 2, columns 2025-26; and Vol. 6, columns 2233-245.

Porton, Gary. *The Traditions of Rabbi Ishmael.* Vol. 4. Leiden: E.J. Brill, 1982.

Rabinovitz, Zeev W. *Sha'arei Torat Erez Yisrael.* Jerusalem: Weiss Press, 1940.

Rapaport, Solomon. *Erekh Millin.* Vol. 1. 1852. Reprint, Warsaw, 1914.

Rokeah, David. "Zecharya ben Avkulas: Anvetanut O Kanaut?" *Zion* 53, No. 1 (1988), pp. 53-56.

_____. "Be-Khol Zot Mishak Millim." *Zion* 53, No. 3 (1988), pp. 317-22.

Rosental, David. "Pirka de-Abaye (Perek Sheni Shel Bavli Rosh Hashana." *Tarbiz* 46 (1977), p. 108.

_____. "Arikhot Kedumot ha-Meshukaot ba-Talmud ha-Bavli." In *Mehkerei Talmud.* Ed. Yaakov Zussman and David Rosental. Jerusalem: Magnes Press, 1990, pp. 155-204.

_____. "'Benei ha-Talmud Hifsiku ve-Kafzu Lehakshot be-Tokh ha-Baraita': Bavli Ketubot 78a-b." *Tarbiz* 60 (1991), pp. 550-76.

Rosental, Eliezer Shimshon. "Rav Ben-Ahi R. Hiyya Gam Ben-Ahoto?" In *Hanokh Yalon Jubilee Volume.* Ed. Saul Lieberman, E.Y. Kutscher, and Shaul Esh. Jerusalem: Kiryat Sefer, 1963, pp. 284-85, n. 1, and 289-307.

_____. *Massekhet Pesahim Talmud Bavli: Faksimilia mi-Ketav Yad (?) Provinza (?) 1442-1452.* London, 1984.

_____. "Toldot ha-Nusah u-Va'ayot Arikhah be-Heker ha-Talmud ha-Bavli." *Tarbiz* 57 (1988), pp. 1-36.

Russell, James R. "Sages and Scribes at the Courts of Ancient Iran." In *The Sage in Israel and the Ancient Near East.* Ed. John G. Gammie and Leo G. Perdue. Winona Lake, Indiana: Eisenbrauns, 1990.

Safrai, Shmuel. "Tales of the Sages in the Palestinian Tradition and the Babylonian Talmud." *Scripta Hierosolymitana* 22 (1971), pp. 209-32.

Saldarini, Anthony J. "The Adoption of a Dissident: Akabya ben Mahalaleel in Rabbinic Tradition." *Journal of Jewish Studies* 33 (1982), pp. 547-56.

Satlow, Michael L. *Talking About Sex: Rabbinic Rhetorics of Sexuality.* Ph.D. Dissertation: Jewish Theological Seminary, 1993.

Schachter, Jacob. *Sanhedrin.* London: Soncino Press, 1935.

Schwartz, Daniel. "Od le-She'elat 'Zecharya ben Avkulas: Anvetanut O Kanaut?'" *Zion* 53, No. 3 (1988), pp. 313-16.

Schwartz, Joshua. "Tension Between Palestinian Scholars and Babylonian Olim in Amoraic Palestine." *Journal for the Study of Judaism* 11 (1980), pp. 78-94.

Segal, Eliezer. *Case Citation in the Babylonian Talmud: The Evidence of Tractate Neziqin.* Atlanta: Scholars Press, 1990.

_____. "Law as Allegory? An Unnoticed Literary Device in Talmudic Narratives." *Prooftexts* 8 (1988), pp. 249-50.

Segal, J.B. "Arabs in Syriac Literature Before the Rise of Islam." *Jerusalem Studies in Arabic and Islam* 4 (1984), pp. 89-128.

Simon, Maurice. *Baba Batra.* London: Soncino Press, 1935.

_____. *Rosh Hashanah.* London: Soncino Press, 1938.

_____. *Berakoth.* London: Soncino Press, 1948.

Slotki, Israel W. *Yevamot.* London: Soncino Press, 1936.

Sokoloff, Michael. *A Dictionary of Palestinian Aramaic of the Byzantine Period.* Ramat Gan: Bar-Ilan University Press, 1990.

Sperber, Daniel. "Ha-Im Alah Rabbah le-Erez Yisrael?" *Sinai* 71 (1972), pp. 140-45.

_____. "On the Unfortunate Adventures of Rav Kahana: A Passage of Saboraic Polemic from Sasanian Persia." In *Irano-Judaica.* Ed. Shaul Shaked. Jerusalem: Ben-Zvi Institute, 1982, pp. 83-100.

Spiegel, Yaakov S. *Hosafot Meuharot (Savoriot) ba-Talmud ha-Bavli.* Ph.D. Dissertation: Tel Aviv University, 1976.

_____. "Amar Rava Hilkheta–Piskei Halacha Meuharim." In *Iyunim be-Sifrut Hazal ba-Mikra u-va-Toldot Yisrael.* Ed. Y.D. Gilat, C.

Levine, and Z.M. Rabinowitz. Ramat Gan: Bar-Ilan University, 1982, pp. 206-14.

Steinzalts, A. "Ha-Kesharim Bein Bavel le-Erez Yisrael." *Talpiot* 9 (1965), pp. 294-306.

Stemberger, Brigitte. "Der Traum in der Rabbinischen Literatur." *Kairos* 18 (1976), pp. 13 and 26-30.

Stemberger, Günter. *Introduction to the Talmud and Midrash.* 1991. Reprint, Minneapolis: Fortress Press, 1992.

Szadzunski, E.I. "Addenda to Krauss." *The American Journal of Semitic Languages and Literatures* 49, No. 4 (1933), pp. 336-38.

Urbach, Ephraim. "Al Iyun Histori ba-Sippur Al Moto Shel Rabbah bar Nahmani." *Tarbiz* 34 (1963-1964), pp. 160-61.

_____. *Hazal: Pirkei Emunot ve-Deot.* 1969. Reprint, Jerusalem: Magnes Press, 1986.

_____. *Ha-Halacha: Mekoroteha ve-Hitpathutah.* Givatayim, Israel: Yad la-Talmud, 1984.

Weiss, Avraham. *Hithavut ha-Talmud bi-Shlemuto.* New York: The Alexander Kohut Foundation, 1943.

_____. *Ha-Yezira Shel ha-Saboraim.* Jerusalem: Hebrew University, 1953.

_____. *Le-Heker ha-Talmud.* New York: Philipp Feldheim, 1954.

_____. *Al ha-Yezira ha-Sifrutit Shel ha-Amoraim.* New York: Horeb, 1962.

_____. *Mehkarim ba-Talmud.* Jerusalem: Mosad ha-Rav Kuk, 1975.

Weiss, Isaac H. *Dor Dor ve-Dorshav.* 1871-1891. Reprint, Jerusalem, 1964.

Weiss, Moshe. "Ha-Otentiut Shel ha-Shakla ve-Tarya ba-Mahlokot Beit Shammai u-Veit Hillel." *Sidra* 4 (1988), pp. 53-66.

White, Robert H. *The Interpretation of Dreams: Oneirocritica, by Artemidorus.* Park Ridge, New Jersey: Noyes Press, 1975.

Yudelowitz, Mordechai. *Yeshivat Pumbedita bi-Yemei ha-Amoraim.* Tel Aviv, 1935.

_____. *Mahoza: mei-Hayei ha-Yehudim bi-Zeman ha-Talmud.* Jerusalem, 1947.

Zlotnick, Dov. *The Iron Pillar: Mishnah.* Jerusalem: The Bialik Institute, 1988.

Zuri, Yaakov S. *Toldot Darkhei ha-Limud be-Yeshivot Darom, Galil, Sura, ve-Nehardea.* Jerusalem, 1914.

Zussman, Yaakov. *Sugyiot Bavliot le-Sedarim Zeraim ve-Tohorot.* Ph.D. Dissertation: Hebrew University, 1969.

_____. "Heker Toldot ha-Halacha u-Megilot Midbar-Yehuda: Hirhurim Talmudi'im Rishonim la-Or Megilat 'Mikzat Ma'asei ha-Torah.'" *Tarbiz* 59 (1989), pp. 23-73.

II. Medieval Chronicles

Igeret Rav Sherira Gaon. Ed. Benjamin Lewin. Haifa, 1921.

Seder ha-Dorot. Ed. Jehiel Heilprin. 1769. Reprint, Warsaw, 1883.

Seder Tannaim ve-Amoraim. Ed. Kalman Kahan. Frankfurt am Main: Hermon, 1935.

Sefer ha-Kabalah. Ed. Gerson D. Cohen. Philadelphia: Jewish Publication Society, 1967.

Sefer Yuhasin ha-Shalem. Ed. Zvi Philipovsky and Avraham Freiman. Jerusalem, 1963.

Yihusei Tannaim ve-Amoraim. Ed. Yehuda Leib Maimon. Jerusalem: Mosad ha-Rav Kuk, 1963.

III. Critical Editions, Manuscripts, and Collations of Variant Readings

Tractate Abodah Zarah. Ms. Jewish Theological Seminary of America. Ed. Shraga Abramson. New York, 1957.

Feldblum, Meir. *Dikdukei Soferim: Gittin.* New York: Horeb, 1966.

Friedmann, M. *Babylonischer Talmud: Traktat Makkoth.* 1888. Reprint, Jerusalem, 1970.

Herschler, Moshe. *Dikdukei Soferim ha-Shalem: Ketubot.* 2 Vols. Jerusalem: Makhon ha-Talmud ha-Yisraeli ha-Shalem, 1972-1977.

_____. *Dikdukei Soferim ha-Shalem: Nedarim.* 2 Vols. Jerusalem: Makhon ha-Talmud ha-Yisraeli ha-Shalem, 1985-1991.

Katsch, Abraham. *Ginzei Talmud Bavli.* Vol. 1. Jerusalem: Rubin Mass, 1979.

Liss, Avraham. *Dikdukei Soferim ha-Shalem:* Sotah. 2 Vols. Jerusalem: Makhon ha-Talmud ha-Yisraeli ha-Shalem, 1977-1979.

_____. *Dikdukei Soferim ha-Shalem:* Yevamot. 3 Vols. Jerusalem: Makhon ha-Talmud ha-Yisraeli ha-Shalem, 1983-1989.

Melamed, E.Z. *Talmud Bavli: Massekhet Baba Kamma.* Jerusalem, 1952.

Rabbinovicz, Rafael. *Dikdukei Soferim.* 12 Vols. Reprint, New York, 1976.

Index to Biblical and Rabbinic Passages

Index of Modern Scholars

General Index

Brown Judaic Studies

Brown Studies on Jews and Their Societies

Brown Studies in Religion